Striking Out

– ROBERT MATTHEWS –

An environmentally friendly book printed and bound in England by
www.printondemand-worldwide.com

Mixed Sources
Product group from well-managed forests, and other controlled sources
www.fsc.org Cert no. TT-COC-002641
© 1996 Forest Stewardship Council

PEFC Certified
This product is from sustainably managed forests and controlled sources
www.pefc.org

This book is made entirely of chain-of-custody materials

www.fast-print.net/store.php

Striking Out

ISBN 978-178035-026-4

First published 2011 by
FASTPRINT PUBLISHING

Foreword

When my middle daughter, Viki, was about six, she told her teacher that I had a corner shop, played poker and loved porridge. What Viki had said was partially true. I did occasionally play poker and I do love porridge, but I certainly did not own a corner shop.

The story, amusing as it is, got me to thinking. What on earth had possessed little Viki to believe I owned a corner shop? The only conclusion I could arrive at was that my wife had mentioned in passing that Daddy had been born in India. An Indian family, who spoilt Viki with sweeties, had a corner shop nearby. *Ergo,* in her innocent mind, all those from the subcontinent owned corner shops!

My three lovely daughters, Kerri, Viki and Abigail are now grown up and have children of their own. They have known for a long time that, although I'd been born in Delhi both my parents were British. However, it came to me there were gaps in their knowledge about my early years; about which they knew little. And so, thinking they might be interested, I set out to write a short memoir covering the period 1949-1954, dating from when I was despatched by plane from Pakistan to England at the age of eighteen, to the time I first met their mother, five eventful years later. Aided and abetted by my friends and peers in the Hogsback Writers, the writing group to which I belong, the book grew like Topsy.

More than anyone, I have my editor, the eagle eyed, Mary Ellen Foley to thank for putting me straight, encouraging me, chivvying me, and generally holding my hand throughout the long period it has taken me to write this book. I could not have done it without her.

My memory maybe fallible about the exact dates and sequences of events I've described, but in all other respects the story is entirely true. However, I have changed the names of several characters. If perchance they resemble any person living, or dead, it is entirely coincidental.

Chapter 1

At the start of the new school term in March 1948, I was made head boy of The Lawrence College Ghora Gali, my boarding school in the foothills of the Himalayas. I was expelled two months later, having been caught teaching the Headmaster's daughter how to play strip poker. Unsurprisingly, I was promptly packed off home to the Attock Oil refinery at Morgah, six miles from Rawalpindi in the Punjab, where my family lived.

Seven months after the partition of India and Pakistan, there was still considerable unrest and rioting in the Rawalpindi area. British citizens were safe enough, but my stepfather, the chief oil chemist of the refinery, recommended I remain within the grounds of the house. For the next couple of months, instead of preparing for my final exams, I read novels to pass the time, forbidden tomes such as *Forever Amber*, or else sat twiddling my thumbs, hoping the savagery would subside and I could go out again.

One morning, as I sat on the verandah staring into space, my attention was caught by the sight of the oil company's Hindu doctor, fleeing for his life along the road in front of my house. I watched in horror, as a rabble of black-shirted

Muslim peasants, some bearing sharpened spades, others wielding pitchforks, closed in on the poor man.

His hands clamped tightly over his skull for protection, the elderly doctor ran for the shelter of the oil company's head office. As he tried the front door, a spade flashed in an arc, taking his hand off at the wrist. The door opened and someone from within pulled the screaming doctor into the sanctuary of the building, leaving the bloodied mess of his severed hand, fingers still fluttering, lying in the dust. Denied of their prey, the howling mob hammered on the door, before rushing off to search for other Hindus to murder.

Over the ensuing months, I suffered nightmares over the tragic events I saw at first hand, such as a bus load of Sikhs slaughtered on the banks of the Sohan River, their bodies left to be picked over by vultures and jackals. Then there was the smoke all around, rising from funeral pyres; the homes of innocents reduced to ash and rubble. Men, women and children, the Sikhs and Hindus who had lived in harmony for generations with their Muslim neighbours, all killed without qualm.

Eventually, in late December, I was allowed back to my school to sit my Cambridge School Certificate exams, for which I was completely unprepared. At that time, exam papers were sent by boat to England to be marked and so it was not until the following March that I got my results. Miraculously, I found I'd passed.

The riots finally subsided and it was safe to be out and about again. But by this time, most of my classmates and friends, who, like me, had been born and brought up in the sub-continent, had left with their families for Canada, Australia and New Zealand to make new lives for themselves.

I had hoped the Royal Air Force would take me when I finished school, but scuppering any such ambition, the British army and Air Force had also left Pakistan. Now eighteen, I had no prospect of a job, no money, and as far as I could see, no future either. The only way out for me was to get to England somehow, where I could join up, or find some kind of work. Living in Pakistan was not an option. After what I had experienced, I had no wish to live there.

My kind stepfather, Maurice Cuell, would certainly have stumped up my boat fare to England, but he was drying out in a clinic in Devon. My mother had no money of her own and, because she'd started an affair with Maurice's best friend, my interests were far from her mind. As the summer progressed, I became more and more despondent and desperate. What was to happen to me? What could I do with my life?

On a particularly hot and humid day in August 1949, I sat sweating under a fan in the drawing room of our bungalow. I dreamt of England, my mind filled with images of pretty green countryside, thatched cottages and baronial castles, when Colonel Nick Grahame-Carter, wearing a crumpled, sweat-stained, khaki uniform sauntered into the room with my mother on his arm.

Catching sight of me lounging in an arm chair, he flung his hat on a table by the door and barked, "Stand up, boy, when your mother enters the room." I clambered to my feet and stood mute with surprise facing the colonel, who seemed like a louche version of David Niven. I struggled to contain my dislike of the man.

"Cat got your tongue?" he enquired. His words, larded with heavy sarcasm, were punctuated with jabs of his swagger stick into my chest.

"No," I replied, fighting to hold my temper in check.

"*Sir*!" shouted the colonel, snarling, his pencil-thin black moustache twitched at an absurd angle, rage distorting his mouth. "When you speak to me you address me as 'sir'."

With that, he slapped me hard across the face. Blinded with anger, my instinctive reaction was to lash out. The colonel, caught flush on the jaw by my clenched fist with all my weight behind it, was sent sprawling across the marble floor. Semi-conscious, he came to rest at the feet of two servants, one holding a tray with cut glass tumblers, the other a jug of iced gin and lime. Standing stiffly to attention, their lips trembled with concealed laughter, though their eyes gave no hint of having witnessed this most extraordinary event. Meanwhile I, in a state of shock, stood panting over the inert body of the colonel.

Given the circumstances, I expected a theatrical outburst, at the very least, from my diva mother in response to her eighteen-year-old son's behaviour. After all, she'd once been on the stage and could conjure the entire gamut of emotions, from hysteria to helplessness, at will. Her face remained surprisingly expressionless as, without a single glance in my direction, she stretched a hand down to the floor and calmly picked up the colonel's cigarette. Without a word, she stubbed it out on the silver tray held by one of the bearers before reaching into a brass plant pot to retrieve her lover's ivory cigarette holder. The force of my blow had made it fly from between his discoloured teeth, and it now lay in a perhaps more hygienic resting place at the base of a dwarf palm.

My mother eventually straightened up to look me directly in the eye. "Bob," she said in an icy voice, "there'll be hell to pay when Nick recovers. What possessed you to hit him?"

"He hit me first, Mum," I protested. "He had no right to do that."

"Well, I think it best you beetle off for a couple of hours while I see to Nick." She hitched her thin shoulders to her ears, transforming into a despairing waif-like figure, albeit one who wore an expensive summer frock. Her lover's situation clearly of secondary importance, she allowed me a full minute to appreciate her bravura performance before instructing Victor, our Christian head bearer, to help the colonel into a chair.

Deciding not to be audience to another thespian show, I scooted from the room. Running from the house, I climbed on my bike and set off blindly.

With my bicycle wheels bumping across scrubby ground, I rode for a couple of miles beyond the oil refinery's walls. The occasional partridge whirred up in front of me and hares bobbed in all directions as I pedalled on faster and faster. Disturbed by the noise, fat monitor lizards basking in the sun heaved themselves up on their stubby legs and sought shelter in deep crevices as I flashed by.

Eventually, I arrived at the banks of the Sohan River where the air was clean, free from the tarry smell of bitumen coming from the oil refinery and from the presence of Colonel Grahame-Carter. By now I was drenched with perspiration. I undressed and swam naked in the cold, clear river water, drying off in the sun afterwards. I sheltered for the rest of the day in the dark shade of the ochre cliffs until the light faded and my stomach cried out for food. Then I cycled home in the gloom to face the music.

The colonel's staff car was no longer outside the bungalow, so it was safe to assume he had left. The *chowkidar* who stood guarding the house asked me in Urdu where I'd been, adding that *memsahib* was worried.

"She is in the house," he said, adding slyly, "Colonel *sahib* left some hours ago." In the yellow light coming from his reeking oil lantern, I detected a smile on his wizened old face. "*Tik heh, sahib*, everything okay."

Victor opened the front door and beckoned me into the drawing room. Somewhat relieved, but still concerned about what my mother would have to say to me, I entered and saw my mother curled up in her favourite high-winged wicker chair. Her face appeared to have aged well beyond her forty-two years. Nonetheless, with her emerald-green eyes, dark hair, pale complexion and trim, ballet-dancer's body, she was still a very attractive woman, although now, as she peered at me through eyes smudged with mascara, she resembled a mournful clown. She'd obviously had more than a few gins, for her speech was slightly slurred.

"Where have you been, Bobby?" she whined, sipping from the glass in her hand. "I've been worried stiff." She took a swallow before her words came out. "You really shouldn't have hit Nick, you know. He was dreadfully upset. I honestly think you should apologise to him, don't you?" With her glass waving about in the air and in peril of falling from her fingers, she pleaded, "Darling, if only to save face, that sort of thing."

"I didn't start it," I replied defiantly. "He did. Mummy, I'm really sorry I lost my temper, but it was Nick's fault. He ought not to have belted me. He had no right to. He's not my father."

"Whatever you say, dear," my mother responded wearily, "but there'll be a dreadful to-do, if the news ever gets about."

"The news of what gets about, Mum? That you and he—"

My mother's voice shrilled angrily as she put down her glass and rose halfway out of her chair. "That's enough of that! What do you know about anything? Nick and I are just friends. Friends, I tell you! That's all! He's just being kind to us while Maurice is away sick."

"Mum, you know that isn't true! We've all seen how he looks at you. You're always with him and once, I saw him kiss you—"

"*Never!*" shouted my mother, now standing upright. "That's absolute nonsense. When was it you *think* you saw him kiss me?" She looked guilty, nervous, her eyes darting about.

"One night in the garden. Geoff and I both saw you. How could you have allowed Nick to kiss you, Mum, when you are married to Maurice?"

Colour flooded into my mother's cheeks. "It was probably just a goodnight kiss. Nothing more. And anyhow, you're just a child. Eighteen, that's all. You know damn all about these things!"

What she said was true. For the past nine years, I'd been stuck in a boys' only boarding school eight thousand feet up in the Himalayas. Other than for the three-month-long winter school holidays, I was never home. Innocent of what went on in the world, who was I to judge adult behaviour? Innocence notwithstanding, I was horrified by my mother's infidelity. Surely my poor stepfather didn't deserve such treatment, nor the constant nagging to which he'd been subjected throughout their marriage. In the end, to avoid confrontation, he found refuge in the tennis club bar and there drank himself into oblivion every night. Unsurprisingly, his work suffered. His bosses at Attock Oil finally took action, recommending extended home leave and treatment for his alcoholism. No sooner had Maurice been sent home to England than his best friend, Colonel Nick Grahame-Carter, turned up on the scene, ostensibly to care for Maurice's family while he was away, but with a different agenda in mind.

I went over to my mother. Taking her hands in mine, I said, "If it helps, Mummy, I can leave home, stay with friends in 'Pindi until I find some work."

Dismissing the idea with a wan smile, my mother gave me a look of ineffable sadness. "Bobby," she said, "have you any idea how hard it's been for me, bringing up five children after your dear father died?" Her voice faded away. As her tears fell, she whispered, "Dear, dear Arnold, I loved him so." Her hands went to her mouth to restrain a sob. Overwrought by the sight of my mother weeping, I hugged her tight. "Arnold, Arnold," she breathed over and over again. I left her eventually and went out to stand on the verandah, where the image of my father came into focus.

Lahore's air, on the September morning in 1939 that would be my father's last day with us, had a brisk, invigorating feel, welcome after the stifling, unrelenting heat of summer. Shoeless, I sat on a patch of grass playing with a small pi-dog under the canopy of a great peepul tree, whose broad leaves whispered gently in the light breeze. Smoke from a neighbour's bonfire spiralled upwards, its acrid reek unpleasant.

From somewhere in the distance came the satisfying *thwack* of washing being bashed clean on polished stone by washermen. The fate of flimsy buttons and delicate fastenings of no concern to them as they plied their trade at brimming *ghats* of water with unbounded fervour. Nearer at hand, I heard the cries of our loyal *ayah*, who'd looked after me since my birth eight years before, berating the only other servant left in our employ.

In a corner of the garden, bent double over a neglected flower bed, my mother listlessly dead-headed roses, searching out a few unblemished ones to put in a vase. Our garden had once been the jealously guarded domain of our *mali*, but he had long since returned to his village with three months wages owing, as had our cook, along with four other retainers who'd looked after the family for years. As a result, both the twenty-roomed white colonial mansion and its spacious garden were now in a state of neglect.

Hearing the clatter of horse's hooves, I released the puppy. Shielding my eyes, I looked up to see a horse-drawn *tonga* pass through the tall gates fronting the gravelled drive. The two-wheeled carriage lurched to a crunching stop under the colonnaded porch framing the front door.

In itself, the sight of the *tonga* was not unusual for, over the preceding months, vehicles of all sorts had come and gone with increasing frequency. However, the arrival of this particular *tonga* evidently caused my mother great concern, for I heard her voice, shrill with alarm. "Bobby! Bobby! Come here! Now! This minute! Here, to the back of the house. Hurry, my darling!"

I flew to my mother's side in my bare feet, my soles hardened by many weeks of walking about unshod. Indoors, I wore makeshift footwear of thin cardboard, fastened across my instep with cord. The one blessing arising from my shoeless state was that I did not attend school any more. My mother explained my absence to the Cathedral School authorities by saying I had chicken pox. The real truth was that I had grown out of my shoes and there was no money for new ones.

As the family's financial situation continued to worsen, my mother resorted to sending me to the door whenever food vendors called, requesting payment for goods she had purchased on credit. I would stand in front of them, shuffling about in my cardboard shoes, saying with well-practised shrugs, "Sorry, the *memsahib*'s not in." The poor fellows, noticing my makeshift footwear, realised there was little chance of extracting any cash. So they departed, waggling their heads ruefully, plainly upset that the *memsahib* had used her child to fend them off. But, being businessmen, the vendors always returned at a later date, their hands clutching wretched scraps of crumpled paper: unpaid bills of ancient vintage signed by my mother in her extravagant hand.

My mother clutched me close to her, scraped a hand across her eyes to clear the tears and said to me in a low tremulous voice, "Promise me, Bobby, you'll be a brave boy. Promise." Shaking me as she emphasised each word, she added, "One day you'll be so proud of your daddy."

I wanted to say I was already proud of my daddy, when I saw him emerge through a door at the back of the house. Following closely behind came a smartly uniformed Anglo-Indian inspector of the Punjab police, a hugely embarrassed expression on his face. At the rear came an Indian police constable wearing a red turban, khaki shirt and shorts, the latter so stiffly starched, the material crackled like *poppadoms* as he marched. My father stared directly ahead, his face gaunt and whiter than I'd ever seen it. Straight-backed, with his head held high, he led the way down the steps in advance of his guards. His eyes never once wavered in our direction. Before I could call out to him or react in any way, my mother grabbed hold of me. My face pressed to her groin, I gasped for air, gagging from the mysterious, rank odour coming from between her flimsily covered legs. "Oh, dear God, Arnold," I heard her cry. "What have they done to you?"

Wrenching myself away from my mother, I saw my father's eyes fix on us with an expression of profound sorrow before he was led away around the corner of the house. I didn't know it then, but he was being taken off to Lahore Jail. At the same time as he disappeared, I spotted a thin trail of blood running down my mother's legs.

"Mummy!" I shouted, pointing a finger, "You've cut yourself. Look, look, there's blood, Mummy."

My mother gave a great gasp. "Oh, my God, my God! My period." Stuffing a handkerchief into her mouth, she ran, weeping hysterically, into her bedroom.

Meanwhile, my old *ayah*, who'd arrived at my side, took hold of me. Since she was several inches shorter than my mother, I now found my face pressed deep into the cleft of her capacious bosom, smelling of sweat and cheap bazaar perfume. She rocked back and forth on her heels, her silver bangles tinkling, singing the song she'd sung to me when I was a baby.

"Bobbee, baba, meeri peeri bucher." (Bobby, my dear, my beloved baby.)

The *ayah* stroked my head with her heavily ringed fingers before releasing me. Her glistening cheeks ran with perspiration and tears sluiced from her eyes. I stood looking at her with affection, until I heard the loud tongue-clacking sound that *tonga* drivers used to urge on their skinny horses. I ran to the front of the house and then onto Abbott Road where I saw my father sitting on the rear seat of a *tonga*. The police constable was squeezed in beside him, with the inspector perched up in front alongside the *tonga wallah*. The poor horse was failing to make any forward motion and had to be assisted by the driver. Alighting from his seat, the *tonga wallah* put a shoulder to one wheel, managing to get both wheels rolling after a couple of heaves. Leaping back on board, the driver cracked his whip over the bony flanks of his horse. Its hooves, finding little purchase on the metalled surface spent sparks flying as it lunged forward between the shafts. Finally, under the enthusiastic use of the *tonga wallah*'s whip, it finally broke into a tired trot. I watched disconsolately as the *tonga* receded into the distance.

I was only ever to see my father once again, a few months later in February 1940, when my mother took me to visit him in Lahore Jail. I'd often asked my mother why the "nasty policemen" had put my father there, but she had always deflected the question by shushing me quiet. All she ever said was, "You'll be proud of your father one day. It won't be long before the nasty policemen realise they've made a big mistake. You'll see, Daddy'll be home soon, I promise. So show Daddy you're a big brave boy when you see him. He wants to say goodbye before you go off to boarding school next month."

It was a final goodbye, for I never saw my father again. He died of typhus a few months later, aged forty.

I later learned that in 1939, when the Quit India campaign by the Indian Congress Party and the Muslim League against the British, was in full spate, my father was falsely accused of fermenting riots amongst his students at the Forman Christian College in Lahore. He naively decided to defend himself in the High Court but was found guilty of sedition under the Defence of India Act and was sentenced to nine months in jail.

Chapter 2

I stood for a long while on the verandah lost in my thoughts. My eyes searched the night sky for a particular star, one my father had singled out for me when I was very small.

"That's my star," he'd said, pointing at the heavens, as we sat together on the roof terrace of our house in Lahore, where we often went to cool off on hot nights.

"It's where you you'll find me when I die and go to heaven," he told me. "Can you see it? Look, son, look, it's there, just by the North Star, the brightest star in the sky." He held me close. "Bobby, you too will have your own star one day. We all do."

When I found my father's star, I told him how much I missed him, before creeping back into the house. My mother still sat in her chair, her half-empty glass on the table beside her. She gave a start when she saw me re-entering the room.

"I thought you'd already gone to bed, darling," she said, shifting in her seat. "I was just sitting here thinking of your daddy."

I omitted to tell my mother that I had actually spoken to him. Giving her a goodnight kiss, I went to my bedroom, one I shared with my elder brother.

Geoff raised his head from his pillows. "I heard what happened this morning, Bob," he laughed. There'll be hell to pay for you, but the guy deserved it."

Geoff and I were so completely different in appearance we were never taken for brothers. I was hefty, Geoff was scrawny. His skin was white, mine was the colour of nicotine. I played all kinds of sport, and loved shooting and fishing. His preference was books and anything to do with Hollywood cinema.

Geoff was impressed by everything American, and hung around Flashman's Hotel in Rawalpindi in the hope of meeting U.S. soldiers holed up there. As part of the UN contingent of observers, the GIs' mandate was to report on how well the cease-fire line was holding in Kashmir.

Geoff spent all his free time picking up American slang and copying the GIs' mannerisms. He bummed K-rations and Camel cigarettes off them and dreamt of living in the US. With his padded-shouldered suits and hand-painted ties, he could have been mistaken for an all-American kid, albeit a pallid, skinny one with acne.

"So what happened, man?" Geoff asked.

I recounted how Nick Grahame-Carter had slapped me and I had responded with a punch and knocked him out.

Geoff chuckled. "Hot diggetty dawg! Man, you're the bees. Bet when the news gets out Mum and Nick will be blackballed by that snooty bunch at the Rawalpindi Club. Nick won't find that too cute." Geoff's imagination was running riot as he waffled on about the rest of the family. "Hey, man, its lucky Pam's in Karachi and Richard's still at boarding school. David's just ten, so he won't understand anything." He paused in mid-flow. "And what about poor old Maurice in England? He's bound to find out from his friends here at

Attock Oil. For sure he'll divorce Mum. Most probably get guardianship of Ronald. After all, he's his son."

"Okay, so what's going to happen to me now, Geoff?"

"Guess you'll have to scram, beat it outta here and get a job."

Although the ceiling fan was on full blast, I lay uncovered in bed throughout the night, sweating in the heat, nervous about what the next day held for me. Finally, sleep came at around four o'clock in the morning. My bearer, Shah, woke me at seven with tea. Handing me a cup, he gave me a grin.

"*Memsahib* want see you, Bobby *sahib*," he said. Waggling his head from side to side, he added, "After dressing."

Noticing that my brother's bed was unoccupied, I asked, "Where's Geoffrey *sahib*?"

"Gone 'Pindi, Bobby *sahib*," replied Shah. "Half hour before."

During the summer months, people were up and about by six-thirty in the morning. So, when I appeared for breakfast at seven-thirty, my mother had long since finished hers. I was about to wish her a good morning, when she held up a restraining hand. She was hardly able to contain her excitement, "Bobby, I've the most wonderful news for you! Nick's arranged for you and Geoff to fly to England. You are going in ten days' time!"

Barely comprehending what she'd said, not daring to believe my ears, I mouthed like a fish. In my state of utter bemusement, I heard her repeat, "You're going to England darling. It's true. Really. Cross my heart, it's true. Nick phoned me late last night and gave me the news. He's pulled strings with General Ayub Khan. Yesterday, after—well, you know what happened—he fixed it all up. You're both to fly home on an RAF Transport Command aeroplane. All things considered, it's awfully decent of Nick, don't you think? And, Bobby, it's solves everything for you, doesn't it?"

I looked at her askance. "You're not joking?" I asked hesitantly. "Tell me, I'm really going to England? I mean, Mummy, really going? How did Nick arrange it all so quickly?" Even as I put the question, I knew the answer. The quicker Geoff and I were out of the way, the sooner he'd have my mother to himself. Also, the chances of their affair becoming common knowledge would be limited by our being off the scene. It was a bribe to shut me up. "Nick wants Geoff and me out of the way, doesn't he?" I found myself blurting.

My mother gave me an acid look. "That was uncharitable of you, Bobby," she said. Then softening her voice, she continued, "You should be grateful, Bobby. Just think, yesterday you didn't know what to do with your life. Now you can go home to join the Air Force, like you've always wanted. Or do anything else. England, darling. England! Home! You've a future now. Oh Lord, I am so pleased for you. It's a wonderful outcome isn't it?"

What she said was true. It was indeed an amazing, stupendous outcome.

Now, pacing about the room with unaccustomed briskness, my mother said in a surprisingly controlled voice, "There are lots of things to be done today. But first things first, Bobby." She took both of my hands in hers and said, looking deep into my eyes, "You're to be on the Frontier Mail Express tomorrow, which leaves at five in the afternoon. You are going to Lahore to collect your passports. Freddie Barratt"—this was Nick's second in command—"will be accompanying you to the British High Commission. It happens that Freddie has some business there."

Releasing my hands, she said, "I must fish out your birth certificate, and Geoff's, and... and..." She stood gathering her thoughts. "Oh, yes, you'll need passport photos, too. Go with Geoff to Khan Studios on the Mall this afternoon. Geoff finishes work at four, so you can have your pictures taken soon after."

My mother's voice, once more alight with enthusiasm, echoed around the room. "Nick will be having a word with his friend the High Commissioner this morning. It may surprise you to know, Bobby, Nick has a great deal of influence, because of his family connection with the Bowes-Lyons." Realising from my expression that I had no idea what she was talking about, yet still determined I should be impressed, my mother emphasised, stabbing a finger in my direction, "Bowes-Lyon is Queen Elizabeth's maiden name, darling." She gushed on unstoppably, marching about the dining room.

Ceasing at last, she said, "Major Barratt is sending his car for you at three tomorrow. Geoffrey won't be accompanying you to Lahore because of his job. So, darling, get Shah to pack your things for you." Giving me a coquettish look, one with which I was familiar, she purred, onstage again, "Now come closer, Bobby, and give your Mummy a kiss. Mummy deserves one, don't you think?"

In too much of a daze to dwell on whether she did or not, I simply blinked. The thrilling news of my salvation finally absorbed as the truth, I took my mother in my arms. I kissed her hard on both cheeks, lifted her off the floor and twirled her round and round the room.

Later on, singing my head off, I cycled the six miles down the Grand Trunk Road to Shaw's Electrical in Rawalpindi where I met up with Geoff.

"Hey, man!" he greeted loudly in his cod American accent, throwing an air punch in my direction. "Waddya know? Mum phoned me at the shop with the news. Hot diggetty! It's true we're off to England, yeah?" Passers-by on the Mall looked curiously at the fool gesticulating and whooping. “Weeeow! Man, oh, man, can you really believe it? And, all because li’l bro banged the crap outta that Nick Carter!” Stopping suddenly he said, “Aw, shit, hope we get some dough from somewhere. Mum being Mum, I guess it hasn’t occurred to her that we’ll need some.”

My mother had indeed forgotten Mr Khan required payment. That afternoon Geoff had to pay Mr Khan five rupees from his own pocket for taking the photos on an ancient Kodak plate camera and developing them. He whinged on about it all the way home.

To kill time, I spent most of the following morning fishing in the Sohan River and was lucky to land a ten-pound *mahseer*. Fleshy and mighty good to eat, *mahseer*, known as fighting fish, often grew to twenty or thirty pounds and were rarely to be found in the river after the snow melt of March and April. My catch was big enough for our servants to have their fill that night, the only present I was able to give them before saying goodbye forever.

Booloo, our cook, had been with us for nine years. He could conjure up delicious three- four- and five-course meals that would have delighted Mrs Beeton, whenever *memsahib* requested them. How he managed to recall recipes handed down to him and then prepare complicated dishes in his tiny kitchen, cooking over charcoal in a clay oven, remained a mystery.

Victor, our Christian head bearer was a martinet and ran the entire household like clockwork. Unlike Booloo, who lived with his family in the servants’ quarters at the rear of the house, Victor cycled back and forth from his home in ‘Pindi. Arriving never later than five in the morning, he stayed for as long as he was required, sometimes on duty as late as midnight.

Then there was Shah, my bearer, my pal, more of a brother than Geoff. Shah, who was only a year older than I, had turned up on our door step three years before, asking for work. My stepfather, impressed that Shah had walked 150 miles from his village near Peshawar, took him on immediately, assigning him to look after Geoff and me during the school holidays. The remaining servants—the *malis* who kept the gardens, the sweepers who cleaned the bathrooms and toilets, the *chowkidar* who guarded the house—all came and went. I didn't know any of them too well, but Booloo, Victor and Shah were family to me, and I was desperately sad to be leaving them.

With my big catch in a gunny sack tied to the carrier of my upright bike, I returned home and handed over my fish to a delighted Booloo.

Chapter 3

At precisely three o'clock, Major Barratt's staff car, a dun-coloured Studebaker, pulled into our drive and drew up under the porch. The driver climbed out and opened the rear door. I watched with interest as one highly polished shoe made an appearance, followed by a khaki trouser leg with knife-edge creases. Then, taking the utmost care, Major Barratt allowed his other shoe and trouser leg to emerge. Twisting sideways, he slithered his body elegantly over the leather seats and was out of the car in a single fluid movement. Once he stood upright, he eased his hands over his beautifully tailored uniform. His immaculate appearance was quite unlike that of his superior officer, my mother's lover, Colonel Grahame-Carter, who always looked dishevelled.

I couldn't put a finger on it, but there was something about Major Freddie Barratt that made me uncomfortable. He seemed pleasant enough—a smallish, neat man, with ginger hair, a pale freckled complexion and a high girlish laugh. Most probably it was the looseness of his lips, and the wet mouth he kept dabbing at with a handkerchief, that bothered me most.

"What ho, Bob, boy!" he called out in a genial voice, waving his swagger stick. "Mother in?" Catching sight of her on the verandah, he hailed, "Ah, there you are, Alys. Any chance of a G & T, d'you think? It's so blessed hot."

My mother, charm itself—for wasn't the major escorting her dear son to Lahore?—smiled back archly. "Freddie, don't be so idiotic. Victor's already chilling the gin. Come on in, won't you? I suppose we'd better go over the details with Bob, so he'll understand."

As far as I could see there wasn't much for me to have explained. All we were doing was catching a train at five from Rawalpindi Station, arriving at Lahore around ten, and staying the night in the station hotel there before visiting the British High Commission the following morning. Even a dunderhead like me could take that in. However, I was the dutiful son and did as Mother asked. I learned nothing new, other than that, as my mother divulged in a whisper, Major Barratt was on the board of directors of Heals in London. Not understanding what she was talking about, I failed to muster the enthusiasm she expected regarding the major's elevated status in civilian life.

I was anxious to be away on the first leg of my adventure. But it was to be another forty minutes before my mother and the major had finished talking and I was allowed to get into his car. As I was about to settle myself on the rear seat, my mother pulled at my shirt sleeve through the open window, "Darling, darling," she cried out. "I almost forgot." She extracted a ten rupee note from a purse, handing it to me as if it was some priceless gem. Then she added loudly, more for Major Barratt's benefit than mine, "Ten rupees. In case you have need of it, darling."

I committed my mother's act to fond memory, for it was not often she was so generous with me. "Thanks, Mummy," I said, trousering the note, the equivalent in sterling to ten shillings. "I'll phone you from Lahore tomorrow, let you know what train I'm catching back, so someone can meet me." With that, I blew her a kiss through the window and waved her goodbye.

Major Barratt eased himself into the passenger seat alongside me. "Thought I'd join you in the back, Bob, boy, to keep you company," he said, smoothing down his trousers. Tapping his driver's shoulder, he told him to get going.

It took just over half an hour to reach Rawalpindi Station, with its ornate red-brick Victorian façade and its long platforms shaded by fretted wooden awnings. As usual, a maelstrom of noisy gesticulating humanity surrounded the building. Our driver, accompanied by a porter carrying the major's luggage on his head, threaded his way through the crowd. Freddie Barratt and I followed more cautiously, our feet avoiding streaks of red betel nut juice and other indeterminate bits of detritus on the ground.

When we reached the platform, the colossal steam locomotive that pulled the Frontier Mail Express already sat huffing, panting and wheezing on the track. The major's driver waited for us by the open door of our reserved first-class compartment, the luggage already installed inside by the porter.

Turning to me and patting me on the back, Major Barratt urged, "After you, Claude."

"I'm not Claude. My name's Bob, or didn't you know?"

The major rolled his eyeballs to the sky. "Of course I know you are Bob," he replied. "Didn't anyone tell you 'After you, Claude' is just an expression? It just means you go first and I'll follow."

Properly put in my place, I stepped into the compartment.

"Love the smell of that leather," the major said, sniffing the air like a hound as he followed me in.

I'd recently had my nasal septum displaced during a game of soccer, so was unable to distinguish one smell from another. Wishing to be back in the major's good books, I replied, like the funk I was, "Terrific, sir. Just terrific."

"Oh, for God's sake, Bob! My name's Freddie. Just call me Freddie," he laughed. "Go on, take a pew."

I refrained from turning the tables on Freddie and correcting his silly mistake. He really ought to have known that pews were to be found in church and not on trains.

The compartment of our carriage was entirely faced in pale green leather, including the bunk beds, the two club chairs and a table. A door at one end opened onto a small bathroom fitted with a shower, WC and hand basin. At the other, another door led to a small kitchenette, where Freddie's driver was busy cramming an icebox with bottles of Murree Brewery beer. Air conditioning, which I'd never before experienced, fed cool air into the compartment from ceiling vents, a heaven-sent relief from the sultry atmosphere outside. I wished the journey would take five days and not five hours, just so I could continue to enjoy the luxury of my surroundings.

"Nice to relax in the cool," remarked Freddie, interrupting my musings. "Fancy a beer?" Without waiting for my answer, he shouted, "Raman! Bring beer!" Moments later, like a genie uncorked, Freddie's driver materialised bearing a silver tray with two pewter tankards.

"Good chap, Raman," murmured Freddie, reclining back in his chair. "Driver, batman, cook, bottlewasher, you name it. Go on, drink up, Bob, boy." He took a swig himself and then watched me closely from under lowered eyelids as I reached for a tankard.

I could count on one hand the number of times I'd tasted alcohol. I took a hesitant swallow. Deciding the bitter taste was to my liking, I had just about polished off my drink when the train slid away from the platform, the engine making a deeply satisfying chuff-chuffing sound as it got up speed. It was not long before the rhythmic noise of the train's wheels passing over the rails sent me dead asleep.

Freddie shook me awake some four hours later as the express clunked slowly across the iron bridge over the River Ravi, one of the five great tributaries of the Indus. "Wake up lad," said Freddie. "We'll be at the station in a minute or two."

We had hardly come to a stop before the maniacs festooning the roof of the train peeled off, along with hordes of others clinging precariously to the sides of the carriages, Poised with their feet over the platform and then, as agile as monkeys, they jumped, landing at a dead run and disappeared hugger-mugger into the crowd. Hawkers, food sellers, purveyors of fruit and water, passengers, porters, bystanders massed around our carriage door as it opened, their raised voices an almost unendurable cacophony. Raman parted the throng like some latter-day Moses, hissing epithets at anyone standing in his path. In seconds, he had obtained the services of a porter to assist him with the luggage. Then Major Barratt, the wealthy Director of Heals of London, and I, with ten rupees in my pocket and therefore by my standards rich beyond avarice, followed on closely behind.

We passed through the grubby entrance of the station hotel and into the foyer. Freddie asked me to wait while he dealt with the hotel manager, whose office was elsewhere.

He returned soon afterwards, a broad grin on his face. "All settled," he said, rubbing his hands. "Wonderful what a ten rupee tip will get you. We've been given a room at the rear of the hotel away from all the noise. So, chop, chop, Bob, boy. Supper ready.

I was getting pretty fed up with Freddie referring to me as "Bob, boy" all the time. I wondered if I had the guts to tell him over supper how objectionable I found it. Deciding I hadn't the courage, I figured out a subtle ploy.

"Do you know, Freddie, boy," I said brightly. "I had no idea I was so hungry."

Catching on immediately, Freddie's eyebrows rose in surprise. "No, Bob, boy, neither did I," he chuckled.

After a splendid meal of chicken curry, pilau,nan bread, dhall and curried vegetables chased down with cold beer, we made our way out of the old fashioned dining room. With dark furniture that had seen better days and with faded photographs of railway dignitaries lining the walls, it all looked in need of attention. Together with Freddie, his small feet pitter-pattering, I walked past a man seated at Reception, whose knowing, inquisitive eyes followed us all the way into a long corridor. Through a door at the very end we entered a bedroom. Mercifully, a ceiling fan rotated at full speed over the double bed. Besides a wardrobe and two small cane chairs, there was no other furniture in the room. The place was as basic as our train compartment had been opulent.

"Is this where I am to sleep, Freddie?" I asked. "This is my bedroom?"

"No, no, dear boy, it's for both of us," he replied offhandedly. "Sorry, old chap, there were no other suitable rooms available." Fingering the tatty embroidered coverlet on the bed he said, sounding apologetic, "All taken, I'm afraid, so we'll just have to make do and mend with this one."

"What! Sleep in the same bed?" I asked nervously. The idea was wholly repugnant to me, even if we topped and tailed. Furthermore, since I never wore pyjamas and had brought none with me, I found the prospect of lying naked in bed with a stranger horrifying.

"Share the bed? Well, yes, of course. Nothing to it, old chap. Up country or in the field, frequently have to do it, don't you know? Though I must say, hardly ever with such a good-looking chap as you." Bringing his face into close proximity with mine, he gave a girlish giggle as I cringed away from him. Still laughing, he continued, "So sorry, Bob, boy, but needs must. Seeing it's late, we'd better get on with it and have a bit of kip. Bags I take the left side of the bed." With that, Freddie sat himself on the bed and removed his shoes and socks. He then proceeded to remove all his clothing, which he carefully folded before swiftly getting under the covers.

Hopelessly embarrassed, I turned my back on him, quickly tugged off my jacket and shirt, and, leaving my trousers on, ripped the shoes from my feet and got into bed. Moving crabwise to the very edge of the mattress, I slipped my trousers off and threw them on the floor.

Enjoying the pantomime, Freddie lay with his hands clasped under his head pretending to stare at the ceiling. "Shy little chap aren't you," he remarked, casually. "I mean to say, whatever for?"

Rolled over on my side of the bed, with my eyes shut, trying to keep myself from trembling, I called out, "Goodnight, Freddie."

"Goodnight, Bob, boy," he replied, switching off his bedside lamp.

In the dark, with the whirr of the fan above and crickets making a racket outside, I lay absolutely rigid, desperate to avoid any kind of contact with Freddie's body. Unable to relax, I had curled myself into a tight ball, when I heard

Freddie whisper, “May I kiss you, Bob?” For a brief moment I thought I’d imagined it, but then I heard his voice again. Grasping my shoulder, he attempted to turn me over. “I want to kiss you. Cuddle you.”

I was instantly out of bed. Wrenching the top sheet off the bed, I covered my nakedness, moved well out of distance and bellowed, “Kiss me? Cuddle? What do you mean, Freddie?” Gesticulating angrily at him, I was painfully aware how ridiculous I looked in my white cotton shroud.

Freddie snapped on the light. Lying back on his pillows, he said mildly, as if there had been nothing unusual in his request, “I just wanted to give you a kiss. Cuddle you, that’s all.”

“No you bloody can’t,” I raged. “You think I’m a pansy, don’t you? Well, you’re wrong, chum. Try anything on with me and I promise you’ll get this.” I shook my clenched fist at him. “C’mon, c’mon, Freddie boy,” I taunted. “I’m not scared of you, you dirty bastard. Try a knuckle sandwich.”

Freddie grinned as I ranted on, making me even more furious. “Calm down, calm down,” he soothed, “you’ll disturb the natives. There’s no harm done. I’m very sorry. Made a small mistake, that’s all.”

Hating the man, I shouted, “Bloody big mistake, I’d say.”

“Tell you what, dear boy,” Freddie interrupted, paying little regard to me, “I’ll sleep on the floor if it makes you any happier. You take the bed. How’s that? Removing the pillow from under his head, together with the under sheet, he pointed at the carpet. “That’ll do me. I’ll switch the light off now and you get some sleep. You have my word, you’ll be perfectly safe.”

Deciding Freddie would not try to molest me again, I got back into bed. By now my fury had subsided. I no longer felt apprehensive. Nevertheless, I remained disgusted with his behaviour.

I had heard that tribesmen from the North West Frontier, who walked about holding hands, some with flowers in their mouths, enjoyed sex with boys. Apparently, they had a saying: "A woman for pleasure, a donkey for exercise, a boy for paradise." But these were ignorant wild Pathans, weren't they? That an educated European adult could be similarly inclined beggared belief.

At my boarding school, the boys had been completely isolated from the opposite sex for many months at a time, so it was unsurprising that reports of homosexuality surfaced on the campus from time to time. It was never condoned. Those who indulged were soon found out, laughed at, and made fun of as pansies until they pleaded to be sent home. I had always assumed they'd grow up to be normal. Now Freddie Barratt had proved how wrong I was.

For my part, I could not begin to understand how a man could be sexually aroused by another. I was only ever interested in girls. But having been segregated from them for so long, my knowledge of sex extended to snatched, furtive kisses during the school holidays in the back seats of the Regal Cinema in Rawalpindi. In all other respects I was an innocent, fearful that if I so much as fumbled a girl's breast, she'd become pregnant. In school, rumour had it that fiddling about with nipples was certain to do the trick. It is credible to assume that nonsense of this sort was fostered, even encouraged by the school authorities, whose job it was to restrain their horny charges and keep them at arm's length from young women.

As a consequence, the girls of Rawalpindi remained virgins for an inordinate length of time. Their parents slept easy in the beds, unaware their daughters' virtue remained unsullied thanks to adolescent myth and flagrant lies.

I awoke at seven and discovered Freddie already gone. He'd left a letter for me on his bedside table, attached to which was a ten rupee note and the return half of my train ticket. My eyes raced over his carefully formed handwriting.

Dear Bob,

Truly sorry about last night. Sorry, too, for cutting and running before saying goodbye. Raman woke me before six, saying my adjutant had telephoned. I've had my meeting with him (scheduled for midday) brought forward to sparrow's fart at eight. Thus I can't make it to the High Commission for your ten o'clock appointment. Don't worry, everything's been arranged. Just go there and collect the passports. When you are done, use the telephone in the Passport Section to ring your mother. Tell her you'll be on the 3 p.m. train out of Lahore, arriving Rawalpindi eightish. I'll have the reservation made for you by one of my slaves.

I've left you ten chips to get you through the day. Tonga fare (tonga wallah will know the way to the British High Commisssion), lunch, etc. The hotel's settled. Have a safe journey back.

Freddie

P.S. I'd be most grateful if you do not speak to anyone about last night.

Consumed now with mixed feelings about Freddie, my first thought was that he'd conjured up a lame excuse to avoid the embarrassment of facing me, but as I read and re-read the letter, I concluded he'd told the truth. The benefit of the doubt I gave him was doubtless assisted by his thoughtful gift of ten rupees, or chips. I now had twenty rupees to my name, more chips than I'd ever been blessed with in my life.

Chapter 4

I decided getting about alone in Lahore would be great fun. So I folded up Freddie's ten rupee note and put it in my pocket, resorting to amnesia about the previous night. I ventured out at eight o'clock and went directly to a *tonga* rank at the front of the railway station. I selected one of them and proceeded to haggle with the driver to take me to the Secretariat buildings—in which my grandfather, Richard Matthews, ISO, Superintendent of the Punjab Secretariat had once had his office—and thereafter to the British High Commission. The *tonga wallah* was obviously in need of a fare, for he agreed a price of one rupee, which was ridiculously cheap. Looking askance at his bony horse hanging between the shafts, I wondered if I'd made the right choice, the poor animal already looked dead beat.

Nonetheless, it surprised me by taking off with an unexpected degree of panache at the sound of the *tonga wallah*'s clacking tongue, sending sparks off the metalled surface of the road. I shivered inwardly, recalling my father being escorted off to jail in a *tonga* whose horse, too, had sent sparks off the road. Brushing my tears away I cheered at the thought of revisiting Zam-Zammah, the great cannon dating from the Afghan wars, which guarded the Secretariat and was made famous in Kipling's novel *Kim*.

When I was a small boy it was rare to own a car and considered very grand. On the way to his office, Grandpa frequently took me to the Secretariat in his 1930, canvas topped Pontiac. Nothing made me prouder than sitting in the back alongside him, with his uniformed driver at the wheel.

I would climb up on Zam-Zammah's cast-iron gun carriage, sit astride the barrel and slide down its enormous length. There, much to the amusement of onlookers, I'd whoop and shout at mythical Afghan invaders and make booming noises, imagining cannon balls flying from the gaping muzzle down the Mall.

Ten years had passed since I last set eyes on the Secretariat. As imposing as ever, the buildings formed three sides of a grand square, in the centre of which Zam-Zammah sat glowering. The fourth side of the square opened out into the Mall. Unfortunately, there were a number of Pakistani Army soldiers on guard, putting paid to my ambition of sitting on Zam-Zammah one more time. With an hour to kill before my appointment at the British High Commission, I asked my *tonga wallah* if there was enough time left to also take me to my old house in Abbott Road.

"*Jee hai sahib, tik hai*," he agreed. ("We have, just".)

Giving me a toothless smile from a mouth reddened with betel nut juice, he cracked his whip and off we trotted again, down the broad boulevard of the Mall. Marble statues of Queen Victoria and of viceroys such as Elphinstone and Curzon stood at the intersections, where policemen on point duty controlled the desultory traffic. None of the vehicles on the road—*tongas*, cars, hordes of cyclists—appeared to be taking any notice of their commands as the policemen, swivelling about and looking fierce, blew shrill futile whistles.

Our route took us past the Anarkali bazaar, where food vendors proffering chopped sugar cane sat cross-legged on the pavement, cheek by jowl with others offering sheaves of corn roasted over charcoal braziers. Together with the aroma of myriad exotic spices rising up from vividly coloured mounds of the stuff piled up in front of shops lining the narrow entrance to the bazaar, the sights, the smells combined to overwhelm the senses.

A few turnings after the bazaar, the street widened into quiet Abbott Road, lined with plane trees. A row of substantial, single storey villas with colonnaded porches sat well back behind a low wall on one side of the road. On the other were open fields of yellowing grass. Number 19, where my family had once lived, looked in much better shape than it had been when I was shunted off to boarding school. Apparently my family had been relatively well off prior to that, but when my father was sent to jail, the comfortable world we had known was no more.

I left the *tonga* and crossed over the road to get a better view of the house. Taking in the well-ordered garden, my eyes ranging over the big, newly whitewashed house with its shaded verandas I realised I should never have returned. All the sad memories of my childhood suddenly engulfed me and I started to cry.

A servant, who had been standing by the front door, hidden in the dark shadow cast by the porch, came down the gravel drive. I quickly dried my tears. He hesitated, looking puzzled. I called out in my best Urdu, *"Subchis, bilkool tik hai."* (Everything's all right.)

He replied in English. "No problem, *sahib" and* returned to the house, scratching at his cheeks as he shuffled off.

All this time, my *tonga wallah* had sat immobile in the driving seat of the carriage with his eyes closed, pretending that the private business of his young passenger was of no concern to him. However, when I got in the back of the vehicle, he was instantly alert, proving he'd missed nothing. I showed him my wristwatch and he got the message to get moving. When we arrived, I tried to pay him off, but he said he'd wait for me outside, take me wherever I wanted afterwards, for just one rupee more. At that price, I was not about to argue.

We'd reached the British High Commission with a few minutes to spare and I went straight in. The young Pakistani clerk behind the desk in the Passport Section was expecting me. I declined his offer of tea and handed him the passport photographs. Thanking me, he led me through a door into a comfortably furnished room set about with plump-cushioned cane sofas and chairs.

"Plenty magazines, *Daily Mirror*, et cetera," he said. "Sit down, sir. Not long waiting." Smiling, he backed out in obsequious fashion, affording me the pleasant sensation I was not just a kid, but a person of some importance. As I was about to pick up the hefty yellow-covered volume of an entire month's *Daily Mirror* newspapers, shipped over from England and highly coveted, the door opened. A tall man of about fifty entered, hand outstretched in greeting.

"Young Robert Matthews, I presume," he said with a genial smile, shaking my hand. Sitting down opposite me, he continued, "Allow me to introduce myself. I'm Charles Heyworth, High Commissioner."

Instantly warming to the friendly gentleman with a crop of short white hair and searching eyes, whom I'd presumed would be a stuffy old buffer, I replied, " Yes, sir. I'm hoping to collect my brother's and my passports. My mother told me that Colonel Grahame-Carter is an old friend of yours and that you offered your help in issuing them."

"That's correct, Nick did contact me," replied the High Commissioner. "A bit short notice, but you're right, I did promise him." He slapped his thigh. "Old friend, Nick. Tell you, did he, we were at Wellington together?" Seeing from my baffled expression that Nick had not, he said, "Ah well, no matter," before adding in a much more business-like voice, "Gulab Khan, the chappie you met, is getting on with preparing your passports. Has he your photos and so on?"

Nodding, I replied, "Yes, sir."

"Well then, young man," he said, still on his feet, "let me explain the situation. Because of time constraints and the absence of supporting documents proving whether any or all of your antecedents were born in the United Kingdom, we are issuing you with British Nationality passports. I'm sorry, but you do not qualify for those issued to British citizens. I mean, if only we'd had more time..."

His voice drifted away like smoke.

"I don't understand what you mean, sir," I ventured, lamely. "My Grandmother was born in Glasgow and my mother in Tenterden."

"But on the male side, the male side?" the High Commissioner questioned, sounding as if the discussion was wearisome to him. "What of them?"

"Well," I replied, hesitating before imparting the information I was sure would work the oracle and doubtless impress him hugely, "my great-grandfather was the son of the Earl of Llandaff's sister. Then there's my grandfather. He was Superintendent of the Punjab Secretariat and was awarded the Imperial Service Order for his services at the Delhi Durbar." I folded my hands in my lap and gave him a smile of great satisfaction.

"Perhaps so," replied the High Commissioner, who did not appear in any way overwhelmed by my disclosure. "Notwithstanding all that, have you their birth certificates at hand? Or even confirming evidence from the India Office in Whitehall to support your claim?"

Savagely put down, or so I thought, I slowly shook my head.

"Well, that's the rub," said the High Commissioner. "You can see how my hands are tied." Soothingly, he added, "Look, Robert. There is no difference between the two types of passport for your purpose. The British National passport will get you into the UK, which is the object of the exercise. So, not to worry, eh? Now, if you'll excuse me, I'll go and find out how far Gulab has got with the documents." With that, Charles Heyworth, OBE, British High Commissioner, late of Wellington School and doubtless a Guards regiment, too, wafted out of the room. I was left to feel I wasn't quite up to snuff in his eyes, all because I'd been born in India and couldn't prove my parents were of British stock. Although I was unaware of it at the time, he'd lightly planted a chip on my shoulder which had not lain there before.

I hadn't long to wait. Gulab, the clerk, came into the room bearing two British National passports both duly stamped and signed by the High Commissioner. "All done, *sahib*," said the clerk, "HC sends apologies. He busy now. Good luck *sahib* and goodbye."

"Just a moment," I said, as he made to leave. "May I use your telephone, please? I need to ring my mother and tell her what train I am on."

Permission granted, I quickly dialled up my mother, saying I'd got our passports and I'd be on the 3 p.m. train. "Shah will meet you, darling," she replied. "Sorry I can't. I'm off to the club tonight with Nick. Cheerio, darling. Bon voyage."

My precious documents now safely ensconced inside my jacket pocket, I went out again into the scalding sun, to find my *tonga* awaiting me under the shade of a *peepul* tree. There were still four hours to waste before my train, so I asked the *tonga wallah* if he knew the whereabouts of the

Anglican cemetery where my father was buried. I would go there, I decided, and pay my last respects.

When I arrived at the cemetery, I found the gates unlocked. I looked to see if anyone was about, someone who could be of help in finding my father's grave, but there was no one. Pushing the gates open, I saw before me row upon row of plain headstones with tall strands of spiky grass growing up in between. Plainly, the graves were not being looked after. All were untended, some with black crows hopping about on them. Crouching down, I went from tombstone to tombstone, to discover which was my father's. I moved slowly down the rows, sweating profusely in the heat.

Many were the graves of very young European children who had perished from the heat, pestilence and disease in the savage climate of the Punjab. As a sobering comment on how tough life had been for the Lahore residents of the past, only a few of those buried in that place appeared to have lived much beyond middle age. Picking my way on my knees, I came upon a black marble plinth in a small clearing, where the grass had been mown and the surrounds were tidy. There was a rusty tin can beside the gravestone in which flowers, perhaps only a couple of days old, had been placed. Under my breath, I read out the words scored in faded, gold lettering:

Professor Arnold Monteath Matthews M A (Oxon)

Born 1900–died 1940

I was intrigued to find my father's grave in so much better condition than the others. Who had been responsible and why had it been given such special attention? Frustratingly, there was no one to give me the answer. As I pondered on the mystery, I got down on my knees beside the plinth and, with my forefinger, traced my father's name. I felt no grief or sadness as I did this, only a comforting sense of being at one with my father again. I smiled to myself, remembering things he had taught me. One example immediately came to mind. 'When you decide you are in the right, fight with all your might for what you believe and never, ever give in.' A host of memories crowded in, such as his marvellous expositions about the one true God, the universe, the planets, the stars and in particular, the star he called his own. Suddenly, I choked with emotion at the thought I'd never visit his grave again. I got to my feet, said a small prayer of farewell and left the cemetery.

My *tonga* took me straight back to the station hotel. I paid the driver off with the rupee I owed, but he stood there waggling his head from side to side, looking woebegone, and begging for a few more annas to keep his horse in hay. He looked so sorrowful, my heart softened. I put another rupee in his outstretched palm. Whereupon, he clasped my hands and said that Allah would regard me as a hallowed prince for all time. Thus, with Allah's beneficence bestowed upon me, albeit by a humble *tonga wallah*, I went into the refreshment room, ate lunch, and fell asleep until my train arrived at the station.

Chapter 5

The Frontier Mail Express from Lahore arrived in Rawalpindi just a few minutes late. Shah, his face wreathed in smiles, greeted me with a bear hug on the station platform. Eyebrows were raised on the faces of several Europeans alighting from the train. Such familiarity between servant and master was considered distasteful. But what did they know? Shah might have been my personal servant, but he was also my best friend.

Shah had a *tonga* waiting outside the station ready to take us home to Morgah. We both climbed onto the rear seat, setting the wooden carriage rocking on its two wheels, before the *tonga wallah* got us going. Perched up front, he sat silent as his horse clip-clopped slowly through the dimly lit streets. Meanwhile, Shah chattered non-stop, full of questions about my trip to Lahore. I made no mention of Major Barratt, but watched his eyes widen as I elaborated on Zam-Zammah, before they saddened when I told him of my visit to my father's grave.

Relapsing into silence, he sat with a mournful expression on his face as we came to the brightly lit cantonment. For generations, the tree-filled area had been home to the British Army. Now the neat lines of bungalows set in trim gardens housed the Pakistan military, together with some British officers who had remained behind to train Pakistan's nascent army.

Things had changed a great deal in the two years since Partition. Even the exclusive Rawalpindi Club, the last bastion of the Raj, had been forced to relax its rules and admit senior Pakistani officers. Several of these had passed through Sandhurst and served in Africa and Europe with the Indian Army during the war. Other than for the colour of their skin, in their immaculate jackets and cavalry twills they were indistinguishable from their fellow British officers downing their Black Label whiskies with hearty cheers and chin-chins at the bar. They joined in everything on offer with the same enthusiasm as the rest of the British members, with only one difference: their families rarely accompanied them to the club. The British—including those civilians such as my stepfather, whose families resided in Pakistan—used the Club's facilities to the full.

Shah's voice broke into my musings. "Bobby *sahib*, I sorry you go to Blighty," he said. "What happen to me now?"

It was a chilling question for which I had no answer. Work was hard to come by, now that the British had left. Doubtless he'd be forced to return to his village near Peshawar, a hundred and fifty miles on foot, just as he had when he came to us. He earned a pittance as my houseboy, equivalent to about three pounds sterling per month, with a room provided in what were called the servants' lines—their quarters at the back of the house. Since I did not know what to say to Shah, I kept silent and turned my head away.

As we passed Flashman's Hotel, whose ballroom, facing the Grand Trunk Road, was ablaze with light and filled with United Nations personnel dancing to big band music, Shah nudged me. "Bobby *sahib*, have you ever had a womans?" he asked, in a serious voice. Without waiting for my reply, he added, "I think you have not."

I felt my face redden. I blustered, humming and hawing, "Well, er, no. British *sahibs* don't go in for that sort of thing. At least, not 'til we're older."

In the yellow light cast by the overhead street lamps, I made out Shah's grin. Giving me a cheeky look, he questioned, "Is that why *memsahibs* so old, is it?" His grey eyes, fixed on my face, were innocent but, at the corner of his mouth, a tiny smile played.

I couldn't help laughing at him. "That's rubbish, you bugger," I replied, visualising the yellowing, sun-dried complexions of the stuffy suburban English *memsahib*s who lived in company-owned bungalows on the compound of the Attock Oil refinery.

"I have had many womens," Shah commented grandly, lolling back in his seat, no hint of a boast in his voice. "Many, many."

Humouring him, for I didn't believe a word of it, I agreed, "Sure, sure, if you say so."

"No, *sahib*, it is true I'm telling you," insisted Shah, sounding hurt. "But I am thinking, you must have a womans before you go to Blighty. You must be real man."

"Don't be so damn silly, Shah," I responded, squirming on my seat as a passing *tonga* attracted my attention. Its occupants, a UN soldier in uniform and a pretty Eurasian girl wrapped in his arms, encouraged me to think Shah's recommendation had a lot going for it. The prospect, however hopeless, of being that close to a female sounded most attractive.

After a lengthy pause, I heard Shah say again, "Bobby *sahib*, you must have womans before you go. I can fix it up for you."

"Fix it? How?"

"Easy, *sahib*, we can do it at Chakla."

Utterly bewildered, the sensation compounded with a stab of fear, I countered, "Where's Chakla? What's Chakla?"

Shah's response was to guffaw helplessly. The noise made the *tonga wallah* jerk up in his seat with alarm and the horse to flatten its ears in fright. "You not heard of Chakla? It famous place, near Raja bazaar. Men go there to *jig-a-jig* with womens, Bobby *sahib*." His pale eyes searched my face. Seeing I was intrigued, he ceased laughing.

"But you have to pay for these, these, women, don't you?" I stuttered awkwardly. "Actually, I've no money left," I lied, "so even if I wanted, which I don't, there's no point in thinking about it." The truth was I had fifteen rupees left over from my trip to Lahore. Making it sound more of an afterthought than a serious question, I put it to him in a casual-sounding voice, "By the way, how much is it?"

Shah was not taken in. He replied, "Bobby *sahib*, do not be worried for this, because I will pay! It will be my present to you. It is only sixty rupees." Placing his right arm across his chest, he declaimed: "Truly my friend, I mean what I say. Allah strike me dead if I lie."

I protested, but only half-heartedly, for by this time I was definitely interested in the proposition. "Shah, don't be ridiculous, sixty rupees is your entire month's wages. I could never allow it."

"Believe me, no problem, *sahib*," Shah responded, eagerly. "I have plenty money. Please let me do this small favour for you, Bobby *sahib*."

That Shah was ready to spend a month's pay on me, just so I could lose my virginity, was kindness itself. To have discovered how much he cared for me was positively humbling. Even though I knew he really could not afford to pay and would impoverish himself by borrowing from a moneylender, I still didn't offer to make a contribution. To my undying shame, I accepted Shah's proposal. I lied to myself that I would never have done so but for his insistence. My behaviour towards my friend was unutterably shabby. It made a mockery of our friendship.

"Good, I am glad," said Shah, looking relieved. "Then we go day after tomorrow, after I've finish work..." He paused. "*Sahib*, you will have to wear one of my spare *shalwar kameez*. It would not be seemly for an *ingrezi sahib* to be seen in Chakla."

Exhilarated, thrilled by the prospect of having sex, it never occurred that there was also danger attached, besides the possibility of catching some nasty disease. I shook Shah by the hand.

"I do not know how to thank you," I said.

"No problem, *sahib*," he replied, waggling his head from side to side.

When I arrived home, my mother was waiting for me. "Just got back, darling?" she asked, giving me a kiss on the cheek. "How did it all go?"

Showing her the two passports, I replied, "Fine. Here, take a look at them."

"Nice picture of you," she said, "not so good of Geoffrey."

Geoff, who had been on tenterhooks waiting for my arrival, bounded onto the verandah. In his cod American accent, which veered wildly from the Deep South to the Bronx, he shouted, "Hey, man, let me take a gander at my passport, willya?" I held out the one in his name. He grabbed it and retreated into the house.

Meanwhile, my mother was saying, "I'm so glad for you, Bobby. I just know you'll do well in England. Much, much better than you could have ever done in Pakistan, thanks to Nick." At the mention of her lover's name, I froze. Even more so, when she added "So glad Freddie Barratt went with you to Lahore. He must have been a great help. I must remember to thank him."

Before she could even finish her sentence I was off to my bedroom, leaving her looking bewildered. I found Geoff lying on top of his bed, still examining his passport photograph as if obsessed with his own image. Even though I was dog tired, my mind was occupied with the events of the past two days, so it was going on midnight before I slept.

I awoke very early for me, just before six o'clock. I knew that Shah started work at five and would be busy in the kitchen fixing *chota hazri* for the family, comprising tea and a digestive biscuit for each of us. Loathing myself for allowing him to shoulder the entire burden of converting me into "a real mans" as he put it, I thrust fifteen rupees into his hands. At first, he refused to take the money. Only after I threatened to bow out, did he reluctantly accept. Shaking his head, he said, a sorrowful smile on his face, "Bobby *sahib* that was to be my present to you." But having salved my conscience, I felt altogether more cheerful about my initiation the following night.

Afflicted by a combination of apprehension, excitement and sheer terror, the ensuing hours dragged by. Only when Shah came into my bedroom after ten o'clock at night bearing a freshly laundered set of his clothes—baggy pants, long shirt and a black embroidered waistcoat—did I finally realise there was no turning back. I closed the bedroom door and dressed quickly. Shah stepped back to admire the effect.

"Bobby *sahib*," he chuckled, "now you look like perfect Pathan bearer."

More like perfect twerp, I thought, as we slipped out of the house by a back door.

Shah, who had borrowed a bike from a servant, waited for me to climb on mine, before we pedalled off together into the pitch-black night. I was filled with dread and riddled with self-revulsion. Shah, on the hand, was finding the enterprise very funny indeed. He laughed all the way into Rawalpindi, making ribald comments as he cycled alongside me. For him, the charade, my disguise, and his determination to have me deflowered were all part of a great game. It only served to make me huffy with him.

Half an hour after we started out, we threaded our way through the teeming, clamorous Rajah Bazaar and then out again on the Murree Road. By this time I was all for going back. Not so Shah: he was hell bent to get to Chakla and encouraged me onwards with great enthusiasm.

"Just soon we are getting there," he kept on shouting, using Urdu so as not to attract attention. Following closely behind, I was beginning to get concerned we'd ever reach our destination when Shah turned off the tarmac road and lurched onto a muddy track. Now that we were off the main road, even the meagre light coming from sparsely spaced street lamps vanished altogether. There was no moon. The darkness made it impossible to avoid deep potholes, rubble and foul-smelling refuse. I fell off my bike a couple of times, which set *pi-dogs* barking somewhere in the gloom ahead. Other than small pinpricks of yellow light coming from a row of stunted mud huts directly in front of us, there was no illumination of any kind. Shah, who obviously knew his way from previous forays, dismounted suddenly and handed me his bike to hold for him.

"This is Chakla, Bobby *sahib*," he said, pointing to the huts. "Please wait here for me."

With that, he entered the nearest of the mean dwellings and was out again within seconds, his exit heralded by loud abuse from a woman. Head down and determined, he strode through the open door of the next hut, only to emerge again almost instantly to the accompaniment of angry screams. Flinging aside the beaded curtain of the third hut, he went inside with a flourish. The occupant pushed him out, this time with foul curses.

It was only at his fifth attempt, when he reached the very last hut in the line, that Shah found success. He gave me a thumbs up sign from the doorway before calling out, "So sorry. All the other bloody womens is wanting much money. This one okay. She will be doing *jig-a-jig* with both of us for sixty rupees! But please, Bobby *sahib*, okay I go first?"

I watched Shah disappear inside the hut. Shuddering at the thought I would soon be required to follow, I wished fervently that he would stay in the brothel forever. But he reappeared a quarter of an hour later. Giving me a cheeky look, he chuckled, "She very good. You will like."

Reluctantly, with lead in my legs and none elsewhere, I stepped into the hut. The small room within was surprisingly clean and lit by a single oil lamp dangling from the ceiling. In one corner, a *lotha*—a clay vessel—full of water stood in a shallow earthen recess. On the facing wall, King George V stared back at me from a faded picture on an old calendar, promising dire consequences if I let the Raj down. Beneath a tiny window, was a string *charpoy* bed spread with a filthy, disturbed coverlet. The thought of my body coming into contact with it revolted me.

Facing me was the occupant of the room, a wizened, bare-breasted woman wearing a long patterned skirt of yellow cotton. Probably no more than thirty, to me she appeared ancient and repellent. Giving me a gap-toothed smile, she began loosening the drawstring of her skirt.

I watched in horror and fascination as she stripped naked, her skirt dropping to her ankles. In the lamplight, her skinny brown body gleamed with perspiration, from her recent labours or else from the hurried application of coconut oil. Whichever it was, I averted my eyes. The silence between us grew and became monstrous. It seemed an age before the woman addressed me in Pushtu. Seeing that I did not understand a word of what she was saying, she indicated with the clearest of lewd gestures, what I was meant to do next. Seeing I still hadn't budged and remained fixed to the spot, she reached out a hand to unfasten the drawstring of my *shalwars*—whereupon I fled.

Shah was waiting for me outside. "How was it Bobby *sahib*?" he cried in glee. "Did I not tell you she would be good? Now, *sahib*, you go Blighty as real mans."

Naturally, I did not put him right. How could I? So conjuring up a false enthusiastic laugh, I gripped his hand and pumped it up and down. "It was brilliant!" I lied. "How can I ever thank you enough?"

It would be fifty years before I could repay him.

Chapter 6

Three days before Geoff and I left for Karachi, from where we'd fly to England, my mother had her tailor come to the house and measure me up for a Kashmiri tweed blazer and a pair of thick flannel trousers. "You'll both need something warm. It's cold at home in the UK," she said.

Geoff gave a dismissive snort, saying he wasn't interested in home-made stuff. Instead, he went to a gentlemen's outfitter in Rawalpindi and acquired an off-the-peg, beige gabardine suit with wide lapels and padded shoulders. In this style, in vogue in Hollywood, he aimed to slouch about in the UK looking like Robert Mitchum.

Having run his tape measure over me, Ali, the tailor, set up his treadle Singer sewing machine on the verandah and got to work. He deftly chalked out a pattern on the material my mother had selected, before getting down to scissoring it into panels suitable for sewing. By early evening, he was ready for my first fitting. My mother had often used Ali to copy clothes she'd seen in English magazines, and was delighted Ali had made an equally good job of mine.

"Finish off, tomorrow, *sahib*," Ali promised, speaking through a row of pins hanging from his lips. True to his word, he delivered my blazer and trousers, ready for me to wear the following afternoon. Now, with Maurice's old dinner jacket and black trousers which he'd given me the year before, plus a couple of white cotton shirts, my mother assured me my wardrobe was entirely adequate for the UK.

"You're sure to be invited to black tie events, like those at the Rawalpindi Club," my mother stated with absolute certainty. "That's after you've found your feet, darling."

In my mother's fanciful dreams, her son Robert was sure to make his fortune and be someone important in no time at all. Much in demand, he'd swan about with debutantes at Queen Charlotte's Ball in London, dressed up in his dinner jacket and black tie. Alternatively, if he fulfilled his ambition to join the RAF, he'd soon be a wing commander and look equally spectacular in his mess kit.

By now almost as excited as I, my mother, in a fit of extravagance, had a Chinese boot maker come to the house. He drew the outline of our feet on a piece of newspaper and returned the following day with two pairs of black brogues in the softest of leather for her two sons. Other than for making a slight squeak when I walked, they were perfect. My shoes were infinitely kinder to my toes than the Army boots, soled and heeled with metal inserts, I wore throughout my days at school.

All my belongings now went into my old tin trunk, one that had travelled back and forth with me to school for the past nine years. Geoff, on the other hand, was bequeathed our grandmother's battered leather suitcase, stuck all over with P&O and Cunard stickers.

While all this was going on, Colonel Nick Grahame-Carter kept well away from the house. His name was mentioned just the once, when my mother announced he'd generously paid for our train tickets to Karachi. "It'll be a long trip," she said. "Two nights and two days. You'll be met off the train by a chap called Sam Windsor-Brown. By the way, his nickname is

Soupy. He works in Attock Oil's Karachi office. You'll recognise him immediately. He's about six foot six with a yellow fluffy moustache."

"Soupy?" I asked. "Why Soupy?"

"Brown Windsor. Play on words, darling," my mother replied. "You know, like the Brown Windsor soup cook makes." Noting my blank expression, for I couldn't recall cook ever making anything of the sort, she continued with a show of irritation, "Oh, never mind, Bobby. Let's get on, shall we? Soupy has rather a lot of money for you. It's from Maurice's company account. You'll each be given eleven pounds sterling. Should see you through until you join up or get a job."

Even before finishing her sentence, I had already calculated I'd soon be very rich. Rich! Eleven pounds converted to two hundred and twenty rupees. Unbelievably rich!

"That's incredibly generous of Maurice," I said. "Fancy him thinking of us when he's so ill. I really ought to write and thank him, don't you think?"

A strange, wary expression flitted across mother's face. Turning away, she replied, "Yes, darling, both of you must. You'll find Maurice's address in the bureau in the drawing room."

At eight o'clock on the evening of August 21, 1949, the servants lined up to say goodbye to Geoff and me. Each one of them had been wonderfully kind to us: Victor, the head bearer; Booloo, the cook; the two gardeners, Kasim and Riaz; the lavatory cleaner and water carrier, a Christian called Joshua; and, of course, my friend Shah. Taking both of our hands between theirs, they bowed their heads in turn and wished us well in Blighty. They all had tears in their eyes except for Shah, who stood proud and upright, looking directly at me. "I coming to station with you, Bobby *sahib*," he announced. "*Memsahib* say I can come in car." My mother nodded her assent. "Yes, Shah can help with the trunks."

An Army staff car, one of General Ayub Khan's fleet of American automobiles put at Colonel Grahame-Carter's disposal, stood ready by the porch. The driver saluted us into the rear, while Shah sat up front. I'd only been on a train on two previous occasions, once, years before en route to school from Lahore, and the second, more recently in the company of Major Barratt to collect my passport. But this train was different. It was taking me from a life I knew to an uncertain future in a strange country, which everyone called home, but wasn't home for me. Although I'd been longing for this day, I felt terribly nervous as the car pulled away.

As soon as we arrived at the railway station, my mother handed Geoff our train tickets. "My God, Mum!" he exclaimed, his eyes wide with horror. "Third-class tickets. Holy shit, Mum! Third class! We'll be with a bunch of Pakistani villagers and all their crap. There'll be no room to move, let alone go to the john." Geoff grimaced. "If there is one, it'll probably be one of those bloody squat-down jobs."

"I'm sorry, darling," my mother replied unsympathetically. "Nick's paid for them out of his own pocket. I'm afraid you'll have to make the best of it."

"Two third-class tickets to Karachi would hardly make a dent in his colonel's salary," I retorted bitterly. "The bastard's getting his own back on me."

"Now then, Bobbie, that's enough of that," my mother interrupted, anger sparking in her voice. "After what you did, you should be thankful Nick is having you flown home. At least I am grateful to him for giving you the chance of a future in England. There was none here for you." Pulling a handkerchief from her sleeve, the actor in her came to the fore. Conjuring up tears, she moaned softly, “My boys, my boys, when shall your poor mother see you next?”

I was certain Shah had heard what was being said, for he appeared stricken at the thought of us travelling in third class. *Sahib*s never travelled third class. Never. He quickly hopped around to the car boot and removed our luggage, saying as he passed me, “Bobby *sahib*, don’t worry, I will get you best compartment I can.” With that, carrying my tin trunk on his head, leaving Geoff’s case for the driver, he scurried into the crowd and was soon lost to sight in the melee. As we fought our way to the waiting train, hearts pounding, fearful of what to expect, we heard Shah shouting from the front of the train, “Bobby *sahib*! Here, *sahib*, refreshment car. Come on here.”

We found him standing by the open door of the third-class refreshment car, coupled two carriages back from the locomotive.

“We can’t go in there, can we?” I questioned uncertainly.

“*Sahib*” he replied, with a grin. “Pakistanis never buy food from refreshment car. They too poor. They take own food on train. So this carriage will be empty. Only few peoples in it.”

To the last, Shah was looking after my interests, seeing I had the best on offer. Even so, I felt dubious as I climbed the steps into the carriage. Shah urged Geoff and me on, while standing to one side to allow my mother to follow us in.

“It okay, *sahib*,” he assured me. “I had word with driver, he told me it good place. He Pathan like me. Never tell lie.” Laughing aloud at his own joke, he suddenly turned serious once more. As he took me into a crushing bear hug, I felt his entire body tremble. I pushed him away. His eyes were filled with sorrow.

“My friend,” I said, “I will never forget you. Never. Thank you for everything.” Pausing, I repeated, “Everything,” aware he'd understand I meant Chakla and the prostitute he'd paid for. "*Inshallah*, we'll meet again. Now go, please."

The tears he'd been trying so hard to restrain flooded his cheeks. "Okay *sahib*, okay," he choked, giving Geoff a swift handshake before jumping from the carriage to the platform.

Heartbroken, I was left wondering what was to become of my best friend.

My mother's face wore a perplexed frown. "How very odd," she said. "May I ask why you are being so emotional about leaving Shah? You shouldn't worry darling. We'll look after him." Her words had the ring of truth, yet I knew she lied. Shah was due for the chop. My mother no longer had need of him.

A tremendous hiss of steam followed by two loud hoots from the huge locomotive brought me down to earth. "Mummy," I said, "It's time to say goodbye."

"Yes, my darlings," she replied tearfully. She flung her thin arms around me before doing the same to Geoff. "You've got Major Tipping's address in London, haven't you? Write from there, darling. Let Mummy know you've arrived safely, won't you?" Pain in her voice, she murmured, "Oh God! I shall miss my boys so much. So too, will Pam, and Dick and David and little Ronald. All of us."

I could tell she meant it. Sniffing, my mother returned to the platform, where she stood waving a lace handkerchief as the great beast of an engine gave out a tremendous huff. Slowly, it gathered speed. My mother, cloaked in billowing white smoke, vanished from our sight as the train drew away from the station. I had left Rawalpindi forever.

The refreshment car was as bare as Major Barratt's first-class couchette had been luxurious. Slatted wooden settles ran the length of the carriage on both sides beneath large, grimy, open windows. Tables, fixed to the floor at intervals, looked barely wiped. There were only two other occupants. Dressed in brown shalwars and kameez, I noted the brass badges on their tunics, denoting they were railway employees. They glanced away when I looked at them, and went to the far end of the carriage where a small iron stove stood. Balanced on a shelf by a window, a basket topped up with unsavoury-looking *chapattis* lurked. I presumed from the smell that the large aluminium pan beside the basket was filled with curry of some sort. I saw Geoff's nose twitch in distaste.

"I wonder if these guys have any water on the train," he asked, "It's so bloody hot in here."

What he said was true. It was stifling. Under my thin, soaked shirt the sweat ran down my body.

"Sure to have, Geoff," I replied, picking at the material, hoping vainly that a draught of air might cool me. "Let's ask them, shall we? It's five hours to Lahore, where I know we can get some."

Fortunately, the two railwaymen were able to supply a couple of glasses of water with ice in it. Refusing payment, they shyly asked if we wished more, but as I watched the ice melt rapidly, I realised Geoff and I had been foolish to accept.

Seeing how nervous I looked, one of the men smilingly reassured me, "Do not worry, *sahib*, ice okay. Railway Policy Memo, reference 256, chapter four in manual."

Thankful the men were still hostage to the bureaucratic railway procedures of the Raj, we retreated to our luggage and there figured out somewhere to sleep for the night. There was nothing for it; the wooden benches had to do. So, dragging out my new blazer from my trunk, I rolled it into a pillow, stretched out, said goodnight to Geoff and promptly fell asleep.

Woken by Geoff's snores, I checked my watch. It was ten in the morning. We had both slept through the night. I got up on one elbow and looked through the window onto parched, flat terrain outside, stretching to the horizon, so different to the fertile Punjab. Obviously, we were well beyond Lahore.

"My God!" cried Geoff, as he stirred into life. "That's amazing. We'll soon be at Multan. How in hell did we sleep through Lahore?"

The train had indeed stopped at Lahore, and taken on additional passengers as well. Startled, I looked about. Occupying a large area, but still distanced from Geoff and me, there were some fifty other people in the carriage. Lolling on the tables, squatting, spitting, moaning softly to themselves, women and children, their pathetic bundles wrapped with string beside them, returned our gaze with blank eyes. They looked like refugees fleeing. If so, from what?

Geoff shrugged, suggesting we scoff one of the sandwiches Shah had prepared for us, which were in his case. The railwaymen were good for cups of tea, which cost us three annas for two. Feeling guilty under the eyes of our fellow passengers, we drank from the small metal vessels we'd been handed and devoured our sandwiches, as far away from them as was possible. Returning the empty containers, Geoff asked the railwaymen if there was a lavatory. Grimacing, Geoff returned.

"No john here, at all. We'll have to cross our legs—and, boy, am I busting. I guess I'll have to wait until we get to Multan. Don't know how far that is."

"I should have done for Nick," I laughed. "Bastard had it in for us, knew what would happen. But we'll show him."

My brother was staring out of the window, lost in thought, his pale face dripping with sweat. "What will you do when we get to England?" he asked. "Join the Air Force or the army?"

"I don't know," I replied. "If the British hadn't left Pakistan I would have joined up just to get out the country. No, deep down what I'd really like is the chance to be a singer. Y'know, sing on stage. Musicals, that sort of thing."

Geoff was taken aback, making me realise just how little we knew each other. "I had no idea," he said. "Sure, you've a good voice and all, but hell, have you thought how to go about it?"

"No, not really. I'll take any old job first. Find out how later, I guess."

I saw the uncertainty in Geoff's eyes. "Are you sure you've a good enough voice?" he asked.

"I don't know. My choirmaster at school seemed impressed. He said I had the makings, encouraged me to take up singing as a career."

I nudged Geoff, "What are you going to do, though? Work in a shop, like you did in 'Pindi? You could try Heals. Mum told me Freddie Barratt was a director. If you mentioned he's a friend, who knows, it might help?"

"Not without a school cert it won't. You've got yours, I haven't. When I was living with Gran in Lahore I had private tutors and did damn-all work, so I've got no qualifications at all..." He turned his face to the passing scene again and, almost in a whisper said, "Actually, I'd like to be a writer like Dashiell Hammett. I've always enjoyed writing you know, same as Dad."

Further discussion on the subject of what we'd do in England was soon quashed as one of the dreaded sandstorms of the Sindh Desert struck with alarming velocity. The sky darkened as it developed. Great swirls of sand appeared beyond the windows, striking the train, peppering the glass, seeping into every crevice, until the inside of the carriage was covered with a coating of grainy brown particles. Soon everyone was cloaked with the stuff—our hands, faces, eyes, mouths, every orifice invaded—until we could hardly breathe. Those who had blankets or wore loose clothing used these to cover their faces as they wailed loudly. With my new jacket held to my face, I shouted over the noise of the storm, which roared above the sound of the rattling, rocking train, "Geoff, are you okay?" His gabardine suit pressed into service as a mask, he gestured that he was.

The storm continued unabated for four hours. Some passengers hunkered down, their faces pressed hard to the floor; others gripped their bodies tight and rocked; babies clasped to their mother's bosoms cried, their weeping drowned out by the terrifying racket. Then, as quickly as the storm had come upon us, the sky lightened, the wind softened, the dust-laden clouds swept past to wreak their devastation elsewhere. Quietly, we all got to our feet. Somehow, our shared experience had emboldened the Pakistanis to smile at us, to grin sympathetically with bared, brown teeth and reddened eyes. Geoff and I appeared just as dishevelled, but we smiled back at them in relief. As best we could, we dusted ourselves down to make ourselves presentable and waited for the surcease that our next stop would bring.

Alighting from the train in Multan, where the train stopped for an hour, Geoff and I legged it to the restrooms. As luck would have it, the first-class lavatory was clean. Taking our lives in our hands, we drank copiously directly from the taps.

Eyeing us, a British Army officer, a lieutenant aged about forty, sauntered over to the stall to pee. Looking over his shoulder as he relieved himself, he drawled, "I say, hope we don't have to go through all that again. Bloody sight worse than the Western Desert." Fixing his flies, he ventured, "Mind if I ask where you chaps are going?" His eyes flitted over Geoff, taking in his white complexion, before sweeping over to me and resting briefly on my duskier visage. I thought I detected the merest frown of puzzlement before he returned his attention to Geoff.

"We're going to Karachi," Geoff replied, quick as a flash. "My brother and I are catching a plane home from there. Arranged at the last minute, so couldn't get a train seat in first class. So we're bunked up in the refreshment car." I noticed immediately Geoff's adoption of a classy British accent and the fact he'd cleverly avoided the phrase 'third class'.

"But that's dreadful!" gasped the astonished lieutenant. "You can't possibly travel to Karachi in there. Now, look, I've a first-class couchette all to myself. You'd be most welcome to share it with me."

Playing along, my brother protested, "No, we can't possibly incommode you." I was absolutely taken aback by his nerve, his almost Woosterish response, as I heard him repeat, "No, we really cannot."

"But you must!" answered the officer. "I insist. Anyhow, it'd be terrific to have some good English company. So, what's it to be then?"

Geoff and I looked at one another. Hunching his shoulders, Geoff assented, "Okay, we accept. That's jolly decent of you."

"Well, that's settled then, fetch your luggage and we'll have a G & T. I'm in carriage four, middle of the train, reserved sticker on the window. Shall I send my batman to help?"

"No, no," replied Geoff. "Thanks, but we can manage." Taking my arm, he shunted me along the platform. Reverting to his more usual faux-American accent, he muttered, "If that guy's batman had discovered we were in third class, we'd have had it."

The officer introduced himself as Lieutenant Roger Beamish. We travelled in luxury for two more days and a night, all the way to Karachi. Even more spacious than Major Barratt's compartment, Roger's four-bunk leather-covered couchette was similarly blessed with a highly efficient air-conditioning unit. In addition to his Pakistani Army batman, Roger also had another servant to look after our every need. For us to drink, there was a choice of India pale ale or the ubiquitous Murree Brewery beer chilling in the ice box; to eat, sliced cold chicken, fresh bread, mangoes and other fruit.

"If you'd like something hot, my chap Feroze is a first-class cook," invited Roger. "He can rustle you up a curry from the kitchen, if you wish."

Thanking Roger for his splendid hospitality, I smiled, thinking of how Colonel Nick Grahame-Carter's scheme had been thwarted thanks to Geoff. We were travelling in railway train heaven, instead of mucking in with Pakistani peasants in dusty third class. Let the heavens roar, the sandstorms flay, we were insulated from it all in our sealed capsule.

Roger Beamish was envious of us flying home, for his destination was a holding camp in Deolali, where he was to await transport by ship to England. "Your father must be pretty high ranking to get you on a plane," he commented.

"Yeah, well," replied Geoff, loftily, instantly promoting my mother's lover to the role of father, "he's a colonel in Intelligence. G2 to General Ayub Khan."

Roger whistled. Giving us a bow, he laughed, "That explains it. I didn't know I was so honoured." If only he'd known the truth.

The two long days passed, with desultory conversation mainly between Roger and Geoff interspersed with relays of beer and food at intervals. Roger might have been surprised to discover that neither of us had been born in England; if so, he didn't comment. Instead, he talked mostly of his longing to be home with his family in Kent—"The Garden of England," he said wistfully—adding he'd been away for three years on active service. "Lucky you chaps were too young to join up," he said at one point, adding, before he relapsed into a beer-sodden stupor, "War's a shitty business."

Mostly my mind was on other things, such as what I'd do in England, whether the Air Force would take me and, if not, how I'd manage. I remained optimistic, for the prospect of simply being there, in a country I'd read and heard so much about, was terribly exciting.

When we finally reached Karachi at ten on the morning of August 24, we thanked Roger, our benefactor, and said goodbye. It seemed as if I was constantly saying goodbye to someone or the other these days.

"Think nothing of it," said Roger. "It was good to have your company. Now, if you're ever in need of help, here's my address in the UK." He scribbled it on a page from a notebook, and handed it to Geoff, saying, "I mean it, chum."

The man's kindness to us was altogether overwhelming. I hope our gratitude showed as we shook his hand before looking about to see anyone resembling Soupy, the Attock Oil person who was supposed to be meeting us.

We had been waiting for about ten minutes or so when a tall, spindly looking man, adorned with the fluffy yellow moustache we had been told to look out for, came running up to greet us.

"I say, terribly sorry," he lisped. "You must be the brothers Matthews? I'm Sam Windsor-Brown from Attock Oil.

So, so, sorry I'm late," he said in a rush. "Held up by a dead water buffalo on the way here. Dashed thing just keeled over and died in the middle of the road. Caused havoc to the traffic." Waving an arm, he called out for a porter, who placed our luggage on his trolley and came after us as we walked.

As we were to discover as the hours progressed, Soupy—as, after he'd caught his breath, he insisted we call him—was constantly in a flap. Rushing about, weaving in between Geoff and me as we passed out of the station to his waiting car, he fired questions and answers at speed, such as, "Like some lunch, would you? Gymkhana Club do you? Or shall we try the Boat Club? Yes, yes, the Boat Club, on the river. That's it, you are sure to like that. Well, that's settled then, Boat Club it is."

Neither of us had had a chance to speak, have an opinion, demur, or anything for that matter, before we got into the car, at which point, I said, "I'm Bob, and this is Geoff."

"Windsor-Brown," he blathered, taking our hands. "I answer to Soupy for the obvious reasons. Now, chaps, your plane leaves from the airport at two this afternoon, so we'd better get a leg on, if we are to have a bit of scoff. Hungry, are you?" We had no chance to reply before he was off again, talking at headlong speed and gesticulating as we crawled down the busy road. "Got some cash for you from your stepfather, er, er, Maurice Cuell, but of course you already know that. Poor man's not well I hear." Finally, Soupy caught his breath and slowed down. "Dashed hot, isn't it?" he groaned, falling back on his seat, wiping the perspiration from his brow with a large handkerchief as he did so. "Heavens, must be 100 degrees already, and what's it?" he glanced at his watch. "Only eleven."

Brunch at the Boat Club, a rickety wooden structure overlooking a tributary of the Indus, consisted of a fine array of curries to which we helped ourselves. I drank orange juice, having refused the lethal-looking Bloody Marys that Soupy and Geoff were downing. A slight breeze ruffled the surface of the water. The rising heat haze made it impossible to see beyond the muddy foreshore, where fishing boats of various shapes and sizes were moored. I was tired out after the long journey and desperate to be on the plane and be off, whereas Soupy and Geoff carried on animatedly as my eyelids dropped. I heard little of what was said and only became alert when I saw Soupy fish his wallet from his jacket pocket and withdraw two envelopes. I wasn't too sleepy to take the eleven pounds he had for each of us, or to sign the receipt.

Soupy settled the bill and ushered us back to the car. "Right, chaps, off we go to the airport," he said.

I looked across to Geoff in the back seat of the car. He appeared as tense as I felt and doubtless just as jubilant.

At the airport, there was just one aircraft to be seen, a beautiful, silver plane with RAF roundels on the tail fin. It was our plane! Our plane! I dug Geoff in the ribs.

"That's our plane!"

"Yeah," came Geoff's laconic reply. "It's a twin-engined Convair. It's real fast, bud."

Soupy accompanied us to the door of what passed for Immigration and Passport Control, a small brick building by the hanger, and said goodbye. Yet another goodbye. We carted our luggage inside. A duty officer checked our passports. Running his eye down the passenger manifest, he called out, "Matthews, Geoffrey. Matthews, Ian." The man's use of my first name caused me to hesitate momentarily. From as far back as I could remember I'd always been known by my second name Robert, or Bob.

"Okay, proceed," said the duty officer, "I'll get someone to take your luggage from you. When you board in half an hour, please give a steward both your names. Your seats have already been allocated. Meantime, take a seat in the lounge, it's cooler in there."

I counted twenty or so other people in the lounge, who I guessed were also passengers. We were by decades the youngest. Some of the men were dressed in drill uniforms, others wore civilian clothes. All looked fearfully important. Even the women, presumably the officers' wives, appeared full of themselves, haughty, definitely unfriendly. Not given a second glance, we slunk to a far-off sofa and looked out of the window.

Fifteen minutes later, a Tannoy announced it was time to board. Geoff and I stood uncertainly, wondering what was expected of us. Only after everyone else had filed out did a man in RAF uniform suggest we follow them or else we'd be left behind. Deflated, we crept out onto the hot tarmac and then up a ladder into the plane. As we'd been instructed, we gave our names to a smiling Goan steward standing in the open doorway at the front of the plane. He led us to our seats at the very rear of the aircraft, which was less than half full. I could barely contain my excitement as I heard the captain's voice over the Tannoy, saying we were ready to take off. A minute later we were aloft, banking hard to the right over the Arabian Sea and on to England.

England. England. England...

Having flown over sea and desert for about three hours, our plane made a short refuelling stop at Shahjar, an RAF base in the Middle East, before taking off again for Cyprus. After we disembarked in Nicosia, we were driven by taxi to the Dome Hotel in Kyrenia for the night

As soon as Geoff and I settled into our shared bedroom, a maid sent to collect our dirty laundry knocked on the door.

We asked her to wait, allowing us time to change our shirts, which had been on our backs ever since we left home five days before. We put on the only spare shirts we owned before handing over our soiled ones to the maid. She asked if there was any more clothing to be laundered, suggesting with a shy smile that perhaps we might also wish to have our undergarments washed. In our experience, it was only women who wore underwear, so we just shrugged in response. The maid stood looking perplexed. After a moment, she recovered her composure, promising to have our laundry ready by morning.

Although neither of us was hungry, having stuffed ourselves with biscuits and an unending flow of soft drinks on the plane over, the fish on offer in the hotel dining room looked so enticing we both decided to try some. We'd not seen or eaten fish from the sea before. Our previous acquaintance with fish was limited to the *mahseer*, caught by me in the Sohan River. Although the *mahseer* is an extremely tasty fish, I found the pan-fried hake the waiter brought to the table to be even more delicious. I promised myself to try some more of the same when I got to England.

To walk off supper, Geoff and I took a stroll along the promenade directly in front of the hotel, built on a rocky outcrop overlooking the Mediterranean. We stopped by an ancient fortification dominating the harbour and looked out over the water. We stood enjoying the view; fishermen squatting on the sand repairing their nets, their boats moored at the quay, swaying and rocking on a dark blue sea ruffled by a freshening wind. The scene was so different from the dusty plains of the Punjab and the familiar views of the Himalayan mountains. We just stared and stared until the sun set, silently absorbing the beauty of it all.

Eventually, I heard Geoff remark, "Do you realise, Bob, other than from the window of our plane, this is the first time either of us has ever seen the sea?"

"Or for that matter, older bro, boats bigger than a rowing boat," I replied. "Or stayed at a proper hotel, or been on an island, or eaten fish from the sea." I dug Geoff in the ribs. "Or for that matter, seen so many pretty girls as the maids in our hotel."

We walked on towards the steep cliff adjoining the promenade, where I'd spotted a small bar set in a cave. From its open doors and windows, light streamed out, together with wild music accompanied by rough laughter, vigorous handclapping and the loud stamping of feet. The aroma of meat grilling on braziers mingled with the perfume of pine and rosemary wafting down from the hills, making each breath an intoxicating experience. Was England as magical a place as this?

On the following day, en route to Athens for another refuelling stop, we were delayed for six hours by a technical problem and finally arrived in Rome in the early evening. The Hotel Quirinale turned out to be even more sumptuous than the Dome. We handed over our passports and signed in. A bell boy with lots of gold braid encrusting his uniform led Geoff and me to adjoining bedrooms. As I looked about my vast, luxurious room, I figured that I would be better off joining the Army than looking for a job in England, if this was the kind of life officers enjoyed as a right. After taking a long bath in a free-standing, gleaming, enamel tub with gold plated taps, I joined Geoff in the hotel's magnificent dining room.

In space enough for a ball, officers and their wives, all dressed up for dinner, sat at fifty or so tables covered with fine white linen. Heads turned as we entered, and we were given searching, sniffy looks. Shrinking nervously, we followed a waiter to a table in a corner.

Before we had time to take our places, one of the stewards from our plane approached. At first, I didn't recognise him, for he had changed out of his white uniform into a grey cotton suit.

"It is Shiv, gentlemen. You know, steward from plane. Captain tell me to look after you, so permit me to join you, if okay by you. You can eat and drink anything, it is all paid for."

"Why not? You are welcome," I replied. "And thanks for telling us we don't have to pay. I was just wondering if we had enough cash to pay for all this.

"No problem. Thank you, sir," smiled Shiv. "Some officers very stuffy, not like you."

As if by magic, a waiter brought a chair for Shiv, who sat down opposite me. It turned out that Shiv, along with the other stewards, were civilian employees of a firm providing catering staff for a couple of aircraft used by the military, to transport serving officers home from the subcontinent. Shiv had done the Karachi to London run several times and, fortunately for us, had some acquaintance with Rome. He also knew more than a thing or two about the Italian menu at the Hotel Quirinale, which he translated for us.

He suggested antipasto to start with, which I really enjoyed, followed by a dish of pasta called carbonara. Since I'd never set eyes on pasta before, I found the slithery, squirmy, creamy stuff, tasty though it was, impossible to handle. Shiv came to my aid. He demonstrated how to swivel a fork laden with pasta into the bowl of a spoon, then bring it to our mouths without making a mess. Geoff and I soon got the hang of it and polished off a plateful with gusto.

Offered wine, I asked the wine waiter for a glass of red. Passing me a wine list, he asked me in English which one I'd like. Humming and hawing as if I knew great deal about wine, though in reality I had never tasted it, I pointed to one called Barolo. The waiter assured me I had made a fine choice and, with Geoff saying he'd like the same, rushed off to get a bottle.

Pasta was followed by veal Milanese, a gorgeous fruit salad, and finally cheese, which I'd tasted only once or twice before. Now absolutely stuffed with food, I finished my glass of wine. Watching Geoff sink a third glass of wine, it was obvious he was more drawn to it than I was. As we finally came to the end of our lavish meal, I speculated that since the Italians had been on the losing side in the war and could still produce such meals, it was conceivable that the English, who had won the war, might do even better. Cheered by the thought, I had a cup of coffee and suggested the others hurry up, so we could see the sights.

Since he knew the way, Shiv suggested we first visit the Coliseum. We set off together, ogling everything on the way, gasping at the scale and beauty of monumental buildings, at the broad piazzas, at the lavish use of white marble everywhere. A sense of history pervaded every corner of the city.

Sadly, since it was after ten o'clock when we arrived, there was nobody to show us around, but the grandeur of the immense outer walls of the Coliseum left me in awe, and Geoff, who had previously boned up on Rome, gave me a vivid description of Christians being devoured by lions and gladiators fighting to the death in the arena. As he rained facts down on me for a full five minutes, I heard the sound of a band playing in the piazza just ahead. Persuading the others to join me, we headed to the Piazza Venezia, which had been turned into an outdoor nightclub thronged with noisy, laughing Italians, sitting at tables or fox-trotting on a makeshift wooden floor. On a small stage sat a quartet of musicians playing great swing; a banner flapping above their heads proclaimed the venue to be the Casa Della Rosa.

"Hey, Bob, let's sit down here for a bit and listen to the music," said Geoff, ever the precocious sophisticate. Shiv looked as dubious as I was, and shifted his feet about uncertainly. However, Geoff persuaded us to stay for just a while, so we sat on the edge of our seats at an unoccupied table to hear the band. We were joined by a smiling blonde waitress in a short skirt and blouse, over whose dangerously low neckline large creamy breasts billowed. She held a writing tablet, evidently expecting us to order something to drink.

"*Vino*," said Geoffrey promptly, holding up three fingers, indicating drinks all round. As soon as the waitress departed, appearing unamused, perhaps because her usual clientele were in the habit of ordering champagne, I rounded on Geoff.

"What the hell are you doing? We don't have any lira. All we've got in the world is eleven pounds each. We haven't even reached England yet and you're already spending our dough."

Shiv looked on, embarrassed. "It is okay, sir," he said, waggling his head, speaking in a sing-song accent. "I was given some lira by my captain for my expenses. Kindly let me pay for the wine."

I could have hugged the man for his kindness, but since I was sweating profusely and wasn't into that kind of girly stuff, I shook him by the hand instead.

Geoff, normally polite, gave a dismissive shrug. "Thanks, but no need, Shiv. These Eyeties take pounds here." Stretching his legs under the table, he folded his arms behind his head and continued in his put-on American accent. Sounding like some small-town big shot, he said, "I heard in the hotel the Wops will take any currency. After all, we won the war didn't we?"

It was a crass remark, making me mad with anger. "Geoff, that was a bloody stupid thing to say. How about thanking Shiv?" I blazed. "This place is right out of our league and we should bugger off after we've drunk our wine."

Our waitress reappeared with our wine on a tray. "Tree a-tousand-a lira, *signore*," she said, looking Geoff squarely in the eye. Shiv peeled off a few notes from his money clip and asked for change. The waitress glowered back at him and handed Shiv a few coins, which he pocketed.

Geoff, who was evidently drunk, tapped Shiv on the shoulder. "Hey, man," he said. "I think the young lady deserves a tip, don't you?"

Not wishing to make a scene, Shiv handed the waitress a small gratuity. She flounced off, mouthing a stream of colourful Italian obscenities and leaving Shiv looking extremely put out.

After a short interlude, the band struck up a fanfare and from the far corner of the piazza, a white stallion with a plume of scarlet feathers on its head pranced into sight with a beautiful bare-breasted young woman sitting astride it. At first glance she appeared to be completely naked, but as she came closer I saw to my disappointment that her lower half was covered in thin flesh-coloured material. She made an enthralling sight as her mount reared on its hind legs, pirouetted and then high-stepped around the dance floor in time to the music. Enchanted by the vision, I sat slack-jawed, gazing at her. Shiv and I were so absorbed, neither of us took any notice of the woman who had slipped into a chair beside Geoff.

Shiv and I polished off our wine. Light-headed, we began to giggle like schoolgirls. He slapped my thigh delightedly, and I his, as the horse performed a sequence of astounding manoeuvres and the gorgeous woman did a handstand on its back. The music reached a crescendo. To a roll of drums, the horse, with the woman now draped across its saddle, trotted from the dance floor. Applause echoed around the piazza. I looked around to see if Geoff was enjoying the spectacle, but his seat was vacant. I spotted him some fifty yards distant in the unlit part of the piazza, walking hand in hand with a woman, before he vanished into the darkness.

"Shiv, where the hell has Geoff gone?" I shouted. "Come on, after the silly sod!"

With that, we legged it after him, but of Geoff there was no sign. Together, Shiv and I searched the length and breadth of the street, then up and down the brightly lit Via Veneto, lined with cafés, in case he had taken the woman for a drink there. Cursing Geoff, we marched here and there, up and down, past the Spanish Steps, the Piazza Barberini, the Via del Tritone, the Via Sistina and other places I lost track of.

By two in the morning, I had a more than a passing acquaintance with central Rome. Shiv and I were now seriously panicked, thinking Geoff could have come to some harm. Shiv considered contacting the police, saying that he was responsible for our safety and if Geoff didn't show up in time for the plane, he'd lose his job. However, I persuaded Shiv to continue looking.

We gave up in the end out of sheer fatigue and made it back to the hotel, where I stuffed Geoff's few scattered belongings into his case. I did the same with mine, before trying to get some sleep. The phone at my bedside brought me out of a half-slumber at six in the morning. Geoff had still not made an appearance. I was unable to think or eat my breakfast, wondering what had become of him, at a loss as to what to do next.

Half of the passengers on our plane were already waiting in the hallway, and a coach to take us to the airport stood outside the hotel. It was already six forty-five. Our plane was scheduled to take off at eight. In desperation, I was about to ask the concierge to contact the police when Geoff burst through the revolving doors of the hotel and collapsed in a chair in the lobby.

I was about to give him hell, but he waved a hand at me, attempting to catch his breath. “Sorry, Bob,” he said finally, still panting. “God knows how far I’ve run.” He took a deep breath. “Don’t tell me, I know I’ve been a bloody idiot. I’ve been walking around most of the night trying to find my way back here. And the worst thing is, I had all my money stolen.”

“All your cash?” I asked, disbelievingly. Geoff nodded, his face a picture of misery.

“My God, do you realise what this means?” I said. “How will we manage when we get to London?”

“Christ, Bob, I am so sorry,” said Geoff, crying.

Chapter 7

I had no chance to question Geoff further. The passengers were already filing onto the coach. "Leave it," I said, feeling sick. "Tell me about it on the plane."

Despite our leaving the hotel a quarter of an hour late, our plane took off from the airport exactly on time. "What made you go off with that dame?" I asked, as soon as we had taken our seats on board. "What happened after you disappeared with her?"

"I was a bit drunk," muttered Geoff, staring out of the window, unable to look me in the eye. "Bloody taught me a lesson."

"Yeah, me too, Geoff," I replied acidly. "That's never to trust you again. You do know we've got just over five pounds each now. What got into you? Was it because you hadn't had it off with a woman before?" Out of curiosity, I added, "Did you get to poke her?"

Sounding utterly wretched, Geoff replied, "You're right, Bob. I never had a woman before. Still haven't." I watched Geoff clenching and unclenching his hands, as he fought to explain himself. Sighing heavily, he began speaking in short sentences, taking a deep breath between each one. "I got taken for a ride. She—Isabella, that's her name—thought I was an American. I didn't tell her I wasn't. Told me I was such a handsome guy. Invited me home to meet her parents. Said she had never met an American before. Wanted to be my friend, that's all."

By no stretch of the imagination could Geoff be called handsome. He'd always had problems dating girls. I guessed Isabella's flattery had gone to his head. And there was I thinking my older brother was much smarter, more worldly than I was.

"Come off it, Geoff," I scoffed. "Meet her parents? Didn't you realise she was a prossie?"

"No, honest. I thought she was just being nice to me," Geoff wailed.

"Bloody fool. Okay, so what happened then?"

"She took me down this street and that... I really don't know where, and I finally ended up at her flat. She told me I had to pay her money to sleep with her. Hell, bro, I was so drunk, I didn't see this big guy come in. I was scared stiff. He took my coat off me and went through all my pockets. Isabella just stood there laughing. The guy took all my money...and my Shaeffer pen. Left me with nix. After that, the guy slung me out on the street. Didn't know where I was."

By now I was almost feeling sorry for Geoff. "How did you get home?"

"I have no idea. All I knew was the name of our hotel. So, I gesticulated, saying 'Hotel Quirinale' to everyone I passed, hoping someone would figure I was lost. None of them understood me. All they said was *ciao*, or meow, some word that sounded like that, and walked off. I gave up in the end and tried retracing my steps to the Coliseum, but I got hopelessly lost. It was about five when I eventually saw a policeman, who understood a few words of English. He gave me directions, but still it took me more than an hour to find my way back."

"You must be dead beat."

"You said it. Jeez, Bob, I am so sorry."

"You bloody should be. There's no point in going on about it, though. What's done is done. Better get some sleep now. I'm pretty tired out, too."

There were several empty seats in the cabin, so I took one by a window and curled up. Geoff did the same, and we slept the rest of the four-hour flight to London. We both awoke just as the plane landed at RAF Northolt. I should have been thrilled to be finally in England, but I was suddenly scared stiff. I had so little money, and not the slightest idea of how or where to start looking for a job. I had no friends in England, indeed didn't know anyone at all. It was hardly the best preparation to start a new life.

As the forward doors were opened, Geoff and I exchanged nervous glances. We remained in our seats until all the officers on board, together with their families, left the aircraft. Eventually, shepherded by Shiv, we walked across the tarmac to a corrugated iron hut.

"Your passports an' all will be checked in there," Shiv said. "Then after, we will go by coach to Gloucester Road, West London Air Terminal to pick up luggage. Then, sorrs, we will say goodbye." He wagged his head from side to side, looking sadly at us, "It has been a pleasure knowing you."

I looked into Shiv's eyes, wondering if he was just being polite. If I had been in his shoes, I'd have been happy to see the back of us.

The immigration formalities were concluded very quickly, our faces and passports given the barest of glances, before we found ourselves led to a waiting coach. Geoff and I were the last to take our seats before it pulled away. On the approach to London, I noticed how narrow the streets were, and how small the terraced houses lining them—a far cry from the fine buildings and piazzas of Rome.

It was a bright, sunny day, which should have lifted my spirits. However, because everything looked so scruffy, it made me feel depressed. All the surrounding buildings needed a lick of paint to cheer them up. Where were the green fields and thatched cottages I had dreamt about? Nothing in the grim passing scene met any of my expectations.

The coach stopped directly in front of the glass-fronted West London Air Terminal building on Gloucester Road. I sat, flinching from the noise of the traffic, my hearing more attuned to the clip-clop of horses and only occasionally the hooting or honking of a car or bus circulating around the cantonment of 'Pindi. I waited until the very last moment, and had to be marshalled off the coach into the baggage hall where our luggage was being unloaded.

Geoff, who was more in charge of his wits than I was of mine, found a porter who told him the simplest way to get to Streatham, our ultimate destination, was via the Underground. Conveniently, Gloucester Road Tube station was just across the street from the terminal building. Carrying our luggage, we dodged through the traffic and entered the station. Too timorous by half to ask for directions, I handed Geoff a pound note to buy our tickets and get us on the right train. Geoff used his American accent at the ticket office to ask the price of the fare to Streatham, I imagine because it somehow boosted his confidence. Returning with two tickets, a ten shilling note and a fistful of change, he said, out of the corner of his mouth, forgetting he was still in Yankee mode and now talking to his brother, "Baab, the guy told me we gotta check out the Underground map and find the District line, which goes to Victoria. We have to buy another ticket there for the Overground railway. So let's haul."

Having never before seen an escalator, I stood fascinated, as people casually stepped on the moving contraption without a thought. I stood at the top, trying to follow their example, timing the precise moment to climb on it. But hampered as I was by my tin trunk I missed my footing and was forced to clutch at the clothing of the person ahead of me to prevent myself from tumbling downwards. Red in the face and full of apologies, I held on to the rail with one hand and with the other grasped my tin trunk, stepping off in a rush at the bottom. Geoff had not fared much better, so the two brothers Matthews made themselves as inconspicuous as possible and shuffled to the far end of the platform.

The Underground train was a revelation. Digging Geoff in the ribs, I grinned, "I can see why they call this the Tube." From the sidelong glances I received from my fellow passengers it was clear they thought me a fool. As the train rocked and rattled on, Geoff shrank inside his coat trying to make out he was nothing to do with me.

Happily, the train made just a few stops before we alighted at Victoria and made our way to the main station. This time I had got the hang of the moving steps and, with a sense of triumph, I made the top of the escalator without making an idiot of myself. Handing in our tickets at the gate, Geoff and I made our way into the main hall, where we stood like a couple of lost orphans, I with my black tin trunk at my feet and Geoff hanging on to his battered leather case, both of us jostled by a press of people on their way to work.

I noticed that a great many of the men shuffling past were clad in drab suits and dirty raincoats. Others wore bowler hats and were dressed in black jackets and striped trousers. Striding purposefully, furled umbrellas in hand, they were animated versions of cartoons I'd seen in *Punch*. There was none of the exuberance of the Italians we'd encountered in Rome. As for the women, most were young and wore flouncy summer frocks. With piled-up hair, sticking-out breasts and scarlet lips, they made a wondrous sight. My eyes had never before seen so many glamorous white women in all my life.

So taken was I, Geoff was forced to shout in my ear to get my attention. "Bob, I hope you've remembered the address in Streatham? I seem to have mislaid it."

The news shocked me out of my reverie. I fished in my jacket pocket for my small wallet and, with a sigh of relief, found a scrap of paper with the name and address of the person in Streatham with whom we were to stay until we got our bearings.

"Yeah, I've got it. Major Tipping at 72 Downton Avenue, Streatham, wherever that is. Good job I made a copy."

"Well, can you let me have it? We need to find which station we go to," Geoff said. "Give me some dough. Wait here while I buy the tickets."

Geoff returned a few minutes later, tickets in hand, saying, "We go to Streatham station. Platform six. We're just in time. The train's due to leave in ten minutes."

Our train was already standing at the platform. We claimed a couple of seats in a third-class compartment at the rear of the train. Cigarette butts littered the floor; the entire carriage reeked of smoke. Furthermore, the fabric-covered seats were stained and grimy, much dirtier than those of the trains we'd travelled on in Pakistan. We sat in silence, staring out of the murky windows, while our companions on the train had their heads buried in newspapers. My eyes strayed to the *Daily Mirror*, which I recognised from the bound copies we received in Pakistan once a month, but *The Times* and the others being read were foreign to me.

Instead of being interested in the view outside, my mind was entirely occupied with how we'd manage with what was left of our money. As I struggled with the complexities of sterling currency—twelve pence to a shilling, twenty shillings to a pound, half-crowns and crowns—our train slid out of Victoria, gathering speed, rolling and rocking past boarded-up buildings, with here and there the skeletons of bombed-out structures surrounded by mounds of rubble. I had a sinking feeling that all of London might be the same. But on leaving central London behind, I caught sight of several quiet leafy squares surrounded by fine houses, proof that not all of London was a wasteland.

We finally pulled into Streatham station at midday. As Geoff and I piled out onto the platform with our luggage, we were confronted by a uniformed porter with a trolley. Touching his peaked cap, he asked if we wished assistance. Geoff piped up and asked for directions to Downton Avenue.

"Just dahn the road it is, sir. Up the steps, outta the station, turn left, then after the lights, first right and you're on Downton Avenue. Come on, I'll give you hand with your belongings."

Instructing us to follow him, he placed our luggage on a trolley, before scuttling off at a rate of knots. He negotiated a flight of steps, totalling four in all, and stood waiting for us at the top. "There's where you go out," he said, pointing to the entrance just a few yards away. As we removed our stuff from the trolley, we found our way out baulked by the porter, who was clearly expecting to be paid for his services. I was embarrassed, for I was unused to having a white man waiting on me. Furthermore, I had no idea how much to tip. Gulping, I extracted a ten shilling note and handed it over to him. For an instant, a look of consternation came over the porter's face, but seeing we were making ready to move off, it was replaced with a huge smile.

"Thank you, sir, thank you. Gawd bless you sir," he said, touching his cap, his day, perhaps even his month made by my largesse.

"How much did you give him?" Geoff questioned, as soon as we were out of the main door of the station.

"Ten shillings," I replied, turning away.

"Christ! That leaves us with about four pounds five shillings. You bloody idiot! Why did you do that?"

Feeling more and more foolish by the second, I mumbled something to the effect that an English porter would certainly expect greater remuneration than a Pakistani one.

"Yeah, man, but he only carried our luggage up four steps. Four bloody steps," Geoff raged, looking disgusted. "That's two shillings and sixpence per step."

"I'm sorry, Geoff," I replied, feeling abject. "But remember, it was you who lost your share in Rome. Anyway, let's stop arguing and find this place where we are supposed to be staying."

I looked down at my tin trunk and then at Geoff's leather case, which had a shoulder strap. "Tell you what," I said, "Downton Avenue could be quite a way from here, so I'll take one end of my trunk and you take the other. I'll carry your case over my shoulder. That way, we should manage all right."

We emerged from the station and, dodging trams and double decker buses trying to mow us down, we crossed over the road into Downton Avenue. Geoff kept an eye out for the house numbers on the right. I watched those on the left. We'd been led to believe England was cold, but wearing clothing more suitable for winter than high summer, it was stinking hot and hard going. Sweating profusely, from time to time we were forced to lower my tin trunk and take a breather. Puffing and panting as we staggered along, we finally arrived outside the house we'd been looking for.

We stood on the pavement outside number 72, part of a small, shabby terrace, trying to pluck up the courage to knock on the door. Finally, Geoff braced his shoulders, saying, "Let's go," and opened the gate. He led the way and I squeezed in behind him. Geoff rapped on the door and stood back, looking highly nervous. Just as he raised his hand to knock again, the door suddenly opened wide, exposing a man of about fifty with thinning white hair and a quizzical expression on his face. Wearing slippers, unpressed flannel trousers, and a cardigan over an open-necked shirt, he removed a cigarette from his lips, breathed out blue smoke and asked unthreateningly, "'Oo yer looking for?"

Geoff and I replied in unison: "Major Tipping."

"I am Major Tippin' and I can tell you Major Tippin's not expecting anyone. 'Oo are you anyway?"

"Geoff and Bob Matthews, sir," Geoff answered, colour fleeing from his face. Pointing to himself, Geoff stuttered, "I'm Geoff and he's my brother Bob. Colonel Nick Grahame-Carter said he'd written from Pakistan, asking you to put us up for a while. He told us he'd received a telegram from you saying it would be okay for us to stay for a few days."

I piped up. "We arrived by plane from Karachi only a few hours ago, sir."

Major Tipping looked at us and sighed heavily. "Boys," he said, "I did know a Colonel Grahame-Carter, some time ago, before I retired from the Indian Army." Scratching his head, his cigarette wobbling loosely in his lips, he said, "An Intelligence *wallah*, as I recall, but I haven't set eyes on him or heard from him in years. Anyhow, I never sent him a telegram saying you could stay here with us. There's been some dreadful mistake, I'm afraid. We've no space for you, what with my four sons and missus living here. We've only three bedrooms. So sorry, boys, there simply isn't any room."

At my side, I heard Geoff making "er, er" noises as he tried to digest the awful news. It was unimaginable that we'd travelled so far only to find we'd nowhere to go, nowhere to stay.

"But we have nowhere else to stay, sir." As I pleaded, I realised that Nick had landed us in the most terrible fix, perhaps as a means of getting his own back on me.

"Don't know what to say. All I can suggest is the Salvation Army," replied the major.

A woman's voice interrupted from behind the major, "We'll find room for them somehow, dear. Poor things, we can't leave them out on the street." The woman had been standing in the hall, hidden behind the major. "Come in, boys, bring your luggage into the house and we'll have a cup of tea."

Major Tipping swung round to look at his wife in amazement, threw his hands up and said, "If my wife says you can stay, you can stay. But God only knows where."

Stepping out of the house, a big smile on her face, our saviour, Mrs Tipping, a small, round bustling figure whose grey hair was tightly fastened in a bun, wiped her hands on the apron she was wearing and greeted us. "I'm Emily, David's wife," she said. "Now, come on in and tell us all about yourselves."

My relief was so palpable, I could hardly restrain myself from hugging Emily. Major Tipping lit another cigarette. Sucking smoke deep into his lungs, he removed his cigarette and wheezed, "Follow me chaps, we'll have a confab in the parlour and decide what we are to do."

As we passed through the front door into a narrow, dark hallway, Major Tipping pointed out a tiny dining room on the left, where we deposited our belongings on the floor. The parlour, as he called it, was on the right, with a window overlooking the street.

"Park yourselves, boys," he said, before excusing himself. "I'll give the missus a hand with the tea."

It was obvious he wished to have a private chat with his wife, perhaps give her hell for taking us in. But then again, it was patently clear she was the boss in the house and would give as good as she got. Geoff and I gingerly took our seats on the edge of a chaise longue and waited for them to return, wondering what was to befall us.

Compared to our spacious house in Morgah, the Tippings' residence was miniscule. I found it hard to believe so many people could live there, or in such poor circumstances. The parlour had not been decorated for some time, and was filled with so much shabby furniture, there was hardly room enough to move around the centre table without knocking something over. Four chinaware ducks in flight, fixed to the wall above head-height, were the only items out of danger.

The major entered carrying a tray, placed it on the centre table, and levered himself down into a leather club chair.

"Never leaves that chair, does my David," laughed Emily, following her husband into the room. "Now, boys," she said, pouring the tea, "David and I have had a chat. As you heard, we have four sons—John, Derek, Andrew and Bill—who share the two bedrooms upstairs. David and I are in the other, so what we thought was, and it's up to you..." She paused briefly, tea pot held up in mid-air. "Toss a coin for who sleeps in the dining room, under the dining table, and who sleeps on the landing."

I'd have accepted anywhere to put my head down, at least until an alternative solution presented itself, so I answered for both of us, "That's fine by us, isn't it, Geoff?"

Major Tipping fumbled about in the pocket of his cardigan and extracted a sixpenny piece. "Right," he said, flicking the coin between his fingers. "Heads the dining room; tails, the landing. Temporary measure, mind."

Geoff called out heads and got the landing. I won the dining room table. I didn't know it at the time, but I had the best deal. The landing area at the top of the stairs was barely five feet long by three feet wide, whereas my space under the table was well over six feet.

"That's settled then, boys," said Major Tipping, leaning back in his chair, pulling on yet another cigarette. His face now in repose, I noticed his skin was almost transparent, the expression in his pale eyes soft and gentle. "Give us the griff. What's the story?"

Geoff and I took our time describing the entire sequence of events that had brought us to England, and then Emily suggested a nap and got us settled with bed-clothes. I managed to make myself very comfortable. Covered with a bed sheet and lying on top of a pile of blankets, I examined the underside of the table, counting the knots in the wood grain before falling asleep—much more effective, I thought, than counting sheep.

Emily Tipping woke me with a cup of tea at four o'clock. "Bob, drink your tea," she said, handing me a cup with on hand and a thin towel with the other. "The bathroom's free now, so if you want, have a wash and brush up before the boys arrive. When you've finished come on down."

The bathroom barely accommodated the toilet, let alone the bath and hand basin. At half the size of bathrooms I'd been used to, it catered for six adults routinely and now for two more. But it did have several advantages over the three bathrooms in our house in Morgah, whose toilets did not have flush systems and had to be disinfected with chemicals after use. They were cleaned daily by a low-caste servant, who also carried in buckets of hot water to fill the bath, since hot water did not come straight from the tap.

Removing my shirt, I turned on the tap and washed the top half of my body with hot water, thinking that there were some advantages in living in the Tipping household. I only had one other shirt, so the one I'd been wearing for the past two days went back on again. After which, now marginally less malodorous than before, I returned to the dining room, folded up my bedclothes and lay them in a corner next to my trunk. Geoff brought his bedding down, saying there was no room on the landing, and piled it on top of mine.

The four brothers all arrived home at much the same time and were immediately taken to the kitchen by the major, doubtless to be apprised by him of the two interlopers in the house. There was a mirror on the wall facing the kitchen, enabling Geoff and me to see each one emerge into the hallway, where they gathered, looking very put out. A head shorter than his strapping sons, the major ushered them into the dining room to be introduced to us. John, who was about my age, grinned, "Hello, "I'm John." I took to him immediately. Derek glowered and muttered something unintelligible under his breath. Andrew and Bill, who looked to be in their mid to late twenties gave out with surly grunts before retreating to the parlour. Clearly, we were not welcomed by the brothers, with perhaps the exception of John. Given the same circumstances, I'm not sure I'd have behaved otherwise.

Breaking the awkward silence, the ever-cheerful Emily clapped her hands together. "Now that's over and you've all met, I shall go and fetch supper.

How the eight of us managed to squeeze into the parlour for a meal I shall never know. With our chairs pushed up against each other and plates on our laps, the meal, such as it was--a slice of pie, bread and cheese—progressed in virtual silence until John asked "How long are you guys intending to stay here?"

Geoff beat me to the post. "Just until we can find a job and somewhere else to stay," he replied.

"Yeah. A few days at most," I added quickly.

"What kind of a job?" John persisted. "As you see, we're sort of pushed for space here."

Emily cut off that line of conversation, and the Tipping boys trooped off to play football at the local rec, leaving us to the major, who had said it was time for "a little chat."

"Just to put matters straight boys, Carter never contacted me and I never sent him a telegram. However, if you give me your mum's address, I'll send her one tomorrow saying you're okay. But, if you ask me, this Colonel Carter sounds a bit of a rum bloke. Another thing that puzzles me, how did he get hold of my address? And why choose me?"

Since neither Geoff nor I could provide an answer, we sat bemusedly gazing at the major. We were lucky God led us to the door of the major. If it had been someone else, I don't know what we'd have done.

The major looked across at his wife and said, "I suggest Geoff and Bob take a trip around London tomorrow."

"Oh, yes," agreed Emily, giving us that sweet smile of hers. "You may not get another chance for a while, if you're busy looking for a job. My boys leave at half past seven, so lie in until after they've gone. The bathroom will be clear by then."

The major leaned back in his chair and said, flicking ash off his cardigan, "We'll breakfast at 0830 hours. When we're done, I'll tell you how to get around town, get your bearings. See the sights, that sort of thing. The day after, unless you've other plans, I'll take you both to the Army Recruiting Centre down the road. The Army will have you like a shot." He laughed, this time without coughing. "They offer permanent bed and board, which can't be too bad."

Geoff, who I was certain was not a candidate for the Army, interrupted quickly, "I've a friend from Lahore who lives in London. He's in the consular section of Indian High Commission. Maybe he can help me find a job."

I was both angry and astonished he'd kept me in the dark, "Geoff, you never once said. Who's this guy?"

"Didn't I tell you about Peter Arratoon?" Geoff replied, looking shifty.

He was lying. He knew it and I knew it. He'd told me on the train to Karachi that he'd no idea what he was going to do, never once mentioning Arratoon and Indian High Commission. I determined to have it out with him when we were on our own.

Geoff continued, "Years ago, Peter told Grandma that I should contact him if ever I came to England." Looking me straight in the eye, he said, "Sorry, Bob, thought you knew."

Disgusted by Geoff's behaviour, I wondered what other surprises he had in store. "Well, anyway," I said, addressing the major, "I'm game to give the Army a shot, if I can't get a job."

"Good lad," said the major, "Now go off and have good night's kip. Tomorrow, like I said, beetle off round London."

Even though it was only seven o'clock in the evening, I was suffering from the effects of all the time changes I'd experienced. I was absolutely fagged out and ready for my bed under the dining table. So, saying goodnight to our hosts, Geoff and I left the room.

Chapter 8

The following morning, after we had breakfasted on tea and toast, Major Tipping sat us down in his parlour. Pulling from his pocket a map of the London Underground, he instructed Geoff and me on how to use it to get about. Handing the map over to me, he suggested I should aim for Piccadilly Circus, from where I could easily walk to Hyde Park and thence to Buckingham Palace. Both should not be missed, he said. He omitted to mention that it would be an ordeal walking for miles over baking hot pavements in the steamy heat of late August. Geoff, on the other hand, only had to walk about a hundred yards from the Strand Underground station to visit his friend at Bush House, where the Indian Embassy was located.

But before we separated I gave Geoff something of a tongue-lashing. I said that he should never come to me for help if he was ever in a jam. I left Geoff visibly shaking and carried on to Piccadilly where I spent about three hours aimlessly sightseeing. Fagged out by midday, I faltered to a stop in front of an imposing building in St James's Square and sat down on the pavement outside. No sooner had I parked myself than a uniformed doorman with a row of campaign ribbons on his chest asked me to move along.

"I know it is 'ot an' all, sir," he said, not unkindly, "but this 'ere is the RAC Club and sitting in front of it is not allowed."

With stammered apologies for defiling the RAC's august premises with my bottom, I got to my feet. "Sorry," I said, "I didn't know. It's just I'm shattered. I've been wandering about looking for Buckingham Palace for hours."

"Well, son," the doorman replied, removing his dark green top hat to wipe the sweat from his brow, "you are in luck, 'cause it's only a short walk from 'ere. Continue dahn St James's to the end of the street, then make a sharp left, pass through the wrought-iron gates and you'll be in the Mall." Fingering his left nostril, he confided in a whisper, "Don't let on, sir, but from the Mall you'll observe the residence of His Majesty George VI quite clearly in front of you. But Mum's the word, eh, son?"

Why he had asked to keep the whereabouts of Buckingham Palace secret was deeply mystifying. However, I thought it best to just thank him for his help and be off.

"Think nothing of it, son," said the doorman, offering a hand, palm uppermost.

How very friendly, I thought, pumping it vigorously.

The doorman looked puzzled for a moment before his face broke into a huge grin. "Away with you lad, an' good luck," he said, patting me on the back. "Now don't forget what I told you."

Rounding the wrought-iron gates as I'd been told, I found my view of Buckingham Palace partially obscured by a well-dressed gentleman standing directly in my path. Having materialised from God only knew where, he stood hopping about from one foot to the other as if performing some strange tribal dance. There was a wide-enough berth on the broad pavement for each of us to pass without difficulty, but he appeared bent on making physical contact unavoidable.

When we were about two feet apart, the stranger, a man of about fifty, doffed his bowler hat with a flourish and ceased his curious jig. His headgear removed, there was exposed a pink scalp and neatly parted white hair, before the hat was firmly returned to his head. Tamping down on the curly brim until satisfied he'd got the angle just so, he unhooked a tightly furled black umbrella from his bent right arm and gave it a couple of practised twirls. He was very important-looking in his striped trousers, black jacket and highly polished shoes. I watched as he unbuttoned his coat to show off his pearl-grey waistcoat and the solid gold fob watch suspended on a heavy gold chain stretched across his swelling belly. Evidently his exertions had affected him, for his chest heaved with each breath he took. However, he soon recovered himself and stood with one foot delicately placed in front of the other as he regarded me with quizzical eyes.

I felt awkward under his scrutiny. My hands ran involuntarily down my blazer to smooth out the creases and one shoe came up behind the other for a quick shine on my flannels.

I hardly had time to gather myself when I heard him question in a loud bray, "I say, are you lorst?" The man's tone of voice was at once pompous and condescending. Articulating every word as if he regarded me either as an imbecile, a foreigner, a mental defective, or perhaps all three, he continued, "Because, if so young man, I daresay I can be of some assistance to you." He obviously noticed my perplexed expression, for he added nasally, his vowels full and rounded, "All right, old chap, I can tell you are a stranger to London."

His beaming smile made his pink, smoothly shaven cheeks bunch like russet apples. But his pale, almost colourless eyes radiated evil, reminding me of Canon Coleman, principal of my old school, whose eyes had been similarly repellent.

Canon Coleman was loathed by all the boys. No one could accuse him of mollycoddling, for even the slightest misdemeanour qualified for six of the best. A whippy Malacca cane was his instrument of choice.

Canon Coleman informed me of my father's death on the June 14, 1940. I had imagined the principal had called me to his office to administer a thrashing for some fault I'd committed. I was wrong. As I entered, Canon Coleman barely rose from behind his desk to utter in a voice devoid of any emotion, "I have bad news for you Matthews. I have just been informed by telegram of your father's death in gaol, which occurred yesterday. I gather he died from typhoid."

I watched his thin bloodless lips shaping the words. I felt, rather than heard, what he was saying. It was a long time before anguish allowed my mind to absorb the dreadful news. Only later, as I lay on my dormitory bed, did I begin to weep at the realisation I'd never see my father again.

The principal's words had been as painful as blows from a hammer. Clearly compassion was a stranger to him, for how else could he have been so uncaring about the feelings of a nine-year-old boy who'd just lost his father? Why could he not have shown even a modicum of sympathy and said he was sorry? Why did he have to emphasise that my father had died in gaol? For nine years my hatred of that mean-spirited bastard burned unabated.

"You are new to this country, aren't you?" I heard the stranger on the Mall repeat in a loud voice, bringing me back to the present.

I dragged my eyes away from his. "Yes, I only arrived in London yesterday." I replied. As an afterthought, I added "by plane" as a pathetic attempt to impress the intimidating stranger and to elevate myself to his status.

To have travelled to England by plane in those days was rare, something only the most well-breeched families or senior military personnel were able to do. Surely, a person of substance, such as he, would appreciate the fact. So, just in case the stranger had misheard me, for he seemed distinctly uninterested, I repeated, “I came over by plane,” stressing the word ‘plane’. It was not every day one encountered a genuine air traveller, I wanted him to know.

“Ah, so you flew over?” the man questioned, fingering his bottom lip. “Pray, may I ask where from?” Before I could respond, he giggled like a girl, “No, no. Don’t tell me, let me guess.”

Cocking his head to one side, he cupped his elbow with one hand and, sticking his forefinger against his chin, he surveyed me with the intensity of a scientist examining a laboratory specimen under a microscope.

“Got it!” he exclaimed at last, as I shifted uncomfortably under his gaze. “Philippines? Bet you’re Filipino, eh?” Even before I had time to register an adamant denial, he proceeded in a headlong rush: “Dashed if you aren’t, sir! Said it to meself the minute I set eyes on you walking down the Mall. Much too handsome to be Anglo-Saxon. No offence, sir, but I recognised your ethnicity from having served in the Pacific during the war. Lovely chaps, Filipinos. Lovely chaps.”

I was hugely offended by the man’s bloody cheek. It had never entered my head that anyone could imagine I was anything but British.

“No, I’m British,” I flared, through clenched teeth. “Father Scots. Mother Italian, maiden name Belletti.”

The damned man had me behaving defensively. I was furious he’d forced me into explaining my background which, if I got down to it, proved my antecedents were infinitely more illustrious than his. Surely, it was obvious to everyone I was a European? Dammit, anyone could tell I wasn't a wog, couldn't they? Okay, I was heavily suntanned, but so what? I had just arrived from sunnier climes and my tobacco-coloured skin was much nicer than this fellow's lily-white complexion, wasn't it?

"Quite so. How very interesting," said the stranger, moving closer. "I am emboldened to ask what you intend doing, now that you are in England? College perhaps?" Pointing his umbrella in the direction of Buckingham Palace, he continued affably, "Do forgive me. Most interesting all of this. However, must dash, tempus fugit, as they say. But hang on..." He fished out a business card from his waistcoat pocket and handed it to me with a smile. "Do please take tea with me tomorrow if you have the time. We could continue with our chat then?"

I examined the man's beautifully embossed card. I couldn't put a name to it, but something akin to fear still nagged as he stood at my shoulder wafting expensive cologne. Reaching over, he traced the name on his card with a forefinger. "That's me," he said, tapping his chest. "Cyril Goodall, Lord Netherwood. My London address is 174 Shepherds Market." I looked at him uncertainly, unsure as to whether he was telling me the truth, but he just chuckled amiably, "Now you have my name, what's yours?"

"Er, it's Ian Robert Monteath-Matthews," I replied, reddening up for no good reason.

"Hyphenated?"

"Well, er, yes, actually."

"Oh, very grand, very grand, old man," said Lord Netherwood, clutching my arm above the elbow. Squeezing hard, he said, "Now we are introduced, promise you'll come to tea."

Seeing I looked dubious, he wheedled, "Oh, come on. Do say yes."

Finally, despite my misgivings, I gave in to Lord Netherwood's persuasion and accepted his invitation, thinking my introduction to him might have its uses—for instance, on the job front. I needed a job in a hurry, any kind of work to support me. Maybe the noble lord could be of help?

"Good-oh," said Lord Netherwood, placing an arm around my shoulder as if he had known me forever. "Excellent. I shall instruct my butler to put together a feast of Madeira cake and other goodies, eh, Mr Monteath-Hyphenated-Matthews?" Pausing, he pulled on a pretend cigar, parodying Winston Churchill. "Nevah will so few, er, evah again, consume so much food, for so, er, lengthy a time at tea."

Lord Netherwood's mention of a butler suggested he was very rich, but unaware that food rationing was still in place, I failed to appreciate the munificence of his offer.

"Okay, thanks," I said. "It's very nice of you to invite me, Lord, er..."

"Call me Cyril," he replied, "It's what friends call me. And anyway, who knows, I might be of some use to you? After all, we all need friends in this world, Ian."

"Bob."

"Bob?"

"Yeah, nobody calls me Ian."

"Bob, that's fine by me, Bob."

Cyril grinned, reaching to shake my hand. He startled me by stroking my palm. "Now, hear me, Hyphenated-Matthews," he said, with such emphasis it made his bowler hat wobble. "I shall expect you on the dot of three tomorrow."

My dislike of Cyril momentarily put aside, I flushed with gratitude for the interest he had shown in me. The inviting lifeline I'd been tossed had come at just the right moment. He said goodbye to me and strolled off, twirling his umbrella as he went. I stood for a long time gazing at Lord Netherwood's retreating back, congratulating myself on my good fortune. Perhaps now I could avoid the Army Recruiting Centre.

I walked down the Mall towards Buckingham Palace, hoping to see the Changing of the Guard, which A A Milne had written Christopher Robin was wont to do. But there were no guardsmen in scarlet uniforms to be seen anywhere, nor did I hear any bands playing. So, rather despondently, I walked to Hyde Park Corner, where I found the noise and weight of traffic so threatening, I sought refuge in the quiet of the park.

Having cooled off on a park bench, my eyes were taken by a bunch of pretty girls in summery dresses, whom I assumed to be office girls. Wondering if they'd be taking the Tube as I had planned to do, I followed them towards Marble Arch at a discreet distance in the hope I might get to talk to some of them, and in the process get some pointers as to where and how to meet girls. But they all went down Oxford Street instead, leaving me vaguely disappointed.

I arrived back at Streatham in the afternoon. Avoiding trams hurtling along the middle of Streatham High Road, keeping clear of buses determined on crushing me, I reached the terraced house of my benefactor, Major Tipping, who offered me a cup of tea. Over the teacups in the parlour, he nodded with approval as I related the day's adventures. Only when I casually mentioned I'd been invited to tea by a total stranger did he freeze in his chair.

"Tea, Bob? Are you sure? Tea?" he queried, concern on his tired face. Emitting a bronchial bark, the result of his forty-Woodbine-a-day habit, the muscles surrounding his mouth went into a spasm as he fought to speak. Not unnaturally, I figured that smoking was also responsible for this. I watched in horror as the poor man continued to mouth in silence. Finally, it became apparent that the major was engaged in a contest between what he actually wanted to say to me and the impropriety of discussing matters best left unmentioned, leaving him desperately scrabbling around to avoid using the word 'homosexual'. I could almost see the workings of his brain as it searched for a suitable alternative, a word I'd understand and not find embarrassing. I was unaware that polite society shrank from acknowledging the existence of homosexuality, let alone mentioning it.

Being ex-Army, Major Tipping was certainly not blind to what went on in the world, but as he attempted to warn me of the dangers I faced from homosexuals prowling London looking for prey, he became hopelessly inarticulate. I realised that in his kind, fumbling way he was only trying to protect me. Fiddling about with an unlit cigarette, tamping down the tobacco with his thumbnail, he kept glancing out of the window as if he expected help from some outside agency. At last, he croaked, "Bob, just how old are you?"

"Eighteen," I replied, surprised by the question. "Why, sir?"

"No need to call me 'sir'," he said gently. "'David' will do nicely. Eighteen, eh? Pity you aren't twenty-one. If you'd been older, you might then have understood why I am concerned about you visiting this Lord fellow's house for tea tomorrow."

"It isn't because you think Lord Netherwood is queer, is it?"

The major's body immediately straightened upright in his chair. His Adam's apple jerked up and down in his overlarge collar, his neck sprouting up from it like blanched asparagus.

Avoiding my eyes, he lit his cigarette. Puffing out acrid smoke, he whispered, “Bob, son, where did you hear that word? Do you really know what a queer is?”

“Oh yeah, sure I know,” I boasted. “We had a couple of them in school. Called them pretty boys, we did.”

The major looked relieved. “Ah, yes, of course. You were at boarding school weren’t you? Well then, young man, you know what I am trying to get at. Bob, this whatchamacallit, Lord chap—I doubt he is a real Lord—sounds to me has ulterior motives. Don’t you think it’s a bit unusual to be stopped in the street and then be invited to tea? To be offered help out of the goodness of this— this bloke’s heart?” He clenched both fists tight, and stressing his words, said, “Seriously, Bob, I don’t think you should go, however important he sounds. Really, I don’t.”

“But he can help find me a job!” I protested. “He said so in so many words.”

“That’s as may be. But it’s all a bit iffy, if you ask me. I advise against anything to do with him.”

It was obvious David was only trying to do his best by me. He’d only known of my existence since yesterday and here was I repaying his kindness with ingratitude. At least, that’s how I imagine it must have felt to him. But there was no avoiding the fact I needed to find work quickly, and could not turn away any opportunity that presented itself.

I said, “I am sorry, sir. Don’t you see, I have to find out for myself? Maybe you’ll want to kick me out of your house for not taking your advice, but you have my promise I’ll be very careful. Cross my heart. You have my word.” I gave David a reassuring smile, saying I’d leave Lord Netherwood’s address, just in case. I gave out a false-sounding laugh, “You can come after me with the cops if I’m not back here by six.”

Having taken note of Lord Netherwood's immaculate appearance, I took a great deal of care over my own prior to meeting him. Wearing my blazer and newly pressed, grey flannel trousers, and with my feet shod in black brogues, spit and polished to a high shine, my reflection in the hall mirror pleased me mightily. I looked more than good enough, I thought, to be offered a very decent job.

The virtue of good timekeeping having been drummed into me at school, I turned up at 174 Shepherds Market precisely at three o'clock. On the wall alongside the tall black-painted front door facing me, there was a small, shiny brass nameplate simply inscribed with the name Cyril Goodall. I pressed the bell push adjacent to it. Almost immediately, the door opened, disclosing a very tall man wearing a black tail-coat, a wing collar and striped trousers.

"Ah, I assume, Mr Monteath-Matthews?" he enquired in a deep, graveyard voice, his sunken eyes fixed somewhere above my head. Before I could even respond, he waved me inside with a flourish of his white-gloved hands. He then turned about and without a further word disappeared through a door at far end of the hallway. I was left standing nervously twiddling my thumbs.

The butler returned a few moments later and led me into Cyril's immense drawing room. Overawed by the room's lavish furnishings, the rich carpets, the long satin drapes, I failed to notice the significance of the silver-framed portraits lining the ornate mantelpiece.

"Ah, Hyphenated-Matthews!" cried Cyril Goodall, entering the drawing room with a flourish. Approaching me with twinkly, ballet-dancer's steps, he was all neat and pinkly scrubbed. "Punctuality, politeness of kings," he enthused, taking my hand in his. "Well done, old chap. Now, Bob," he commanded, patting the silk-covered chesterfield on which he had delicately perched himself, "you sit here beside me.

We have so much to talk about haven't we? First, allow me to divulge a secret. To be truthful Robert, I did not exactly bump into you by chance. I noticed your presence quite five minutes earlier. I thought to myself, 'Now there's a—'"

Cyril was interrupted by his butler's delicate cough. "At what time shall I fetch tea, your Lordship?"

Scowling at his butler for having disturbed his train of thought, Cyril waved an impatient hand. "Half an hour, say. Then take the rest of the afternoon off, Butteridge."

"Thank you, m'lord. Will that be all?"

"Yes, yes, Butteridge," Cyril replied testily before returning his attention to me.

Having witnessed how Butteridge fawned in front of Cyril, I wondered if I was expected to be as deferential. Sucking up to him with a disingenuous smile, I ventured chummily, "Gosh, Cyril, what's it like being a Lord? The only ones I've ever seen were in films." I continued eagerly, "Fancy my meeting up with a real lord, with a butler and all, and only the day after I got here."

"Well, let me tell you, Bob," laughed Cyril. "Being a lord doesn't count for much these days. It's useful to get a table at the Atheneum or a Lyons Corner House, but that's all." I heard his girlish-sounding giggle again. "Silly of me, Bob, I don't imagine you've heard of either of those. Now, down to business. I want to hear all about you."

I chatted animatedly about how I'd been born in Delhi, but had spent most of my life in the Punjab and the Himalayas, not far from the wild North-West Frontier. Cyril surprised me with his knowledge of the area, explaining it away offhandedly, revealing only that his job in the government of the day had something to do with policy over the Partition issue. Proceeding with all sorts of searching questions about my early life, he interrogated me, which I imagined was to ascertain where best to me place in a job.

He pressed me for information about my late father, whom he had assumed to be Indian Army. Correcting him, I told him my father had been professor of English at the Foreman Christian College in Lahore and before that had held several important positions in the government of India in Delhi. In order to impress Lord Netherwood, I added casually that my father had attended the Round Table Conference of 1933 in London, convened to settle the future of the princely states of India, adding that he'd also been a friend of Gandhi.

Throughout, Cyril had betrayed nothing other than affability. "Didn't actually know Gandhi myself, chum," he said when I'd finished, "but, you know, I might well have met you father at the very same Round Table Conference." Edging up closer to me on the sofa, he said, "You see, Bob, I happened to be a Member of Parliament at the time, similarly engaged in resolving the business of those very disputatious Indian princes."

Cyril's proximity made feel uncomfortable, so I shuffled some distance away from him. Lolling back on his cushion, he sighed, looking at me directly, "My word, how interesting your story is. How very interesting. What a small world, Robert. Indeed, what a small world."

My presence momentarily ignored, he cast his eyes upwards to the ornate plaster work decorating the ceiling and stared at it for several minutes. Then, as if some spell had been broken, he straightened himself and smiled. "Sorry, Bobby," he said, sounding apologetic. "How very rude of me. I intended to comment on how smart you look today. Quite the young gentleman. Definitely, a real gentleman. And very handsome, very handsome indeed."

I flushed with embarrassment under the weight of Cyril's compliments, not knowing how to deal with them.

Apprehensive now, I saw his wet lips shape into a grotesque pink pout. He squirmed this way and that to show off his attire, clearly expecting me to compliment him on his appearance with equal effusiveness.

"See, Bobby?" he said, smoothing down the braid lapels of his green velvet jacket with one hand, the other picking at imaginary vagrant threads from the matching silk cravat around his neck, "I dressed up for you, too." He extended his small feet for my inspection. I noted they were encased in black velvet slippers whose uppers were woven with a crest of some sort. Reading my mind as I gaped at his footwear, Cyril commented archly, "My dear, it's my family crest. So come on, tell me," he urged, "do I meet with your approval?"

I responded with a lame, "You look very elegant, Cyril." Tempted by his promise of employment, I remained blind to his intentions. As I wondered what was coming next, Butteridge entered the drawing room, pushing a trolley laden with a fine bone-china tea service and a burnished silver cake stand. I spotted slabs of Madeira cake on the top tier and, on the one below, thinly-cut cucumber sandwiches and neat rows of digestive biscuits. For an instant, I thought I detected a knowing look on the butler's face before he averted his eyes. With his back turned away from me, Butteridge set a side table with small plates, silver cutlery and folded napkins, after which he silently retired, coat-tails flapping.

Cyril asked, "Shall I be Mum?"

The expression was unknown to me. It was only after watching him pouring the tea that I twigged what he'd meant. As I munched away on a piece of cake, Cyril told me that umpteen jobs were open to me. All of them, he added, would suit a fine fellow like me down to the ground.

"They are mostly in the Civil Service," he continued. "It's the area in which I have some influence. It so happens I know personally several departmental heads. They are all friends of mine, and will overlook the small matter of your having being schooled abroad." I made to interrupt, but Cyril waved his hand and silenced me. "Do not take offence, Bob. It's just that a public school education is a requirement for what I had in mind for you. I'm sorry to say your school in Pakistan doesn't quite match up, you see. That's the truth of it," he finished, bringing the flat of his hand down on my thigh, too close to my crutch for comfort. When His Lordship's hand showed no signs of stirring from my upper leg, I took hold of his wrist and removed the offending article, hoping against hope I'd not misread his intention and blighted my chances.

Cyril seemed not to notice. Instead, he casually reached for an exquisite silver cigarette box sitting on the table. Retrieving from it an oval-shaped Passing Cloud cigarette, he put on a small pair of spectacles before handing the box over to me. "Go, on, young man," he said. "Lift the lid and look at the inscription. It's from the Dean of Canterbury, a gift to me. He's known as the Red Dean, because he's a leftie. Now, how would young Robert feel if I gave him the box as a keepsake?"

So startling was the offer, I was thrown completely off balance. "No, no. I can't. Thank you, Cyril, I just couldn't," I stuttered wildly.

"Well, no matter. If you wish to be stupid, my beautiful Bob—"

Even before Cyril completed his sentence, I screamed at the top of my voice, "I am not your beautiful Bob!" Maddened by the implication, I raged, "Bloody hell! Who do you think you are?"

"Oh, come, off it, boy," Cyril snarled, casting me a vicious, evil look.

In rank disbelief, I watched him rapidly unbuttoning his trousers. Fumbling about in his underwear, he withdrew his erect penis. "You weren't born yesterday, sonny boy," he growled menacingly. "Now, you do something for me and I'll do something for you, like getting you a job. That's how the world works, Bobby, dear."

Shuddering with disgust, I shouted, "You fucking bastard! "Major Tipping told me to watch out for queers like you. But no, I didn't listen to him, did I? I said you were a decent bloke. Ha! *Decent*? *Like bloody hell, decent!"*

I thrust my clenched fist under Lord Netherwood's nose. Getting to my feet, I stood over him as he hurriedly stuffed his rapidly deflating appendage back into his trousers.

"Look here!" he blustered. "Whom do you think you are addressing? You can't talk to me like that. Why? Let me tell you why. It's because you're nothing more than a scruffy-arsed, Anglo-Indian wog with pretensions. I should have known better than to class you with my other bum boys. Yes, those boys," he pointed with a quivering forefinger, "those in the picture frames there. At least those young buggers were grateful for what I did for them."

I turned to look at the silver picture frames flanking the mantelpiece. I'd barely given them a second glance when I entered. Every one of them featured a photograph of a smiling youth, none of whom appeared to be more than fifteen or sixteen years old. Recalling my unpleasant experience in Lahore with Major Barratt, I said, "It seems the world's full of people like you, trying to take advantage of young chaps like me."

I enjoyed the spectacle of Cyril shrivelling in his seat. He looked so small, suddenly, puffing wild-eyed on his cigarette. Everything about him I'd admired had vanished. His eyes now darting about the room, he asked cautiously, "What do you propose to do now, Matthews? Is it your intention to blackmail me? Because if so, blacky, I warn you, you'll never be employed in this country if I have my say. Hear me? Nevah! Evah!"

His confidence restored, he threatened, "Take my advice young man, cut your losses and get out of here while the going's good." Fishing inside a pocket he withdrew a white five-pound note the size of a small bed sheet. "Here," he sneered, flinging it in my direction. "You were in line for ten more of these, if you'd have let me stick it in you."

Goaded by Cyril's jibes, I lost control. Stepping over to where he lay half-sprawled on the sofa, I grabbed a hank of his white hair in one hand, forcing him to look up at me. Bunching my fist, I slammed it down on the bridge of his nose with all my strength. I felt the cartilage crunch under my knuckles as the metal frames of his spectacles cut deep. Cyril gave a piercing screech before falling to the floor.

The minute I got back to Major Tipping's house, I sought him out, saying, "Hey, sir, you were wrong about Lord Netherwood. He turned out to be a really good guy."

"Thank the Lord for that," replied Major Tipping, in between coughs, as I ruefully concluded I would never put my trust in anyone ever again.

Chapter 9

The Tipping boys, who'd heard from their father that I was meeting a real live lord, asked me how I'd got on and what kind of chap he was. I told them everything, requesting they keep the details from their parents' ears.

Bill, an office clerk and the eldest at twenty-four, said he wasn't a bit surprised someone had tried it on with me. "It happens all the time," he said with the air of one who had inside knowledge of such things, adding sagely, as he pulled on his cigarette, "A couple of chaps I know are homos." Standing wreathed in cigarette smoke, he warned, "Better watch out."

The two younger brothers, Andrew and John, were all for giving "that bastard, that Lord bloke, a good thrashing." Puffing away on their Woodbines, they punched the air in a show of violent shadow-boxing. Throwing right and left hooks at an imaginary target, they fell, sprawling across the dining table under which my bedclothes lay, in a fit of coughs and giggles.

When Andrew and John recovered, they invited me to the hop at the Locarno Palais. So at seven that evening, in the company of the two Tipping brothers, I was launched into Streatham society. Straining at the leash, I paid over my one and six and entered the venerable, gilded, red flock-wallpapered Locarno Palais de Danse.

I wore my blazer and flannels and one of Geoff's gaudy hand-painted ties featuring Betty Grable, one he'd bequeathed to me before he'd said goodbye the day before. The Peter Arratoon he'd mentioned so casually had found him a clerk's job in the Indian High Commission. His departure was sudden and unexpected, but even so, I had been happy for him as he'd stood, anxiously looking out of the front door at his friend who was waiting in a small car. Giving my hand a perfunctory shake, he said, "Got to dash. I'll be in touch," and was gone. Only afterwards did I realise he'd not left a contact address.

I forgot my troubles in my awe at the wonders of the Palais. Couples jived on the brightly-lit sprung surface of biggest dance floor I'd ever set eyes on, to jazz played by a twenty-piece orchestra. Ringing the walls, young women in party frocks slouched on chipped gilt chairs, affecting boredom, ignoring the attentions of youths in drape jackets blowing cigarette smoke in their direction. Some sat drinking and whispering; others swayed silently on their perches, never to take the floor.

A beautiful blonde creature sitting at the far end of the hall by the stage immediately drew my eye. A bit older than the other girls, with big hair and prominent breasts, she was certainly the prettiest and altogether too much for a poor boy from the hills like me. As I stood gawping at her, John swung past with a girl in his arms and gave me a wink. The blonde still avoided my eye, doubtless casting about for a more suitable dancing partner.

I spent an hour being turned down for a dance by one girl after another, not having the courage to ask the blonde to join me on the floor. But finally, when the last dance was announced and the band struck up Glenn Miller's *Moonlight*

Serenade, I threw caution to the winds, raced across the smooth chalk-dusted expanse separating us and slithered to a stop in front of her.

"May I have the pleasure of this dance with you?" I addressed the blonde formally, as I might have done at one of the Rawalpindi Club's balls.

"May you what?" the blonde asked. She giggled, putting her hand over her mouth, her creamy breasts heaving with mirth.

"Have the pleasure," I replied, hopelessly mystified by her behaviour.

Seeing how crestfallen I appeared, she said, "Sorry. All right. C'mon then, m'lord." She got to her feet and stood towering over me, nearly a head taller.

Almost on tiptoe, I tried gliding away with her into a slow waltz, but found myself tripping over her feet instead. I apologised profusely, saying "Sorry, sorry, sorry" over and over again. From her great height, she gave me a sweet smile. "That's okay," she said, "I've danced with lots of blokes who are much worse dancers than you are."

"Really? Gosh!" I preened.

Damned by her faint praise, yet encouraged by the way she pressed her bosom against my chest and nuzzled my cheek with her strawberry-scented lips, I found myself asking, "May I take you home?"

"Maybe," she replied, her mouth widening into a smile, "but only if you tell me your name. Mine's Carol."

"It's Bob."

"Bob, Bob," she said, rolling my name around her mouth like a marble. "And how old's old Bob, then?"

"Eighteen."

"And never been kissed?" Carol laughed, her pink tongue moistening her lips.

"Yes, of course I have, many times."

"Well then, you can take me home." She licked the lobe of my right ear; the sensation sizzled down to my toes.

The number of girls I'd kissed could be counted on the fingers of one hand. So as soon as the dance music stopped and even before the National Anthem commenced, I steered Carol out of the dance hall and into Streatham High Road to catch a tram heading for Gypsy Hill, where she said she lived.

"Bob, I'm not in any hurry, you know," whispered Carol, digging her fingers into my arm as we stood on the pavement outside. "We've time to go in here."

"Where?" I asked in a strangled voice.

"Here, come with me," replied Carol, dragging me along in the dark through a small gate and down a narrow path. At the very end, obscured from view by tall bushes, was a small cemetery laid out in front of a church

By this time, I was torn between being ready for anything and taking headlong flight.

"Come, sit here," said Carol, lowering herself down to a gravestone.

I did as she asked, and sat facing her on the cold stone.

"Now give us a kiss," commanded Carol.

Though her lips tasted of strawberries, I didn't much enjoy her exploring the inside of my mouth with her wet tongue. The sensation was dizzying, but wasn't it unhygienic? Taking my right hand, Carol placed it on her left breast.

"Go, on, Bob," she breathed, "unbutton my dress. Feel them."

With trembling fingers, I fumbled with her buttons and, finding an opening, plunged my hand deep into her brassiere.

"Oh, my God, they're crinkly!" I cried, extracting my hand, my fingers enmeshed in yards of tissue paper dredged from her bosom.

"Oh, Christ!" cringed Carol. "I'd forgotten the bloody padding!"

Without warning, the yellow beam of a flashlight cut through the blackness. For an instant, it played on the paper streamer flapping about in my hand. Then the beam moved, illuminating Carol, who sat cupping her naked breasts with her hands. By the light of a faint moon, I could just make out the outline of a policeman's helmet.

"Oi, Oi! What 'ave we 'ere?" tolled the policeman's doom-laden voice. There was a short pause before the voice spoke again. "Blimey, Carol, you're not whoring again, are you? And as for you, son," a circle of light steadied on my face, "you'd better scarper, before I have yer inside."

Chapter 10

I had had enough of sleeping under Major Tipping's dining room table and sharing the single tatty bathroom with his wife and four scruffy sons. Down to my last ten shillings, I desperately needed to find a job—any kind of job, anywhere, doing anything at all. But I hadn't any idea where to start looking. Major Tipping was no help whatsoever. He simply said, as he reclined in his worn armchair chain-smoking Woodbine cigarettes, his watery blue eyes expressionless in a gaunt face yellowed by years of Army service in India, "Try the Army."

Feeling miserable, I wandered from the Major Tippings's terraced house down to the small park off Streatham High Road and sought out a vacant park bench. All around was the rattle of trams, the terrifying shriek of wheels cornering on metal rails at speed, the unabated thunder of passing buses and cars, the general cacophony that constituted life in London. My thoughts drifted to the Himalayas, which I had so recently left: tall mountains, distant horizons, clean pine-scented air, blue skies, warm sunshine, a comfortable home with servants waiting on me hand and foot. The contrast was depressing. Had I the choice, I knew where I would rather have been.

After perhaps half an hour of daydreaming, I was distracted by a stranger asking if I had a light. In view of my recent experience with a peer of the realm, I was instantly wary. Without replying, I fished about in my trouser pocket and handed over the box of matches lurking there. The man relieved me of it.

"Thanks," he said, lighting up, eyeing me from behind his cupped fingers. "D'you mind awfully if I sit down here?"

Without waiting for my reply, he lowered himself down and began puffing away contentedly, his eyes closed, seemingly at peace with the world. He'd smoked about an inch of his cigarette, when his eyes snapped open and he turned to look at me.

"Awfully rude of me," he said, "would you like a fag?" He flicked open a silver cigarette case. Proffering it, he said, "Do, please. That's if you like Player's Navy Cut."

"Thank you," I replied, selecting one. My previous encounter with a stranger had commenced in a similarly innocent fashion, so I remained on guard.

"Live in Streatham, do you?" the man asked casually. He was no more than about thirty or so, with an open, ruddy face. I decided to give him the benefit of the doubt, if only to bum another cigarette off him later.

"Not really, just for a few days," I replied. "I arrived in England only ten days ago. From Rawalpindi, in India. Well, it's Pakistan now."

"You're kidding!" exclaimed the man. "That's extraordinary. I was born in India. Delhi. What a bloody coincidence. Me, I had the bad luck to come home to England with my parents, aged eighteen, just in time to be called up. Served in Burma, prisoner of war for two years." He smiled. "But hey! You don't want to listen to old soldier stories. Let me introduce myself. The name's Norman Conquest."

Seeing my look of disbelief, he burst out laughing. "No, really. It is Norman Conquest. What's yours?"

I couldn't resist it. "Adrian Wall" I replied with a straight face.

"You're having me on..."

"Yes, joke, joke. I'm Bob Matthews, broke and looking for a job."

"Maybe I can help," said Norman.

"Seriously?"

"Well, if you've got your school cert and can add up, yes, I think so. I work in Personnel for Remington Rand in London. It so happens I know our wages office in Weybridge is short of a clerk. Might you be interested? I could phone and put in a good word. Better still, if you can pay my train fare to Weybridge, I'll accompany you on Friday morning. I've someone to see there. Kill two birds at once. Wouldn't ask, but it's the end of the month and I'm a touch short." I flinched from him as he tapped my thigh. "See, Bob, that way we'll each be doing ourselves a favour."

"Will the train fare be more than ten shillings for the two of us?" I enquired nervously.

"No, you'll get change out of that," Norman laughed.

Before parting, Norman gave me instructions as to how to get from Streatham to Waterloo station to catch the 9.10 train to Weybridge from platform one. The rest of the day was spent in a state of delirium. Not once did it occur that I might not be offered the job Norman had mentioned.

Making doubly certain that I wouldn't be late, I missed breakfast and hurried down to Streatham station the following morning. As luck would have it, the train was late leaving. Instead of getting to Waterloo with half an hour to spare, I arrived desperate for a pee with just seven minutes left to buy two tickets, meet up with Norman and catch the train.

After hopping frantically from foot to foot in front of a gentleman's lavatory in a state of panicked indecision, I finally belted down the stairs and relieved myself. In my haste to fasten my fly, the wretched zip fastener attached itself to a particularly sensitive, highly vascular part of my nether regions. Caught there, the zip refused to budge. In desperation, I wrenched at the zip. Yelping with pain, I ripped away a small piece of flesh as the zip finally meshed. Unaware that I had started to bleed, I ran blindly to the ticket office, then dashed headlong to platform one where I found an agitated Norman Conquest pacing about at the gate.

"Christ!" he shouted. "Thought you weren't coming."

He gave me a fierce look, before steering me into the last carriage of the train, which moments later slid away down the line. "What kept you?" Norman asked, after we had settled down in the compartment.

As I explained what had occurred, I saw his eyes waver over my fly. "My God, man, you're bleeding," he said. "See for yourself. Your trousers are stained."

I was certainly in some pain, but I had no idea how much I'd bled. "Norman," I wailed, looking down at myself, "I can't go to the interview looking like this. What am I to do?"

"God only knows" he answered, looking disgusted.

It was then that I spotted a newspaper on the seat beside me. "I know," I said, "I'll cover myself with this paper. Walk in casually. Like, you know, holding it in front like this." I gave Norman a demonstration. "It might work."

"Whatever," grunted Norman Conquest. He stared out of the window, clearly having lost interest in Adrian Wall.

Not a word passed between us until we drew up at Weybridge station. I was abashed and he was obviously embarrassed. I understood how he felt, since he had recommended me to the manager of the wages office as a suitable recruit. Patently I'd let him down, but there was no way I was ducking out of the interview now. I had to have the job. The alternative did not bear thinking about.

We took the bus to Addlestone and alighted at the entrance of a large industrial estate on which the Remington Rand Corporation had the most impressive factory of all.

Norman left me sitting on a hard wooden chair in front of the personnel office, the newspaper pressed against my trousers, feeling highly nervous. I had not long to wait. Someone emerged from the office almost immediately.

"Ah! Er, Mr Robert Matthews, is it? I'm Mr Randall. Do come in, please," he said pleasantly.

I got to my feet very carefully, manoeuvring the paper in such a way that the stain was completely hidden, and entered Mr Randall's untidy office. "Sit down, sit down, my boy," said Mr Randall, as he lit a pipe and settled back in his chair. I spread the newspaper over my lap and awaited the coming inquisition.

"You a communist by any chance?" enquired Mr Randall at last.

"No sir. What's a communist? I don't know what a communist is." I really didn't.

"I just wondered, my boy," said Mr Randall mildly, "I only asked because I see you take the *Daily Worker*."

"*Daily Worker*? What's that, sir?" I was truly mystified. I glanced at my newspaper. *Daily Worker* was the banner headline on the front page. Clearly I had committed some kind of faux pas, so I pulled the paper tight across my knees and awaited summary rejection.

"It's all right, son, you can admit it to me." I heard Mr Randall's comforting tones as if from a great distance. "Being a communist is nothing to be ashamed of. I don't shout it to the skies, but I happen to support the Communist Party."

From that moment, the interview proceeded apace, and ten minutes later I had landed the job of wages clerk, at the princely sum of four pounds ten shillings and sixpence per week gross, three pounds nineteen and six net, starting Monday. Before I left, the company fixed me up with digs at three guineas a week, including breakfast and an evening meal. At last, I would now sleep in a real bed.

On the train back to Waterloo, Norman plied me with cigarettes, saying how pleased he was that I'd been successful. He suggested that, after we arrived back in London, I accompany him back to his flat to celebrate my good fortune with a glass of beer. "I've got bottled mild beer and also bitter," he said. "Or, if you prefer, mild and bitter mixed together, which seems to be all the rage these days. Do come, you needn't stay long."

I was intrigued because I'd not heard of mild beer, or for that matter, bitter. In fact, I'd not drunk any kind of beer in England, so I agreed.

Norman's small flat in Streatham Park was on the ground floor, with a short path leading from the pavement through a wrought-iron gate. As Norman opened the gate to allow me in, I noticed a beautiful green racing bicycle chained to a post. "That yours, Norman?" I asked. "It's a beaut."

"It's a Claude Butler, actually," replied Norman. "It's got eight gears. Lovely bike."

Norman led me into his simply furnished living room and asked me to take a seat while he opened the beer bottles in the kitchen. He reappeared soon after with a couple of tankards and passed one over to me.

"Cheers," he said, sitting down next to me, after which he gave a great sigh and stretched his arms above his head.

Curiously, when he lowered them, I found one of his arms had fallen casually across my lap. I was immediately on alert. I shifted my body away. It did not seem possible that Norman, who had been so helpful to me, was trying anything on. I sipped my beer and eyed him, ready to take flight the second anything untoward happened. Meantime, Norman, saying nothing, lay slumped with his eyes closed, occasionally levering himself up to gulp his beer.

Finally, when his tankard was empty, he smacked his lips and said, "Did anyone tell you what a good looking chap you are?" Unzipping his trousers, he exposed himself. "Bob, get a load of this," he said.

I shouted out, "Christ, Norman! Is every bloody Englishman a homosexual? I've had enough. This time, I'm going to the police."

"But, but, I thought...," stammered Norman. "When I asked you home, you must have known."

"Fuck you, Norman!" I screamed. "I bloody trusted you. As soon as I leave—and don't try and stop me—" I continued, thrusting a clenched fist under his nose, "I'm down to the police station. You deserve to go to jail for this."

"You wouldn't do that, would you, Bob, after all I've done for you?" Norman whined. His ruddy face had gone deathly white. "Listen, I'm sorry. I just thought—"

"Well, you bloody thought wrong," I replied, making for the door.

"Please, Bob, can't we talk this over? How can I make it up to you?"

"You can't. I'm going. No doubt a copper will be here soon."

Clasping his hands together, Norman pleaded, "If you promise not to go to the police, I'll give you my bike. You can ride it away now, but only if you give me your word."

I did not hesitate. "Done," I said before he could change his mind. "You have my word." Even as I spoke, it suddenly struck me that if Norman notified the police himself and accused me of stealing his bike, they'd believe him rather than me. So with a flash of inspiration I said, "I need you to sign a note saying you've given it to me."

He nodded. "Okay, okay, just get out of here."

He unclipped a fountain pen from his breast pocket and scribbled quickly in a small notebook, mouthing as he did so, "I gift this bicycle to Mr Bob Matthews, signed Norman Conquest." Dating the paper, he savagely tore it out and handed it to me.

I went outside with Norman and watched as he unchained the bicycle. He stood aside as I pushed it through the gate. Slinging a leg over the saddle I cycled off.

Figuring Norman had got what he deserved, I did not dwell on the fact I was guilty of blackmail and just as bad as he was. I now had the means of getting to work from my digs and, at that moment, that was all that mattered to me.

Back at the Tippings' house, David shook my hand and Emily kissed me, delighted at my good news. We mouthed meaningless pleasantries as a matter of form, until finally I said, "I'll be off to my digs in Weybridge on Sunday, so you only have to put up with me for one more day."

David shook his head silently. His eyes wandered to the window, through which he could see my new bicycle propped against the fence. “Where did you get that thing?” he asked mildly.

“Oh, that?” I replied. “The bloke who got me the job loaned it to me, so I can cycle down to Weybridge. You see, I don’t have enough money left to cover my train fare. I’ve only four shillings left. Norman said that was enough to send my case ahead of me on the train. So that’s what I’m going to do. I’ll take my case down to the station and see what they have to say.”

“It’ll cost you about two bob, I think,” said the major, sticking a fresh cigarette in his mouth.

“That’s okay, then,” I replied. “That’ll leave me enough to last the week. I get breakfast and an evening meal at my digs. I can get by without a midday meal until I get paid.”

“But you don’t even know the way to Weybridge. It’s about thirty miles you know,” puffed the major.

“Don’t worry, sir,” I said. “I’ll manage somehow.”

In the event, putting my tin trunk on the train cost less than David had thought, and I was left with two shillings and sixpence change jingling in my pocket.

When I returned from the station on Saturday evening I found that the major had written out a route to Weybridge for me. It looked simple enough, following road signs for Streatham, Mitcham, Merton, South Wimbledon, Raynes Park, then down the A3 to Walton and Weybridge.

After saying my goodbyes on Sunday morning, I set off on my bike. Streatham itself was easy enough, but having missed the sign to Mitcham, I found myself in Croydon, miles out of my way. Someone gave me directions back to Mitcham, but I got hopelessly lost again. Only after discovering the A3, did I finally arrive in Weybridge at three in the afternoon, where I asked a passerby for directions to my digs in Portmore Park Road. Terribly saddle sore, I guessed I'd ridden about fifty miles in all.

Chapter 11

Portmore Park Road was located in an affluent part of Weybridge, a couple of hundred yards from the River Thames. Substantial houses, all of them far superior to the Tippings' house in Streatham, stood on either side of the wide, quiet road lined with chestnut trees in full leaf.

I dismounted outside number 52, a three-storied red brick Victorian villa. Remington Rand had an arrangement with the landlady, Mrs Parsons, to put up new employees. The door was opened by a large cheerful-looking woman wearing a pinafore.

"My name's Bob Matthews," I said. "I believe Mrs Parsons is expecting me."

"Yes, I'm Mrs Parsons," she said. "Come in, come in. Please, do come in. It so happens I was just cleaning your room. Mr, er..."

"Bob Matthews."

"Right, Bob. Bring your things in and I'll show you to your room."

"'Fraid my case is at the station. I rode down from London on my bike."

"You cycled all the way? Poor thing, you must be tired out. Don't stand on the doorstep. Come in, have a cup of tea."

I followed my new landlady into the gloomy hallway and into a room on the right. "Mr Parsons' and my parlour," she stressed, raising a finger in the air, making it plain the room was her private domain. "Take a seat and I'll bring you some tea." With that, Mrs Parsons bustled out.

Still overheated from my long ride, I loosened my tie and sat down on an overstuffed chair with a lace antimacassar. As I sat reflecting on the room's dejected air, Mrs Parsons entered with a mug of steaming tea.

"There," she said, putting it on the table beside me. "Drink that down. You'll feel better after that."

She waited for me to take a few sips, before asking if Remington Rand had made me fully aware of the arrangements.

"The rent's three guineas a week," she said. "Wake up call's six-thirty in the morning. Breakfast is at 7 a.m., tea at six in the evening. There are three other young men living here, nice chaps, all Vickers apprentices at Brooklands. You'll meet them this evening. The bathroom is shared between you. You take turns in the morning according to the rota on your bedroom wall. I'll provide you with one bath towel and a hand towel. Dirty laundry is collected each Wednesday and returned on Friday by the laundryman. The cost for each item you'll find on a note in your bedroom." She paused, as if searching her mind, "Oh, yes, before I forget, you'll have a key to the front door. If you bring any male friends to the house, they must leave by nine in the evening at the latest. I'm afraid I don't allow ladies."

Mrs Parsons slapped her thigh. "I think that's all for the moment. Now, have you any questions to ask?" From the brusque manner in which she had intoned the rules, it was clear Mrs Parson did not intend them being broken.

I shook my head. Excited at the prospect of having my own room and starting work the next day, it all sounded very fine. "No, Mrs Parsons," I replied. "It's all okay by me."

"Well then, young man, let me show you to your room," she said.

Mrs Parsons occupied rooms on the first floor. Two apprentices were on the second and I, together with one other, lodged on the topmost floor, up three flights of steep creaking stairs.

My bedroom was tiny. It had one small window, a narrow bed, a bedside table and a small cupboard. There was hardly enough room to move around. Nonetheless, I was content. It was better than sleeping under Major Tipping's dining room table. I told Mrs Parsons everything was okay and said I'd be back with my case in an hour, after picking it up from the station.

"Rather you than me, going all the way back there," she smiled. Pausing for a moment on the front doorstep, before seeing me off, she said, "Don't mind my saying, but Remington Rand never mentioned I'd be taking in a foreigner. Not that I mind," she added hastily. "No, not at all."

It irked that everyone questioned where I came from, sounding as if I was some sort of inferior being. It put me on the defensive and I hated it. "I'm British," I replied fiercely and this time left it at that, without going into a long rigmarole about my antecedents.

"I didn't mean any offence," said Mrs Parsons. "It's just that—"

"None taken, Mrs Parsons," I grinned, interrupting her.

As I mounted my bike, she called after me, "Remember, Bob, tea's at six."

As I rode up Weybridge High Street, heading for the station, it suddenly occurred that I had no idea how I would manage to cart my trunk home. In the end, I had no option but to balance it on the frame between the seat and the handlebars and push the bike the two miles back. I finally arrived in a state of exhaustion, and was shown into the dining room just in time for tea, as Mrs Parsons referred to the evening meal.

Sitting round the table were three youths about my own age, all scrubbed clean and staring curiously at the dishevelled stranger in their midst. Mrs Parsons went round the table introducing me.

Each of my fellow lodgers rose from his seat to shake my hand muttering "Pleased to meet you" before sitting down again. I took the only vacant chair, replying, "How do you do?" as I'd been taught. "Pleased to meet you" was considered a touch low-class where I came from. In the centre of the table was a mound of sliced fresh bread surrounded by four small plates. There were portions of something vaguely resembling tinned meat on three of them and, on the other, thinly sliced hard-boiled eggs. A larger plate at one side featured a plain cake, already cut into four pieces.

Mrs Parson reappeared bearing a tray with a large tea pot. She poured tea into our cups, which already had some milk and sugar in them. Leaving the teapot on the table, she said, "Just shout if you want more tea, and I'll bring some hot water."

As soon as her back was turned, urgent hands reached out for the food. My boarding school experience had taught me to fend for myself, so my hands were just as quick as the others. Famished, I piled my plate and set to. Not a word was spoken as jaws munched noisily, hungry beasts at the kill. The smell of the eggs and the meat was faintly nauseating, but not sufficient to put me off my food. Finally, I pushed my plate back and got to my feet. Excusing myself, I said I was fagged out after cycling from London. Three surprised faces turned up to look at me, but I was gone before anyone could comment.

Despite being tired, I tossed and turned all night, wondering how I'd manage on my first day at work. I was fully awake even before Mrs Parsons knocked on the door, telling me it was time to get up.

My name was last on the rota to use the bathroom. I ignored it and was in and out again before I heard any sound coming from the others. Out of habit, I'd laid out my trousers under my mattress, so they had a crease of sorts in them. After dressing quickly and giving my dirty shoes a rub with a cloth, I found myself in the dining room well before seven. I said good morning to Mrs Parsons, who was busy laying the table. I mentioned I wasn't sure of the way to Remington Rand and since it was my first day at work I'd best be early. "Well then," she said, "you'd better get stuck into the bread and jam and I'll bring you tea."

As I ate my breakfast, Mrs Parsons told me how to get to the factory estate, a bit over two miles away.

I was at Remington Rand by seven-thirty and was forced to cool my heels outside the personnel manager's office for a good half-hour. When Mr Randall showed up exactly at eight o'clock, he gripped my hand like a long-lost friend.

"Welcome, Mr Matthews, welcome." he said, smiling. "Come inside and we'll fix up your paper work, then we'll pop down to the wages office and I'll introduce you to your colleagues, Frank and Mary. Mary's looking forward to having some help. She'll show you the ropes."

Frank Jones, the supervisor of the wages office, was a dour man who simply tipped his head when Mr Randall introduced us. Mary Perkins, on the other hand was very garrulous. Smelling of lavender and constantly beaming as if God had poured sunshine into her, she was a joy to meet.

"Robert, pay no attention to Frank, his bark's worse than his bite. Come, Robert"—Mary insisted on calling me Robert—"sit by me and I will teach you the mysteries of calculating weekly wages for those on an hourly rate."

As hard as I tried I never mastered the art and it was just a matter of a week before Mary rumbled how hopeless I was at maths. My inability to figure out time sheets, and to calculate the number of hours someone had worked, times so many pence per hour, caused ructions when some workers found they were short-changed in their pay packets. Others were delighted, having received too much. All in all, rather than being a help to Mary, I proved to be a disaster.

Mr Randall, still of the opinion I was a fellow traveller and communist sympathiser, was chary of firing me. Instead he moved me to the Goods Inward department where he figured, quite incorrectly, I could do no harm.

Actually, I didn't much care where I worked or what I did as long as I had enough to pay for my digs. Since I was pocketing the princely sum of three pounds nineteen shillings and sixpence net, I was left with sixteen shillings and sixpence, after shelling out three guineas to my landlady. Squandering some on twenty Woodbine cigarettes and settling my laundry bill, left a surplus just sufficient to put in the meter for the occasional tepid bath.

My landlady had her eye on my sweet-ration book, but I soon learned the coupons could buy me free lunches in the works canteen. "Must be tough for furriners like you," remarked the two kitchen ladies, whose hot, pink, sweaty faces glowed as I handed over my coupons. In return, they awarded me dollops of shepherd's pie, Spotted Dick pudding and similar indigestible fare every lunch time. But for this satisfactory exchange, I'd have gone hungry until six in the evening.

It did not take long before my communist boss starting questioning me about my political beliefs, and encouraging me to join the Young Communists to appreciate what communism was all about. To keep in with him, I took to attending their weekly meetings in the village hall.

It was there that I met an older woman of twenty-one. Francine was simply gorgeous and made a dead set for me. Flattered by the attention, I walked her home every Friday night to St George's Hill, where we petted on her front porch. After three attempts at fumbling inside her blouse and planting wet kisses on her mouth, she casually dispensed with me, saying I was too inexperienced for her. She was right, of course, but it was a blow to my ego. I asked myself why she hadn't shown me what to do. That way I could have got experience.

Communism now struck from the agenda, I joined the Young Conservatives, having been recommended by Charley and Ben, two of the apprentices who shared my digs. Both maintained that the Young Conservatives not only had great parties, but also had scads and scads of terrific-looking girls with rich parents. This was sufficient of a magnet to draw me to the YC monthly gatherings in Gower Road. There, young men of my own age, dressed in expensive blazers and flannels, and girls in chiffon party frocks with nipped-in waists and pointy, pushed-up breasts, only very occasionally discussed politics and spent most of the time having fun.

During four months leading up to Christmas, I made a lot of friends. Perhaps because, YC's were better educated than most I'd previously met, no one ever questioned where I came from, and simply took me at face value. It was a new experience for me, and it made me warm to them.

Sharing in their gilded existence, I swanned about in their parents' huge, pseudo-Tudor mansions on the St George's Hill estate, polishing off their Pimms and pints of beer, flirting with numerous pretty young women some of whom wanted me to go a step further than heavy petting. Still a virgin, though now more experienced than in my communist era, I remained scared of getting any one of them pregnant. I existed in a state of perpetual hopeless, helpless sexual frustration, all because I did not have the wherewithal to buy a packet of Johnnies from the barber.

Chapter 12

My first Christmas in England was the quite the most miserable time of my life. My landlady, Mrs Parsons, decided with her husband at the very last minute to spend it with relatives up north, leaving me to fend for myself.

A week earlier Mrs Parsons had spoken of cooking a turkey, which I'd never before tasted. She promised Christmas pudding as well, and the prospect of a glass of sherry if I kept my room tidy. I also harboured the hope Mr and Mrs Parsons would invite me to join them around a log fire in their sitting room after lunch and listen to music on the radio. However, Mrs Parsons scotched the idea by saying that both she and her husband always slept after lunch until teatime. But if I wished, she said, I could always join them and kip down on the sofa. Then, when I awoke, there'd be piles of turkey and dripping sandwiches to tuck into. Just the thing after a good sleep, she said, particularly when there were mince pies to look forward to, as well. Such was the dream she put in my head.

Though food rationing was still in force, it never stopped Mr Parsons acquiring all kinds of delicacies unavailable to others. If asked how he managed it, he'd change the subject with a nudge and a wink. He was the archetypal spiv, ferret-faced, always on the lookout for the main chance, not that I was ever invited to share in Mr Parson's spoils.

"You'll manage all right without us, dear, won't you?" enquired Mrs Parsons solicitously. She stood at the front door and tugged her brown felt hat down over her ears before firmly securing its crown with a metal hatpin. Slipping on a tweedy overcoat with a rabbit fur collar, she made ready to join her husband, who stood waiting on the pavement outside. As a parting shot, she said, "Bobby, you know where everything is. Hubby's chopped a bit of wood for you, so you can have a fire in the lounge. There's apple pie in the cold box and sixpence in the bathroom boiler so you can take a bath. Mind you, in this weather..."

The last of her sentence was lost in a blast of icy wind as she waved goodbye at the open door. A sudden gust made her skirt flare up, exposing a large expanse of mottled white flesh. Hugely embarrassed, she half-stumbled down the steps, before mincing along the path to the gate, clutching her clothing tight about her stout calves.

The news of the apple pie and firewood was very welcome indeed, for all the money I had was three shillings and threepence, which had to last me until I went back to work on the day after Boxing Day. Thereafter, the canteen ladies at Remington Rand would see to it I'd not starve by providing me with free lunches every day.

Eking out the sliced apple pie and casting Mr Parson's timber on the fire like a miser, I went to bed very early on the night of Christmas Eve. The last thing I did before drifting off into a deep sleep was to count out all my money, place two shillings and sixpence on the top of my bedside table and put the balance in a drawer. A spendthrift, I'd allocated the cash to be spent on Christmas night in an orgy of bacchanalian excess in *The Ship*, a public house a short distance away, at the foot of Monument Hill.

When I awoke the next morning, I discovered icicles decorating the glass on the inside of my bedroom windows. Since there were no presents to be opened or Christmas cards to be read, and nobody in the house whom I could greet with a "Happy Christmas", I pulled the covers over my head and snuggled down until midday. There I remained in a disconsolate daze, wondering how the three younger brothers and a sister I'd left behind in Pakistan were doing and what presents they'd been given. Geoff was living somewhere in London. Was he as lonely and unhappy as I was?

My thoughts drifted to my mother, my poor mother in whom God had not invested a single maternal instinct. I asked myself if she was still offending the prim sensibilities of the Rawalpindi Club's lady members, still outraging them with her open affair with Colonel Nick Grahame-Carter while her husband, my stepfather, was recovering from DTs.

Perhaps it was these gloomy musings, coupled with the sound of my stomach growling, that forced me out of bed. Teeth chattering, I dressed quickly in the freezing bedroom, wolfed a slice of apple pie, washed it down with a huge mug of tea, climbed on my bicycle and went for a long ride down the empty Surrey lanes.

The cold tore through the wholly unsuitable clothes I was wearing: a blazer, white shirt and grey flannels clipped at the ankles. Other than for my dinner jacket and a spare shirt, on my back was my entire wardrobe. But wheeling away at speed, I'd warmed up by the time I reached Virginia Water on that sunny Christmas afternoon. It was dark by the time I returned to a house as chilly as a morgue.

I gave my face a quick sponge-over with cold water and I was ready to party. With my two shillings and sixpence jingling in my trouser pocket and my teeth rattling like mah-jong tiles from the cold, I hurried down the street to *The Ship*.

Consoled by the knowledge that the pub would have a huge log fire roaring, and for an hour or two at least I'd be warm, I walked there with a light step.

The pub was virtually empty, with just a couple of displaced persons like me at the bar and a few others sitting at tables, flushed with booze and filled with noisy bonhomie. I kept my head down and clattered over the dark, stained wood floor to a dim recess at one side of the carved fireplace, over which a stag's head looked down. The massive logs burning in the cast-iron grate sent tongues of yellow light flickering on the panelled walls, creating a marvellously welcoming atmosphere.

I flashed the attractive young woman behind the bar one of Bob Matthews's most expansive toothy grins, which she returned with a shy smile from under a lowered head. I sat myself down on a comfortable club chair to dwell uneasily on the vast array of alcoholic beverages on display. I wondered which one of them I could afford and could stretch out to closing time.

My eyes settled on the selection of whisky bottles and then rested awhile on the price list below. There they remained, pondering, gauging, calculating whether a double with a lot of water added could be afforded by me. From somewhere behind me I heard a woman's voice, "I'll have a rum and pep, please." The name of the drink had an appealing ring to it. No sooner did I observe the thick brown rum, topped up with emerald peppermint being poured into the woman's glass, I was undone. That was it. A rum and pep it had to be, if my cash could run to it. I listened with bated breath as the drinker of this beautiful potion asked how much it cost, and nearly expired with relief when I heard the woman behind the bar reply, "Two bob to you, dear."

I stepped up the bar and asked for the same, leaving me with change for a bag of crisps. Returning to my seat, I took a cautious, tiny sip of my precious liquid and thrilled to the peppermint taste, the warmth in my throat, and the heady realisation that this was first time I'd drunk hard liquor. I crammed a handful of crisps into my mouth, and took another sip. Carols were being sung on the radio, and it was all wonderfully cosy. The bar lady was turning fuzzy and more beautiful by the minute. Even the model Father Christmas by the front door was smiling at me.

No more did it matter to me that my mother had not sent me a Christmas card or mailed me the money to buy an overcoat as she'd promised in her only letter to me. I didn't care any more. I took another small sip and started to sing quietly along with the radio, *God Rest Ye Merry Gentlemen*. Suddenly all was well with the world. I smiled to myself and, without envy, imagined my brothers and sister at home opening their presents. In my mind's eye, I witnessed them scoffing Indian sweetmeats before sitting down to a resplendent Christmas lunch made by Booloo, our cook. They would be dining, perhaps, on venison—not turkey—and curries. They'd have sweetmeats and trifle, and crackers, and, and... I started to sob quietly. Hanging my head, I did my best to disguise my tears with a handkerchief.

At my side, a woman's soft voice asked gently, "Are you all right, sir?" I looked up to see the girl from behind the bar. She placed a rum and pep on the table, saying, "Happy Christmas. Can't be having you sitting there all alone without a drink on Christmas Day, now can we? It's on the house." She retreated to the bar again and from there stood smiling at me. The drink I'd intended to last all night had gone, the glass that had contained it, empty. Overcome by the young woman's generosity, I swallowed half the fresh glass of rum and pep in one go and put my head down. In no time at all I was dead asleep.

I was gently shaken awake by the young bar lady. "Sorry, sir. Closing time," she said softly. "Take care as you go, love."

She came forward to give me a quick, darting kiss on the cheek. “Happy Christmas.”

Chapter 13

Fred, one of the Vickers apprentices who shared my digs, convinced me that the girls who frequented the Young Liberals were a great improvement on those of the Young Conservatives. An aficionado of Hollywood films, he said to me, “Man, oh, man, so many gorgeous broads, so liberal.” He flicked the brim of the grey fedora that seemed never to leave his Brylcreemed head and gave me a knowing wink. No more encouragement was needed. As a result of my laissez-faire, feckless, fickle attitude to politics, I now found myself in the village hall on Thursdays being bored witless by vapid rhetoric spouted by pimply-faced Young Liberals in duffel coats.

On one such evening, a ravishingly pretty girl with long auburn hair, scarlet lips and curves to drool over sat down beside me and asked if I enjoyed the meetings. I admitted that I did not, expecting to be put down for such a heresy. Instead, she said, “I only come here because my brother does. I’d rather be at my drama society, the Desborough Players, but we haven’t anything in rehearsal ‘til next week. We’re doing *Hay Fever*. D’you know it?” I said no, I did not. She then asked if I had ever acted onstage, because the Desborough Players were short of juveniles, and I’d be perfect as Simon Bliss, the son.

Thus enticed, I joined the Desborough Players and was immediately cast as Simon in their forthcoming production of *Hay Fever.*As I told the producer, other than for the odd school play, usually lipsticked and playing a girl, I had no acting experience. Undeterred, she said I'd be perfect, just perfect for the part, because I was pretty and dark haired, much as she supposed Noel Coward had perceived Simon to be. "Pretty?" I questioned, more than a bit aggrieved. "Well, yes," she replied. Seeing my expression, she went some way to mollify me by adding, "Oh well, Bob, let's say good-looking, then."

The play went off very well at the Playhouse in Chertsey and I found myself being avidly courted by the Nomads, a local drama group, and the Ashley Players in Walton-on-Thames. I began to fancy myself as something of an actor, unaware that I was in demand not so much for my fine thespian qualities, but for the reason that I had just turned nineteen and was male.

Socially, I was having a great time with the people in the drama group, though I was finding it more and more difficult to accept their hospitality, simply because even mild ale at a dizzy nine pence a pint was beyond my means. I had no alternative other than make my excuses after rehearsals and cycle home, while the rest of the cast headed for the pub.

Finally I decided something had to be done to improve my lot. Having spent nine boring months working in the goods inwards department—fiddling through oiled-paper parcels of typewriter parts from the US, collating minute cogs, tiny wheels and thingies sufficient to assemble thousands of Remington typewriters—I cast about on the Addlestone factory estate for a higher paid job.

In no time at all, I discovered that Peto-Scott, a television manufacturer, had a vacancy for an unloader-cum-clerk in their goods inwards department. Obviously, Peto Scott had found it difficult to employ a labourer who could also write, for they snapped me up at a weekly wage of five pounds, nearly twenty-five per cent more than my previous earnings. My new boss, Mr Herzog, an apple-cheeked Swiss who—having discovered I could shoulder large cardboard cartons from delivery lorries with comparative ease and, more to the point, list their contents in a ledger—took to snoozing most of the day, hidden amongst the stacked boxes in the warehouse. I minded not a jot, since I easily coped with the number of incoming deliveries. Besides, in the vastness of the warehouse, I could pretend I was Frank Sinatra and sing at the top of my voice while Mr Herzog snored away like a flugelhorn.

The stultifying business of humping cardboard cartons on and off lorries palled after six months or so, and the call to better myself consumed my waking moments. Early one morning, pleading a toothache, I sought Mr Herzog's permission to go home. As soon as I was off the premises, I hurried to the local Labour Exchange.

Scanning through a list of job vacancies, I came across one from the Army Operational Research Group (AORG), based in West Byfleet. The advertisement read, 'Assistant Scientific Officer required immediately. Age range 18-30. Minimum educational standard, School Certificate, including one science subject.' That was more like it, I thought, having seven credits, including chemistry and biology to my name. The salary was stated as being Scale 8, Grade 14, whatever that was, and payable monthly.

"Monthly, monthly," I muttered over and over to myself. How could I survive without any money for an entire month? Financial problems notwithstanding, I decided to ask the glum-looking clerk, just visible behind his small window, if he'd make an appointment for me with the bracket-AORG-close-bracket asap. Maybe if they were interested in employing me, I'd do a deal with them—like getting an advance of salary.

"Out of the question," replied the clerk when I asked if the AORG would consider such a thing. "But you've a good chance of getting the job, I think. It's been on and off the vacancy board like a yo-yo. I keep sending blokes and they keep turning down the job. Can't understand why when it's paying £350 a year."

"Why, that's about seven quid a week, isn't it?" I said, pleasantly surprised to learn how much the job paid. The clerk nodded. "Well then, sir," I said to him, "could you kindly fix me up with an appointment at the soonest opportunity?"

The clerk picked up the receiver of his black Bakelite phone and dialled out. I was unable to hear anything of the brief conversation. Replacing the receiver, the clerk filled in an appointment card and handed it to me through his window.

"They'll see you this afternoon at two," he said.

"That quick?" I asked.

"Yeah, that quick," came his reply.

To avoid being late, I set off on my bike at twelve-thirty to cover the five miles to West Byfleet and arrived at the Army Operational Research Group headquarters a full hour early. I mooched about, pushing my bike up and down outside the tall iron gates fronting the entrance to a large building. Eventually, a soldier in uniform emerged from a pill box and asked my business.

"I've got a two o'clock appointment with a Mr Pinfold," I replied.

"Okay, son," the soldier said, opening the gates to let me through, "go to the main door and press the bell. The commissionaire will help you." The soldier opened the gates and let me in.

The soldier must have phoned through, for I found the commissionaire waiting for me outside the building. After examining my note from the Labour Exchange, he opened the door and requested I follow him up a broad flight of stairs facing me. No sooner had I reached the top, an office door, one of several lining a corridor, opened wide and I found myself facing a short, tubby man who peered at me short-sightedly.

"Ah, you must be Mr Matthews," he said, thrusting a hand out. "I'm Tom Pinfold. C'mon in, c'mon in. You've come about this assistant scientific officer job, haven't you? Well, of course you have," he finished breathlessly, sitting down behind a table. "Sit yourself down, won't you? Now let me tell you what we do here and what the job entails. You've gathered by virtue of its name that the Army Operational Research Group does a kind of work that is confidential. Official Secrets Act, that sort of thing applies." Tom Pinfold stopped. "Not going too fast for you, am I?" he asked.

The truth was that I was overwhelmed, hardly able to catch a breath, let alone get a word in edgewise.

"Well...," I said lamely.

"Oh, jolly good," said Pinfold. "I take it you have the required qualifications? Oh, course you have. The Labour Exchange wouldn't have sent you, otherwise."

How was the poor man to know that the clerk in the labour exchange had never once questioned me about them? I nodded to Mr Pinfold. "Yes, sir. I've got my Cambridge School Cert with me." I reached inside my jacket pocket to withdraw the folded document. "I got seven credits and two distinctions."

Mr Pinfold flopped back in his chair. “Brain box, eh?” Seeing the confused expression on my face, he quickly added with a laugh, “Just jokin’, just jokin’, lad.” He waved away my prized school cert. “Don’t need to see those,” he said, sounding out of breath. “Question is, when can you start? A week Monday all right for you?”

I was completely taken aback. I hadn’t learned anything about what was required of me and here was Mr Pinfold offering me the job, without even asking what experience I had. It did not occur to me to question why he seemed to be in such a hurry to recruit me. I was much too excited to go into details, but since Mr Pinfold was so eager for me to join the AORG, I thought I’d come clean and request a loan to tide me over.

“I could start Monday week,” I replied cautiously, “but, sir, it says the job pays monthly and I can’t afford to live for a month without money, sir. Is there any chance...?”

“Course there is, my boy,” said Mr Pinfold, anticipating my question. “I can arrange a temporary loan. Yes, yes, of course we can in exceptional circumstances.” He looked at me sympathetically, his fingers drumming on the table top. “Now, if that’s all, Mr Matthews, I’ll say welcome aboard and get you to sign the Official Secrets Act.”

Everything happened with such rapidity that it was only when I was outside the gates and on my way home, with a song in my heart and lightness in my head that it registered I had no idea what my job was to be.

On the Monday following, having given in my notice to Peto-Scott, I cycled up to AORG at ten to eight in the morning and proudly presented the official card I been given by Mr Pinfold to the corporal at the gate.

"Assistant scientific officer," he said, handing me back the card, "Well, well. Bleedin' good luck to you if you can stick it." He winked before letting me in.

The corporal's words filtered through my brain all the way to the main building. I clocked in, along with a stream of other employees, before the commissionaire escorted me outside again and to a dilapidated Nissen hut.

"Dr Cosmo Payne, chief scientific officer, will be along shortly," he said, leaving me to cool my heels outside.

A few minutes later a voice hailed me from within the hut. "Are you Mr Matthews? Come on in and let me show you around." I peered into the gloom beyond the open door and saw a slightly built man beckoning me in. "Don't be shy, come inside. I'm Doctor Cosmo Payne, chief bottlewasher."

As I ventured into the hut, Dr Cosmo Payne took me by the arm and steered me into a small partitioned-off area in the large space.

"This is my office, outside's my lab," he said, "and you're here to assist me in my experiments." Cocking his head to one side, he stroked his bearded jaw with a gloved hand. He noticed my look of curiosity. "Ah, the gloves," he smiled, "they're just for protection. He paused, giving me a quizzical look. "You've been apprised of what we do here, haven't you?" Seeing I was mystified, he gave a wry smile. "I see from your expression you've not been told. Suppose Personnel thought you'd be off if they elucidated. C'mon, young man, let me demonstrate and you can then make up your mind."

He led me deeper into the cavernous area, whose floor was littered with bales of cloth and woollen material. "This here is my pièce de résistance," he said, stopping alongside a strange wooden contraption that resembled medieval stocks. But instead of having three holes to accommodate an unfortunate's head and arms, Dr Payne's device was set on wheels and featured a single aperture in the centre of the frame.

"Now pay attention," said the scientist, poking me in the chest with a forefinger, "because this is what you'll be doing from time to time."

Going to the rear of the frame, he removed his gloves, unbuttoned his right shirtsleeve, rolled up the cuff and placed his bare forearm hard against the opening. Gripped by what he was doing, I noticed that the skin on his arm, from his fingers to his elbow, was peeling in parts and marked with reddish blotches as if he'd had too much sun.

I was about to comment sympathetically when he swivelled his head to say, "You'll notice, Mr Matthews—"

"Bob" I blurted, interrupting him. "Please call me Bob, sir."

"Right, Bob it is" he said. "I'm Cosmo to you, okay? Now, to continue. You'll have noticed the wheels of this fiendish device are set on rails, allowing it to slide backwards and forwards thusly." He leant against the wooden frame and eased it along the rail for a foot or so. "Being bright, my dear Bob, you'll also have spotted the calibrations painted on the floor. Each one represents a thousand yards."

Since my gaze had been fastened on his face throughout, the neat white markings had escaped my attention.

His arm still pressed against the stock-like apparatus, Cosmo pointed to the far wall with his free hand. "Bob, that round metal thing you see there happens to be an oxyacetylene furnace. It heats up to thousands of degrees Celsius and simulates, on a small scale, the heat generated by an atomic bomb dropped on the centre of London."

"An atomic bomb?" I questioned, shivering at the thought.

"Yes, Bob. What we do in this place is calculate how many survivors there'd be following such an explosion."

I chanced an interruption. "Sir, I thought nobody could possibly survive."

"You're wrong, boy. Nagasaki and Hiroshima showed us that at a distance of a thousand yards from the epicentre and beyond, many Japanese survived. But in the aftermath they suffered horrific burns. These could have been avoided if rescue teams wearing flame-retardant clothing had been quickly on the spot. Which is where we come in. In this laboratory we are trying to develop flame-retardant materials for the armed forces so that a similar catastrophe may never be visited on the people of Greater London."

Cosmo relaxed his arm. "If you care to examine that chalk drawing on the wall surrounding the furnace, you'll make out that it's a rough map of Greater London. The red bit in the middle represents Westminster. Those concentric circles you see, radiating out from the centre, are drawn to scale a thousand yards apart." His arms now at his side, Cosmo asked, "Are you with me so far, Bob? You look puzzled."

"Sort of, sir. What's my work to be?" Puzzled didn't come close to what my feelings were.

"You're to be a guinea pig, like me, lad, guinea pig in the cause of science. Saving lives, that's what. C'mon, enough of this talk. I'll give you a demonstration." He strode over to the oxyacetylene furnace and switched it on. Within a minute it glowed white hot, looking like some bulbous, malevolent eye, its heat concentrated in a cone aimed at the contraption. "Warm enough for you?" he laughed, as he swept up a piece of stray cloth from the dusty floor, before setting about baring his arm again. Only this time, he bound the material around his forearm, before holding it tight against the hole.

"This is some cloth I was sent from Halifax. The makers say it is flameproof. Well, let's see if they are wasting our time, shall we? I've set this device at three thousand yards and I can't feel a thing at this distance. So I'll move in closer and see what happens."

I watched, hypnotised, as Cosmo eased the machine forward, the material covering his arm exposed to the heat. The furnace was by now roaring. Raising his voice above the din, he bawled, "Nothing yet, I'll chance moving in to a thousand yards. Oh, Christ! Bloody stuff's charring." Cosmo pulled the frame backwards at some speed and, leaping away from it, disgustedly flung the burnt cloth away. "Effing cloth manufacturers, they never stick to the spec I give them."

"Are you all right, sir?" I asked.

"Fine, Bob, fine. Just a wee scorch, that's all," he replied, in a surprisingly cheerful tone of voice. "Happens all the time. Nothing to it really. Happily, once in a while we get a result. See those bits tacked to that board? They passed this test and are ready for more, elsewhere in this establishment's labs." Cosmo clapped his hands together. "Well, Bob, what d'you think? Are you up for this? You and I will take turns, with you recording my experiments and vice versa. I won't think any the less of you if you say no. Several others before you did."

Without hesitation I replied, "I'm your man, sir. It sounds as if it could be fun."

"Fun, eh? That's your idea of fun is it, Bob?" laughed Cosmo, patting me on the back. "Believe me, it's not fun, but the work's necessary. You'll soon find out my boy. Anyhow, glad to have you on board."

Chapter 14

My job title at the Army Operational Research Group was Assistant Scientific Assistant Grade 1. Grade One Idiot would have been more appropriate, for had not Cosmo warned me in advance that during his experiments my arms might be burnt on occasion? Only a complete idiot, or someone desperately short of cash, would permit their limbs to be scarred by a mad MoD scientist.

Almost from the first minute I joined him, Cosmo and I spent all of our time trying to set fire to batches of woollen cloth sourced from manufacturers in Halifax. The aim was to find at least one that improved on the flame-retardant qualities of material currently used in the manufacture of military uniforms. If the cloth we tested charred or burst into flame at the minimum range of a thousand yards from an atomic bomb blast, it was deemed to be unsuitable. Unfortunately, the only means at our disposal to simulate this was by using the good doctor's oxyacetylene-fired furnace.

After a very few days, it became apparent that Cosmo had had enough of having his arms burnt, for he now asked me to stand in for him. There was I, a lamb to the slaughter, the perfect patsy, having my arms wrapped in cloth, ready to have them scorched daily in the cause of science.

It seemed that until I turned up on the scene, Dr Cosmo Payne had despaired of finding anyone to assist him. There had been previous incumbents, but they had lasted only a few days, whereas I stuck the pain inflicted on me by his fiendish device for three months. The others could not have been as hard up or as gullible as I was; why else would anyone do such a stupid thing for a wage of seven pounds a week?

Eventually Cosmo came to the conclusion that my forearms had been burnt enough times. Bearing in mind that he would now have to find a replacement for me, he advised, reluctantly, that I be moved to another department so my skin could heal.

"Bob, I'll have a word with Personnel and tell them you warrant a wee rise for all this," said Cosmo. In a way I was sad to be moving on, for as bosses went, he was a kindly chap and treated me very well. But to continue working with him was no longer an option. What if, for example, some daft general ordained that Army boots required testing to destruction and mine were the only feet available to wear them?

"I'll tell the office *wallahs* to find you something interesting to do," Cosmo said. "For instance, working for Colonel Marriott. He's the Army trick cyclist in the main building. Now, he's doing some very interesting work, he is." He paused, fixing me with his sharp eyes. "That's it. I'll have a word with Colonel Marriott *sahib* myself. He's sure to want a bright young fellow like you as an assistant, eh? Nothing like grasping the moment, so I'll be off to see the wizard this minute. That's if I've your permission, Bob?"

Before I could reply, Cosmo was already half out of the door.

If I'd been given the choice, I'd have rather have taken a job in the shed adjacent to the one in which I'd worked.

There the staff engaged in all kinds of exciting experiments, such as testing a revolutionary semi-automatic rifle and designing a new helmet. The helmet that evolved in that inauspicious place, a hideous pressed-steel and plastic scuttle, eventually came to be standard issue. However, I'd recently blotted my copybook with the scientist in charge of those secret projects after entering his private domain without permission and inadvertently wrecking one of his experiments.

The reason for my clandestine visits to the hut next door was primarily to check whether my friend, Martin Squires, the assistant *in situ*, had brought his scrumptious sandwiches to work. Since I never had anything to eat and he was prepared to share his lunch with me, we became the best of pals. As small recompense, I allowed him to thrash me at ping-pong after I'd demolished his food. "Cupboard love" he used to say, his soft brown eyes on mine as I munched away on triangles of fresh bread and filling. So intent was I on scoffing his largesse, it never occurred that Martin wanted to share more than his sandwiches with me.

On one occasion when I visited him in his den, he plonked the new style helmet on my head and took Box Brownie photographs of me. "Gosh!" he said admiringly, "you don't half look the part, Bob. Really, you do." And so, the very first person to be pictured sporting the new British Army helmet was none other than yours truly.

As a further claim to fame, I unwittingly performed an act of vandalism that came to save the MoD thousands of pounds. My little diversion and it was no more than that, made me highly unpopular with Martin Squire's boss, who had spent months developing and testing a new trigger mechanism for his pet rifle.

With an electrically operated jig to pull the trigger smoothly, the mechanism had worked perfectly for an uncountable number of times: pull, stroke, click; pull, stroke, click. Then the mechanically dyslexic Robert Matthews turned up in the hut one day and said to Martin, "That looks interesting." Putting my finger through the trigger guard, I pulled the trigger manually, just the once. Horrified, Martin witnessed the entire contraption fall apart leaving nuts, cogs and screws in a pool of machine oil. I heard him squeal as his fluttering fingers went to his mouth in horror, "Now look what you've done!"

Martin was roundly reprimanded by his boss for failing to guard his secret project, as was I for wrecking it. My intervention on Martin's behalf was dismissed out of hand even though I claimed my "crime" had actually been a blessing in disguise.

"After all," I said to the enraged scientist, "if it hadn't have been for me discovering it was faulty, that new trigger might have gone into production. Imagine if it had jammed when some poor guy tried firing it at the enemy."

My protestations and pleas fell on deaf ears. Furthermore Martin refused to play ping-pong with me ever again and, more seriously, clamped the lid of his lunch box tight whenever I hove into sight.

After Dr Payne had asked Colonel Marriott to take me on, I was requested to present myself for an interview with him. It was with some trepidation that I faltered into the psychiatrist's office to be confronted by a bluff, ruddy-cheeked, extremely tall man clad in an open-necked shirt and yellow corduroys. I stood in silence as he took a step forward, his eyes scanning every inch of me. After a thorough examination, he finally spoke from his Alpine height, scratching the snowy white hair dusting his scalp as he did so.

"Know what I do, young man?" he asked. "Know what a psychiatrist is, do you?"

I replied that I did not, on both counts.

"Well, let me enlighten you, Mr Matthews," he continued. His tone was agreeable, his manner jovial. "My work as an Army psychiatrist is to investigate the psychological and mental states of my patients, that is, soldiers sent for my opinion as to whether they should remain in the Army or be released from it. In short, Mr Matthews, we weed out the genuine psychopaths from the cunning, sane buggers trying to work their ticket by using false pretences. Sheep from goats. Sorting the wheat from the chaff, that sort of thing. The aim is that the sick ones go home and the others get put on a charge. Get me?"

"Yes, I think I understand," I said, "but may I ask, sir, what'll be my job?"

Colonel Marriott steepled his fingers, whistled tunelessly for a moment, then surprised me by asking, "Mind speaking a bit more?"

"What about, sir?"

"Tell me a little about yourself, for example. Cosmo Payne has a good opinion of you. Do you have a good opinion of yourself?"

Perplexed, I didn't know how to answer, but I decided to tell him that I'd been brought up and educated in India and gave him details about how, by chance, I'd wound up in Weybridge. I was well into my story, when he put up a broad hand and stopped me in mid-sentence. "Sorry to interrupt, Mr Matthews, very interesting. It so happens you've confirmed what I thought when I first heard your voice."

"Sir?"

"Deep, sonorous-sounding voice. Almost hypnotic I'd say."

"I beg your pardon, sir, I don't understand."

Cosmo Payne had done for my arms with heat. What designs did Colonel Marriott have on my voice box? The thought did not bear entertaining.

"Nor would you understand, dear boy, and there's nothing to be afraid of," chuckled Colonel Marriott. "It's like this. One of the tests we conduct is to determine just how susceptible to suggestion some of my patients are. Psychopaths are known to be ultra-susceptible to suggestion and, suffice to say, your voice will come in very useful when testing them."

Seeing my look of incomprehension, he added, "Don't try and understand, my boy, all will be revealed in time. Be here early on Monday and I'll explain. All right? Very well then. Welcome aboard. I'm sure you'll find the job very interesting. And—before I forget—Personnel have agreed to up your grade by one, which means another ten bob a week for you."

Colonel Marriott shook me by the hand. "Ah, yes," he said as an afterthought, "you don't mind being promoted, do you? You see, for practical purposes it'll be helpful if I can introduce you as Second Lieutenant Matthews when we meet the inmates at Banstead Mental Hospital. That's where we put the old sweats through their paces. The seniority will be of great help to you when interviewing the lower ranks and the like. So for the moment, young fellow, have a nice weekend."

Chapter 15

I left Colonel Marriott's office in a state of high elation. The ten shillings a week increase I'd been awarded, coupled with the prospect of assisting the psychiatrist in the guise of a second lieutenant, even if it was a fake commission, had made my day.

Singing my heart out, I cycled the five miles to my new home on the Hamm Court Estate along the towpath by the Thames. Frankie Laine's version of *I Believe* might have been all the rage, but he had nothing on me in terms of volume as, bellowing the maudlin lyrics of the song, I swerved and skidded down the thin ribbon of mud at speed.

My friend and landlord, Dick Purkis, whom I'd met at the Young Conservatives, had invited me to share his home, Willow Cottage, which stood alongside the Thames facing Pharaoh's Island. I was just twenty and Dick thirty- one, actually a year too old to be a Young Conservative. But so reluctant was he to leave the association, the committee had made an exception in his case and allowed him stay on.

Conscripted at eighteen, Dick had survived the war unscathed for more than five years of service in the desert with the Eighth Army. Then, on the very last day of hostilities, by now in Italy, a sniper's bullet shattered his shoulder, just as he'd taken a helmet-full of water from the River Po to give a thirsty child. Hospitalized for eighteen months, he was finally discharged at the age of twenty-five. Now, in a forlorn quest to recover his lost youth, he had taken to attending the YCs in the hope of forging a relationship with the opposite sex. Hopelessly shy, he was uncomfortable in women's company and finally admitted that he'd had an ulterior motive when he suggested I live with him.

"You see, Bob, I wanted to learn how you get all those girls," he said, with a hopeful expression on his heavily freckled face.

Taken aback, I replied, "Dick, I don't know *how*. I just like girls, you see," adding cautiously. "Maybe that's all there is to it?"

"I like girls, too, but I need to know what line you use," Dick persisted, his voice earnest and full of yearning.

"*Line*? I don't have a *line*," I answered truthfully.

Dick looked disbelieving. "Why do they fall for you and not me?"

I could not bring myself to tell Dick that he was a bit on the old side to capture the affections of girls in their late teens. It didn't help that he had thinning ginger hair and a pock-marked face covered with freckles, added to which his habit of stomping about the YC meeting hall in Gower Road in red cords and fleece-lined jacket, with a brass-topped cane to help him along, was considered eccentric. Clothing coupons were in short supply, so it was rare for young men to be seen wearing anything other than scruffy grey flannels and old tweed jackets. Dick Purkis stuck out from the rest of the YCs like a poppy in a field of cropped corn. Certainly his sartorial approach was no way for an aging virgin to get his oats. Even the mousiest of lasses from St George's Hill were sure to rebuff him, but I could not repay Dick's kindness towards me by telling him so.

My contribution towards the household expenses was a pound less than I'd paid for my previous digs. Now that I was earning a respectable salary as well as enjoying reduced rent, I could afford to buy girls the odd Babycham and not disappear to the loo when it was my turn to pay for a round. At last I was not reliant on handouts. Surely it was a fine day to be singing *I Believe* and giving thanks for my prayers being answered.

Dick was standing outside the back door when I came flying up the drive. He held a bucket of chicken feed in one hand and his cane in the other, while several of the Rhode Island Red chickens he kept pecked at his brogues.

"You look pretty pleased with yourself. Had good news, have you?" he asked with a smile.

"Yes, Dick, you'll never guess what! I've had a ten-bob raise and been made a second lieutenant."

"Bollocks! You're a civilian. And being no gentleman, either, you could never be an officer. So it's impossible, matey."

Laughing, I told Dick what had occurred and for a moment, judging by his puce face and heaving shoulders, I thought I'd provoked a heart attack.

Finally, he spluttered, "Well then, Bob, old chum, when you go back to work on Monday we'll have to see you looking the part, won't we? Officers can't be seen going about without a hat and coat. I'll let you have my dad's old Burberry and that green trilby of mine. How's that?"

"Seriously?"

"Seriously. I don't need either of them. They're hanging on the coat hook inside the outhouse. Try them on and we'll have a shufti."

The pale cream-coloured Burberry fitted perfectly and, after stuffing some newspaper into the trilby's headband, it sat nicely on my black thatch, too.

"What d'you think, Dick?" I asked, spinning around in front of a crazed mirror hanging precariously from a nail in the wooden planking.

Dick came to attention and saluted briskly. "Top hole, sir," he chortled. "A wee brush down and you'll be fine on parade on Monday. Now come along inside the house and we'll celebrate with some of that sloe gin I made last year. But hang on, I've forgotten something. You can't go on wearing that tatty old blazer of yours any longer. I've got a three-piece demob suit that's too small for me. You never know, it just might fit you."

The jacket of Dick's grey chalk-striped suit fitted me perfectly; however the wide trousers with hefty turn-ups were altogether too large. But with Dick's Army braces to hitch them up to somewhere near my armpits, and all the surplus material hidden under a buttoned-up waistcoat, the general effect was more than satisfactory.

"Thanks Dick. Thanks," I said, swallowing hard, "It's the best present I've ever had."

"Think nothing of it, Bob," said Dick gruffly, handing me a glass of sloe gin. "Cheerio, old son, and good luck in the new job."

The weekend flashed by. At seven-thirty on Monday morning, with a stomach full of Dick's slow-cooked porridge oats and tea, clad in my cream-coloured Burberry, I rode my bike along the towpath. Under my top coat I wore my new chalk-striped three-piece suit, with Dick's trilby forced down on my skull to keep it from flying off. Completing the alluring picture, my recently acquired cherry-wood pipe was firmly gripped between my teeth. Gold Block tobacco smoke leaked from the corners of my mouth, funnelling back over my shoulders in a blue shroud as I pedalled along. On that sunny morn, when all was well with the world, I was absolutely the bee's knees.

To my surprise, Colonel Marriott was already at his desk when I arrived at his office.

"Ah, jolly good show, Mr Matthews. Good to see you on time," he said, rising from his seat, "and, if I may so, looking very smart, too." I preened under his friendly smile. "Hang up your coat and hat," he said, pointing to a tripod stand in the corner, "then I'll show you the ropes. Oh, by the way, it is Robert, isn't it?"

"I'm known as Bob, sir."

"Bob a job, eh?" Colonel Marriott laughed at his own joke.

I'd never heard of bob a job, so had no idea what he was getting at. Since it seemed expected of me, I just grinned.

"You'll have noticed from my appearance, my boy," continued Colonel Marriott, "no one in this establishment ever bothers to dress up. Boffins, you see. All of us. Round the bend, that sort of thing. By all means, if you wish to wear a suit, please do so. I rarely do, myself, other than when I see my patients in hospital. You might think that a good idea, too. Eh, what?"

Thoroughly deflated, I managed a straight face and lied through my teeth. "Absolutely, sir. I'm much happier wearing casual clothes anyway."

"That's the stuff," said the colonel. I noticed that he was again wearing his yellow cords, though today with a snazzy blue flannel shirt and a paisley neckerchief tucked into his collar. "You save your clothing coupons for the gels, my boy!"

The psychiatrist rubbed his large hands together. "Now, apropos of nothing, old bean, allow me to show you some photographs of what flame-throwers can do to human beings in warfare. Know about flame-throwers, do you?"

"Not much, sir. Only that they were mostly used by the Americans in the war."

"Not only the Yanks. The British, too, in Malaya," Colonel Marriott corrected. "The Jerries in Holland and the Japs in the Philippines as well. Nasty things, flame-throwers. Range fifty yards or so when used by infantrymen. Much farther when fitted to tanks. Either way the end result is horrific. Not only for those on the receiving end, but it's hard, too, on the chaps aiming the stuff at the enemy. During the war flame-throwers not only caused terrible burns, they also reduced some of our own soldiers to gibbering idiots. Especially when those soldiers witnessed at close quarters what they'd done to their fellow human beings."

The colonel ceased speaking for a moment. His mind seemed to have travelled elsewhere. He stroked his jaw absentmindedly. Catching himself, he said sadly, "Yes, young man, I observed flame-throwers at first hand in Germany. Made many a brave man turn tail and run." The colonel's voice trailed away, before it became impassioned once more. "Few of these men were the cowards the Army thought them to be. Some of these poor chaps were court-martialled and have lived with the stigma of cowardice ever since. Our job, yours and mine, is to go through all the field reports. Scour what evidence we hold in the files with a fine-tooth comb. As the Army psychiatrist in charge of the investigation, it's my aim to discover what effect the use of flame-throwers had directly on the morale of our troops. Was the inhuman behaviour they'd witnessed sufficient to unhinge their minds? That sort of thing."

I had listened, rapt and in silence, to Colonel Marriott. The expression on his face had been harrowed throughout, whereas it was normally genial. In time I learned that beneath his bland mask lay hidden a complex mind of great intelligence whose depths few were allowed to plumb.

Banging a hand on his desk, he said, his face once more layered with his habitual, disarming smile, "No more of that, eh? Can't afford to be maudlin. Objectivity is what science is all about. Come along now. Off we go to have a look-see at what my picture library of horrors has in store for you."

I followed the enormous, shambling bulk of the psychiatrist into an adjoining room furnished with a plain deal desk and a single chair, with metal filing cabinets lining its four walls. Pulling open the top drawer of one of the cabinets, Colonel Marriott fished out a bulky file and tossed it on the desk. "C'mon on, young Robert, this is to be your place of work. Sit yourself down and I'll quickly show you the ropes."

When he flipped open the cover of the file, I could see it held a wad of photographs clipped together neatly. Unfastening the clip, the colonel warned, "These are pretty unpleasant to look at."

Nothing could have prepared me for what I saw in the topmost photograph, let alone the ones beneath. I sat transfixed as, one by one, the colonel spread the photographs across the surface of the desk. Each grisly picture featured soldiers—Japanese, German, American and British—either lying spread-eagled in the glutinous mud of forgotten atolls or else emerging from caves and holes in the ground, their hands raised in surrender. All were disfigured, burned beyond belief, their skin hanging in drapes, some with eyeballs hanging out of their sockets, their limbs reduced to charcoal, mutated by flame-throwers into obscene, blackened caricatures of mankind.

As if from a distance, I heard the quiet voice of Colonel Marriott. "Just think, young man, a few moments before these pictures were taken the poor sods were alive. To coin a phrase, cut down in the flower of their youth. No matter they were our enemies and we theirs, this was a ghastly way to die."

Unprepared for the horrors I was witnessing, I realized that working for Colonel Marriott was going to be much different from what I'd expected. As if reading my mind, Colonel Marriott laid a comforting arm across my shoulder. I looked up questioningly. In a gentle, quiet voice he said, "Son, I know you must have a lot of things to ask of me. For instance, why did I show you these photographs? Isn't that so?"

I nodded. "Yes, sir."

"Well, I had to observe your reaction to them. Because when we interview the patients in Banstead Hospital, you'll have an understanding of what some of them experienced during the war. It'll help your comprehension of what my tests are all about. From a purely medical perspective, our job is to separate the cheats from the sick. There are those who have been irretrievably psychologically damaged and are of no further use to the Army. On the other hand, we also have to weed out psychopaths who shouldn't have been in the Army in the first place. Then there is a third category, as I think I mentioned to you before, hiding somewhere amongst all these patients: clever buggers trying to work their ticket, as they say in the Army, faking mental illness, and up to all the tricks that God made. They get released from the service on full disability pensions. We've got to winkle them out and ensure the rest get the proper treatment they deserve. Understand?"

I did not. But again I nodded, as if all was clear.

"Good," said the colonel. "I shall leave you alone now. Spend an hour or so marrying up the photographs with the various reports relating to each action. The number on the reverse of each tells you in which cabinet you'll find the relevant personnel files. Fish these out. There are about fifty of them, alphabetically listed. Acquaint yourself with their contents. After which, write down the names of the servicemen, their ranks and numbers, not forgetting to note the date and site of each specific action: the Ardennes, Malaya, wherever. When you've finished come and see me like a good chap, will you, please?"

The colonel shuffled out of the room leaving me slumped over my desk and alone with my thoughts. What had started out as a fine day for singing my heart out had suddenly turned very depressing indeed. I felt very alone and inadequate.

The task I'd been set took all day to complete. So absorbed with what I was undertaking that I forgot about the time; everything beyond the confines of my office. I extracted file after file and tried to make sense of what I read, but it was to no avail. Although my eyes were riveted by the imagery, the insanity of war was so vividly portrayed in the photographs that, at just twenty years of age I was too juvenile, too inexperienced, to comprehend what was required of me. Obviously, the colonel had some agenda beyond my shuffling papers into order, or else what I was up to was surely a waste of time.

At five-thirty I heard the colonel's booming voice. "Still here?" I looked up to see his face poking around the door. "Time to go home, young man. If you've not done, it'll keep 'til the morrow."

"Just finished, sir," I replied. "Well, at least, I think I have. Hope I've done as you wanted."

"Sure to have, sure to have, dear boy. Now hurry along." The psychiatrist stood by the open door smiling at me. "Bit of a harsh baptism today, what? Never mind, tomorrow we'll go through the service records and set up some appointments for next week."

As I got to my feet, the leather Army braces Dick Purkis had lent me to hold up my trousers detached themselves from their fastenings. I watched in dismay as folds of flannel trousers settled over my shoes. Red-faced, I clutched at my waist in a vain effort to curtail their embarrassing descent. Colonel Marriott affected not to notice and, over his shoulder, bade me goodnight as he left the room.

Chapter 16

After my first day, my boss, the colonel hardly put a foot on AORG's premises for a full two weeks. On the odd occasions he deigned to show up, he burst into my office, smiled disarmingly and said something like, "Sorry to have left you alone, old chap, something came up." Beyond that he gave me no clue as to where he'd been. By now I'd finished scrutinising the horrific photographs in all the filing cabinets. I'd also noted down, as instructed, the relevant details of patients still to be examined by the psychiatrist. The fate of those confined to Banstead Mental Hospital in Surrey rested entirely upon Colonel Marriott's diagnosis; he was the main arbiter of whether the Army retained them or pensioned them off. There seemed to be nothing more for me to do, but before I could ask for instructions he'd whirl off like a dervish and vanish. I'd be left looking bemused, twiddling my thumbs, passing the time by reading his discarded copies of the *New Statesman*.

Utter boredom set in. Just as I was considering whether it was time to move on again, Colonel Marriott called me into his office one morning and fired up my enthusiasm once more. Asking me to pull up a chair, he said without preamble, "We're off to Banstead Hospital tomorrow, my boy. There you'll be introduced to my patients as Second Lieutenant

Robert Monteath-Matthews. Don't think Bob has got enough bottom to it, so Robert you shall be. Now, what do you think to that?"

"Whatever you say sir," I replied, pleased as punch.

Colonel Marriott climbed to his feet. His smile grew ever more expansive. "Yes, we go on the morrow, Robert, at sparrow's. Shortly I'll hand you the questions you'll be putting to these chaps. On your own, you know. But before that, let me demonstrate to you my method of determining how susceptible some patients are to suggestion. That's where that voice of yours comes in"

I gulped uncertainly. "Sir?"

"Yes, yes, your voice" the colonel replied, a touch testily I thought. "Don't you remember my telling you it's your voice I'm primarily interested in? Now then, I'd like you to repeat after me: *You are standing on the edge of a cliff and you are falling forward. Forward, forward, forward. You are standing at the edge of a cliff and you are falling forward, forward.* Kindly repeat the sentence for me in as deep a voice as you can."

"Who is this 'you' person, sir?" I enquired cautiously. Clearly, he was off his rocker.

The colonel gave me a tart look. "Come on, Robert," he said. "Who else but the patient? Now give it a try for me, will you please?" Striking an orchestral conductor's pose, he stood with his arms outstretched and commanded, "Now from the beginning, repeat after me, *You are standing...*"

Feeling rather foolish, I dredged up my deepest ten-cigarettes-a-day basso profundo. Even I was surprised how deep I could go. Paul Robeson himself might have envied my bottom G.

"You are standing on the edge of a cliff and you are falling forward," I growled, stressing 'forward' as the colonel had done. Then again, but louder this time as I got the hang of the mantra, *"Forward, forward."* I dare say if the colonel hadn't stopped me, I might have gone on and on declaiming for ever more as the ham actor within me took firm hold.

"That's it!" exclaimed Colonel Marriott excitedly, "I knew you had it in you. Exactly right. Now do it once more and then afterwards in your office. Repeat it all day long. *Forward, forward, forward.* Emphasise 'forward'. Got that, Robert?"

My eyes lit up. "Yes, sir." However mad the psychiatrist appeared to be, I could see there was fun ahead after all and I was very much up for that. "Well then, Second Lieutenant," said the colonel, "kindly tell me how and where, and to what use those words you've been repeating can be put. Where does your voice come into it? How does it help us ascertain what we need to discover?"

I shook my head. "No idea, sir."

"All right," said the colonel. "Let me show you."

He walked swiftly over to the wall behind his desk, fumbled about in one of his trouser pockets and withdrew a stick of charcoal. I watched, fascinated, as he made a horizontal mark about two inches long at a height of roughly five and a half feet from the floor, then another one six inches beneath the first. Whistling tunelessly, he drew a third line, parallel to the others and halfway between them.

"Voila!" he exclaimed, with a flourish of his charcoal. "Now, Robert, here comes the tricky bit."

Puzzled as to what on earth the colonel was up to, I repeated "Tricky bit" after him like a budgerigar.

Conjuring a tiny metal eyelet from his shirt pocket, the colonel held it up close to my eyes. "Devoid of a hook, it's a pretty useless object, wouldn't you think?" His ability to read my mind never ceased to amaze. "Just watch."

He swept both hands across the surface of his desk before proceeding to rummage about on the floor. He followed this up by stomping all over the carpet, after which he crouched down like a colossal bear, his fingers searching the tufts. Failing to find what he was looking for, he opened all the drawers of his desk and then slammed them shut again with a series of deafening bangs.

"Where's the blessed thing gone?" he demanded loudly. "It was here just a moment ago." Finally, he discovered what he was looking for under an untidy pile of papers. "Thank the Lord for that!" he exclaimed. Triumphant, he held up a piece of thin cord for my inspection. At one end of it there was attached a small brass bob, at the other, a safety pin.

"Now, pay attention, Robert," he said, with a gleam in his eye. Dipping into a receptacle on his desk he came up with a fist-sized lump of Plasticine. "Sticky stuff this," he said, squeezing hard. "Mould it thus and it adheres to most surfaces like mad."

Walking over to the wall he'd marked, he forced the Plasticine against the surface above the topmost line, before giving it a tweak to ensure it was stuck fast. He thrust the eyelet's threaded end deep into the softened Plasticine He then unfastened the safety pin, ran the free end of the cord through the eyelet, and left the brass bob swinging like a plumb line. Giving me a quick glance, he pointed to his handiwork and ordered me to stand with my back to the wall.

"Now, Robert," he said, "I'm going to pin the cord to the back of your shirt, like so." He came round behind me and thrust the safety pin into the cotton material at a point between my shoulder blades. "Don't move," the colonel growled as I shifted my feet. Taking up a position a short distance from where I stood, he began to bray, *"You are standing on the edge of a cliff and you are falling forward.* Now, Robert, do you see what we're getting at?"

Standing rigidly to attention, I replied, "Not really, sir."

"Well, I have threaded the cord through the eyelet. The wee bob is hanging straight down the middle of your spine. Now if you rock forward or backward on your feet, however small the movement is, I shall be able to register the distance exactly. How? By using the marks on the wall. Thus I can assess the patient's susceptibility to suggestion or alternatively his resistance to it. In some cases you'll observe patients actively resisting suggestion. Cunning little shits, they'll have figured out what we're after. So instead of tilting forwards, they rock backwards on their heels. Others will stand steady, knowing that however hard we cajole them to do otherwise, they will remain unaffected. Then there are those, a few, whom you'll see stumble and pitch flat on their faces. So susceptible to suggestion are they that I can, without hesitation, categorise them as being psychopaths who qualify for discharge. Remember, this exercise is simply to weed out genuine psychopaths."

"And the other fellows?" The colonel shrugged. "Who knows? Disability arising from stress is always tricky to diagnose. I leave it to others to decide the fate of those I can't figure out. Any questions?"

"No, sir," I replied, deciding that my boss was completely batty.

"Well then, young man, I've prepared the questions you'll be putting to patients I've allocated you. Take a shufti at these will you?" Colonel Marriott handed me a couple of sheets of buff coloured paper. "Nothing too onerous. All you have to do is fill in each one's name, rank, serial number, regiment, corps, et cetera in the appropriate places on the form and check it with the patient. When done, hand the papers over to an orderly. After that we'll get on with the test. Suit you?" The psychiatrist looked at me quizzically. "You look a touch despondent, young Robert. What's up?"

"Well, sir," I ventured, "is that all I have to do?"

"Yes. And...?"

"I just thought you wanted me to go into greater detail, ask more personal questions and things, sir."

"Things, things? Whatever gave you that idea? Mustn't rush you on your baptism, eh? Next time round perhaps, but for now, let us see how you cope. Anyway, you're vital to me in other ways. Your voice, remember."

Colonel Marriott paused, his eyes roving over my open-necked shirt and baggy trousers. "Oh, yes. Proper kit tomorrow, wear your suit."

Chapter 17

At eight o'clock the following morning a staff car drew up outside the office. The colonel climbed into the back of it and asked me to join him. "It'll take about forty minutes to the hospital," he grunted, squeezing his huge frame into the back seat. "Nervous are you?" he asked, patting my thigh. I flinched reflexively. "Nothing to it, you'll see."

Under my breath, I repeated for the umpteenth time, *"You are standing on the edge of a cliff and you are falling forward."*

Our driver obviously knew where we were headed. We slowly rolled forward out of the gates and accelerated away from West Byfleet. I noticed that the trees we passed were already turning russet. Heralding an early autumn, there was a chill in the air.

Huddled in Dick Purkis's Burberry, I allowed my mind to wander. My thoughts turned to my mother. Almost for the first time, in the two years I'd been away from home, I found myself missing her, my brothers and only sister, too.

My mother wrote to me every three months or so. I replied with even less frequency. My excuse was that I could not afford the postage. It must have sounded lame to her, but it was true nevertheless. Her last letter said my stepfather had divorced her. True to form, she blamed him for all her woes, castigating him for leaving her without a penny. I found myself unable to sympathise. I remembered all too clearly that it had been she who had cuckolded him.

Still I did have her to thank for the cheque she'd enclosed for six pounds. The money, she said, would buy me a warm coat for the winter. But since I already owned a voluminous Burberry, I'd made other plans for the cash. The old dinner suit I'd brought with me from Pakistan was horribly stained and fraying at the collar. Now I needed another and a friend of mine wished to dispose of his old one. Buying a dinner suit was not the extravagance it might have seemed; without it I couldn't attend the Friday night dances at the High Pines Club in Weybridge with the Young Conservatives.

Colonel Marriott interrupted my musings. "Robert, ready for the fray are we?"

"Yes, sir. I think so," I replied, with some trepidation.

"Good-oh," said the colonel. "That's the stuff."

Moments later we pulled off the road and drove down the long curved driveway leading to Banstead Mental Hospital. Set in what appeared to be acres of well-tended lawns, the massive red brick building featured contrasting facings of grey stone, softening its otherwise glum frontage.

"Follow me," said the colonel as the car came to a stop. Huffing and puffing, he forced himself out of the rear door and gestured in the general direction of the hospital. "The clinic is in that small block at the side. It's reserved for military personnel only, but I'm sure the civilian canteen *wallahs* will be pleased to rustle up a cup of tea for us. Tell you what, I'll detail the driver to get us some." Apprehension had turned my throat dry as kindling wood. A cup of tea would do nicely, whoever got it. Summoning our driver, the colonel ordered him to organise our refreshment, then loped off at a great pace. My rapid, short staccato strides alongside his great long ones must have looked comical to the many onlookers standing about, but none of them smiled. Their eyes were blank, their expressions vacant.

At ten o'clock a white-coated orderly showed me into a small windowless office furnished with an unadorned desk and two chairs. "I'll send the first patient in when you are ready, sir," he said.

"Now's fine." I just stopped myself in time from adding "sir" and giving the game away.

I sat down in a chair, holding my back stiff and upright. With my face fixed in what I hoped would be perceived as a stern military expression, I waited anxiously for a knock on the door and my first victim to enter. Moments later, I heard a loud rap on wood. With an effort, I kept my voice steady. I called out "Come" as Colonel Marriott was prone to do.

A tall, broad-shouldered man entered briskly and took three paces forward before snapping to attention. "Sergeant Ripley, sah," he shouted in a parade ground voice, his heels coming together on the wooden floor with a thunderous sound. He stood facing me, his jaw thrust out, his arms held rigid down the seams of his trousers. His glinting dark eyes, set in a hard-bitten pock-marked face, swept the entire office before coming to rest on me. Sergeant Ripley was not a man to encounter on a dark night, I decided.

"At ease. Stand easy," I replied. If nothing else, my old school's army cadet force had taught me the correct responses. "Please take a seat."

"Sah!" came the shout again. The sergeant, who was wearing a grey civilian suit too small for him, pulled a white handkerchief from his breast pocket. Dusting the seat of his chair prior to placing his bottom on it, he offered by way of explanation, "Germs, sah. Can't be too careful, sah." Facing me, he continued to glare as if he were the interrogator and I his prisoner. I cleared the sudden constriction in my throat with a cough.

Unnerved by Sergeant Ripley, I avoided his X-ray eyes. Concentrating on the sheet of paper in front of me, I said, "I shall run through your service details now, Sergeant. Please stop me at any point if you have anything to add or comments to make." I then proceeded to read out his Army record as laid down for me by Colonel Marriott. Throughout, the sergeant sat unblinking, not saying a word. When I arrived at the end, I looked up and asked him, "All correct, Sergeant?"

"Sah, permission to ask a question, sah?"

"Yes, sure. What do you want to ask?"

"I've gone through this kind of thing before. I thought I was going to see a quack, er, doctor. A psychi—, er, whatchamacallit?"

"A psychiatrist?"

"That's the chap. I was hoping to get a clean bill today, sah, so I could get me discharge and go home shortly. I know I went a bit round the bend after D-day an' all. The docs said it was those bleeding flame-throwers in the Ardennes what did it. But that was six years ago, sah, and I'm okay now. See, I ain't set eyes on my wife or my wee bairns for a long time. They live in Somerset and it ain't easy for them to get up here. I'm missing the poor buggers. Pardon the expression."

"That's okay," I said, feeling helpless, hopelessly at a loss. "I'm so sorry, sergeant. But you will be seeing Colonel Marriott later and, well, let's hope." I didn't know what else I could add.

As I sat confronting the formidable Sergeant Ripley, I saw his shoulders slump suddenly and his head bow. Pulling his handkerchief from his pocket again, he dabbed at his eyes before blowing hard on his nose. "Sorry, sah," he sniffed. "Bit overcome, see?" Pulling himself together, he said, his voice gritty once more, "Wouldn't think I'd seen active service in the desert, Italy, France and Germany, would you, sah? Behaving like a bleedin' baby, an' all, and me forty years old."

I had the sudden impulse to put my arm around the sergeant's shoulder, but fortunately I managed to restrain myself.

"That's fine, sergeant," I said standing up, keeping my eyes well away from him, "I've done. You're dismissed. I'll see that the orderly gets you a cuppa."

The sergeant was in charge of himself again. "Thank you, sah," he said, getting to his feet. He saluted, turned on his heel, opened the door and marched out.

My encounter with the formidable Sergeant Ripley had left me feeling distressed. I prayed the orderly would allow me time to recover my equilibrium before the next man on my list entered. But no, almost immediately after the sergeant had left the room, a small mean-looking fellow barged in without knocking. Unshaven, wearing creased corduroy trousers and a shirt that had seen better days, his shoes were worn down at the heels and caked with mud, the antithesis of the immaculate sergeant in every possible way. I knew from my notes that my scruffy visitor was a Private Amos of the Royal Artillery.

"Can I sit down, mate?" asked the private, a little squirt no more than five years older than I was. Without waiting for my response, he hitched up his trousers and sat down on the chair facing my desk.

"Kindly address me as 'sir', I said stiffly. Private Amos had taken liberties with me and I was annoyed. "In future, you will ask my permission to stand, sit, or have a pee. Understood?" I was full of myself, using my rank to deal with the private's insolence, unaware of how pompous I sounded.

"Don't have to call you 'sir'," smirked Private Amos in reply. "I ain't in the Army no more. I was medically discharged six months ago. Got a measly forty per cent disability pension, didn't I?"

Colouring up, I quickly scanned the man's Army record but could find no reference to his having being discharged from the Army. If he was telling the truth, and there seemed no reason for him to lie, then, embarrassingly, Colonel Marriott's notes on Private Amos's medical history were well out of date.

Ignoring Private Amos's insubordination, I said, "I see you served in Malaya in '49 against the commie guerrillas. Took some shrapnel to the head. You were hospitalised in Singapore before being sent back to Blighty for rehab. That's right?"

"Yeah," agreed Private Amos, his manner now more reasonable. "Then I was put in hospital again, down in Plymouth, because I began to get these headaches, blackouts and twitches. The medics discharged me when they couldn't find anything wrong. I ain't been able to hold a job since. So I applied to the Board for 100% disability. They gave me some more tests. Now they've sent me here. I tell you, I've really been frigged about, mate, and I'm fuckin' pissed off." Private Amos leant back in his chair, his eyes fixing me with me a baleful glare.

It was apparent that, prolonging the meeting with Private Amos was of no value whatsoever, so I told him to leave.

"Okay, Amos," I said, "you can go now, you're dismissed."

"Too fuckin' right, I am. What nah?"

"The orderly will take care of you. You'll be seen by Colonel Marriott, who is a psychiatrist, sometime this afternoon."

Without waiting for any more snide remarks from Private Amos, I got up and opened the door wide. "Off you go then, Amos." I said, standing aside, allowing him to slink past me into the corridor. Putting my head round the door, I called out in a loud voice, "Orderly! I'll have the next one in, soon as you're ready."

I saw six more men that morning. Two of them, Corporals Tanner and Whistler, were regular soldiers like Sergeant Ripley and each had done twenty or more years in the Army. They'd both been on active service in almost every campaign, which I found very humbling. On the surface, there didn't appear much wrong with them now and so I wondered why they had been ordered to be examined. If these proud men were to be diagnosed as psychopaths, then I was convinced the system was wrong. But then again, what did I know about anything? There was I, wet behind the ears, an inflated incompetent, searching for any inconsistencies in their stories, any statements that failed to match their records. It was an absurdity for me to interrogate these men who had been through so much.

Even I could tell that, of the remaining four soldiers, Privates Gordon, Melhuish and Rippon of the Armoured Corps were feigning symptoms of mental illness to obtain their discharges. They certainly weren't going to deceive Colonel Marriott with their rolling eyes and sudden twitches.

The last soldier to be seen, Sergeant Jobson of the Gordon Highlanders, a tall, gaunt Scot who had twice been wounded before being returned to the front, entered the room like a ghost. He sat down and thereafter completely ignored my presence. His eyes seemingly set on some far distant loch, he sat fully upright on his chair and refused to answer any of my questions. After ten minutes, I called for the orderly and had the sergeant led out. The walls of the small office closed in around me. I buried my head in my arms and sobbed.

Chapter 18

After lunch in the hospital canteen, I was shown to a large room where Colonel Marriott prowled the floor.

"Well then, Robert, me lad, I've read your notes and I think we can wheel the chaps in now. I've set up the experiment, so all I need the orderly to do as they come in is fix the safety pin to their coats and line 'em up there." The colonel pointed to the wall opposite, in front of which were a desk and two chairs. "Keep your eye on me," he said, "when I raise my hand do your stuff. Any questions?"

I shook my head. I was still feeling too miserable to display any enthusiasm.

The first patient in was Sergeant Ripley. The orderly, who obviously knew the ropes, spoke quietly to the sergeant, fixed the safety pin to his coat, and asked him to stand with his back to the wall, with his feet lined up to a chalk mark on the floor.

"Now, Sergeant," said the colonel in a friendly voice, "you might think what we're doing is a bit daft." He looked to me for confirmation, then at the orderly and lastly the sergeant, before laughing. "Suppose it is daft, really, but I'll learn a great deal from it." He studied Sergeant Ripley's face for a reaction. There was none. But for a slight twitch of his eyelids, the sergeant's expression remained inscrutable.

"Righto, then," said the colonel, lifting a hand.

I cleared my throat and, forcing my voice down to previously unknown depths, I chanted, *"You are standing on the edge of a cliff and you are falling forward. Forward, forward, forward."*

Quite unexpectedly, the sergeant's eyes flicked wildly from side to side as if in a state of near panic. I watched, in horror, as his head began to sway like a cobra's as I said, *"You are falling forward."*

I had hoped that, of all the men I'd seen that day the sergeant would not be labelled a psychopath, for surely he was not. But as I continued to repeat my words like a gramophone, the effect of my voice on Sergeant Ripley was plain for all to see. Stiff as a board, he rocked on his heels until the colonel called on the orderly to restrain the sergeant. "Thank you, Sergeant Ripley," said the colonel, "I'll have word with you later."

The sergeant gathered himself together, saluted, and with arms swinging marched out noisily. Was I dreaming? Or had the sergeant dropped an eyelid in my direction as he left? I could not be sure. But the colonel certainly was.

"Humph," he shrugged, not in disdain, but curiously, in a sad kind of way. "The poor sod was having us on," he said quietly. "He's no more a psychopath than a fly with fleas. Nevertheless he's suffered terrible trauma and I shall recommend him to be discharged with a full disability pension on medical grounds."

So the psychiatrist had a heart after all. "I, for one, am glad," I said.

"How so?" quizzed the colonel.

"Well, sir, he hasn't seen his family for a long time."

"Ah, so he hasn't. Quite true, actually. Perhaps because he hasn't any family now. Wife ran off to New Zealand with a fellow from his regiment, taking the children. Ripley's never accepted the reality, which is part of his problem."

I sat with my mouth open, looking at the colonel in disbelief. The more I got involved with his work, the more discombobulated I became.

"Well, Robert, shall we get on before we drown in syllabub?" said the colonel, cracking his knuckles. "Can't allow sentiment to interfere."

Private Amos was brought in next. He sauntered rather than walked, clearly uncaring of the proceedings or of the fact that the increased pension he was looking for depended on the psychiatrist facing him.

"Blimey, mate, what you doin'?" he asked the orderly as his coat was pinned through.

"Just you be quiet in the colonel's presence," replied the orderly.

"Don't give a shit, mate," said Private Amos. "I ain't in the Army nah."

Watching the proceedings, the colonel tipped his chair back and, from under lowered eyelids, viewed Private Amos with obvious distaste. Wafting a languid hand he rapidly explained that all that was required of the hapless one was to stand still and be quiet. Signalling me to carry on, I cleared my throat. To my utter consternation, I found my vocal cords, for no good reason at all, refusing to produce the deep, hypnotic notes, the colonel sought.

I tried again: *"You are standing on the edge of a cliff and..."* Lower this time, but in nothing like my usual voice. Private Amos had not budged an inch. I glanced across at the colonel, who looked very tetchy. Glaring at me, he fiddled around with his Adam's apple as if to say "get on with it, you're wasting time." Once more I tried, *"and you are falling forward, forward..."* and to my astonishment, saw Private Amos sway, then totter on his heels. Encouraged now, I raised my voice a few decibels louder, to a near falsetto shout. On and on I went, repeating: *"and you are falling forward, forward..."* Private Amos, his eyes popping from his head, abruptly put his hands out to save himself, then sprawled full length at the feet of the colonel. Picking himself up, he stood awkwardly, shorn of all bravado.

"Orderly, take this man out, will you, please? I think we've done with him," commanded the colonel. The orderly took Private Amos by the arm and led him out.

Turning to face me, the colonel asked, "What on earth is the matter with your voice, boy?"

"Don't know, sir" I replied, shamefacedly. "It sort of just went. Still not right. Sorry, sir."

"Bad timing to get a sore throat," said the colonel. "Well, anyway, let me tell you I'm amazed it worked the oracle with Amos. Bloody little twerp. Total psychopath, he may be, but I'm dashed if I'll let the Board give in to his demands. We'll take a ten minute break now. Off you go and smoke that infernal pipe of yours. Hopefully, it'll lubricate your vocal cords."

I was just about to take leave of the colonel, but stopped short when I saw his face go ashen. Clutching his skull in both hands, his knuckles white with tension as he applied pressure to his temples, the colonel howled in pain.

"My God!" I cried, "are you all right, sir?"

After about a minute the sudden spasm subsided and Colonel's features relaxed somewhat. "Fetch me a glass of water," he croaked. "There, on the table."

I made a quick dash to the table, poured a glass of water and handed it to the colonel, who downed it in one. "Another, please, Robert," he said, again in control of himself. "Now if you'll kindly leave me alone, I shall be ready to continue in a little while."

I was stunned. Clearly the colonel was ill and, for an instant, I considered calling on one of the hospital's doctors to examine him. But fearing the colonel's certain ire for disobeying him, I took myself off, sat down on a bench outside, lit my pipe, and gazed over the sunlit lawn, my mind riven with uncertainty.

As it happened, on my return to the room the colonel appeared to be his old self again—cheerful, bantering and eager to get on. By this time I had come to the clear conclusion that the tests we conducted were valueless. For the life of me, I could not see how they could possibly separate sheep from goats, as the colonel had once claimed. Furthermore, he'd said my deep voice was an imperative for achieving results. Yet the effect had been the same even when my voice had gone funny on me. So where did that leave me?

"Got the voice together now, Robert, have we?" asked the colonel. "Baccy nicely fouled up your pipes, eh? Kindly get the orderly to wheel the next chap in, please."

One after another, the remaining men had their coats pinned and were subjected to my voice, which had been magically restored.

Corporals Tanner and Whistler stood as still as monuments throughout their tests. Privates Melhuish, Gordon and Rippon staggered drunkenly in varying degrees, whereas Sergeant Jobson ignored everyone in the room. His body was present, but his mind was somewhere far, far away; he was a sombre pine-tree of a man, whose sap had long since dried.

By five in the evening when we'd finished for the day, I was more than ever convinced by the evidence of my eyes that the colonel's experimental tests were certainly unreliable. How he concluded some of the men we'd seen that day were psychopaths and others not—well, it beat me.

Chapter 19

Colonel Marriott never again asked me to accompany him to Banstead Mental Hospital. Since he did not explain why, I assumed my Paul Robeson-ish rendition of *You are standing on the edge of a cliff* had not been up to snuff or hadn't achieved the results he'd hoped for. Whatever the reason, I sensed I'd let the Colonel down. Being too reticent to ask, I was left puzzled, miserable and disillusioned. I was left to fiddle about in my office with next to nothing to do.

Where once Colonel Marriott would poke his head around the door and greet me affably, now he hardly ever did. It was if his mind had moved to a loftier plane and my presence was a distraction. In a bafflingly short time, the hugely personable character I'd come to revere had changed into a hulking, gloomy figure I was rather scared of. So, for a while, not having him around was something of a mercy.

I eventually found his lengthy absences frustrating. Since I was still receiving my pay, I decided things could be worse and so kept my mouth shut. But as the weeks went by, I was forced to field telephone enquiries as to the colonel's whereabouts. All I could do was say, "Sorry, I've no idea where Colonel Marriott is or when he'll back." Doubtless the callers thought the colonel was a fool to be putting up with such a dolt as me. I guess I could have discovered my boss's whereabouts, but I was scared of asking Personnel in case I was made redundant—especially likely if it came out that I had nothing to do all day.

I asked some of my friends, over lunch in the canteen, what they'd do in my position. To a man, they acknowledged I was a lucky sod, adding how much they envied me my indolent, unsupervised days.

"What are you worrying about, Bob?" they all said. "You're getting paid, aren't you?"

"Yes, but what happens if Personnel finds out?" I replied.

"Deal with it then," was what they advised.

I decided they were right and thereafter kept my mouth shut.

Whatever project Colonel Marriott was now embarked on, it was plain I didn't figure in his plans. And, after the middle of October, he vanished as if he'd never been more than a figment of my imagination.

In spite of this, I continued to cycle along the Thames towpath, signing into work each morning dead on eight o'clock as usual. My daily ritual was to head for my office, make a pillow of my Burberry and lay it down behind the filing cabinets ready for my rest later in the afternoon. After which I made pretence of working, but I soon gave up on that, for no one ever visited me. From time to time, I'd get down to the floor and do a few sets of one-armed press-ups, with the object of keeping in shape. Otherwise, each day was as aimless and stultifying as the one before

Now that I had my dinner suit, most Friday nights Dick Purkis and I went to the High Pines Club with the YCs. To finance my evenings, I took to challenging any man in the bar to do as many one-armed press-ups as I could. The bet was a half crown. I was never short of takers, for many of the Young Conservatives were massively built rugby players. I was never beaten and the cash I won bought several glasses of foul custard-yellow Advocaat and fizzy Babychams for the girls I fancied, with enough left over to buy a couple of mild and bitters for Dick and myself.

I had learned how to perform one-armed press-ups from the Army PT instructor at my school. He'd proved to me that it wasn't just a matter of muscle and was largely a matter of balance and technique. Also, because my power to weight ratio was pretty good, I didn't find the press-ups at all difficult. After practising for years and showing off at the slightest opportunity, I realised, after once beating someone twice my size at the High Pines, there was money to be made. Naturally, I never explained the mechanics to those queuing up to show the cocky Bob Matthews a thing or two. There were regulars who always insisted on having a go, imagining that pure strength would be enough to beat me. They were wrong. Despite losing face in front of their pals, they continued to brag, "Okay, Matthews, we'll sort you out next week." But no one ever did.

The tedium of not being occupied at work was briefly relieved at around midday, when I headed for the recreation room adjoining the canteen, and played ping-pong with some of the other scientific assistants. Freddie, he of the soft brown eyes and delicate hands, whose boss's trigger-mechanism experiment I had ruined, had forgiven me. Once again, he was always on hand at lunchtime, offering to share the tasty sandwiches his mother had made up for him.

"Have one, Bob. Go on, have one. Plenty here for me," he said, eyeing me, venturing out a hand in which was gently clasped fresh bread stuffed with ham, sometimes even chicken.

"Thanks, Martin," I said, accepting his largesse, at the same time distancing myself from him as I ate.

Martin just looked on and smiled, his face filled with something akin to love. One time he plucked up the courage to ask, "Fancy going to the flicks with me?" When he saw that he'd surprised me, his lisping stammer faded to a halting whisper. "Mario Lanza's on at the Regal, Walton, this week. I know you love singing. What about it Bob? My treat." Not wishing to put my sandwiches at risk, I rejected Martin's kind offer, but assured him that I'd take him up on it another time. I had no intention of doing so, but accepted another sandwich from him nevertheless.

The lunch hour over, I'd scrape up all the discarded newspapers I could find and repair to my den where I'd read them from cover to cover. Then I'd sleep some more until it was time to leave. Eventually, I decided enough was enough.

I asked Dick Purkis for his advice. "Should I hand in my notice and look for another job? I can't stand the boredom any more.

Scratching at the ginger stubble on his cheeks, he replied, "Don't know, old chap. November's a bad time to look for a new situation."

Coming from an older, stuffier generation Dick always called a job "a situation." Going to work was "going on business". A salesman for a greetings card company, Dick insisted his situation was that of commercial traveller, as if being called a salesman was somehow inferior.

"I'd hold on until after Christmas if I were you," he continued, "but I'll not deter you if your mind's made up. If you are worrying about paying me for your keep, don't. Really, don't, old chap. We can always work something out, can't we?"

Dear old, kind old, Dick was right, of course. Christmas was just around the corner and it was about the worst time to find a new "situation". It was also coming up to the worst time of the year to cycle to work on the towpath. Dark when I left home in the mornings, dark when I returned, it was hazardous in the extreme to negotiate the narrow, slippery strip without a cycle lamp to light my way.

The night I skidded off the towpath and landed myself in the swollen Thames proved I should have splurged a shilling or two and acquired a lamp. Fortunately, I fell down a gravel bank into the very edge of the river, where the water was no more than four feet deep. Nevertheless, weighed down by my heavy Burberry, holding on to my bike with one hand, with the other scrabbling around in the murk reaching for a tree root, anything at all on the bank to give me purchase, was a scary fifteen minutes before I managed to clamber out onto the bank where I lay like a landed fish, gasping for air. After I had recovered somewhat, although now shivering with cold and wet through, I pushed my bike the rest of the way home and fell into a tepid bath.

Good time or bad time, I knew I had no choice now other than to leave the AORG. So the following morning I informed the personnel officer that I wished to resign.

"May I ask you why you wish to leave, Mr Matthews?" he asked. "I thought you were happy with us."

"Well, sir, I'm bored. I haven't seen Colonel Marriott since mid-October and he's left me no work to do. He's not been in contact with me since then and I don't even know where he is now."

"What? Didn't you know the colonel's been ill in hospital?" asked the personnel officer. "You mean to say no one told you?" From the rising colour in his face, I thought he was about to self-ignite. "It's bloody ridiculous!" he raged. "Surely, you got a note to the effect? Brain tumour, that's what the colonel had, and you mean to say no one told you? Moved you on to do something else?"

My mind reeled from the news. After I left the personnel officer it occurred that it was his responsibility to keep me notified and find me something productive to do elsewhere.

The die now cast, Bob Matthews had to find another job, and fast.

Chapter 20

The Labour Exchange came up trumps almost immediately. The weasely man behind the small glass window, in his bleak cream- and dark green-painted hole of an office, peered out at me as if I was some detestable object.

"Mr Matthews. Two t's is it?" he asked, giving me a sniffy look. "If you consider a temporary, manual kind of job, working alongside women on the same piecework rate as them, I have something that pays well."

I had no idea what "piecework" meant. For the moment I was only interested in what the rate for the job was. Working with women, I thought, could be fun. Different, anyway.

"Sure," I said, "but what kind of work is it and how much can I earn?"

"Up to you. Depends how much you turn out."

"Of what? What do I have to do?

"Flatting."

"Flatting?"

"That's the company's description. The firm's called Panelite and they are up on the right, halfway up Monument Hill in Weybridge. They make cladding panels for railway compartments. Interested? I can make an immediate appointment with the forewoman if you are."

Thinking "beggars", I took an introductory note from the weasel and headed off straight away.

If Panelite Ltd had any intention of complying with the Factories Act, their premises, consisting of a flimsy timber shed with a corrugated roof, gave no indication of it. Gritting my teeth, I opened the front door and entered a kind of workshop, filled with a dozen long trestle tables on which were laid lengths of wood, laminated with an unfamiliar shiny, hard material. Women wearing grimy cotton coats were bent double over the wooden boards, dipping sponges into buckets of water standing at their feet, before sanding down the surface of the laminate.

My sudden appearance at the door was the cause for much hilarity from the twelve or so women in the place. I watched nervously, as one of them, a beefy creature of about forty, straightened up before approaching me. Placing her hands on her stout hips, she faced me with a huge grin on her blotched red face.

"Oi, you," she bawled. "You the chap from the Labour?"

"Yes," I replied, half-wanting to make run for it. "They told me to see a Mrs Blodgett."

"Well, that's me, mate," the woman said. "You come for the flattin' job, innit?"

There was a sudden hush in the room. Every eye was fixed on me.

"Yes," I said, handing Mrs Blodgett the piece of paper I'd been given. She barely gave it a glance before saying, "So you are Mr Matthews. Well, we can't be doin' with surnames here. What's your Christian name"

"It's Bob," I said.

"Oh, la-di-da, are we, Bob?" said Gwen. Then hastily, in case she had caused me offence, "Don't mind us, we're always ones for a laugh, aren't we girls?"

"Yeah, always game for a laugh, Gwen," the women cried.

From my first day, laughter in Panelite's misbegotten factory was to be at my expense.

Exposing a mouthful of uneven tobacco-stained teeth as she smiled, Gwen reached out a hand and pinched my left cheek. "You'll be all right here, mate," she said, "just so long you got a sense of 'umour. You have to have one to be a flatter. Otherwise you'll go mad here, son."

"Flatter?" I asked. "What's that?"

"Didn't the Labour tell you nuffink?"

"Well, the man just said the job was called flatting and it was on piecework, but I'm not sure what that is either."

"Blimey O'Reilly, Bob. Where you bin all your life? From the looks of it, I don't think the job's going to suit you, mate. Office job's what you want." Gwen's eyes softened as she looked me over. "Best you don't work here, son," she said kindly. "It's not for the likes of you. It's hard. Really hard, Bob."

With a total of six shillings to my name, rent to be paid, and two tickets for the YC annual ball on D'Oyly Carte Island to think about, I was not about to be put off by Gwen or anyone else. "Look, Gwen," I said, keeping my voice low, "I need this job. I don't care how shitty or how hard the job hard is. I'm ready to do anything."

Seeing that I meant every word, Gwen looked at me and said, "Right mate, if your mind's made up, clock on Monday morning at seven. But first I'd better fill you in about what you have to do. If you still fancy starting here, give me your P45, and I'll have the office sort you out. Okay?"

"I'm game," I replied, my voice sounding more certain than I felt. "Go on, show me how to flat."

"Your funeral," said Gwen, taking my arm. "C'mon, just come with me." As Gwen walked me over to a vacant trestle table, I saw, reflected in a window ahead of me, every eye in the room focussed on my back. "Right," Gwen said, "see those panels stacked against the wall? Fetch one and put it on the table. C'mon, c'mon, no time to waste. Be quick! You're on piecework, remember."

The panels were surprisingly heavy. At about thirty pounds each, they were much heavier to lift than I'd anticipated and their length made them awkward to carry. I strove to be casual, insouciant even, as I heaved one of them off the pile and laid it on the table. I suspect I hadn't fooled Gwen who watched me in silence, albeit with the tiniest of smiles on her face.

"Right," said Gwen, "nah what you do is this. Run your hand over the surface of this effing thing and tell me what you feel. C'mon, Bob, jump to it!"

I leapt forward. Stroking the biscuit-coloured laminate with my fingertips, I was surprised to find minute pimples marring its otherwise pristine surface. "I expected it to be smooth, and it's not," I replied. "I couldn't see the little bumps, but I felt them all right."

"Sanding down them piddling little bumps, as you call them, is what's called flattin'. Got it nah, mate?" Gwen cackled. "Pick up that sponge, dip it in that bucket of water there and wet the claddin' down before sandpapering it. Called wet and dry, it is. You ain't got all day, Bob. It's piecework, mate, so get on with it."

I resented being treated like a child by the bossy forewoman, but still I jumped to the task. I sponged the laminate with icy water, folded sandpaper over the small wooden block Gwen handed me and began to work it up and down the length of the piece. It was surprisingly hard work and, as I got a rhythm going, despite it being very cold, I began to pour with sweat as the sandpaper hissed and scratched at invisible projections.

After about five minutes, Gwen told me to stop. "That's enough, Bob," she said. "What you just done was flattin'. Nah, I'm going to have a feel to see how well you did it. The idea's to get it as smooth as a baby's bum, mate."

Not a square millimetre of the laminate escaped Gwen's scrutiny, as her eyes searched and her coarse work-hardened palms scoured the surface. Every now and then, as I stood by following her movements, she pointed an accusative finger at me and scorned, "You missed that one...and that one..."

In all, I'd missed smoothing out, or flatting, about five imperfections and Gwen made it quite plain to me that I'd have to improve—that is, if I wanted to earn decent money.

"Bob," she said, "I'm serious. At the end of each shift I check all the claddin' you done. Each piece that don't pass, you don't get paid for, geddit?"

"How much money for each do I get paid?" I asked, turning round to see if anyone was eavesdropping. All the women were hard at work, heads down, arms flailing, some singing to Henry Hall's band on the radio, but most were quiet, concentrating on what they were doing.

I tried to picture myself amongst these working-class women, in the awful conditions in which they were obliged to labour, and wondered how I'd cope. The situation was far removed from the comfortable offices and tonsured lawns of the Army Operational Research Group, and the women themselves as remote from the Young Conservatives and the well-bred girls of St Georges Hill I was used to mixing with. In my head, I'd already planned to fabricate a story that Dick

Purkis could swallow, one that would persuade him, a snob and a founder member of the Keep the Class System Intact Brigade from being outraged about the lowly job I was about to embark on.

"'Ow much you get?" Gwen answered, tossing an imaginary coin. "Sixpence for each one I pass, mate. That's two sheets for a bob. Forty sheets, one quid. My girls earn on average about seven quid a week, that's about two hundred and eighty pieces a week." As I dwelt on the mind-numbing figures, I heard Gwen call out, "'Ere Beth! Tell Bob how many pieces you flat a week."

I saw a tiny sparrow of a thing lay down her sander. Drying her reddened, wet hands on her headscarf, Beth replied, "Gwen, you knows 'ow many I flats. About four hundred a week, give or take." She turned to me. "That's ten quid, mate."

"Four hundred?!" I cried, rapidly calculating that Beth flatted eighty sheets a day over a five-day week, or one every six minutes in an eight-hour day. "Impossible!" I shouted in a falsetto voice.

The workshop went silent. The *scrape scrape* sound of sandpaper ceased, as did the accompanying chatter. Then one of the women piped up, one I'd already noticed as being younger and prettier than the rest. "Nah, it ain't, impossible, Bobby. Honest, it ain't impossible." Others joined in, "Nah, it ain't impossible," one adding cheekily, "but maybe for a man it is." I could not help laughing. "Yeah, you're probably right," I said, in between giggles. "I don't think I could flat anything like four hundred."

"Yeah, Bob, sure you can," interrupted the pretty one. The rest joined in, crying, "Yeah, Beryl's right, you can. When you're one of the gang, we'll larn you the tricks of the trade, won't we, gels?"

Warmed by their unexpected, unaffected friendliness towards me, I knew that instant that flatting was not going to be as daunting as I had first thought.

Gwen brought me down to earth. "Bob, do you want the job?" she asked. "Can't hang around, mate. I'm on piecework, too, remember."

I reached inside my jacket and withdrew my P45 and National Insurance card, which I held it out for Gwen to take. "Yes, Gwen. If it's okay, I'll be here at seven on Monday."

"Right then, Bob. See you then, and don't be late. If you are, it'll be the first and last time you'll see Mr Jones, the gaffer," she smiled, holding out her hand.

As I cycled home, I questioned whether I'd done the right thing. I was desperate for money, but did I really have to sink that low? It was depressing to think that, over the two-year period I'd been in England, my career prospects had steadily dwindled.

The problem was that I had no ambition to do anything other than be a singer in a West End musical. But I still had no idea about how to go about being one, other than for entering talent competitions in the hope that some discerning soul in the audience would recognise my talent and take me under their wing. The first competition I'd entered was put on by the Weybridge Chamber of Commerce in the local village hall. Even though the audience was small in number, their enthusiasm for my version of *Old Man River* won me first prize. The second, held as recently as a month ago was at the Playhouse at Walton. Again I won, making me richer by three pounds. Although my confidence had soared, my plan to be a professional singer remained a distant dream.

Dick Purkis kept urging me to get a junior position in an office somewhere. "I'd work my way up, is what I'd do, Bob," he said. Considering that he'd already been stuck in his job as a greetings card salesman for the past three years, his well-meant advice didn't carry much weight. I spent the rest of the day thinking about how I could avoid telling Dick the truth about my new job, and by the time Dick returned from work at five, I had concocted a story.

Cheerful as ever, Dick climbed out from behind the wheel of his old Standard Ten. "How did you get on, Bob", he boomed, giving me a resounding clap on the shoulder.

"I got it," I replied, mustering good cheer.

"Jolly dee, what d'you have to do? Office situation, like I suggested?"

"Not quite," I lied. "It's more like supervising a team of women in the factory. Bit of a mucky job to start with, but after a bit of training, the bloke said I'd go on to dealing with customers in the sales office. So it's not too bad, and the money's good. With bonuses, could be about ten quid a week." I looked Dick straight in the eye, my heart quailing at the prospect of flatting four hundred sheets.

"Well, that sounds bloody damn good to me, old chum. More than I earn. So when do you start?"

"Monday at seven."

"Then you can make me a cuppa before you leave," Dick chuckled. "But right now, old chum, I'm starving, so I'll fix some supper for us." Cocking an eyebrow, he asked, "Fancy a piece of haddock?"

Dick, Surrey's biggest snob, had swallowed my story wholesale and I wasn't about to be kicked out for joining the working class.

A stickler for punctuality, Dick made sure supper was always taken in the tiny kitchen at six in the evening. We ate off a small trestle table graced with a jar of Dick's own pickled onions, a crusty loaf, home-made raspberry jam and a pot of tea; the main course was usually Spam. Occasionally, providing variety to our rich repast, Dick conjured up a small piece of stewed oxtail or liver, which were not rationed. We finished off with either rice pudding or apple crumble, which we took turns to make. As a rare treat, we munched on a couple of ginger biscuits as well. Although Dick's chickens were prolific layers, he sold most of the newly laid eggs to neighbours and preserved the remainder in isinglass or water-glass for use during the winter months. It was even more of a rare treat when Dick allowed us a couple of fresh eggs for our breakfast.

Once supper with Dick was over and done with, there were still chores to be completed, such as feeding the chickens and tending to the vegetable garden. By the time all the jobs were finished, there were only a couple of hours left to view television. Few people owned a set, Dick's nine-inch Murphy black and white television was the first I'd ever set eyes on, even though I'd previously carted cases of them off delivery lorries. I found the flickering images of news, variety shows, even pictures of fish swimming about in tanks during the ten-minute intermissions, a source of constant fascination.

Promptly at ten o'clock the BBC went off the air. Then it was off to our bunks: I in the top one, Dick in the one below. In the dark, to the accompaniment of Dick's nasal snorts and grunts, I lay wondering what had become of my family.

Most nights I endured painful memories of my mother and my younger brothers, Richard, David and Ronald, all of whom were still living in Rawalpindi. And what had become of my only sister, Pam, trying to survive on her own in Karachi? Colonel Nick Graham-Carter, my mother's lover, the architect of the family's woes, I cursed every night without fail.

Chapter 21

Dick left the house early on Saturdays, supplementing his meagre income by driving patients to and from various hospitals for treatment. Paid a few pence per mile by the Hospital Car Service, he was always on the lookout for jobs as far away as Buckinghamshire, and so earned a handy sum most weeks. Left to my own devices during the day, I filled in time washing and ironing, making sure my shirts were pristine and my trousers had a knife-edge crease. I always tried to look smart, having recently acquired a new girlfriend, Marion, a YC who was a nurse at St Thomas' Hospital near Waterloo.

It was a tradition, Marion told me, that nurses were sometimes offered free tickets to West End shows as a perk of the job and asked if I'd like to see Jack Hulbert and Cicely Courtneidge at the Lyceum in a comedy. Since I'd never before been inside a theatre, I had accepted Marion's offer and agreed to meet her at Waterloo station at seven in the evening. I'd earned five shillings from my one-armed press-up challenge of the previous Friday and had put it aside for my date. The train fare from Weybridge was one and nine, which left me plenty to buy her a drink before or after the show. I knew that Dick wouldn't be back in time to give me a lift to the station, so at a quarter to six, I walked the couple of miles there to catch the six-thirty train.

Arriving a few minutes early, I mooched about the platform savouring the colourful posters on the wall adjoining the waiting room. One of a Great Western steam train puffing out great clouds of smoke, signed by the artist Terence Cuneo, I found particularly appealing. Another, extolling the virtues of an orange drink with the slogan "Idris when I's dry", I thought very clever. I mouthed "Idris when I's dry" as I walked up and down the platform, delighting in the pun. I thought it almost as good as the one I'd dreamt up as a schoolboy when asked to pun on the word Japanese, and had come up with 'can't you give a chapaneasierone?'

My train left on time. Half an hour later I emerged at Waterloo. Marion was waiting for me by the gate, smiling and looking very pretty indeed, in a blue off-the-shoulder dress under a smart wool coat. After a moment's indecision, I kissed her gently on the cheek, aware that we were under the gaze of a smirking guard. Sitting close beside Marion on the Underground, with our hands entwined and her dark-lashed blue eyes on mine, I thrilled at the softness of her body pressing against me. I knew then I was in love. I was absolutely certain of it, just as sure as I'd been at some time or another with all the other girls I'd previously dated.

The condition of being in love, as opposed to infatuation, was a malady I suffered from. Psychiatrists would have had a field day with me. If all the females had responded by saying they were also in love with me, I dare say I'd have faced a line of fathers armed with shotguns. As it was, I could never restrain myself from going overboard the minute a girl showed the slightest interest in me.

I'd only been out on a couple of dates with Marion. It was juvenile, innocent, unrequited stuff—jiving at the *High Pines Club* and at a hop at the Walton Playhouse. Any minute now I was about to ask her to marry me. I was sure of it. I sincerely felt I loved her, overwhelming emotion coming on like a tidal wave, and I was unaware of how silly I might sound to her. "Marion," I breathed in her ear, I—"

"Oh, look, Bob," Marion interrupted. Cruelly, the spell was broken, the magic moment lost.

Marion's free tickets were for the front circle of the theatre. "Aren't we lucky?" Marion said, as we were led to our seats, "Nurses get lots of tickets to shows. If you'd like it we can see all of them together."

"That would be wonderful," I replied. "I'd like nothing better than to be with you." I was about to add 'always', when the orchestra started playing, the lights dimmed, and the great drop curtain lifted, exposing the set of a country-house living room. Being inside a real theatre left me awestruck. Riveted by the sense of occasion and by the baroque red and gold décor, I fantasised being onstage. I hummed quietly to myself Novello's, *'Waltz of my Heart'*. In my reverie, I saw myself costumed as a Ruritanian prince, singing to my adoring, swooning public. Lost in my dream, I consigned poor Marion to some faraway Green Room as the curtain rose and the show got under way.

I'd no idea who the principals were. Jack Hulbert wasn't one of them, nor Cicely Courtneidge for that matter. Famous he might have been, but Jack Hulbert's pallid features and lantern jaw made him look like a dejected horse, as he delivered inane jokes and Cicely cackled wildly in response. The second-rate comedy progressed apace, leaving me singularly unimpressed. What did impress, however, was Jack Hulbert's beautifully cut electric-blue suit. There and then, I decided to own one just like it.

I nudged Marion's arm and whispered in her ear, "What d'you think of Jack's suit? Nice, isn't it?"

"Do you really think so?" said Marion, "I think that blue is a bit, well, common, don't you think?

Her put-down was enough to keep me silent for the rest of the first act. During the interval we fought our way to the bar, where I bought an Advocaat for Marion and a half of mild beer for myself. Horrified at the price, I stood looking casual, whilst my right hand nervously picked about in the recess of my trouser pocket, assessing the value of coins that jingled there by their size and shape. I found rather less than I'd hoped for. I figured I'd found about three shillings, barely enough to buy another drink and pay for a return tube ticket as well.

Marion stood looking around the bar, oohing and aahing at the dresses the women were wearing. She waved her glass about as her eyes swept the room. She was taking far too many sips of her drink for my peace of mind. Any second now, I was sure she'd request another Advocaat. I flinched as she came up to stand close beside me, nuzzling her face against mine. As I struggled to find a reason to refuse her without being thought of as a cheapskate, she whispered, "Bob, would you think it awful of me if I had another?"

That was it. All ideas of falling in love with Marion dissipated as speedily as her drink had vanished. Just then the five minute bell for the second act rang out and saved me. "What a pity, Marion," I stammered. "Don't think we've enough time, d'you?"

I found the second act as unfunny as the first, but after we'd stood for the National Anthem at the end of the show, I gave Marion a peck on the cheek and lied about how much I'd enjoyed the performance. "Oh, I'm so glad, Bob," she replied, clapping her hands.

It was about eleven o'clock when the Tube pulled into Waterloo station. The last train to Weybridge was at three minutes past twelve, enough time to linger for a bit on the

Embankment before walking Marion home to St Thomas' hospital, half a mile distant. We held hands as we walked, and every now and then stopped to kiss. The kisses became increasingly frantic the further we went in the dark night. After a quarter of a mile of ambling, I decided I was in love again. My hands searched for her breasts under her coat and her tongue found mine. We'd found a metal bench by the Thames, standing in deep shadow cast by the hospital's walls. Spreading ourselves on the cold surface, I fumbled with Marion's dress, perplexed and frustrated that she wouldn't allow me to slip my hands between her thighs, or go beyond playing with her nipples. "No, Bob," she protested, "not here. No, please. Please, no, Bob."

At first I did as she asked, saying, "Sorry, Marion. So sorry," before I made another attempt. Marion thrust me away from her. Giving me a parting kiss, a chaste brush of her lips on my cheek, she said, clambering to her feet, "I've got to go now. What's the time? I'm sure to be in trouble if I stay any longer."

I looked my watch. "My God! It's ten to twelve! C'mon, Marion, we'd better step on it or I'll miss my train."

Fortunately Marion's nurses' home was only about a hundred yards away. She adjusted her clothes as she walked beside me, and I gave her one last kiss as we stood on her doorstep. "Thanks, Marion," I said. "It was a great evening. If you are still on for the YC Ball, my friend, Dick Purkis and I'll pick you up in his car. Is that okay with you?"

"That's super. I'll be home that weekend, so come to the house. But, Bob, I'll see you before that, won't I?"

"Sure, if you like. I'll phone, yeah? Must dash. See you."

Giving Marion a wave, I sped headlong down the street and made it to platform one at Waterloo station in time to see the last carriage of my train vanishing down the track.

I dashed frantically up and down the main concourse, scrutinising all departure boards to see if I could find a train going anywhere near to Weybridge. There was none. By buttonholing a guard, I learned that the earliest train the following morning was the three-fifteen to Strawberry Hill, which left me little option other than to find a vacant bench to sleep on until then. Finding an unoccupied bench was surprisingly difficult. Most were already taken by tramps who'd covered themselves with newspaper and lay fast asleep. Eventually, I came across one by the cinema at the far end of the station. As the vagrants had done, I collected discarded newspapers and covered myself with them, before stretching out full length on the bench.

It was a very cold night. Each time I adjusted my position, the papers fell off me to the floor. Dozing off and on, I kept one eye on the hands of the big station clock until it finally moved to three o'clock. Now stiff as a board, I staggered unsteadily over the platform and climbed on the Strawberry Hill train. Since I fell fast asleep immediately, it was fortunate Strawberry Hill was the end of the line, or else I might have ended up anywhere.

It was three forty-five in the morning when I was shaken awake by a railwayman. When I came to, I asked him the way to Weybridge. He looked at me as if I was mad. "Son," he said, his shoulders heaving with laughter, "at best, Weybridge is about thirteen miles from here. What's more, no chance of a taxi this time of the morning."

"Then I guess I'll just have to walk there," I said, quailing at the thought.

"Suit yourself, son," smiled the guard. "D'you know the way?"

I shook my head.

"Okay, mate, I'll write it down for you."

With the guard's directions in my jacket pocket, I slipped into the Scout's pace, which I'd been taught by Akela, my pack leader at school. This involved taking thirteen steps at a fast walking pace, then another thirteen at a run. It was a remarkably efficient method for covering ground quickly, and being fit from cycling everywhere, I actually began to enjoy the challenge of a half-marathon.

After I'd covered about five miles and was heavily sweated up, I tried thumbing lifts from the few cars and trucks passing by, but the drivers averted their heads, ignoring my existence. By the time I reached Oatlands Park, between Walton and Weybridge, I guessed I'd covered ten miles. Now faltering with fatigue, I slowed to a walk for the final leg through Weybridge. Finally, I took the turning to the Hamm Court Estate. Lurching drunkenly past the little river cottages that made up the community, I was in a state of exhaustion when I reached home. The front door opened with a loud squeal.

"That you, Bob?" I heard Dick shout.

"Yes, it's me. Sorry I woke you."

"I was worried stiff. Expected you back about one, you silly fool. Christ! It's bloody quarter to six. Been catting again, I bet. I hope she was bloody worth it, you silly sod."

I thought it best to stay quiet. Quickly removing my shoes, I crept into our tiny bedroom. Climbing the short wooden ladder to my bunk, I pulled the covers over my fully clothed body and passed out.

It was well after midday when I awoke. On Dick's return from church, brimful with holiness and sanctimony, he harangued me for a good hour about my transgressions. He chided me for my obsessive pursuit of the opposite sex and my persistent straying from the path of righteousness. It would be my undoing, he said, before he stomped off to feed the chickens.

He was right about my fixation with girls, but at the same time I suspected his ire was directed at me because of his own lack of success with them. I'd once suggested that he join the Young Liberals or the Young Communists, as I'd once done, if only to widen the choice of females available to him. That Dick was outraged by the very idea was not entirely unexpected.

"Communists! Liberals!" he thundered, his face flaming at the appalling prospect. "What a preposterous bloody idea. I'm a Conservative. Born a bloody one. Always will be one. I'll die one."

"Well, it was just a thought," I said, with a straight face.

Prudence dictated that I stay out of the way of the Grand Master of Conservatism for the remainder of the day. I waited until just before supper-time before offering to prepare the meal, but Dick had beaten me to it and had already finished the preparation. Amazingly, he seemed to be his old self again. After we had finished, Dick pushed back his chair and wagged his forefinger at me. "Bob, me lad, no dame is worth the fag," he said. "You must be crackers, is all I can say. Let last night be a lesson to you."

After what I'd been through I figured Dick had a point. So, taking advantage of an early night, I took myself off to bed. The rigours of flatting awaited me, and I hoped that when I woke I'd be in better shape.

At six-fifteen on Monday morning it was still pitch dark. I pulled on my clothes, tossed cold water in the direction of my face, made a quick cup of tea for Dick, downed one myself and beat it to Panelite's workshop on my bike. I pedalled with leaden legs, but still I arrived there a good ten minutes ahead of time. Bracing my bike against a wall, I opened the rickety door of the workshop and entered hesitantly.

The time clock at the far end of the room was already surrounded by women wearing head scarves and loose work coats. Each had a cigarette hanging from her lips, already blueing the air with acrid smoke and even bluer humour. It was cold as death, and I was thankful for the warmth coming from my recently smoked pipe, which lay deep in my trousers pocket. Rubbing my hands together, stamping my feet on the concrete floor in that awful draughty space, I waited for Gwen Blodgett to hand me my time card.

I found it curious that none of the women standing around had taken any notice of me, when previously they had been so vociferous about having a male in their midst. I put the lapse down to the cold and the early morning. As I pondered this with my brain still half asleep, Gwen made a sudden appearance through a door marked Females.

"'Ello, Bob," said Gwen, smoothing down her skirt. "Bin 'ere long? Sorry, mate, I was just having a quick pee. Always happens when it's so bleedin' cold. 'Ere's your card."

With that, Gwen pulled a beige card from a side pocket before slotting it into the brass-framed time clock. A bell rang as my card was stamped.

"Now you're clocked in, follow me to your place," said Gwen. You're next to Beryl. You know, the one you 'ad your eye on." Seeing my face redden, Gwen burst into laughter, and the rest of the women joined in. "Think we didn't notice, mate," she said, holding on to her sides as my eyes searched the floor, the ceiling, looking every which way in silent embarrassment. Gwen took my arm. "Come on, cock, no harm's done. Just havin' you on, like."

I caught Beryl nodding at me as she commenced sanding. She was about thirty, I guessed, a fair old age for me, but still undeniably attractive, with her mass of dark curly hair, vivid mischievous blue eyes and wide smiling mouth. I watched, fascinated, her breasts swinging giddily beneath her coat as her arms worked up and down. Bent double over the board she was sanding, her work coat did little to conceal the curve of her slender hips and buttocks. Diverting though it was, the vision was hardly the best prescription for a horny chap like me on his first day. I tried to remind myself that I wasn't there for the chicks, I was there to make money. Beryl's presence, almost within touching distance of me, was a distinct impediment to that.

"Nah, cock," said Gwen interrupting my brief romantic reverie. "I showed you what to do already, din' I? Dip the sponge in the bucket, give your board a good wettin', fold the sandpaper over the block and sand it dahn. If you put your back in it, ten boards an hour for eight hours a day gets you ten quid a week, mate. Not to be sniffed at." Looking me in the face, she continued kindly, "Bob, love, I'll get you an overall. The clobber you're wearin' is too good for here."

Gwen returned with a long khaki overall. "I think that'll fit," she said, watching me as I slipped it on over my blazer.

"It'll be too warm for both of those, soon," she said, pointing. "You'll see."

For the next three hours, other than for the rhythmic hiss of sandpaper, the sploshing sound of water, and the odd burst of song, there was little to be heard before the radio was switched on at ten o'clock, when Gwen called a halt. A trolley with a tea urn perched on top was wheeled into the workshop by a diminutive old crone. Hardly larger than the urn itself, she forced herself forward on incredibly bowed legs, her feet in worn-down shoes too big for her.

"Tea's up!" bawled Gwen. She glanced in my direction. "Come and get it, Bob. Hurry, if I was you."

Even though I was quick off the mark, putting my sandpaper block down instantly, I found myself at the end of the line of sniggering women already wreathed in cigarette smoke.

I reached for my pipe, tamped down the tiny strands of tobacco closeted in the tarry bowl and lit it with my Zippo lighter, a gift from an American UN observer in Rawalpindi.

No sooner had I taken my first puff, than came shrill protests from the women.

“Blimey, Bob, you’ll stink the bleedin’ place aht with that pipe.”

“Phwaorh, what a stench!”

In my hurry to remove the offending article from my mouth, I sent bits of smouldering tobacco flying, forcing those standing in front of me to hop away with screams of alarm.

Over the resultant din, I heard Beryl shouting, “They’re havin’ you on, Bob. Take no notice. Go on, mate, light your pipe.”

Beryl’s intervention on my behalf had come too late. Friday, payday, was the earliest I could afford to replace the few ounces of tobacco I’d lost. Giving Beryl a smile, I mouthed my thanks.

The women had indeed been having me on, for they broke into raucous laughter. In that madcap moment, I bathed in the warmth of their matey bonhomie and grinned back at my workmates like an idiot.

Returning to my trestle, I was dismayed to find that I’d only managed to finish off fifteen boards in three hours, when my target was around twenty-seven.

“Beryl, how many have you done?” I asked.

"When I've finished this one, it'll be twenty-eight." Beryl sounded almost apologetic. "And you?"

"Only fifteen," I replied.

"Better get on with it then."

By the time twelve o'clock came around and the bell rang for the dinner break, I'd completed twenty-five in all. It would have been five more, but Gwen had rejected them for imperfections I could neither see nor feel. "You ain't done bad for a bloke," she said, before asking, her ham-sized face and tiny eyes screwed into an expression of solicitude, "You all right, Bob? You look a mite peaky. Come, dear, come to the canteen and have some dinner. Brought sandwiches, 'ave you?"

Over the past two years I had got used to not eating at lunch-time. On occasions I had broken down and had some, but only when I was either feeling flush or someone had offered to share theirs with me. Otherwise, I generally took myself off and read a book in some quiet corner.

"I forgot," I replied.

"Liar," said Gwen, taking me by the arm. "You're bleedin' skin and bone you are. Now, no nonsense, you just come with me. I bring so much grub with me—see?" she swung a small basket, "I can't finish it. Feed it to the sparrers, I do. What a waste, eh? Nah then, no nonsense, eh? Follow me."

I stood my ground for a second and then marched off behind Gwen's broad back and her heifer's buttocks that hunched and bunched with every purposeful stride. As she led me past the female toilet into a small room beyond, it occurred, since I was getting close to needing one, that I hadn't seen a lavatory for men. Thankfully I found one later in a small shack outside our workplace.

In the room serving as a canteen, all of the women sat crowded on benches on either side of a long table. A small kerosene-fired stove sat in the corner. Graciously donated by the management for the benefit of their female staff, it had raised the temperature in the room to marginally above shivering level.

I squeezed in beside Gwen. I was an orphan at the table, sheepishly looking down at the floor. Peering inside her basket, Gwen asked, "Fancy a bit of cheese and bread?" Before I could reply, she had placed a thick margarined slice of bread and a small piece of cheddar on the scrubbed table top. "Nah get that inside you. Made the bread mesel', I did."

The bread was wonderfully fresh, though the cheese had seen better days. Nevertheless, I munched away and soon both were demolished. Facing me, watching my every move, sat Beryl.

"Would you like some pie?" she asked, pushing a slice of meat pie across the table. "This is too much for me."

A similar refrain was taken up by a number of others at the table, and very soon a veritable feast, some of it unrecognisable as sustenance, was mounded in front of me. With my mouth full, I nodded my thanks to those whose largesse I'd received. In return, I was treated to the sweetest of motherly smiles from the older women and shyer responses from those who were younger. I sat, choking with emotion, thinking what a kind, generous lot they were for sharing their food with a near stranger. They were probably needier than I was, with children to look after and other mouths to feed.

My eyes ranged over their careworn faces, pale as ghosts. With the exception of the fewer younger women, most of the others looked to be in their fifties, but all were bone thin. Later on, I learned from Beryl that the majority were war widows.

"Poor ducks," she said, "their hubby's pensions are just a few shillings a week. Not enough to bring up their families. So they do anything to live."

"And you?" I asked.

"Oh, I'm married. Well sort of. Husband fucked off a couple months ago. I needed the money. The Labour sent me here." Beryl shrugged, "I'll just do it 'til after Christmas, then find something better."

"Like me," I said, "I only intend to stay here until then".

"I wondered why you were here," ventured Beryl. "You ain't the type." She gave me a luminous smile. I melted.

The afternoon passed unremarkably. Working up a rhythm, I shed my blazer as Gwen promised I would. By five-thirty I was dripping with perspiration, but in the icy atmosphere my breath condensed in puffs of mist. My right hand was blue with cold, my forearms and biceps ached, my legs hurt from my long hike, but I was not unhappy, for I had sanded down seventy boards. Just ten short of my target, I had earned the munificent sum of one pound fifteen shillings, for eight solid hours of hard labour on my first day. It augured well for earning ten pounds, less tax, for the week.

Clocking off, I found myself encircled by Gwen and several others. Congratulating me for proving them wrong, they admitted to taking bets I wouldn't last the day. As I biked off, I forgot my aches and pains and glowed with pride all the way home.

Chapter 22

Endured is perhaps too strong a word to describe how I actually felt about my flatting job. On one hand my surroundings were dismal. But, on the other, the warm affection I received from my workmates more than compensated for the awful, freezing conditions in the shed. So, if blessings were to be counted, my current employers, whom Dickens might have used as a template for a Victorian workhouse, served me better than the Army Operational Research Group.

In the month-long run up to Christmas, I had finally got the hang of smoothing down the panelling sheets in double-quick time. My take-home pay had recently averaged ten pounds a week, the most I had ever earned.

Even the formidable, but sweet-natured Mrs Blodgett seemed impressed by how well I'd got on. "Blimey, cock," she said, in her foghorn voice, "didn't think you had it in you. Honest I didn't. Shows you what being trained by women does for a man."

"Hey, Bobby!" Ada Blewitt shouted. A war widow from Chertsey with five kids under the age of eight, she often took the mickey. "When you leave 'ere, find us another pretty foreign bloke, will you?"

The shed once again resounded with merriment, before Mrs Blodgett hushed everyone quiet. Putting a finger to her lips, she said, "Better get on, gels, or the boss will give us what for." With everyone's eyes upon her, she began to giggle. Hard as she tried to contain her laughter, the amusing thought got the better of her. A sound like a football rattle drawn across a metal railing burst from her throat in an explosion of hilarity. "Gels, I've got an idea!" she yelled, her breath gusting plumes of white mist. "Nah that our Bobby's rich, he can buy the beer for our Christmas do. Can't he? All in favour?"

Every hand in the place shot up in the air as Mrs Blodgett advanced towards me like a Sherman tank. Clasping my face between her huge work-reddened palms, she planted a kiss on my cheek. "Only kiddin', son," she said. "All of us chip a few shillin's into the kitty. Someone goes dahn to the off licence, buys beer and cider, and we have a booze up here when we finish Christmas Eve. "

"I can run to a couple of quid," I heard myself say, "if that's all right, Nora? It'll be my last day and, well, I'd like to, anyway." I felt my face redden with embarrassment as I awaited Mrs Blodgett's response to my hasty, foolhardy offer. My mind raced as I recalculated exactly how much I'd have left to buy Christmas presents.

"That's really nice of you, Bobby," she said, her face creasing into a smile. "I think we can accept. Can't we, gels?"

"Yeah, yeah!! Three Cheers for Bob!!" yelled Mrs Blewitt, setting the others off.

I flushed again, a not uncommon experience for me in that place. Jokes were usually at my expense, but they were unfailingly devoid of malice. The working-class women with whom I worked might have been ill-educated and desperately poor, but they displayed a generosity of spirit I never encountered amongst the St George's Hill crowd I mixed with socially.

With the exception of the nubile Beryl, who responded to my lustful gazes with similar glances at me, the rest of the women treated me like their collective son. Their affection and kindness was overwhelming. Not once did they allow me to go hungry. As if competing with one another, they shoved the food they'd brought for lunch under my nose. They brooked no refusal and almost resorted to pleading with me to share their food as if, by doing so, I bestowed honour upon them.

I planned to start a new job in January, or at least the minute the man at the Labour Exchange came up with something less arduous than flatting that paid enough for me to live on. I hoped the bigoted idiot who'd previously dismissed my Cambridge School Certificate as being of little value, on the basis that I'd sat for the exam in Pakistan and not England, had moved on by this time. As much as I had protested that the examination I'd taken was identical to the one students sat in England, the blinkered fool deciding my fate had remained obdurate.

He'd added insult to injury, by telling me that my spoken English wasn't half bad for a "darkie" before typing in the letter 'C' at the end of my new National Insurance number. Sometime later, I read a newspaper article that said that the classifications A, B, B1, C1 and C were used by officialdom to assign social status in the community demographically. The letter 'C' I'd been so kindly bequeathed classified me as being of the labouring class, at the very lowest rung of the ladder. Once applied, the letter was irreducible, unchangeable, a label appended for the rest of my life. I dare say even if I'd known what the man had done I'd have been impotent to do anything about it. I'd bridled at his insult, but since I was powerless to do anything as far as jobs went, I'd kept my mouth shut and gave him a weak smile.

The days progressed, with chilly starts in the pitch-black mornings. It was so cold that only hours of vigorous sanding got my blood circulating. All the while I dreamt about a singing career. Thus far, all I'd achieved was winning small amounts in talent competitions, which seemed to be all the rage. But the theatrical agent who was to pluck me from obscurity remained as elusive as ever. Such was my unswerving confidence, I convinced myself that someone, somewhere, was bound to recognise my talent. After all, if Mario Lanza had been discovered working as a commis chef in an Italian restaurant in New York, why couldn't a flatter like me be the new Dick Haymes?

In November, I'd hiked home on three occasions after missing the train. As intent as I was on losing my virginity to the delectable Marion, the nurse at St Thomas' hospital, I was no closer to my objective. Having expended so much energy on the pursuit of the unattainable, I decided to stop seeing Marion. I had to find a girlfriend closer to home and where better than at The Young Conservatives Ball? Held at the D'Oyley Carte Hotel, a Victorian pile built on an island in the middle of the Thames at Weybridge, the annual function was certain to be packed with unattached, pretty females. My problem was that I'd asked Marion to partner me, and at this late stage I could hardly opt out.

As I ticked off the days, I regretted more and more having invited Marion. Thinking that I was still enamoured of her, Dick went on and on about how lucky I was to have Marion partner me.

"Unlike me," he said, ruefully, "I couldn't find anyone to ask." On the evening of the ball, he repeated the same remark as we drove up to collect Marion from her family home in St George's Hill. If only he had known, I'd have been more than happy for Dick to escort Marion, which would have left the field wide open for yours truly.

Although we were a few minutes early, the moment we pulled up outside Marion's house, she emerged wearing a mink coat over a long dress.

"Good job you're wearing that coat," Dick called, opening the car door for her, "it'll be damn cold on the blessed chain ferry to the island."

"It's Mum's old mink," said Marion, climbing into the back seat. "Did I hear you say ferry? I thought we went over to the island by boat."

I butted in quickly. "No, no boat, a chain ferry. You stand on a kind of wooden platform sitting on the water. There's a chain and pulley system which makes it work. Someone pulls on the chain and the thingies drawn across the river. You do the same to come back."

"I'll be the ferryman," laughed Dick. "If Bob tried we'd land up in the drink."

"What a lark. I can't wait to see this," Marion giggled.

Dick parked his car by the tow path and together, we walked in the dark the short distance to a landing stage opposite The D'Oyley Carte Hotel. There was already a bunch of partygoers standing in line waiting for the ferry to return to the Surrey bank.

As we joined the queue, I spotted Guy Anderson, a friend of mine, accompanied by a stunningly, beautiful girl. I edged closer to get a better look at her as the ferry finally clanked back to our side of the river and we all climbed aboard the rickety contraption.

By day, it was obvious that the Victorian hotel was badly in need of attention. But, by night, with the light shining through the mullioned windows of the gothic building, reflected in the dark waters of the Thames, it looked simply magical.

Marion took my arm as I led her into a panelled entrance hall, from where a waiter showed us into a dingy room beyond. The ballroom, as the waiter called it, had all four walls clothed in faded damask. Dimly lit by a single chandelier hanging from the ceiling, the room was set with tables and chairs around the circumference of the dance floor. On a small dais, in front of the windows overlooking the river, a four piece band sat tuning their instruments.

I waited until Guy Anderson and his girlfriend found a table, before I quickly nabbed one adjacent to it. I drew up a chair for Marion and sat down opposite her, so I could have a good view of Guy's date. Ever the generous gent, Dick excused himself and set off to the bar. He returned bearing a tray of drinks, an Advocaat for Marion and beers for himself and me. He raised his glass to us, saying, "Chin, chin," and then sat smiling at us like a Cheshire cat, while I continued to feast my smitten eyes on the girl.

Marion held my hand beneath the table and whispered in my ear, "Bags I the first dance," just as the band struck up with a quickstep. We took to the floor, with Marion gazing up at me as if I was the love of her life. I felt a cad, but it still didn't stop me sneaking glances at Guy and his girlfriend dancing within touching of us.

"She's beautiful, isn't she?" said Marion suddenly.

"Who is?"

"The girl you can't take your eyes off. Do you know her?"

"Which girl?

" Come off it, Bob. The girl in the red dress dancing with Guy."

"Oh, her. No, I don't know who she is."

"I think you'd rather be with her tonight, than me."

"That's just plain silly. You sound jealous. Why? You've no need to be."

Marion went quiet. Riddled with guilt, I tried to guide her back to our table as soon as the music stopped, but she shrugged me away. "I'm going to find the loo", she said, flouncing off.

I waited for about ten minutes for Marion to return, by which time the band was well into playing a foxtrot. I looked across to Guy's table and noticed his seat was vacant, his partner absently gazing around the room. Ignoring Dick's frown of rebuke, I asked her for a dance.

Smiling, she got to her feet. "What's your name?" she asked, as I took her in my arms.

"Bob Matthews. And yours?"

"Margot Anderson. I'm Guy's sister."

"Sister! I thought you were his...."

"Girlfriend? No, it was nice of Guy to have brought me tonight. Otherwise I'd have been on my own at home. I only got back from Paris last night, you see."

"Paris? What were you doing there?"

"Oh, I'm a dancer at the Lido. A Bluebell Girl."

I had never heard of the Bluebell Girls or of the Lido, but I didn't let on.

"Which explains why you dance so well," I said, by now already in the thrall of the lovely Margot, in her tight-fitting, scarlet gown.

"Thank you kind sir," she smiled, as we glided around until the band stopped playing. As I led Margot back to her table, she asked, "Would your girlfriend mind if we had another dance later on?"

"No, not at all. Actually, she's not my girlfriend", I said quickly, "she's just someone I promised to bring tonight." Although it was a half truth, I still felt a swine for saying it.

I thanked Margot for the dance and returned to my seat. Dick and Marion were missing from our table. I wandered into the bar to see if they'd gone off for a drink and when I couldn't find them, I returned once more. Half an hour passed. Anxious now, I searched amongst the couples milling about on the floor. But they were making such a din, I could barely make myself heard above the noise, as I went about asking if anyone had seen Dick and Marion. In response, all I got was a shake of the head. Totally puzzled by now, I asked a waiter if there were any other rooms they might be in. He showed me into a couple of anterooms off the bar, but again I drew a blank. Dick and Marion had simply vanished. They were nowhere to be found. Eventually, I began to think the impossible. Had Marion decided Dick was a better bet than me and gone off with him somewhere? After another thirty minutes of fruitless searching, I got myself a beer and sat waiting at the table for them to reappear, when I saw Guy Anderson waving at me to come on over.

Chuckling, a grin spread over his face, he said, "Had you there, Matthews, old sport." He gave me a friendly shove, "Go on, Margot wants a dance with you. Beats me why."

I did not need a second invitation. I took Margot on to the floor and from then on, we waltzed, quickstepped and jived, only stopping for one tune to end, before getting going again when another started. During a short break between dances, Margot mentioned she was moving back to London to perform at The Windmill Theatre in Soho.

"Do they put on musicals there?" I asked, never having heard of The Windmill Theatre. I love musical shows. I don't know if I should say it, but my ambition's to sing professionally on stage"

"You're kidding," laughed Margot. "Really, you want to be a singer?"

"Yes. Nothing else."

"Okay, then," she said, "what if I fix it for you to come to one of our rehearsals? That way you'll find out the kind of shows we do. I'm sure Vivian Van Damm won't mind me asking."

Seeing I had no idea whom she was talking about, she added, "Viv's the owner. He's the one who's made The Windmill famous for variety shows and, er, exotic dancers."

Margot left my heated imagination to figure out what 'exotic' might mean as I swept her round and round. "Many of the big-time variety acts got started at The Windmill—comedians, singers, you know."

"Will you be famous one day?" I asked guilelessly, aware that every male in the room was looking on with undisguised jealousy. By this time amnesia had got the better of me. I had entirely forgotten Marion's existence.

"Not a hope, I'm just part of the scenery at The Windmill," Margot replied, "but tell you what—I can also talk to Viv about an audition for you, if you feel up to it. Would you like that?"

"Would I? Would I?" I squeaked delightedly. "Margot, I've just been dying for the chance. Thank you, thank you." Oh, my God, I was in love again. This time, absolutely certain of it. I held her pliant, dancer's body close to mine, put my face against her soft cheek and nearly expired with longing.

"Can't promise, Bob," Margot said, "but I'll have a word soon after we start rehearsals for the new show." She squeezed my hand gently, "I'm going back to Paris day after tomorrow. I have to finish my contract at the Lido. It's a pity, but it'll be Feb before I get to see you again." She sighed. *"C'est la vie. "*

I looked at her blankly. My brain scrolled through every frame of *Beau Geste*. Nowhere did *c'est la vie* appear in the script.

"C'est la vie," I repeated after Barbara, without the faintest idea what it meant. Aping Ronald Coleman, the lead in *Beau Geste*, I drew my shoulders up to my ears in an extravagant Gallic shrug. If that was what Foreign Legionnaires did, then it was good enough for me.

I hadn't noticed that several of the guests had already left. Margot looked at her diamond studded wrist watch. "Golly, Bob, I had no idea it was this late. "Sorry, but I'd better be off. I can see Guy's waiting for me. *Au revoir*, Bob, promise I'll be in touch. Honest, I will." Margot gave me a peck on the cheek and then swayed her way to the hotel entrance, her figure a perfect, shimmering hourglass.

I was about to return to the ballroom, when I heard the band strike up Glen Miller's *Moonlight Serenade*, signalling the last dance. My hand went to my mouth in horror. Where was Marion? Where was Dick?

By now I was out of my head with concern. As a last resort I headed out into the garden to see if they happened to be there, or on the ferry, now being held steady on the water by a beefy Young Conservative.

"Hurry up, you silly bugger!" he shouted, "Jump on, or I'm off."

Just as I was about respond, I felt my sleeve caught tight and heard Dick Purkis's voice hissing in my ear, "No, you don't. I want a word with you."

Shocked, I turned to face him. Dick was red in the face with anger. "You know something, Bob Matthews?" he said, his face grim. “You have turned into a thoroughly unpleasant young man. In short, a self-centred, self-opinionated, amoral little shit.”

I looked at him with open-mouthed astonishment. Gathering myself, I asked, “What d’you mean, Dick? What’s brought this on? What have I done wrong?” Even as I spoke, I knew what he was about to say.

“Marion,” said Dick, bunching his fists, “your nursie from St Tommy’s. Remember? The girl you brought to the dance? She was in floods of tears, you know. She was so bloody upset by your behaviour; I drove her home two hours ago and stayed with her until the poor thing settled down. You,” Dick unfurled a finger and stuck it into my chest, “you, bastard that you are, didn’t even notice she’d left, did you?”

I could not dispute Dick’s opinion of me. He was absolutely correct. I was every bit as rotten as he claimed. “You’re right, Dick,” I said, full of remorse. “Dead right. I’ve treated Marion appallingly. I’m only thankful you took her home and looked after her.”

Shuffling my feet nervously, I muttered, “I don’t know what it is, or why it is I’m so bloody selfish. Fact is, Dick, I’m stupid about girls. I fancy them rotten, can’t leave them alone and in the end I hurt them.”

Wilting under Dick’s steady gaze, I waited for some kind of response from him. None came. Finally I said, “Okay, if you think so little of me, maybe you don’t want me to share your place anymore? If you wish, I’ll find somewhere else tomorrow.”

It was a high risk strategy, for other than the Salvation Army stumping up a temporary shelter for me, the Great Lover and Putative Star of Stage, Screen and Radio would have been homeless. My fate rested in Dick’s hands. In the end, dear kind, forgiving Dick said he didn't want me to leave, but only if I mended my ways.

"Bob, you're such a silly twerp," he said, his voice betraying the merest trace of humour. "I've been on at you about being obsessed about girls from day one." Tightening his hold on my arm, he added, "You know, I might not be old enough to be your dad, but I damn sure feel like I am. Best thing for you would have been the Army. Might have done you good." He stopped in mid-sentence. Looking at me thoughtfully, he said, "Which reminds me. Funny that you've not had your call-up papers yet. You should have had them a couple of years ago. Do you think maybe it's because you worked for the MoD?"

"No idea, Dick," I replied. "Perhaps I ought to go the recruiting centre at Kingston and find out why?"

"No, let sleeping dogs lie," Dick advised. "It's probably because you were born in Delhi and they haven't caught up with you yet." Dick kicked at a loose pebble. "Where was I? Ah, yes, advice. I want you to do the decent thing as far as Marion is concerned. Bike up to St George's Hill tomorrow morning and apologise before she goes back to the hospital. She won't accept, of course. And quite right, too, but you'll have tried and that's good enough for me. Do I have your word?"

I hung my head. The prospect of facing Marion was not something I relished, but I knew it was what I had to. It was not so much her wrath I feared, rather, it was the certainty of her forgiveness and her tears. I visualised myself standing in front of her in a state of abject contrition, making promises I could never keep. I could see myself missing trains again, indulging in more thirteen-mile hikes, and for what? Certainly, Dick didn't know the half of it. Nevertheless, I gave him my word and for the time being at least, preserved the roof over my head.

In the end, I was too much of a coward to face Marion. I headed out of the house the next morning, telling Dick I was off to make my apologies to her. I took my bike and cycled about aimlessly for an hour or so, before returning home.

When I arrived back, Dick was already waiting to see how I'd got on. He'd been to church and atoned for his sins. Now he was all fired up to discover how penitent I was about mine. "Did you speak to Marion? Apologise, did you?" he asked, in quick fire succession.

"Yes." The lie came easily. "I did. Saw her. Apologised to her."

"And? And?"

"Well, no ands. She said she didn't want to see me again. Understandable, really. Glad I did it though. You were right, Dick, to get me to say how sorry I was."

"No more to be said then, Bob, is there? I hope you've learned your lesson this time."

"Oh, yes, Dick. I have, I have."

Chapter 23

A few days prior to Christmas Eve I received a letter from my mother. Inside the envelope I found a Christmas card and two crisp pound notes. Attached was a message: *"Sorry it's so little, darling. Things are tight. Maurice is still being a so-and-so and hasn't given me any money after the divorce. Just so you'll understand. Love, Mummy."*

The following morning I handed the money over to Gwen Blodgett. "That's my contribution for tomorrow's party," I explained. "I promised, remember?"

"Won't say no darlin'," she smiled. "When we finish work this evening, I'll go with some of the lasses to the off-licence and order the booze. We'll have it delivered tomorrow morning." Looking at me with soft eyes, she said, "We'll miss you, you know."

At precisely four o'clock the next afternoon, Nora straightened up from her flatting and screeched, "Stop! That's it, gels. Dahn tools! Break open the beer. C'mon on Bobby," she hollered at me. "Don't hang about, get the bottle opener going, willya?" She went to the canteen and returned dragging a crate of beer behind her. "There's more where that came from, me little darlin's," she cried, "so, gels, get 'em dahn yer."

Cheers filled the shed, accompanied by loud whoops, giggles and the clink of bottles being passed round. I handed Beryl a bottle of Watneys Red, which she put to her lips and sipped, her eyes giving me the come-on over the rim. As fast as I opened the beer and the scrumpy, the bottles were wrenched from my hands, the contents downed with astonishing rapidity by the fifteen women present. Certainly, as a contrast to the YC ball of a few days before, the flatters' Christmas 'do' could not have been more stark.

"Come on, Bobby, I'll take over nah," said Gwen. "Your turn to get yourself a wet." I sank the contents of the bottle in my fist and was immediately handed another. The women started singing, their flushed pink faces beaming with goodwill as the alcohol got to them. They were letting their hair down, forgetting their woes, having a great time. Their skirts hitched up, they pranced and danced, shouting tunelessly, *Ilkla Moor Baht 'At* and other tunes I'd never heard before. I found the bawdy, wonderfully graphic lyrics hugely enjoyable and picking up on the simple melodies, I joined in the general hubbub, which eventually gave way to carols. Beryl had a hand around my waist. I fondled her rump, joining in to give *Oh, Come All Ye Faithful* full rein and then really let myself go with *Hark the Herald*.

As my baritone soared over the voices of the others, Gwen Blodgett put a finger to her lips, quietening the women. "Blimey, Bobby, didn't know you could sing that well. You're as good that Dickie Valentine bloke, any day."

Beryl disagreed: "Nah, he's more like Bing Crosby."

"Mario Lanza," shouted someone else, as another chipped in to say, "Dick Haymes."

Before I knew it, the women surrounded me, urging me to sing something Christmassy for them. The bare electric light bulbs above, cast yellow light on the beaming faces of my enthusiastic audience. In the heady atmosphere of their unqualified appreciation, I became for them Crosby, Lanza, Sinatra and Haymes all rolled into one. I sang every standard I knew. The women joined in, their loud voices threatening to bring the corrugated iron roof down on them. The management next door clearly knew of their employee's annual ritual and had the good sense to stay out of the way.

After an hour of non-stop drinking, the women were flagging and ready to head for home. That is, they were, until the redoubtable Ada Blewitt—she who cracked jokes at my expense—decided the party needed reviving. Springing to her feet, she began to chant, "Let's get Bobby's breeks orf! Orf! Orf! Orf!"

With that, she leapt forward and wrenched my belt buckle open. Aghast, my hands went to my trousers, as she pulled my belt through the loops at my waist. "C'mon, gels!" Ada screeched, "let's get 'em orf!" A couple of women joined Ada in the fun, then another two, all five surrounding me, doing their level best to drag my trousers down over my hips. I tried fighting them off, roaring at them to stop, but they refused to listen. In a flash, they'd worked my fly open and pulled my trousers down to my ankles. Beryl was screaming, "You stupid cows!" Others shouted her down. Then, saving me from further embarrassment, Nora Blodgett's parade ground voice sounded over the almighty din. "Ada Blewitt! Stop that bloody daftness. You stupid gels, leave Bob alone. Go, on, get away from him this minute."

I took advantage of the hiatus, reached down and hastily pulled up my trousers. My drunken condition had done nothing to assuage my distress. I felt utterly ashamed that the women had seen me naked from the waist down. Doubtless they'd not expected that, since it was customary for men to wear underwear. But since I didn't own any, their eyes had been subjected to more than a glimpse of my nether bits. Given my predicament, I wished it hadn't been so cold.

Beryl, screeching like a banshee, dashed up to shield me. With her back taut against my body and her arms thrust out wide, she threatened to bash anyone who dared to approach. But by now the pandemonium had diminished somewhat. In the face of Nora Blodgett's promised retribution, my aggressors had slunk away. Muttering apologies, they retreated to the back of the shed. Nora, her arms crossed, glowered from under knitted eyebrows, her baleful gaze eventually settling on Ada Blewitt.

"I've a good mind to sack you, Ada, for what you did," she said. "You dun and messed up our 'do'. And that wasn't funny wot Bobby had to put up with. So you just come along 'ere and say you are sorry to him this minnit."

I held no grudge against any of the women and certainly not Ada. True, she'd made fun of me, my posh accent, the colour of my skin, but there was little harm in her and she'd kept me amused for the two months I worked alongside her and her friends. Having recovered some composure, I simply wished to say my goodbyes and leave. It gave me no pleasure to see Ada humiliated or to watch her shuffling towards me, chin buried in her breast, whispering abjectly, asking for my forgiveness, which of course I readily gave.

"Well done," said Nora, giving Ada a pat on the back, "Now pay attention, gels. Time to go home, but before you go, I know you'd like to see me giving Bobby this." Reaching deep into her coat pocket, she withdrew a small package. Handing it over to me, she said, "All the gels chipped in. It's a prezzie for being a good sport, Bobby. Go on, we wouldn't mind if you opened it now."

Not knowing where to put myself, I tore away the wrapping paper to expose a shiny, streamlined Ronson cigarette lighter inscribed with the words, *Xmas 1951. With love from your mates.* Incapable of speech, my eyes brimming with tears, I looked fixedly down at the floor, swallowing hard.

Other than for the odd ten-rupee note given me in Pakistan, and a few pounds in the post now and then here in England, I'd never received much in the way of presents from my mother, not even as a child. Put at its most charitable, she had perhaps forgotten that children loved getting presents; most likely it was because she was both self-centred and lacking in maternal instinct. If once she'd known how to love unstintingly, she'd long ago forgotten the secret, whereas these poor women, who'd only known me a couple of months, and who from the very beginning had been kindness itself, had shelled out their hard-earned cash to buy me a Christmas present. Their generosity was simply overwhelming.

Eventually I got myself together and went round the room thanking each of the women in turn. Dabbing at their eyes, they shyly gave me quick pecks on the cheek as they wished me well. Not daring to break down in front of them, I hugged Nora tight and then kissed Beryl full on the lips. Shouting, "Happy Christmas, all. Thanks again," I removed my Burberry from its hook, quickly opened the front door and stepped into the freezing darkness. Once outside, I leant against the shed's wooden frame and blubbered.

There was a light dusting of snow on the roof and the crunch of ice underfoot, suggesting my bike ride home to Willow Cottage was likely to be hazardous. Having just been paid, I had planned to buy Dick a tie as a Christmas present, from Haslett's, the gentlemen's outfitters at the end of the High Street. They closed at five-thirty, so I had to make a quick decision as to whether I had time to walk there, or take a chance and ride my bike on the slippery roads. As I pondered, the shed door swung open and Beryl stood framed in the light. "Bob, is that you there?" she called, peering into the blackness. "It's so dark, can't see a thing."

"Yes, I'm by the water butt in the corner, where I keep my bike." I replied, "I'm just off to Haslett's to buy a present for my friend. There's lots of ice on the road, so maybe I'll walk."

"C'mon, I'll walk with you, if you like."

"You don't go home that way, do you?"

"Yeah, Haslett's on the turning to Addlestone. It's where I catch the 259 home."

"You sure?"

I liked the idea of having Beryl come with me, thinking that if there was enough time we might get around to some heavy petting in the bus shelter. As I visualised the delicious prospect of it, Beryl came to stand at my side.

"Yeah, sure," she breathed in my ear, following up with a kiss on my frozen cheek. "You could come home with me after you've done your shopping."

"What about your kid?"

"Henry's with my ex's family in London. He's spending Christmas with his dad. I'm all alone, so come. Please."

"Only if you're sure, though."

I could hardly believe my luck. I'd finally been offered a real chance of having sex. I was going to be twenty-one on February 8, just six weeks away, and I was still a virgin, and out of my skin with frustration. My hormones were in a constant frisson of excitement, leaving me at risk of imploding. If coitus was not to occur in the very near future, I feared for my sanity. Now, out of the blue, here was Beryl proposing I go home with her—and I'd had the hots for her ever since we'd met.

Gripping the bike's handlebars with my left hand, I supported Beryl with my right, and together we descended precipitous Monument Hill, slipping and sliding along the icy pavement like uncertain skaters. In austerity Britain the street lamps were on half power, but even so, their scant light helped our progress once we reached the level surface of the High Street. The few cars that were about on the road crunched past at a snail's pace. Other than for the odd last-minute Christmas shoppers—women in head-scarves, wearing drab utility overcoats and shod in clumpy footwear—the pavements were clear of pedestrians. The night was dense with silence, all sound damped by the falling snow, with little by way of illumination or good cheer to indicate it was Christmas.

We continued past the poorly stocked shops flanking the street until Beryl came to a sudden halt in front of a pawnbroker. She stood in front of the window, oohing and aahing, pointing out rings and watches for sale, saying how nice it would be afford one of them. Examining our reflection in the glass, she in her dark tweed coat with fake-fur collar, me in a pale Burberry and holding a racing bike, she quizzed, "Bob how old are you? You look young enough to be my son."

"I'm nearly twenty-one," I replied, for the first time conscious of our age difference, adding warily, "How old are you, then?"

Beryl gave me a wistful look. "Told you so," she said. "I'm thirty-five.

In a childish effort to brighten her gloom, I twittered, "Why, that's not old enough to be my mother. You're only fifteen years more than me. Nothing at all."

"I'm just being silly, Bob," said Beryl, kissing me lightly on the lips. "Forget it. Come on, or we'll never get your shopping done."

Beryl snuggled up to me. Squeezing my fingers, she described her upbringing, her child, the husband who'd walked out on her, just about everything else in her life as we walked. Immeasurably excited now, I concentrated more on restraining the elevation interfering with my gait than with Beryl's animated life story. Older woman or not, Beryl had conjured for me more erotic visions than anyone before. And I, the Great Lover, was not about to disappoint her.

We finally reached Haslett's, where I found a convenient spot to lean my bike. "Shall I come in with you?" asked Beryl.

"Of course, you dope. You'll get frozen outside. And anyway, it's only a tie I'm after."

As an old established bespoke tailor and gentlemen's outfitter, Haslett's had little on display to excite my interest. "We haven't quite recovered from clothes rationing," explained the unctuous shop assistant, his eyes measuring me up for a suit as he'd been trained to do. "Ties? Yes, sir, we have a nice selection of silk ones here, if you'll follow me."

Beryl giggled, "I've never been inside a man's shop before, Bob. Think I can go and have a look around?"

"Why not? But I won't be a minute."

I was led by the shop assistant to a glass display cabinet, inside which were a dozen silk ties laid out.

Dismayed, I asked if there were more in the shop to see. "Sorry, sir," replied the assistant, "that's the lot. You won't find better anywhere, sir, at a guinea."

I gulped. "How much? Did I hear you say a guinea?" I had expected to pay about five shillings at most. "Sure you've nothing cheaper?"

The assistant assuring me that he had not, I returned to the display cabinet to make my choice. Selecting a pale blue silk tie with a faint stripe that looked vaguely military, I heard Beryl call, "Bob, come here a minute." Detaching myself from the assistant, I went over to her. In her hands, held up for my shocked inspection was a pair of underpants. “Only two bob a pair!” she whispered, fingering the material. “Good quality cotton, these. I couldn’t help noticing you weren’t wearing any.”

I searched Beryl’s face. There was not a vestige of a smile and her eyes were serious. She was obviously of the impression that I’d run out of clean underpants, unaware that I never wore them.

“Ah, right.” I said. “I forgot to put them on this morning as I was late getting up. I don’t need any new ones, really. And those are too expensive don’t you think?

“Nah, they are real good value, Bob, You must have them.”

“Okay, then, I’d better do, I suppose.”

I counted out twenty-three shillings from my pay packet and handed it over to the assistant. When he returned with my purchases, nicely wrapped in brown Kraft paper and tied with string, I asked a favour of him. “I wonder if you’d mind if I left my bike somewhere round the back of the shop for a couple of hours.”

He looked uncertain at first, then said, “Well, all right, seeing it’s Christmas, sir. Best place, take it down the side of the shop and stick it by the coal bunker. No one will see it there.”

I did as he suggested and afterwards, Beryl and I ventured out to the covered bus stop opposite. The bus was scheduled to arrive in ten minutes, enough time for some unfinished business.

Snow had blown into the shelter and lay an inch or two deep on the slatted bench seat inside. Stoked up with a desperate lust, I felt nothing of the freezing conditions. Propelling Beryl over to the bench, our feet sloshing mud, slush and discarded cigarette butts underfoot, I grabbed her roughly round the waist and kissed her hard on the mouth. My hands roved over her breasts. What a delicious shape they were, full and round and firm under my kneading fingers.

"'Ere what you up to?" Beryl asked, as my hot breath funnelled into her neck, knowing damn well what I was doing, what I wanted. "Bob, stop it, we can't, no, not here. It's wet and cold, horrible. Anyway, someone might come," she pleaded. "Wait 'til we get home."

"Oh, come on, Beryl, let me get inside your coat at least, have a proper feel of your tits," I said, in a thick voice unrecognisable as my own. Possibly because my mouth was now buried deep in Beryl's fake-fur collar, which reeked of the flatting shed.

"No, Bob! You heard me, not here. Not here! Not now! Someone might see us, then what?"

"Okay, then," I said, guiding her hand, "feel me instead."

"No! Leave me alone, Bob. Didn't you hear what I said, you horny sod? The bus will here soon. It's only a ten minute ride from here to my home."

"Okay, you're right, Beryl," I replied, releasing her. It was plain she meant what she said. I decided not to risk her wrath in case she sent me packing.

A mud bespattered double-decker bus arrived soon after and we climbed on board. Beryl ran both of her hands through her disarrayed hair under the appreciative gaze of the bus conductor, before seating herself at the front of the bus. I held out my palm to the conductor with sixpence in it. "Two tickets to Addlestone, please." His eyes still on Beryl, the conductor rattled off the tickets from the machine hanging round his neck and, absently feeling about in the leather pouch slung across his waist, handed me tuppence change. “Happy Christmas, son,” he said, giving me a sly wink.

The bus pulled away, its front wheels throwing up a plume of snow as we swished slowly down the road. I caught Beryl’s cold hands in mine, rubbing them hard to restore the circulation. “Thanks, Bob,” she said, giving me a luminous smile. “You’ll rub all the skin off if you’re not careful.”

I turned my head around to see if we were being observed, but save for a man in a flat cap peering out of the window and a couple of gaunt old women engaged in deep conversation, there was no one else on the bus. The conductor, too, was talking to the driver, so I took the opportunity to kiss Beryl on the cheek.

“Do you really fancy me?” she asked, shyly. “My hubby didn’t.”

“Then he must have been mad!” I exclaimed, coming to her defence. “Bloody mad. ‘Cos you are a really dishy dame and, yeah, I really, really fancy you.”

“But I’m too old for you,” she said, her eyes now as sad as her voice.

“Who cares? You are a still a corking looker, you know.” It was true, she was very pretty. I guess, even if she had been twice her age, in my priapic condition I’d have lied anyway, so I could make love to her.

“Will you see me again?”

“What do you mean?”

“I mean, after, you know.”

The thought had not crossed my mind. I was so consumed with the thought I’d soon be losing my virginity, there was no room to think of anything other than sex, real sex at last. Not just heavy petting, but actually going to bed with a woman.

"Of course, I'll see you again." I lied, knowing I couldn't face introducing her to my friends. Furthermore, if I ever brought her home with me, Dick would throw a fit. Squirming inside, I repeated, "Yeah, of course I'll see you again, if you want."

"I'd like that, Bob. Really I would, though I know it won't last. 'Cos it can't. Your friends..."

She turned her head to look out of the window.

I hated myself then. She'd seen through me. Reading my mind, she'd accepted the realities. Despite this, she still wanted to see me. Women! How could men ever understand them?

We alighted at a bus stop a short distance from the factory estate where I'd once worked. Flatting was the fifth job I'd had in two and half years. Now that I was unemployed again, it would be six very soon.

"It's along here, Bob," said Beryl. "Come, I'll show you. It's that prefab just beyond the newsagents on the right. Council gave it me."

"Prefab? What's that?" I asked.

"A prefab's a prefab," replied Beryl, clutching my arm, nestling her head against my shoulder as we walked.

I remained none the wiser. We passed the newsagent's shop and then walked down a short path. Ahead was what appeared to be a corrugated iron and plasterboard hut.

"This is a prefab," said Beryl, as she searched inside a pocket for her front-door key. "I've called the house *Chezznew*. It's French. Sweet, don't you think?"

My French didn't stretch to *Chezznew.* Instead, I nodded my head sagely and said, "Yeah, very nice, very nice," hoping that Beryl would shut up and we could get on with what I was there for. Hopping from foot to foot, fretting with impatience, I watched as she plunged the key in the lock, pushed the front door ajar and entered. Switching on a light, she called over her shoulder, "Come on in. I'll go and switch on the electric fire to warm the room up. It's not much, but it's home."

I stepped inside the miniscule hallway and removed my Burberry, thinking, 'Sod the fire, let's go to bed'.

As soon as Beryl taken her coat off, I caught her around the waist. Fastening her mouth on mine, she allowed my hands to rove all over her body. I gave myself up to the bliss of touching her bare flesh. Heady with ecstasy, we kissed open mouthed. I picked her up bodily and croaked, "Where's the bedroom?"

"Through that door," gasped Beryl, as she swiped an excess of saliva from her lips.

"Okay, Tonto," I said jokily, hefting her through the opening.

"Switch's on the left," she said, "You'll have to put me down."

"Not so, baby," I replied, the big Hollywood movie star now. Bending my head down a touch, I flipped the light switch on with the tip of my nose and flopped Beryl, who was still cackling with laughter over my little trick with the switch, down on the bed, before falling on top of her.

Beryl hitched up her dress, exposing her thighs and hips. "By Christ, Beryl," I exclaimed, "you bloody well don't wear knickers either." I guffawed with laughter at the revelation.

"Clothes rationing, Bobby," Beryl giggled. "Half the gels in the flatting shop don't wear them. Imagine the to-do if we all got run over by a bus. So come here, lover boy, and give me a good seeing to."

At other times I'd have considered Beryl's coarse language to be off-putting, but this was no time for quibbling. I released myself from Beryl's embrace, kicked off my shoes and hurriedly removed the rest of my clothing, before turning my attention to Beryl once more. In the interim she'd also removed her clothes, and now lay stretched out on the bed, her sleek limbs alabaster white, a creature of great beauty about to be ravaged by the Great Lover.

I discovered things do not always go to plan. The Greek God Priapus had done the dirty on me. Once so rampant, with Beryl's eyes feasting on the sight and crying out, "Bob, what a lovely, muscly body you've got," that which had jutted out so proudly for the past hour had, of its own volition, become limp and flaccid, a dangling little object of no use to anyone.

Shocked by what I beheld, I could only whisper abjectly, "Bloody hell, what happened to me?" as the shame of it painted my face scarlet.

"Dear God!" cried Beryl, in a pitying wail, "You poor thing," serving only to make me more feel even more embarrassed. "It's your first time, isn't it? Don' worry lover, come to Beryl and see what she can do to put it right."

'Put it right? Put it right?' I wished Beryl hadn't used those words. It implied there was something wrong with me that required restoration. As I looked down at her, I noticed her eyes were filled with concern and sympathy. Now that I'd fallen at the first hurdle, I just wanted to get the hell out of there as fast as possible. But Beryl was having none of it.

"Come on, big boy," she soothed, patting the pillow by her head. With barely enough room for the two of us, I crawled forward on all fours and scrunched up beside her.

Beryl did her best, ministering to me like an experienced courtesan, setting to work with a vengeance, using her mouth and other lovemaking techniques bordering on the dirty, doing things the like of which I thought women incapable. Nothing she did made my slumbering appendage respond.

Ultimately, Beryl resigned herself to failure. Dejected beyond belief, I quickly dressed. Beryl had turned her face to the wall. I kissed the top of her head.

"How often do the buses run?" I asked.

Sobbing, she replied, "'Bout every half hour, but with this weather...? Oh, Bobby, you won't want to ever see me again."

"Sure, I will. Sorry I let you down," I said matter-of-factly, disguising how rotten I felt.

With that, I left the room and fled the prefab. Walking the couple of miles to Haslett's to collect my bike was not a problem for one used to doing half-marathon hikes after missing trains.

Dragging my feet through the snow, burdened by an acute sense of failure, I stumbled on blindly. Adding to my woes, I was still a virgin and a bloody cold one at that.

Chapter 24

At eight o'clock on Christmas morning, there was no sign of life in the bunk below mine. I remembered, in a befuddled kind of way, Dick saying something about going to church and that it was my turn to feed the chickens. Shuffling off my thick eiderdown, I clambered down the ladder, avoiding to the very last moment my feet touching the cold floor.

Although it was freezing, Dick had unplugged the one bar electric fire in the bunk room at midnight on Christmas Eve, saying we had to economise. In the bitter chill, fang-like icicles hung down on the inside of the bedroom window-panes. The flimsy curtains were stiff with frost, crackling as I wrenched them open.

Perched on a withered branch of an apple tree, just beyond the window, a robin fluffed up its feathers. Casting a beady eye in my direction, it sat quite unconcerned, breakfasting on a wriggling worm. Enchanted by the image, I mouthed 'Happy Christmas' to the little bird as I stood shivering, flapping my arms to get my circulation going.

I climbed into overalls, warmed from being under my bedclothes all night, stuffed my feet into my only pair of shoes, and headed out in the snow to the chicken shed some fifty yards away. My teeth chattering uncontrollably, I filled a bucket with seed corn, my breath gusting out of me in white plumes.

All around, as far as my eyes could see, the entire Hamm Court Estate was blanketed with dazzling white snow. Clapboard dwellings similar to ours lined the frozen Thames. By Pharaoh's Island, directly opposite Willow Cottage, a line of swans went slip-sliding over the icy foreshore. Inland, set amongst a stand of tall trees, nestled a few sturdier brick-built houses with wood smoke hazing from their chimneys. The only sound in the silence was the muffled tolling of a distant church bell.

Christmas Day held out the promise of being altogether more enjoyable than the previous miserable ones I had spent in England. In anticipation of good company and a hearty lunch prepared by Dick, I was as happy as Larry, but as I gave the chickens their feed, I wondered which one of the poor beggars' necks Dick was to pull. I hoped it would not be Bertie, a particular favourite of mine, who pecked at my feet as I shooed the chickens back into their coop. Closing the shed door, I retreated to the cottage and brewed myself a cup of tea in the kitchen.

Dick's car rolled slowly through the gate and lurched down the rutted drive, coming to a stop at its regular place, a concrete slab directly under the kitchen window. If the BBC forecast freezing temperatures, Dick's habit was to drain the water from the car to prevent the radiator from cracking during the night; anti-freeze being expensive and hard to come by. In the morning, he'd turn on the kitchen tap and hose hot water into the radiator. The idea might have seemed eccentric, but it resulted from his experience with Army trucks in the Western Desert and, unlike those trucks, his car's engine never failed to start immediately, even on the coldest of days.

Dick bounded up to the back door and gave me a bear hug. "Happy Christmas, old chum!" he boomed, "What a perfect day it is. What a perfect day." The freckles on his ruddy cheeks merged together as he beamed. Removing his navy overcoat, Dick shook snow from its shoulders, before carefully folding it.

After satisfying himself I'd fed the chickens, his brow furrowed, as if he'd been struck by some unpleasant thought. Licking his lips, he said, "Must have a word with the vicar about that so-called wine he dishes up in church. My word, Bob, it was rough. The taste is still hanging about in my mouth. It's probably that awful stuff bottled in Kingston. Ugh."

"That's what comes of being a cannibal, old boy," I retorted, with a laugh. "And a happy Christmas to you, too."

Clearly puzzled, Dick asked, "Cannibal? Cannibal? What d'you mean, exactly?"

"Pagan stuff, communion," I replied, a touch nervously. "You know, transubstantiation, wine into blood, bread into flesh, that sort of thing."

"I shouldn't blaspheme, Robert, if I were you," said Dick, his mouth working, his arms poker stiff at his sides. "Bit of church-going would do you the no end of good, you know."

I instantly regretted my words, seeing I'd upset Dick. Christmas was obviously not the time to get into a discussion about religion.

"You are absolutely right, Dick. Sorry if I offended you," I said. "Anyhow, I've got some tea on the go and a present for you."

"*Pour moi?*" he asked, pointing to himself. Dick had learnt what little French he knew, together with a smattering of

Italian, whilst on active service as an infantryman in France and Italy. "I've one for you, too."

I affected mock surprise, as he'd done, and we both went inside the cottage. He dashed into the bunkroom and I went to the pocket of my Burberry hanging in the hall. We thrust our presents at each other. Dick unwrapped his and withdrew the expensive silk tie I'd bought for him. "Crikey, Bob," he whispered with genuine delight, "its silk. Silk. Crumbs, must have cost a pretty penny. Thanks so much." With that Dick unknotted the tie he wore and slipped on his new one. "Go, on, Bob," he said, "Open yours. See what I've got you."

There was a small card attached to my gift, which read *Happy Christmas, Bob, Lang may your lum reek*." I imagined it was something in French, but not wishing to betray my ignorance, I said nothing. As I carefully undid the paper, layer by layer so it could be of use again, there was revealed a shiny silver Ronson cigarette lighter, identical to the one my mates, the flatters, had presented me with. In my attempt to disguise my disappointment, I stuttered, "Thank you, Dick. I've always wanted a Ronson lighter."

Misinterpreting my hesitancy as emotion, Dick put an arm around my shoulder. "That's all right, old bean," he said, "I've also some baccy for your pipe." He clapped me on the back, "Players Navy Cut. I'll just go and fetch it." He disappeared into the sitting room, leaving me altogether happier, now that I had some decent tobacco to smoke at last.

Dick returned with a four once tin of tobacco in hand, saying, "I've chosen Bertie for our lunch."

"Oh, Dick, not Bertie."

"Why ever not? Time the little beggar got the chop."

Seeing my distress, he gave a hearty laugh. "Oh, all right. Henrietta, it'll be then. I was just having you on, Bob. Henrietta's much plumper anyway. Let me change out of these glad rags of mine, while you be a good fellow and plug in the electric fire. And, because it's Christmas, stick on three bars, will you, please? Get a proper fug up, eh?"

I could not believe my ears. Three bars was unheard of. Before Dick changed his mind, I ran to do his bidding. Moments later, Dick emerged from the bathroom wearing a duffel coat over his gardening trousers.

As he went to open the back door, he said, "Bob, you haven't forgotten Jack Bilbo's joining us for lunch?" Jack Bilbo, our German neighbour, bought most of Dick's eggs. "Besides Henrietta," Dick continued, "I've a decent-sized Christmas pud. But seeing how big the Hun is, we'll also need a stack of potatoes, swedes, and whatever else you can find in the larder. So go it, lad."

Dick in his executioner's role headed off down the garden path to the chicken shed. I, for my part, scuffled around our store of muddied old potatoes and heaps of swedes, grown in our vegetable garden over the summer months. I filled a basket with several pounds of root vegetables. Carrying the basket into the kitchen, I set to work peeling the lot.

Dick entered with the hapless Henrietta, her wings still flailing, gripped in his right fist. "Properly despatched," he grinned, "and with due ceremony. Move over, laddie, I've got to pluck the bird."

The idea of a bath was out of the question; it was much too cold to stand around in the bathroom. Instead, I rubbed a wet flannel over my face and gave my teeth a cursory going over with my forefinger. Applying some of Dick's Brylcreem to my thick black thatch of springy hair in a vain attempt to smooth it down, I shaved with the patented Rolls Razor given to me by my stepfather, Maurice, on my sixteenth birthday. A glance at my image in the mottled bathroom mirror and off I went to press my clothes with Dick's iron, which stood on the hob, already hot.

Jack Bilbo had been told to arrive at twelve-thirty. At precisely that, he knocked on the door. Dick had told me all Germans were punctual, a quality the British should emulate.

"See to him, will you?" Dick called from the kitchen. "I'll fish out some of our sloe gin and elderberry wine for lunch."

I shouted back, "Don't forget the two bottles of beer I bought," just as I heard Jack knock on the door for the second time.

By chance, Dick and I had struck up a friendship with Jack Bilbo after seeing him hammering away at one of his sculptures in the garden of the small house he owned nearby. "I bought ziss place to sometimes get away from London," he explained.

Over time, we got to know one another and he frequently stopped by for a chat and cup of tea. He told me once that his real name was Henry Bausch or something similar, and that Spinoza was his great-great-great-grandfather. I was less impressed by that than by his disclosure that he'd once been the bodyguard of an American gangster. I could believe it, for Bilbo was built like a truck.

It had never occurred to us, until Jack regaled us with stories of his swashbuckling life, that he was also something of a celebrity in the world of modern art. To give credence to his claims, he gave me a copy of the memoir he had published.

Born in Berlin in 1907 to a German-Jewish father and an English mother, Jack emigrated to America at the age of sixteen. At twenty-eight, he left America and joined the International Brigade to fight against the Fascists in the Spanish Civil War. At the start of World War II he came to England to fight the Nazis, but was promptly interned as an alien on the Isle of Man. Whilst there, he founded the University of the People and, for the entire duration, painted, sculpted and wrote. By the time the war ended, he had acquired a reputation in the world of modern art and opened a gallery in Baker Street, London.

Jack's passion was sculpting the female form in various shapes and sizes. The two ten-foot-high examples kneeling in his garden, grotesquely shaped and featuring colossal breasts and buttocks, raised a smile in me each time I passed by his house. On one occasion, when he was out, I took a closer look. To my astonishment, I discovered that between their buttocks, there existed a narrow passageway leading down to a cellar-like space beneath. One day, I asked Jack the reason for this. He replied, with a loud laugh, "Can't you see, *mein lieber* Bob? My statues disguise der bombproof air raid shelter for the der next war. Ven it comes, local people can enter via the big anus into der shelter below. It is not difficult to understand, *ja*?"

I opened the door and Jack entered, carrying a bulging canvas bag. His hulking figure was so enormous, there was barely enough room for the two of us in the minute hallway. Jack's bag made a familiar tinkling sound as he laid it down, before removing his boots.

"Bob, *mein* dear boy! Happy Christmas to you." As was normal for Jack, he conversed in a language all of his own, a cross between German and American, switching from one to the other with bewildering speed.

"Hey, man, take *mein* bag and put it somevere safe," he ordered. "I've got twelve bottles of good beer in there, a bottle of Spätlese wine, and a small one of Schnapps. Enough for lunch, *nein*?" Looking about him, he continued, "Ver is *mein guten freund*, Dick? Bob, you open up some bottles right away, waddya say, man?"

Without waiting for my answer, Jack strode into the sitting room and gripped Dick in a rib-crushing embrace. Dick, being frightfully British, responded more formally than Jack, who shouted his greetings and waved his hands about extravagantly. Dick was not exactly a shrimp, but looked small beside the flamboyant sculptor with the wild mass of black hair and burning eyes. As Jack strode about the room, I noticed for the first time the gold earring he wore in his right ear. If he'd had a hook for a hand he'd have been a dead ringer for Captain Hook.

Our cottage had not yet warmed up, but Jack seemed unfazed by the cold. He'd arrived wearing only a thick woollen shirt tucked into corduroy trousers held up over his broad belly by a plaited cord. Rolling up his sleeves, he exposed ham-sized hairy forearms.

"Aren't you cold, Jack?" I asked.

"Nah, this ain't nuttin'. Not like Chicago. Now, that burg *was* cold, real cold. How you say? Brass balls weather." Roaring with laughter, he said, "Now, young man, vot we wait for? Break open the booze."

I went off to search inside Jack's bag and returned carrying three unlabelled bottles containing dark brown liquid. "Good boy, Bob, that is the stuff," said Jack, taking the bottles from me. "Now, have you a bottle opener? *Ach*, no matter, ve do it zis way." He prised off the metal caps with his teeth and handed one bottle to Dick and another to me. "I learnt how to do that in the US of A. Prohibition time, when I was with dat bum, Al Capone."

Bottle in hand, I stood, mouth agape, whereas Dick's response to Jack's extraordinary claim was the one only he could have made.

"Good Lord, how very interesting, Jack," he said mildly, as if Jack's association with the notorious American gangster was perfectly normal. "Al Capone, did you say? Well, well." He took a swig. "Cheers, chaps. Happy Christmas." Dick shuddered as the beer slipped down his throat. "God Almighty, that was strong. Make it yourself Jack?"

"*Jawohl*. To a good German recipe. Like it?"

Dick took another swallow, a much smaller one this time, as I asked Jack if it was really true he was Al Capone's bodyguard.

He sighed: "*Ach, ja*, in the thirties. When I was young and foolish."

Because Jack was so much larger than life and so very entertaining, I decided I really didn't care whether he was telling the truth or not. I finished off my bottle of beer. As Jack started on his second bottle, Dick shouted out, "Lunch's ready, chaps! Grub's on the table." When and how Dick had managed to find the time to do it was a mystery, but there it was: our kitchen table, usually covered in tattered plastic sheeting, was now graced with a linen table-cloth, proper napkins, polished wine glasses, a bottle of elderberry wine and an armoury of cutlery.

Jack, who had to duck to pass through the door to the kitchen, sat down on the metal chair at the head of the table. Dick requested I give him a hand as he transferred the vegetables to the steaming plates sitting on the hob. Henrietta was carefully drawn out from the oven, crisply browned all over and smelling delicious. Dick had turned his back and was sharpening his carving knife, slapping it back and forth over a leather strop. When satisfied, he fumbled about with the chicken, carefully positioning it on a wooden carving board before placing it before us. A lemon was sticking out of the chicken's bottom. I was astonished to see it. There had been plenty of them growing in my garden in Rawalpindi, but I'd never seen a lemon anywhere in England.

"Where did you find the lemon, Dick?" I asked.

"Oh, that," replied Dick, laughing, with Jack joining in. "It's made of celluloid, you dope. I did it for effect!"

I joined in with the hilarity, figuring Dick's corny Bumper Fun Book joke could be forgiven at Christmas. When the laughter had subsided, I heard Jack ask, "May I please carve? I just love to do it."

"Certainly," replied Dick, handing over the carving knife. I sensed his reluctance, but as a good host, he passed up the duty he considered rightfully his.

Jack ran his fingers over the blade. "Good, sharp thing, zis," he murmured, before expertly dissecting the chicken with delicate, clean strokes. His long spatulate fingers worked the knife through the flesh until, shorn of meat, the bare carcass stood proud in a bed of perfect chicken slices. "My word," said Dick, admiring Jack's handiwork, "where did you learn to carve like that? Brilliant!"

"From that wop, Capone," replied Jack.

Chapter 25

Just after New Year 1952, Dick set off on his annual trek around the south of England and the Isle of Wight.

"I'll be away about a month," he said. "The company requires me to make a goodwill visit to all the stationers who stock our greetings cards. Worry not, old chap, I'll be back in time for your twenty-first in Feb." As he drove away, I heard him shout through his lowered window, "Good luck with finding a job, Bob. Help yourself to anything you need and don't forget to feed the chickens."

I'd been down to the Labour Exchange a couple of days before to see if there were any jobs available within cycling distance. By now, I had more than a passing acquaintance with the man who sat behind the window in his dismal office, the one in whose hands my fate seemed destined forever to rest. As usual, his offensive manner cowed me.

Peering at me through a small opening, he repeated that the few office jobs he had on his books required a higher qualification than my Cambridge School Certificate. He reiterated once again that the exam I'd taken in Pakistan was inferior to the one sat by students in England. I pointed out the fallacy of his argument by reminding him that the Army Operational Research Group had a different view and had employed me as an assistant scientific officer. If my qualifications were good enough for the AORG, surely they had not diminished in value since. His reply, accompanied by a self-satisfied smirk, was I'd got the job with AORG because no one else had been prepared to have their arms burnt during the experiments conducted there.

"I've a couple of manual jobs available," the weasel continued, placing his forearms on the edge of the window and flexing his fingers. Hunching his thin shoulders, he thrust his head forward and fixed his bulging eyes on me. "One is with Woolworths in Walton, shovelling coal. The other is with a maintenance gang working for the Council. They both pay two and six an hour for a forty-hour week. That's a fiver a week, Mr, er," here he referred to his notes, "Monteath-Matthews. Quite a bleeding mouthful for a foreigner, innit?"

Seething, I replied, "I'm not a bleeding foreigner, and no, thanks, I'll come back again next week."

I returned to Willow Cottage and sat down on the freezing river bank to contemplate what the future held. At eye level, mist hung low over the water, clothing Pharaoh's Island with a wispy white mantle. The old Victorian house in the centre of the island looked haunted, dispirited and sad, but no more so than I felt. I stayed sitting for a while, calculating how long I could eke out my savings of just over five pounds. If I forsook bathing, I could save sixpence a week, and by breakfasting on plain oats for breakfast, cutting out anything to eat midday, eating a small evening meal made up of scraps, supplemented by potatoes and the occasional egg, I figured I'd manage a month at most, by which time I was sure something would turn up.

Since finding a job soon was vital for survival, I decided if the worst came to the worst, I could return to flatting for a while. However, the prospect of working alongside Beryl, and reliving my embarrassing experience, soon put paid to that idea.

I then dwelt on the possibility that the delectable Margot Anderson, she of the Bluebell Girls in Paris, might come up trumps with an audition for me at The Windmill Theatre in Soho. However, she had said it would be February before she'd be released from her Paris contract, so I still had a month to wait. She had said she'd phone me but as yet hadn't. Nonetheless, I was so convinced of our mutual attraction, it never occurred that she might have forgotten me or acted on a whim. That certainty saved me from sinking into a state of even deeper depression. If I could have magicked away the entire month of January and found myself in February, I'd have paid any price.

After Dick set off on his rounds I felt very much alone. Miserable, I mooched about the cottage, fed the chickens and went for a long bike ride, to Sunningdale and beyond, until the light began to fail. By the time I returned it was nightfall and the cottage as cold as death. I switched on a single bar of Dick's electric fire, wrapped myself in a blanket and curled up in an armchair in the sitting room. I fell asleep almost instantly and dreamt of dancing onstage with Margot. She was wearing her scarlet evening dress, singing something from Rodgers and Hammerstein, the audience rising to their feet and applauding.

When I awoke early next morning I discovered pus seeping from my left ear onto the cushion beneath my head. My ear had been itching madly for weeks, which I'd tried relieving by teasing a matchstick into it. The greater the irritation, the harder I had scraped at the skin, so that, in protest, the ear finally told me to call a halt. I cleaned out my ear as best I could, and decided to ask the doctor to give me a prescription. His surgery was at the bottom of Gower Street in Weybridge, a shabby place that, judging by the plate glass windows facing the street, had once been a shop. On wooden benches lining two badly scuffed walls, old folk in tired clothes sat staring at the ceiling, the floor, the street—anywhere save at each other. Lips remained compressed, hands stayed folded in musty, ancient laps. Resignation reigned in that silent anteroom. An hour passed before the doctor finally ushered me in.

Everything about Dr Blake was grey. He had thinning grey hair, a tired grey face and was wearing a crumpled grey suit. Unhooking his stethoscope from around his neck, he bade me sit down.

"You are?" he ventured, cocking a grey eyebrow.

"Ian, er, Bob Matthews, sir."

"New patient, and my last one today, eh? Well, what seems to be the trouble, young man?"

"My ear, it's pussing..."

"Suppurating, is it? Let's have a look-see."

The good doctor circled me, pulling on each ear lobe in turn, inserting a device to investigate the problem. He was thorough, if taciturn, in his examination.

"Well," he said at last, "you have otitis externa. That's why it itches. You've been very foolish to dig around with a foreign object. The only thing you ever stick in your ear—d'you hear?—is your elbow. Irritation of the sort you have is usually a manifestation of something deeper." The doctor paused before asking, "Worried about anything, young man?"

I explained I was out of a job, short of cash, lonely and uncertain about my future. I told him how many jobs I'd had and how depressed I was that my life was going nowhere. He listened carefully, asking all sorts of questions about my childhood in India, my parents, how I'd got to England and so on, before he settled back in his chair and sighed, "That's an extraordinary tale. I'm not surprised you are under strain." Then, taking me by surprise, he asked, "Do you consider yourself to be an impressionable person? Let's say susceptible to suggestion, that sort of thing?"

"I don't know what you mean, sir," I replied, now getting nervous, reminded of Colonel Marriott and his tests. "Susceptible to suggestion?"

"Let's put it another way," said Dr Blake peering at me through his faded grey eyes. "Your personality, from all that you've told me about yourself, suggests someone who buries all his feelings. The net result is you'll go along with any idea or suggestion, from whatever source, just so long as you please everybody."

I must have looked blank, for he continued brusquely, "First, we'll give you something for the ear, shall we? Then do something about the underlying cause of it, which I think is psychological." I watched uncomprehendingly as he picked up his phone. "I'll see if I can get you an appointment with a psychiatrist at St Thomas' Hospital. He'll sort out what ails you deep down."

"A psychiatrist?" I heard myself mutter.

"Know what they are, do you?" asked Dr Blake, continuing to dial.

I was about to protest I had first-hand knowledge of them, but was silenced by a testy wave of the doctor's hand. After a brief conversation with Dr Schwartz's secretary, Dr Blake replaced the receiver. "He can see you in two days' time. That's a piece of luck, usually it's about two weeks."

I wasn't listening to the doctor, my mind absorbed with the cost of the train fare to Waterloo and my fast-depleting resources. I'd only gone to see him to fix my ear and here was I being shunted off to see a trick-cyclist.

Dr Blake scribbled a note and sealed it in an envelope, then wrote out a prescription for sulphonamide ointment.

"That'll ease the itch," he said. "Dr Schwartz is a good chap. He'll get to the root of the problem for you."

The chemist on the corner of the High Street made up the prescription and handed me a small tube of ointment, for which, thankfully, there was no charge. As soon as I got home I steamed the doctor's envelope open. The doctor's scribbled note was difficult to decipher. I read and re-read it several times before the contents—written with commendable, if shattering, brevity—sank in.

Dear Doctor Schwartz,

I would be grateful if you would examine my patient, Ian Matthews. He is suffering from otitis externa in his left ear. The causation, in my opinion, is psychological. Possibly a low-level psychopath?

Yours sincerely,

Gordon Blake Mb Chb. MRCoG.

The word psychopath buzzed about in my brain. Me, a psychopath? Banstead Mental Hospital and my mantra of *You are standing on the edge of a cliff and falling forward,* together with the vision of the pyschos I'd interviewed in that place, struck with appalling clarity. Now I had been diagnosed as the same. I began to laugh, a high-pitched cackling laugh.

When I finally pulled myself together, I decided I'd see Dr Schwartz out of sheer perversity. The cost of travelling to London meant I'd probably go short of tobacco. Nonetheless, I figured the fun of finding the boot on the other foot irresistible, an experience not to be missed. Carefully resealing the envelope, I stuffed it in the letter rack on top of the kitchen cupboard and, whistling cheerfully, stomped off to feed the chickens.

Chapter 26

Forty-eight hours after seeing my GP, I stood in front of Dr Schwartz's secretary, dishevelled, hot and out of breath. My train had been late, forcing me to run from Waterloo station all the way to St Thomas' Hospital.

I stood awkwardly in front of the secretary waiting for her to acknowledge my presence. Totally ignoring me for a full five minutes, she fiddled about with her papers before finally removing her glasses to look up at me. "Mr Matthews, I presume?" she rasped. "Well, you're late." I pointed to the clock on the wall behind her, whose hands stood at five past eleven. "No, I'm not late," I stuttered, quailing before her blistering gaze.

"You are, and that's the end of that," stated the woman flatly. Her colourless eyes remained steady on my face. I stood looking foolish as, with a mottled hand, she scraped a stray hair behind her ear. "It's just as well," she went on, her voice sounding like paper being ripped. "Dr Schwartz is running behind."

No sooner had she finished the sentence than an incandescent smile lit up her face. The transformation was so utterly unexpected, I stepped backwards in alarm. Continuing to beam at me, she said in a treacly voice, "Of course, you're one of Dr Blake's patients. We know him well. He sends lots of patients to Dr Schwartz."

'That's my boy, Dr Blake,' I huffed to myself. ' Bad ear? See a psychiatrist. Leg amputated after a road accident? The good Dr Schwartz will doubtless explain why you fell under a bus.'

"Come, sit down, Mr Matthews," said the secretary, rising from behind her desk, leading me to a vacant chair. "There now. He won't be long," she said, her smile still ineffably sweet.

The moment she sat down again, her smile vanished and her grim look returned. I was again of no account, merely wallpaper. Baffled, I picked up an ancient copy of *Punch* from a side table. I concluded that Dr Schwartz's madhouse comprised not only his patients but his staff as well.

I had not long to wait before a bulky figure in a white coat with its tails flapping came bustling down the corridor. Dashing past me, he headed straight for the secretary. I heard him ask, in a deep rumbling voice that seemed to come from somewhere in the region of his boots, "My patient here, Mrs Pritchett?" Instantly obsequious, the secretary fawned, pointing in my direction, "Yes, Dr Schwartz, that's him. Mr Matthews."

Dr Schwartz swivelled around to face me, his plump lips parting in a smile. "So sorry I kept you. You have a letter from Dr Blake for me?" I handed it to him. The psychiatrist fastened heavy-rimmed spectacles on his nose and read the contents of the letter in seconds, his eyes flicking back and forth. Watching nervously, I hoped he'd not noticed the envelope had been resealed. But all he said was, "How is the ear doing?"

It was clear that the two appendages on either side of my face were really of no interest to him, and he'd only asked as a matter of form. I lied, saying, "It's much better," when it really was not.

As if he'd not heard my response, he muttered something to himself before leading me into his consulting room, empty save for a low table and two comfortable arm chairs. Windows, the glass spotted with raindrops, ran the length of one wall overlooking the Thames. I could just make out the blurred image of the Houses of Parliament and, on the waters below, coal barges fastened in tandem, sailing downriver.

"Now, Mr Matthews—or shall I call you Ian?" asked Dr. Schwartz.

"I prefer Bob, sir. I've never been known as Ian."

"Very well. Bob it is, then. Now, d'you know why Dr Blake sent you here?" Without waiting for my reply, he continued briskly, "Well, let me say, he thinks your problem is not necessarily a medical one. Rather, he's of the opinion it stems from something psychological. My job is to see if he's right. Happy with that?"

So saying, Dr Schwartz squeezed his bulk into a chair. As he adjusted himself, he said, pointing, "Take the other one please. Make yourself as comfortable as you can and then tell me all about yourself." Dr Schwartz pulled a note pad from his coat pocket, unscrewed the top a fountain pen and poised it over the paper.

"*All* about myself?" I asked, thinking this was going to be fun, wondering when he was going to get to something like Colonel Marriott's device, *You are standing on the edge of a cliff*, at which point I'd laugh and tell him I knew what he was up to. Poor chap didn't know I was well acquainted with psychiatrists and their foibles.

"Yes, from as far back as you can remember," he replied, smiling. "For most people that's from about the age of two. Take your time, Ian, er, Bob."

As Dr Schwartz waited for me to gather my thoughts, he ran his free hand through his uncombed black hair. His eyes probed mine as he settled back in his chair and gestured for me to proceed.

Caught on the hop by the solicitude in his voice, his warmth, his encouragement, I said, "Well, sir..." and came to a stop. My intention had been to give the psychiatrist the run-around, have fun at his expense. Instead, I found myself doing as he'd asked and began searching my memory. "My earliest recollection is of peacocks strutting on the lawn outside our house."

"Peacocks?" enquired Dr Schwartz, leading me on. "How very interesting. Can you recall where that was?"

"In the grounds of Vice Regal Lodge in Delhi. That's where the Viceroy lived. We had a bungalow on the estate because Dad had some important job in government."

"What was his position, do you know?"

I was now unsettled, for I had no idea where the questions were leading. Racking my brains, I replied, "I don't know exactly. But when I was very small, in 1932, my parents brought me with them to London. That was when Dad accompanied a delegation of Indian princes to the Third Round Table Conference. For some reason—why, I'll never know—my parents left behind my three year-old brother Geoff, to be looked after by my grandparents in Lahore."

"Why did your parents allow that?" asked Dr Schwartz, quietly. I shifted uneasily in my seat, reluctant to allow him dig further. This was not at all how I imagined the interview would go. "Did they ever explain the reason?"

Shrugging, I replied, "Well, sort of. My mother told me much later that my grandparents could not bear being parted from Geoff. Apparently they adored him. I never really understood. I still don't." Then, before I could help myself, I blurted, "Grandma Matthews always preferred Geoff to me."

"Why do you think that was, Bob?" The question came so softly, I barely heard it.

"Well, er..." I hesitated, uncomfortable that the psychiatrist was asking me to remember stuff I'd buried long ago. "It may sound daft to you, but my mother told me that it dates from the time Granny came to visit her in hospital, soon after I was born. Apparently, she lifted my coverlet and seeing Mum had given birth to a dusky-looking baby, left the ward without uttering a word. Mum said that moment was the most hurtful of her life.

"I guess, because Grandpa Matthews was superintendent of the Punjab Secretariat at the time, Granny thought it wouldn't do for him have a grandson who looked Indian. You see, Grandpa's father, my great-grandfather, was related to the Earl of Llandaff. Granny was awfully proud of the connection. Thus my arrival, the runt of the litter, wasn't exactly welcome. In those days, anyone who had a dark skin was regarded an Anglo-Indian, or Eurasian, and placed way down the pecking order of society. According to my mother, Gran simply could not handle that."

"How do *you* feel about being darker than your siblings, Bob?"

The question made me squirm inside, even though it had been put sympathetically. It was not a direction I wanted to go, yet I found myself replying.

"It never entered my head. It was only after I came to England, when some people called me a wog, that I minded being dark skinned. It's because I'd been brought up to, well, if not to despise Indians, to regard wogs as somehow beneath us. And now, here was I being called a wog myself. I took exception to that, still take exception. Now, to anyone who thinks of me as being an Indian, I tell them I'm part Italian which, in point of fact, is true, my maternal grandfather, Hubert Belletti, having come from Piedmont in Italy." What possessed me to do so I'll never know, but I found myself blurting, "His wife was from Copenhagen," as if that gem of information would make all the difference to Dr Schwartz's diagnosis.

Embarrassed now, I went silent and looked down at the floor. I asked myself why on earth I had disclosed so much about myself, my deepest feelings, things I was ashamed of. I wasn't enjoying the experience of unravelling my past one little bit. After all, I'd expected my consultation with Dr Schwartz to be bit of a jape.

Dr Schwartz continued to speak in the same emollient tone of voice, as if there had been no interruption. "Bob, I can see how life's been problematical for you in England. However, if you just think about it, when you tell people you've just arrived from India, it is hardly surprising they pin a label on you, particularly since you don't look exactly English. My recommendation is that you get rid of that chip on your shoulder. Denial is not an option. I don't think your skin's that dark, anyway. It really isn't. Honestly, Bob, you shouldn't let it get you down. I know just how you feel. I am Jewish, so I understand all too well what discrimination's all about. Anyhow, let's leave that for the moment and move on. You haven't as yet told me about your father or mother, your school days, your upbringing."

Now, with Dr Schwartz interjecting here and there to control the flow, all my memories tumbled out of me in an unstoppable flood. This was no longer a joke. Dr Schwartz's sympathy, his understanding of what was going on in my head, enabled me to entirely unburden myself to him.

"Dad was a professor of English, but he also indulged in politics. Apparently, he knew Gandhi, Nehru, Jinnah. He wrote to all three, begging their cooperation to help safeguard the minority communities after the British quit India. I have met contemporaries of my dad, and they say he was a martyr. I'm proud of that.

"If only he'd kept his own counsel until after the war. Then he might never have gone to jail. In 1938, Dad was accused of inciting riots among his students at the Forman Christian College. He was found guilty of sedition under the Defence of India Act and sentenced to nine months in jail. Oh, God, how I wish he'd stuck to teaching. He wasn't cut out for politics."

As it always happened when I thought of my father, I broke down and cried. "Dad died in jail of typhoid at the age of forty."

As if from a faraway place, I heard Dr Schwartz's voice: "Take your time, Bob. Take your time. You may smoke if you wish. Here, have one of mine."

He fished out a pink pack of Passing Cloud cigarettes from his jacket pocket and threw it across to me, at the same time sliding an ash tray to within touching distance. As I caught the cigarettes, the empty pipe I had been twisting in my fingers like a drum major's baton fell to the floor. The psychiatrist had incorrectly interpreted my unconscious twiddling as a need to smoke, but now that he'd given me permission, I took full advantage of his thoughtful gesture and lit up.

"Thank you, sir," I said, inhaling deeply, enjoying the taste of expensive tobacco of a kind I could never afford, "that'll calm my nerves."

Dribbling the smoke from my mouth in tiny blue threads, I continued. "After Dad died, the family was ostracised by Lahore society. Grandma Matthews was mortified, blaming my mother, not her dear son, for having brought the family down so low. For a Scottish missionary, she had little charity in her."

Dr Schwartz laid down his pen. "How so?" he asked. "Why did your grandmother think that?"

I looked blankly at the psychiatrist. "I really do not know. Granny had always hated my mother. Mum and Dad married when he was up at Oxford taking his MA. Mum was a ballet dancer with the Ballet Rambert at the time. When Dad returned to India with my mother, Gran spurned her. She thought Mum was a flibbertigibbet, and much too flighty for her son. My poor, poor, Mum—her own parents cut her off, too. They were Roman Catholics, Dad was Presbyterian. So she got it in the neck from both sides.

"In some ways Gran was right about my mother. She was glamorous, extravagant and spoilt, without any idea how to bring up children. But blaming her for what happened to my Dad was cruel. Wrong. Wide of the mark. Irrational. Mum loved my Dad, I do know that, but she had no maternal instincts. She was thirty-three and had five kids, four boys and a girl, when Dad died. Geoff, my elder brother, was only ten. My sister Pam, nearly eight, Richard, five, and David, a year-old baby.

"Mum was left with no money to support us. Luckily, my Dad had been a Freemason, Master of the Scottish Lodge in Lahore, actually, and they came to our rescue. They paid for Pam and Richard to be sent to a boarding school seven thousand feet up in the hills, whereas I was despatched to a different one, the Lawrence College, a tough boys' school run on military lines in Ghora Gali, a few miles away.

"After I had been in boarding school for a year, my mother found herself a job as a secretary with the Attock Oil Refinery in Morgah. The situation came with a house and a couple of servants, allowing Pam, Richard and me to be reunited once more during our school holidays. Two years later, my mother married Maurice Cuell, an oil chemist, who earned a decent salary. Even so, Geoff and David continued to live with my grandmother until she died and only came to live with us when Geoff was eighteen and David nine."

I had recovered my composure and was beginning to enjoy rattling away to Dr Schwartz, who sat silent, making notes. Outside, the rain had given way to snow. The office was stiflingly hot, with the central heating radiators snuffling and snorting like pigs in swill. I felt a trifle light-headed. I decided the doctor was a really a decent chap to be hearing me out. Throughout he'd not been at all judgmental. I drew my chair closer to his desk and continued to confide in him as if he was my dearest friend.

"My first two years at school were hell. When some of the boys discovered my Dad was in jail, that was it. Not a single day passed without someone beating me up. Every bloody day, I got a hammering from bullies, with prefects dishing out canings, too. Well, sir, in time I discovered a talent for boxing and could handle myself pretty well. I also became the class buffoon. I made fun of the teachers, for which they caned me, or sent me to clean a hundred window panes; stuff like that. All of this made my classmates laugh, and that was all that mattered to me then. It taught me that a sense of the ridiculous works wonders when the going gets rough. Now I can't help seeing the funny side of life whatever the situation."

Dr Schwartz removed his glasses. Interrupting my flow, he said, almost as an afterthought, "Were you aware of any homosexuality at your school? It's fairly common in boarding schools, you know."

Surprised, quite taken aback by the curious path Dr Schwartz had embarked on, I mumbled something about not knowing if there was or not. Other than for the one time, I said, when a school master, Mr Robey, called me into his study for extra class work and tried it on with me.

Dr. Schwartz leaned forward in his chair, showing an even greater degree of interest than hitherto. “How did you handle the situation, Bob? Was it terrible for you?”

“No, but not good,” I replied. “I reported the master to the Head, and Robey was sent packing a day or two later. I remember all of us boys pelting him with stones as he was shown off the school premises.”

“I call that rough justice,” said Dr Schwartz, smiling. “Well done. Now, forgive me for having stopped you just then. Wind the clock forward if you can, and cover the time you’ve been living in England. Bring me up to date. Can you do that for me please? We’ll deal with the rest of your schooldays and your earlier life at a later time.”

I briefly recounted how I’d knocked out my mother’s lover in Rawalpindi, which resulted in my being put on a plane to London. I told of how I’d been very nearly buggered by a member of the House of Lords the day after I’d arrived in England and broke the man’s nose for his trouble. Dr Schwartz laughed and scribbled away furiously. At the close distance I sat from him, his handwriting was clearly legible to me.

“You’ve more than a streak of violence in you, haven’t you?” said Dr Schwartz without looking up. “That you must control. It results from you being bullied. Now then, Bob, pray go on.”

I went on to describe the varied and many jobs I’d had—the rough, the smooth, the bad, the ugly—the discrimination I’d endured, the kindnesses I received, ending with how Dick Purkis had taken me under his wing. All the while, Dr Schwartz rapidly wrote down all I said, with my eyes idly following his handwriting across the page. It was only when I saw him write down 'Dick Purkis' that I really took notice. When he added my name alongside Dick's, with the word 'homosexual' and a query beside it, my brain ceased functioning. My breath held in suspense, I sat motionless, disbelieving. 'Homosexual' swam before my eyes and exploded in my brain.

"I am not a *homosexual*", I protested angrily through gritted teeth. "Doctor, you've got me wrong. I like girls. I *love* girls."

"Ah," breathed the psychiatrist, completely unfazed, "I see humour has deserted you. Apart from a talent for violence, you can also read upside down, I see." Covering the page with the palm of his hand, he said, "Tell you what, Bob, I'll delete it. I don't wish to offend you." With that, he picked up his pen and drew a line.

My eye was quicker than his hand. I saw that he had made a pretence of scoring out the word homosexual and had obliterated the sentence below instead. For being taken for a fool, I became more even more enraged.

"Fuck you, doctor!" I shouted. "All you bloody quacks are the same. There was I thinking you really understood me, but you've no fucking idea at all!"

I fled the room and on the way out stuck up two fingers at his secretary.

Chapter 27

Following my consultation with Dr Schwarz, I decided to be forever done with psychiatrists, quacks, snake oil merchants, shamans: the entire lexicon of raggle-taggle brain tinkerers. On my train journey back to Weybridge, outraged that I'd been thought of as a homosexual, I disguised my feelings from my fellow passengers by staring fixedly out of the window the whole way. Half an hour later, still fuming about how much money I'd wasted on my ridiculous misadventure, I cycled away from the station, tearing at my pustulating ear. En route to my home, I made a detour to the Labour Exchange to see there were any jobs to be had.

Tugging at a metaphorical forelock, my mouth stuffed with humble pie, I asked the weasel sitting at his desk, a cigarette butt behind his ear, if the job shovelling coal at Woolworths was still available. Grumbling, he got to his feet and stuck his head out of the small window before which I stood. Peering out myopically, his face framed in the standard brown and cream paintwork dictated by officialdom, he resembled a fractious garden gnome. "Ah, Mister Monteath-hyphenated-Matthews, thought I recognised you, he sneered. "Nah, wot can I do for you today?"

"I was wondering whether the Woolworths job's taken?" I asked in a timid voice.

No reply was forthcoming. Instead he removed a cigarette from a pack of Woodbines and said, "Gotta light?"

I presented my Ronson lighter. "Nice lighters, Ronsons," he said, flicking the lid to ignite it. I had the distinct impression, from the way he looked at me over the blue flame, that if I'd told him to keep it, he'd have found me a better job.

I was tempted for a moment—after all I had two Ronsons, one a present from the flatters and another from Dick—but pride kept me from sinking so low.

"Yes, aren't they?" I replied, reaching out a hand to take my lighter from him.

I detected a flicker of disappointment on the weasel's face.

"Hang on a tick," he said, withdrawing his face from the window, "Woolworths? I'll check me records." He disappeared into his office and returned holding a buff-coloured folder. "Nah, the job's not been filled yet. Just take this slip to the manager, Mr Armitage, and say we sent you. Sooner the better I'd say." The weasel scribbled on a piece of paper before putting it in an envelope and handing it me. "Here you are, chum."

I couldn't believe my ears. I had been elevated by the weasel to being called his chum. Convinced I'd deluded myself and it was no more than a slip of the tongue, I bowed and scraped my way backwards out of the Labour Exchange and on to the street.

It was already two-thirty in the afternoon. I cycled back to Willow Cottage and there polished off three ginger biscuits, a pitted apple and a pint of water. In thin freezing rain, I climbed on my bike once more, pulled my Burberry's collar high to my ears and rode the three miles to Walton-on-Thames. I already had a good idea of Woolworths's location in the High Street, so went directly there. Once inside the store, I removed my dripping Burberry, slicked down my hair, and asked one of the shop assistants at the nearly empty sweet counter for Mr Armitage's whereabouts. With barely a glance at me, the young girl pointed out an elderly man in a long khaki-coloured cotton coat, standing at the far end of the shop.

My interview with Mr Armitage could not have been briefer. "Mr Armitage?" I enquired, as I came up alongside him.

"'Oo wants to know?" he replied without looking up, his hands busy lining up tiny jars on a counter full of penny knick-knacks.

"My name's Bob Matthews. Sorry to trouble you, sir, but the Labour sent me about the job you haven't filled yet. I've got a note from them for you."

Mr Armitage waited until the jar he was handling was precisely balanced on its base before lifting his head to look me up and down. He took the note I proffered, read the contents and said, his weary face mapped with wrinkles, but smiling nevertheless, "There's not much of you, is there Mr Matthews?" Pausing, he asked, "Like shovelling shit, d'you?"

"Shit, sir?" I was incredulous. "I thought it was coal."

"Don't mind me, son," said Mr Armitage kindly. "Just my little joke. Come with me and I'll show you what has to be done. Then you make up your mind."

I followed at his heels through the back of the shop and out into a dank yard at the rear of the building. A line of cobbles, slick with rain, led to a small brick outbuilding.

"This is the boiler room," wheezed Mr Armitage. Giving out a phlegmy cough, he spluttered, "Blimey, this chill don't 'arf fuck up the tubes."

Opening a door into what appeared to be a room piled halfway to the rafters with coal, he said, pointing a finger, "The boiler's to the right." Standing aside to allow me a view of a large black cast-iron boiler with all sorts of gauges attached to it, he continued, "Well now, old Aggie here, that's what we call the boiler, heats the whole store and the offices behind. Greedy bitch needs feeding a lot. That's what you do, feed it. See the temperature gauges there? The needles have to be kept on the red line by shovelling coal into Aggie's belly from eight in the a.m. 'til we close." Mr Armitage's eyes roamed over me. "If you think you can do it, just say so, and you can start tomorrow. You also have to help out for two hours in the middle of the day with the daily deliveries of coal. We've a woman who comes in to assist, so you can take a rest now and then."

"She? She!" I questioned, astounded that a woman would undertake such heavy, dirty labour.

"Oh, yes, wait 'til you meet our Lorna," grinned Mr Armitage. "Well, what's your answer?"

"I'll take it sir, but if it's okay with you, can I start day after tomorrow? I've things to sort out at home." In actual fact, I had nothing at all to sort out, but Mr Armitage had caught me on the hop and I simply need time to gather myself.

"Good man. No 'sirs' here though," said Mr Armitage, thumping me on the back. "That's all right by me, come along to the office now and we'll do the paperwork."

By the time I left, I figured that no more than fifteen minutes had elapsed since I'd arrived. Now, head down over the handlebars of my bike, I wheeled away, wondering if I'd committed myself to a job I couldn't handle. On the face of it, the work looked harder than flatting and, worse still, at five pounds a week, it paid a lot less. I consoled myself with the thought that, I'd leave just as soon as my beautiful Margot Anderson of the Bluebell Girls in Paris fixed me up with an audition at The Windmill Theatre. Meantime, now that I had a job of sorts, I could afford to eat more than the porridge, biscuits and apples I'd lived on since Dick Purkis left on his sales trip.

It was still dark, and very cold, when I turned up for work on the due date, a couple of minutes before eight. Mr Armitage had arrived ahead of me and was waiting in the yard. In the glow of a lamp, I saw that he held clothing of some sort in his hands. "Good morning, young man. Try this on," he said, tossing me a boiler suit. "You'll need it over that nice clobber of yours. The coal delivery comes at eight-thirty. Ah, here's our Lorna to give you a \hand," he said, turning about, as a towering female strode round the corner. Clad in an overall and wearing black Army boots, she acknowledged my presence with a cheery wave. In a loud voice that went with her size, she boomed, "Pleased to meet you, chum. Glad you're here, I've been fagged out doing this job on me own."

"All right then, Bob," said Mr Armitage. "I'll leave Lorna to show you what to do. If you need to know anything, just ask. Okay?" With that, he walked off, whistling.

"Right, Bob, you follow me," commanded Lorna, as she made her way into the boiler room. Switching on the single overhead light, she said, "I'll give you a minute while you change, eh? It's okay, I promise to turn my back. Just say when you're ready, all right? "

Feeling hopelessly embarrassed, I went round to the rear of the boiler and quickly stripped my clothes off. I was thankful for the heat coming from the boiler as I pulled on the boiler suit over my naked body. "Okay, Lorna, I'm decent," I called, walking into her view, holding my clothes in my hand, "anywhere I can hang these up?"

As Lorna pointed out two massive brass hooks behind the door, she said, looking serious, "Nah then, Bob, I gotta say it. You look like you've never seen a shovel, let alone used one."

"Not true!" I lied vehemently. I gave her a sly look. "Tell you what, Lorna, let's see how you use one."

Lorna was not to be so easily duped. Grinning, she said, "Oh, no. Your turn, chum." She picked up a shovel lying on the floor, as if it weighed hardly more than a toothpick, and handed it to me. Holding it by its wooden handle, I waved it like a cricket bat. Lorna stepped forward, pressed her big red face close to mine and said, "I thought so."

But for the dark smudge of hair on her upper lip, with her bright eyes and curling black hair, Lorna might have been attractive. An intimidating figure, six feet in height, with huge bosoms and mighty forearms, she was certainly not a female to mess around with. Yet I liked her on sight, because she was friendly and marvellously direct.

"Okay, Lorna, I give in," I said with a laugh, passing the shovel over to her. "Go on. Show me how."

Lorna released the catch to Aggie's cast-iron furnace door with a casual flick of the shovel. Giving me a wicked, knowing look, she purred, "Nothing to be ashamed of. I daresay there's plenty things you can teach a girl like me."

I watched admiringly as Lorna swiped her shovel deep into the pile of black nuggets before despatching a sizeable quantity of coal into the glowing furnace. "There," she said, standing back. "Your turn. Easy when you know how, like everything, eh?" Her offhand remark was accompanied by a meaningful stare, her eyes settling on me for an uncomfortable age, before I was forced to turn my head away.

I took the shovel from Lorna, dug into the coal and swung it in the general direction of the furnace. I joined in with Lorna's laughter as I watched the half dozen bits of coal I'd managed to dig out dribbling off my shovel like rabbit poo.

"How you do it so easily Lorna, beats me," I said, full of admiration.

"I was a Land Girl during the war, chum, that's how. Diggin' earth was my job. Day and night it was. *'Digging for Victory'*, like the posters said. Diggin' up potatoes, cabbages, and carrots, is what I did from forty-three 'til the end of the war. I started in this work when I was sixteen. Nearly twenty-seven nah, never known nuffink else."

A look of sadness flickered briefly over her face. She dismissed it with a nonchalant heave of her massive shoulders. "Come on, Bob, just watch me," she said. "You'll get the hang of it in no time."

And indeed I did, in less than half an hour. The weeks I'd spent flatting had bulked up the muscles in my arms, so strength was not the issue; technique, I discovered, was. It all came down to a question of timing, really, of not rushing, but planting the shovel at the base of the pile of coal and then thrusting, using the left leg as a fulcrum, before directing the contents of the loaded shovel, aided by a swing of the hips, directly into the furnace. Rhythm: plant, thrust, swing, plant, thrust, swing. In no time at all, I was a shoveller up there with the best. Wiping the sweat from my brow, I was swelled with pride at how easily I'd mastered the art.

Throughout my labours Lorna sat perched on a heap of coal bags observing me. Eventually, she said, "That's it, you're there. Now, let me tell you about the temperature gauge on Aggie. If you see the pointer, the black needle, move to the red line, tamp down the furnace, or else you'll blow the place up. You must cut off the oxygen. C'mon, let me show you how." She got to her feet and, picking up a metal bar from the floor, hooked its kinked end to a metal slide just above the closed furnace door. Pulling it to the left, she said, "Have a look-see."

Standing on tiptoe, I peered through the thick glass window of the furnace. To my surprise, the fiery redness had turned grey almost instantaneously and the sound of Aggies's roaring belly had dwindled to the merest rumble.

"Okay, that's it," said Lorna, returning the tamping lever to its original position. "It ain't 'ard, Bob, all you gotta do is keep an eye on the temperature, like. When the pointer falls below the black line you stuff in more coal."

"But I thought I had to shovel coal all day long," I said. "At least, that's what Mr Armitage told me."

Lorna's laugh powered out of her like a force eight gale. "Nah! Most of the day you sit on yer bum. The boss was having you on." Her great bosoms heaving, Lorna laughed, "His way of checking if a gent like you would take the job on."

"Gent like me?"

"Yeah. You talk ever so posh, doncha? We've never had gents down here before. You must have been bleedin' 'ard up to take this job."

It was my turn to laugh. "Yeah, Lorna, I'm stony broke. Anyhow, I'm here now and I'll try and make the best of it."

"You'll do, Bob," said Lorna, pinching the skin on my bicep between iron fingers.

I heard a vehicle pulling up outside, followed by the honking of a horn. "It's the coal delivery, Bob," said Lorna. Giving me a wink, she added, "We'll have it off in no time, won't we darlin'?"

As I emerged from the shed, I saw the delivery man standing on bags of coal at the back of the lorry. Waving at Lorna, he shouted, "Mornin', luv. See you got some 'elp today." Pushing his cap to the back of his head, he asked, "Or is he the new boy friend? Bloomin' unfaithful you are, Lorna gel. I thought I was your bloke."

"Shut yer face, Bert!" Lorna bawled. "This 'ere's, Bob. He's a gentleman, so you had better treat him proper. If you don't, I'll 'ave yer." She went to stand with her back resting against the lorry, her left arm cocked, the right one tensed on her hip, ready to take the weight of a coal sack, in what was clearly a regular routine

"Promises," Bert grunted, as he upended a sack of coal, before transferring it onto Lorna's right shoulder.

Calling out to me, "Your turn, now," Lorna headed for the coal shute.

I tried to follow Lorna's example precisely. But unlike the easy manner in which she carried her sack, mine threatened to fall off my shoulder. Forced to support my tottering load with my right arm, and with my knees buckling under me, I staggered after Lorna. As I reached the coal shute, I heard Lorna shouting from the bunker below, "Chuck it down the slide, Bob. You carry 'em, I'll stack 'em."

Unstable as my feet were, I managed to despatch my load down the shute without falling over. "Oi, you! What d'you mean, two sacks?" Lorna protested. "One at a time, chum."

"I didn't know I was carrying two sacks," I mumbled in reply. "I just brought what Bert put on my back."

"That shit Bert! Thinks he's being funny. Hang on, I'm coming up now." Lorna came up the steps in a rush, her hobnailed boots hammering across the cobbles as she made for the lorry. "Bert, what d'you think you were doin', putting two sacks on Bob's back?"

"Just a joke, Lorna," replied Bert sheepishly. "Didn't mean no 'arm." He looked at me apologetically, "You all right, chum?"

I nodded, but Lorna was having none of it. "Do that again, Bert, and I'll have your guts fer garters." She stood, fiercely protective, fists clenched, glaring at the poor driver. "Now let's get on with unloading," she growled. "And no more tricks."

Between us, Lorna and I unloaded and stacked a ton of coal in half-hundredweight sacks. Dripping with sweat on that freezing January morning, I watched the delivery lorry drive off, before returning to the warmth of the coal shed. Lorna was already making ready to leave, her coat buttoned and collar turned up against the cold. "I'll be back at twelve, Bob," she said. "You'll be okay. Just remember what I told you. If you get stuck for any reason, fetch Mr Armitage, and he'll really mess it up for you." With that, Lorna issued one of her hurricane laughs, opened the shed door and vanished outside.

In reality I had little to do except keep an eye on the temperature gauge and every so often, shovel coal into the furnace. It was dirty work but nothing as arduous as Mr Armitage had said.

"How did it go?" Lorna asked, when she returned at midday. Before I could reply, she said, "Told you so. Easy, wasn't it? Nah then, what you goin' to do now, during your break? See, I noticed you didn't have any sangwiches or nothing, so I brought some for you." Ignoring my feeble protests, she thrust a package into my hands and said, "Eat up. If it makes you feel better, come pay day, buy me fish and chips and a pint of mild."

Unfolding a thick cloth in which the sandwiches were wrapped, I gazed hungrily on two thick hunks of crusty bread with slices of spam in between. “Thanks, Lorna,” I said. “It was awfully decent of you to do this.”

“It’s nothin’. You just look like you needed feedin’, that’s all,” replied Lorna. “And, if you fancy a cuppa, I’ve got some in me Thermos ‘ere, and... Oh, yeah, yesterday’s *Mirror* for you to read.”

The next day, Lorna turned up at eight and stayed with me in the coal shed until I left in the evening, explaining that she preferred having me for company rather than being alone at home. To my consternation, she became increasingly affectionate towards me as the hours went by, calling me sweetheart and darling, loading her conversation with double entendres, finding all kinds of excuses to press up against me. However, because she’d been so kind to me, I could not bring myself to tell her how much she embarrassed me and that I wished she’d stop.

Matters finally came to a head soon after Mr Armitage handed me my pay packet on Friday. He said he was pleased with me, adding that Lorna had told him I had worked extremely hard, which was not exactly true. “If you carry on like this, lad, who knows, I might get Head Office to up your wages by five shillings. “Keep it up, Bob, and see you Monday,” said Mr Armitage kindly, his trousers legs neatly furled with bicycle clips, ready to be off home on his ancient upright bike.

As soon as he left, I opened my pay packet and removed three pounds ten shillings in notes, which I put in my blazer pocket. I then shook out a further nine shillings and ninepence in copper and silver coins. Vainly, my fingers continued to fiddle around in the bottom of the sac in case I’d missed some. But hard as I tried, Woolworths’s munificence remained fixed at three pounds, nineteen shillings and ninepence net.

Stuffing the coins into my trousers pocket, I heard Lorna's voice from somewhere behind me, saying, "Goin' to buy me that drink then, darlin'?"

Startled, I swung round. Lorna stood grinning at me from a few feet away. Her plump cheeks were scrubbed and shiny and she'd tied her dark hair back with a red ribbon. Instead of her usual Army boots, she had greenish court shoes on her feet, and wore an all-enveloping brown tweed coat buttoned to the neck. She turned her ankle coyly, as I gaped. "Cat got your tongue sweetheart?" said Lorna. "Or had you forgotten you're buyin' me fish and chips and a pint?"

"No, course not," I lied. "Give me a mo' to change out of this kit. I'll have a quick wash and then I'll be with you. Okay?"

"Don't be long. Can't keep a lady waiting."

Thinking that Lorna looked more like a London bus than a lady, I fled into the coal shed and unhooked my clothes from behind the door. I hastily removed my boiler suit. Hidden behind Aggie, naked as Adam, I stood unbalanced, struggling to pull on my trousers. With them still at half mast, I was suddenly sent sprawling by Lorna's two hundred pounds of muscle landing on my back. Stunned, I fell heavily on my side, where I lay with my bare heels scrambling on the concrete floor. Eventually, I managed to get myself into a half-sitting position with my body supported on my elbows. As my head started to clear, I found Lorna's eyes staring into mine from an inch or so away, before she fell on top of me.

"God, I fancy you," she said, in a thick voice, as I struggled to slither away from under her body. "C'mon, sweetheart, I know you fancy me, too. It's quiet down here, so go on, fuck me."

Still half stunned and unable to resist, I watched aghast as Lorna clambered off me and lumbered to her feet.

Unbuttoning her coat, she flung it aside. She wore nothing underneath. Then, straddling me like some colossal white bear about to feast on a floundering salmon, she attempted to plant her open mouth on mine. I turned my head from side to side to evade her slithery tongue. Lurching forward on her arms, I was very nearly decapitated by her cannonball breasts, featuring aureoles as big as dinner plates. I flinched from her as she breathed into my infected left ear, "Kiss me tits. Lick 'em. Go on. With your tongue, darlin'. Please."

For the two past two years I'd been preoccupied with having sex and now that the opportunity had presented itself, I was scared witless.

"No! Lorna. Lorna, no, please, no!" I pleaded, heaving her off me. Staggering upright, I pulled up my trousers, and stood looking down at Lorna, who now sat cross-legged, rocking back and forth on her haunches. Tears streaming down her cheeks, she mewed quietly to herself, "Oh Christ, what have I done? I'm so sorry Bob, so sorry Bob."

She looked so forlorn, part of me wanted to tell her it was okay and not to worry. Instead, I picked up my shoes and the rest of my clothes and tiptoed out of the shed.

On the following Monday I gave in my notice. Mr Armitage looked at me over his spectacles. "Lorna?" he asked.

I gave a noncommittal shrug.

"Thought so," he said. "Sorry, old man. Same as the last bloke."

Chapter 28

Having severed my connection with Woolworth and Co. and escaped the over-enthusiastic attention of Lorna in the coal shed, I found myself in the not unfamiliar situation of being jobless. However, since I'd only been there a week before, I decided a visit to the weasel at the Labour Exchange would be inappropriate. Instead, I made up my mind to be a famous author and try my hand at writing a short story. The kind of plot Raymond Chandler might have dreamt up had been germinating in my mind for some days. I'd won several prizes at school for the essays I'd written, so I was convinced that *The Sketch*, a publication Dick subscribed to, would readily accept my stuff.

There was also the added attraction of the paper paying a fiver for published stories of a thousand words in length. If I wrote three or four of them a week, I'd make a very decent living for myself in surroundings far more comfortable than a coal shed, I decided. So absorbed was I by the brilliance of my idea, it never once occurred that any of my stories might be turned down. The prospect of rejection never entered my head.

So with my mind overflowing with literary juice and my stomach lined with ginger biscuits, the only edible food I could find in Dick Purkis's larder, I sat down at his old Imperial typewriter and commenced typing. Using one finger at a time I tapped away at the keys on lined paper I'd purloined from Dick's filing cabinet.

I was soon gripped by the substance of my yarn: *Da Brains*, a story about the Sicilian mafia in New York, G-Men, J. Edgar Hoover and nasty goings-on during the Prohibition era. Lost in my fantasy world, impervious to the cold in the cottage, the downpour outside and the unfed chickens, I completed my story by early evening.

I was convinced the narrative was outstanding, the dénouement irresistible. Al, my main character, a mobster, sees his boss gunned down on the street, his skull blown apart, his brains spewing out. "Jeez, boss," Al says sadly, "youse always were da brains." In my overheated imagination, I visualised the story editor of *The Sketch* selling the rights to Hollywood and suggesting James Cagney star.

After reading and re-reading the manuscript, I corrected a few errors with a fountain pen. Unfortunately, some of the worn typewriter keys had made no impression on the paper, so I reformed some words in ink before stuffing the manuscript into an addressed envelope. As an afterthought, I wrote a covering letter to the story editor by hand, in which, to prove I was no amateur, I falsely claimed to have been published in several overseas publications. Too late to catch the post that day, I saw to it the envelope went off the following morning. I then raced home on my bike and commenced writing another story immediately.

Entitled *A Brilliant Smile*, this one, too, had a surprise ending, though it was about an impoverished working-class rugby player who'd lost his front teeth in a scrum. Only by seducing an heiress, who paid for a new set in porcelain, was he again able to face the world. The tale spoke of a dark secret behind the brilliance of the rugby player's smile and only in the last sentence was all revealed.

"Oh, yes," I said to myself as I gummed down the flap of the envelope, "this story has even more going for it than the first one. Oh, gosh, yes."

The scarlet post box at the entrance to the Hamm Court Estate was once again honoured by a visit from the soon-to-be-famous author, Colonel Ian Monteath—the classy pseudonym I had chosen. In the full flush of my boundless naiveté, I was so certain the editor would respond by return of post with a couple of cheques that, in anticipation of them, I cycled down to the nearest grocery shop in Weybridge and treated myself to a tin of bully beef to supplement my meagre rations.

For six mornings thereafter, I stood at the gate in the cold and near dark, watching out for the flickering yellow light of the postman's bicycle lamp rounding the bend. But each day, in response to my supplication "Anything for Matthews?", he called out, "Sorry, no," before vanishing in the gloom and rain. Eventually I gave up, saw to the chickens and retreated back into the warmth of the cottage.

I commenced writing a verse play which I thought my local drama group, the Desborough Players, might like to put on. My pathetic, inept attempt at versification was an idiotic venture, although then I considered it ground-breaking in style and substance. Offstage, an interlocutor opens the drama with these deathless words:

Wouldst I could remove this noxious tumbling in my mind
A mad machine, whose gears engage,
Slowly, inhibited by the grit of fear
It stutters, starts, then grinds,
And falters to a halt.

On and on the play went in the same, excruciating vein. After twenty or so pages, even I, possessed as I was by monumental self-delusion, recognised my worthless writing was better off consigned to the dustbin.

Some weeks later, after Dick Purkis had returned home from his travels, I received two rejection slips from *The Sketch*. Identical, they were unsigned and stated baldly that my submissions were unsuitable for publication. I threw them away in disgust, swearing at the editor for not recognising near-genius when he saw it.

By this time, I had been forced, out of dire financial necessity, to revisit the weasel at the Labour Exchange. In a change from the manual work he'd found for me in the past, this time he secured for me a job as a clerk at Lankester Motors, a Ford agent whose main office was in Baker Street, Weybridge. The company was obviously desperate, for the personnel manager asked me to start that very day.

After a perfunctory exchange of information, I was led to the sales office, where I was placed alongside an attractive young woman called Molly Burns. Her role was to instruct me in the arcane business of costing up work sheets, which she wanted to get on with that very minute. However, the letter I'd received in the post that morning from Margot Anderson, my Bluebell Girl in Paris, which was in my pocket and still unread, was of more interest to me. So, using the excuse I needed to visit the lavatory, I ripped open the envelope as soon as I had privacy. With my eyes racing over the neatly formed handwriting, I read:

Dear Bob,

I started at the Windmill two weeks ago and as promised at the YC Ball in December, I had the chance of speaking to Vivian Van Damm a couple of days ago. I said I had this friend with a wonderful singing voice, (you better had!) who was dying to be onstage. He, Vivian that is, said okay, if he (that's you) would like me to fix it up. Auditions are held every Friday at 1 p.m. and you could have a go. If you wish, come backstage on Thursday afternoon. I'll get you in to see the matinee. I think it'll help if you see the theatre before your audition. Please ring me before I go up to London in the morning, if you can, so I can arrange things. WEY 82346 is my home telephone.

Love, Margot

With '*love*', she'd ended her letter! *With love*! Carefully, I folded Margot's letter, and emerged from my malodorous surrounds to face an impatient Molly drumming her fingers on her desk.

"Got the runs, then, Mister Matthews? First day nerves, I shouldn't wonder."

"Something like that," I mumbled, marvelling at my good luck. Quite unwittingly Molly had provided me with a first-class excuse to take Thursday afternoon and all of Friday off. The runs! How could the management argue with that? No doubt I'd have my wages docked, but it'd be worth it, because on the following Monday I'd hand in my notice, and thereafter be a big singing sensation in London.

"Sure you're all right?" asked Molly solicitously. "You look a bit flushed."

"Yeah," I replied, stifling a giggle at her unintentional pun. With an effort, I applied a brave, yet stricken expression on my face. "I'll be fine soon, if you can put up with me dashing off to the toilet every so often."

"'Course I can," said Molly sweetly. I felt a pang of remorse. She was so gullible, so innocent, with her wide blue eyes and open face.

Thanking Molly for her understanding, I got down to the business of calculating the number of man-hours involved, at so many shillings per hour, for each car repair or service. If Lankester Motors had been aware that my first job had been in a similar capacity with Messrs Remington Rand and how useless I'd been, I'd have been seen off the premises immediately.

Later that night I asked Dick if he could see his way to lending me five pounds. I promised to repay him at a pound a week, if that was acceptable.

"Yes, okay," Dick answered. Then, sounding concerned, he asked, "Are you in some kind of trouble? You've never asked for a loan before."

Quickly assuring Dick I was fine, I told him in some detail about the audition at The Windmill, the cost of travelling up to Soho on successive days, adding that taking Margot out for a five-bob meal somewhere would be a nice way of repaying her.

"All right, since you've finally got yourself a decent sort of job, I'll give you the fiver in the morning." Dick dismissed my thanks with a tolerant smile. "No trouble, old chap." Pausing for a moment, he continued in a more serious vein, "Bob, I've heard you warble in those talent contests at the Regal Cinema in Walton. How sure are you that you're good enough to appear at The Windmill? Isn't that where that Dickie Valentine chappie started his career as a call boy? As a crooner he's dashed good, isn't he?" Seeing my crestfallen expression, Dick added hastily, "Didn't mean to put you down you old chap. Still, it's something to think about isn't it?"

Actually, I considered my voice to be infinitely better than Dickie Valentine's. I kept my conceit to myself, for Dick, in his old-fashioned, very British way, surely believed that it was modesty that separated gentlemen from self-opinionated big mouths. And big mouths like me were not tolerated in his household.

"I've thought about it a lot, Dick," I replied, earnestly, "a great lot. That's all I want to be. A professional singer."

"I imagined you fancied being a writer like your dad."

I burst out laughing. "After those rejections from *The Sketch*, not any more."

At work the next morning, I asked Molly if she minded my making a private phone call from the office.

"Company don't allow private calls," she said, "but seeing it's you, I'll find something to do while you use the phone. But be quick, won't you, please?"

Giving Molly a beguiling smile, I promised her I would. Waiting until she left the room, I dialled Margot. The phone was answered almost instantly. I visualised her lovely face as we spoke, hardly able to prevent myself from telling her I loved her, as it seemed I was driven to say to every girl who showed me the slightest affection.

I listened intently to Margot's low-pitched purr, instructing me how to get to Soho, saying how much she had missed me. Almost faint with the delightful prospect of our meeting on Thursday afternoon, I heard her say goodbye. Overcome with emotion, I kissed the receiver and, breathing a soft adieu, replaced it on its cradle.

"Done, have we?" asked Molly, who had seated herself at her desk without my being aware of it. "What did the doctor have to say?"

"Doctor?" I asked. "What doctor?" Realising my mistake, I said hurriedly, "Oh, yes, the quack, thanks for asking. Caught me on the hop you did, Molly."

"I just wondered," she said, giving me suspicious look. "One doesn't usually plant a kiss on the phone after speaking to a doctor. Unless the doctor's a woman and you fancy her. Do you?"

I gave Molly a rueful smile, put on the famous Bob Matthews charm and, chancing my luck, decided to take Molly into my confidence. If she failed to play along with me, my job at Lankester Motors was up the Swannee. Shifting my seat closer to hers, I asked, my voice now the deepest of deep baritones, earnest, but at the same time, pleading, "Can you keep a secret, Molly?"

"Secret? What secret?" Molly demanded, sitting bolt upright in her chair. "Depends."

Seeing my hang-dog expression, her eyes softened, turned curious as she leaned closer. From her body language, the tell-tale touching of her hair, the intensely inquisitive smile, I knew she could be trusted to help me.

"You were right, Molly," I replied, now deeply penitent. "I wasn't on the phone to the doctor. I'm sorry I lied to you, really I am, but you see, I'd just been given the most marvellous news!" As a ruse to fully engage Molly in my conspiracy, I wrung my hands excitedly, looked about me, and whispered behind my hand, "Molly, just imagine it! I've got an audition at The Windmill Theatre on Friday."

Incredulous, Molly clapped her hands to her face. Her eyes bright and thrilled, she asked, "Audition, what for?"

"Singing. I'm going there to sing. Be a professional singer. It's all fixed. But if I'm to have Thursday afternoon and all of Friday off, I'll need your help, Molly. Please, please, will you?"

Even though I had wheedled with all my might, Molly appeared unsure.

"Dunno how, Bob," she said. "I'd like to, but..." Her voiced trailed away as I gazed at her adoringly. "I mean, you only started day before yesterday an' all."

"Well, if I dash off home after the mid-morning tea-break on Thursday, maybe you can tell the sales manager I've a bad stomach upset. Say I mentioned it to you on Monday, and that I've been running to the loo ever since."

"Talk about pushing your luck," laughed Molly. "Okay, I'll do it, but I can't say if your job will still be open next Monday, unless you produce a certificate from your doctor."

Relieved, I said, "I'll deal with that when it happens. But hey!" I punched the arm of her chair. "You can tell your friends it's through you that Bob Matthews, the famous singer, got his first break."

"You cocky sod," giggled Molly. "C'mon now, if we don't deal with this pile of time cards neither of us will have a job."

I turned up at the office on the Thursday morning looking decidedly peaky. I had the experience of my drama society to thank for my make-up. A touch of Dick's talcum rubbed well into my cheeks, plus a touch of black carbon from a burnt matchstick gently applied underneath the eyes, suggested deathly illness. So pallid was my face, with dark shadows under my eyes, some fellow workers remarked I shouldn't be at work. Giving them a wan smile, I wafted my way over to my desk, where Molly nearly passed out when she saw me.

"Blimey, Bob, you look really shot. Are you having me on, or are you really sick after all?" "

No, I'm fine, Molly, just a bit of powder and stuff. I thought it would help your story."

Shortly after eleven I slunk from the office, took the train to Waterloo, then the Underground and, following Margot's directions to the letter, arrived at Piccadilly Circus at around midday. After a short walk down Windmill Street in Soho, I arrived at the entrance to The Windmill Theatre. To pass the minutes I had in hand, I scanned the billboards outside. Several were filled with photographs of tall, statuesque, virtually nude women posed in Grecian and Roman tableaux. The women's disdainful eyes seemed to follow me as I gazed, shocked and embarrassed by the exposure of so much flesh.

Their breasts took my eye the most. I had no idea that they could be so large, so proud, and so wonderfully upright. I stood for an age, soaking in the vision, in a state midway between horror and lasciviousness, before I caught sight of Margot in one of the pictures. Standing at the rear of a group, coyly masking her naked body with a giant urn of some sort, she obviously appeared nude on stage. I was horror-struck by the discovery. Although I had seen copies of *Variety* magazine advertising the Windmill Girls I really had no conception from the illustrations, which showed the girls in costume, that they also posed unclothed. As I made for the stage door at one side of the building, I asked myself how my Margot could do such a thing.

In a wooden cubicle, an old crone sat guarding the entrance. I said to her I'd come by invitation of Margot Anderson. Asking me to wait, she spoke on the telephone. Just a few moments passed before Margot, clad in a long scarlet silk dressing gown, came out to greet me.

Even more beautiful than I remembered, her carmine lips widened into a gleaming smile the moment she saw me.

"Come on in" said Margot, steering me into a corridor crowded with women in varying stages of undress, all of them flying about at speed, some in sequinned costumes, others whose bare breasts jiggled about wildly as they ran, and a few adorned with tall headdresses who moved more carefully. So dazzling was the kaleidoscopic display of bare flesh and glitter that I dared not let my shy eyes linger as I followed Margot into a small unoccupied dressing room.

"Ta-da!" sang Margot, swivelling about. "This is my dressing room. I share with two other girls, Elle and Zizzie, who came over from Paris with me. Come, you can sit in that spare chair while I put on my make-up. The show's on at two. You can watch it. I've arranged a seat for you in the circle, if that's okay?"

Margot, a huge powder puff in hand, turned on her stool in front of the mirror, framed all round with electric light bulbs.

"It's good to see you, Bob," she said, blowing me a kiss. "Hope you're ready for tomorrow? Just in case, I suggest you lubricate your voice before you come. The thing to do is pop into the *White Horse Inn* in Piccadilly Circus and sink a whisky before you come here. Or two," she added, her long false eyelashes fluttering on her cheeks. "That should do the trick."

Utterly overwhelmed by the colour, the noise, the whirlwind of fantastical theatricality, I was momentarily speechless. Allowing myself to drown in the depths of Margot's violet eyes, I said, "Scotch sounds like a good idea. By the way, I hope I've got the right song. It's *Where is your Heart*? from the film *The Third Man*. Do you know it?" I added that I'd performed the song many times before in talent competitions and it had always gone down well.

"'Course I do," replied Margot, removing her dressing gown. "Everyone does."

Her back now facing me, I revelled in the sight of her breasts reflected in the mirror. Glowing in the bright light, they were perfect white porcelain globes with pink-rouged nipples. I continued to sneak glances whilst her hands worked busily on her face. Enchanted by the sight of her sculptured beauty as she sat, unconcerned by my presence, her hips and lower body enfolded in scarlet silk, my heart beat like a jackhammer. Truly, she was a real-life Titian, a goddess, my angel. I was hopelessly smitten.

Margot turned to face me. "Well, that's it," she said. "What do you think?"

Allowing her gown to fall to her feet, she rose to her feet, clad in no more than a pair of tiny sequinned briefs. Swallowing hard, I replied, meaning every word, "You are the most beautiful woman I've ever seen in my life."

"You're so sweet," retorted Margot, teetering up to me on her high heels to kiss me. I felt the touch of her lips on mine. "So sweet," she said, returning to her dressing table to touch up her lipstick. "So gallant. Now, if it's all right with you, I'll have someone show you into the theatre. Any minute now the call boy will be here." With that, she flung her dressing gown over her shoulders and marched out into the corridor, with me padding behind, a page in attendance to his queen. "Oh, Bob," she called out, before joining a gaggle of similarly dressed women, standing by the wings, "I forgot to say, your audition's at one o'clock tomorrow. You're number four after the comics."

It had not entered my head that there were others to be auditioned, and certainly not comedians. So it was with feelings of unease that I followed a stagehand into the darkened auditorium. Showing me to a vacant seat, he said in a Scots brogue, "You'll get a good view of them tits from here, pal." From my vantage point, I made out the theatre was half empty; the members of the audience, men in mackintoshes or topcoats, seated well apart from their neighbours.

Settling down in my cramped seat, I heard a band in the orchestra pit striking up a stirring piece of vaudeville music. Then on came *les girls*, high-kicking in perfect unison and, unexpectedly, wearing drum majorette costumes. How was I to know that the Lord Chancellor decreed full nudity was banned onstage unless the performers were utterly immobile, as perfectly still as statues?

The high-kicking routine, received with some enthusiasm, was followed by a mime act, drawing hardly any applause. Then it was the turn of a crooner in a shiny padded-shouldered suit with wide lapels. His name was unknown to me, but I thought him to be a pretty decent singer, although someone I felt I could easily match. At first that seemed encouraging, but then he bowed off with hardly a handclap. Was this how it would be for me?

The curtains opened again and there for our delectation was a tableau portraying Aphrodite rising from the sea, surrounded by ten naked acolytes whose tremulous breasts shivered with the effort of restraining their breath. Margot was in the centre, cradling a blue plaster seashell to shield her modesty.

The man in the seat next to me, I noticed, had mislaid something in a trouser pocket. I found his constant fumbling about irritating, so I moved a couple of seats away from him in order to enjoy the acts that followed. The nudes received by far the greatest applause. The most thunderous of all was reserved for the finale, which involved the entire complement of the Windmill Girls, who cavorted, danced and turned handsprings and cartwheels around a half-dozen naked females each of whose only claim to outerwear was a glittering red heart, made from shiny material, covering their groins.

I left the theatre feeling somewhat deflated. My first experience of vaudeville was not as I'd expected it to be. In my fantasy, I imagined the theatre to be grander somehow, more opulent, and the show to be more like an Esther Williams or Betty Grable movie set, with a string orchestra, a mass of beautiful girls and male choirs in white tails. But by the time I got home and had finished describing all the day's happenings to Dick over a steaming plate of fish pie, my spirits had revived somewhat, sufficient to say to Dick, "Well, we've all got to start somewhere haven't we?"

The following morning I rose even earlier than usual to complete my chores—see to the chickens, sweep up dead leaves around the house and so on—while Dick kindly made me a decent breakfast of porridge, poached eggs, tea and toast. "Big days, my boy," Dick chuckled, "require full stomachs, what?"

At just after ten, with my hat pulled down over my heavily Brylcreemed hair, my Burberry buttoned to the throat over my newly pressed blazer and my yellow and gold striped school tie, and with my razor-creased trousers clipped at the ankle, I biked to the station. On the journey up to Waterloo, I pulled out my cherry-wood pipe and, adding to the already-heavy tobacco fug in the compartment, puffed away contentedly on the few scraps of foul tobacco the bowl held. As the train rattled on, I silently sang to myself the lyrics of *Where is your Heart*? over and over again.

Arriving at Piccadilly Circus somewhat earlier than I had anticipated, I hung around Eros, stared in shop windows, and eyed up pretty office girls until I remembered Margot's suggestion of oiling my vocal cords with whisky. I found the *White Horse Inn* easily enough, and after ordering a single whisky, took myself off to a corner overlooking the street. As slowly as the minutes dragged by, so too did my apprehension grow, reaching a point where I found myself trembling uncontrollably. To settle myself down, I drank another whisky, then another, and a fourth one at just on twelve-thirty. Totally unused to drinking hard spirits, I found the warming sensation of it more than pleasant, its heady effect wonderfully calming. Margot had been right about whisky oiling the vocal cords, for by now my I felt wonderfully well-oiled through and through.

With just the slightest of staggers, I made my way out of the pub and was in the foyer of The Windmill Theatre at a quarter to one, in perfect time. At five minutes to, the receptionist picked up her telephone. At three minutes to, she gave me a nod, saying, "You're on. Good luck." A uniformed attendant opened the door to the auditorium, pulled wide the curtains, and said, "I'd take my coat off sir, if I were you." Removing my Burberry with a hasty embarrassed flourish, I entered the place like a reluctant bridegroom. From somewhere in the depths of the auditorium, I heard a female voice call out, "Robert Matthews, please. Down to the stalls in front of the stage."

Lurching unsteadily in the gloom, down the sloping floor that seemed to move under my feet, I was met by a small woman with a tight mouth and a head of coiffed dark hair.

"You have your sheet music?" she snapped, turning my legs to jelly. I nodded, drawing it from my blazer pocket.

The woman ripped the sheet from my hands, "Know who I am?" she asked, her voice a flail.

I shook my head.

"I am Sheila Van Damm and that is," she waved my sheet music in the direction of a grey-haired man sitting in front of the apron, "my father, Vivian Van Damm, the manager of this establishment. After your performance we will decide if you are suitable for us. Is that clear?"

I nodded, now feeling decidedly queasy.

"Very well then," said Sheila Van Damm. "When you get onstage, hand your music to Charlie, your accompanist. Tell him what key you sing in."

Intimidated by the formidable Sheila Van Damm, I went woozily up the short flight of steps at the right-hand corner of the stage. My accompanist was seated at a grand piano which seemed to shrink, then enlarge, then shrink again, the closer I got.

Charlie held out his hand, "What key do you sing this in?" he asked, reading the title page of the sheet music I'd handed him. "A bit boring, *Where is your Heart*?" he remarked dismissively, "but it's okay, I know it. So, Robert, what key?"

"In C," I replied, watching his fingers rippling over the keys in expert fashion, hitting the right chords instantly.

"Okay, I'll play the intro, and then you come in," said Charlie, looking up at me, his fingers poised over the keys.

As I opened my mouth to sing the opening verse, I became aware of the big breakfast I'd eaten earlier welling up from deep inside me. Failing to keep it down, the entire contents of my stomach shot out from mouth like a projectile and landed on the stage in a liquid puddle. There was a deathly silence. The auditorium was a tomb. My tomb.

Tottering about the stage, dragging a handkerchief from my pocket, with which to wipe my mouth, I witnessed Vivian Van Damm attempting to clamber out of his seat, his mouth opening and shutting like a fish. He daughter ran to his side to assist him. The impresario appeared to have only one good arm, the other dangled uselessly at his side. Lurching his way to the apron of the stage, he stood with his good arm outstretched, index finger pointed at my head, purple-faced with rage.

"Out! Out! Damn you, out! Get out!" he screeched.

Sheila stood at his side shouting, “Someone clean up the bloody mess and remove that little shit!”

‘Little shit’ required no explanation. I was the shit. Instantly sobered by the Van Damms’ outburst ringing in my ears, I took to my heels. I collected my Burberry on my way out of the theatre, sat down on the pavement outside and wept.

A hand touched me on the shoulder. “Are you all right lad?” The rough accent sounded Scottish. I looked up and found myself staring into the bloodshot eyes of a grizzled, middle-aged man, whose face wore a concerned expression.

“Come on, I’ll give you hand up,” he said.

He helped me to my feet.

“Thanks, I’m okay now,” I replied.

“Och, well, shake on it, laddie,” said the stranger.

Involuntarily, I stretched out my hand, and felt my fingers squeezed in a vice-like grip.

“Now, you must have a few coppers for me?” he demanded. The Scots accent was now rougher than ever, as he fixed me with a drink-sodden glare and increased the pressure on my fingers, “One good turn deserves another. Go on, son, gimme a few coppers.”

“I’ve only got a few pennies myself,” I pleaded, now terrified. “I need it for the Tube, to get home.” I felt like screaming as my fingers continued to be pulped. Ignorant of my plight, pedestrians carefully stepped around us, before accelerating on their way. “Okay, okay,” I said, finally, “You can have it all.”

“Och, that’s more like it, laddie,” he said, still maintaining his hold as I fiddled around in my overcoat pocket for the change with my other hand.

Almost as if he'd had a sudden change of heart, he abruptly released me and started brushing me down. "Are you sure you're all right, sir?" he said, his voice sufficiently audible to be heard across the street. Stepping away from me, an innocent smile on his face, he touched his forelock as a police constable came round the corner. "Evenin', officer," he said, giving the constable a furtive glance. Nodding politely in my direction, the beggar shuffled off down the street.

"Just in time, was I, sir?" asked the fresh-faced constable as he came to my side. "Did you give Jock any money?" I shook my head. "That's good, then. He's a bad lad, that one. My advice, sir, stay away from Soho. It's a dangerous place for a young bloke on his own."

Chapter 29

After what had occurred at The Windmill Theatre, I could never face my beautiful Margot again. Even if I tried phoning to beg her forgiveness, she would surely cut me off. Who could blame her?

Now poor Margot was certain to be hauled over the coals by the two Van Damms for misrepresenting me as a sensational new singing talent. Even worse, her so-called boyfriend was no more than a drunken, bilious youth, who had defiled their famous theatre. In the annals of London's theatreland, surely my infamous performance was a first.

I debated whether to tell Molly, who had covered for me in the office, the whole truth. I knew she would be dying to know how I'd got on at the audition. However, when I turned up for work the following Monday, with my colleagues remarking on the wonderful recovery I'd made following my debilitating stomach complaint, I told Molly a pack of lies without a mention of the surfeit of whisky, nor of my ignominy. I said the Van Damms had turned me down because I was too young for what they had in mind, suggesting I try again in a year or two's time.

"Bob, that's terrific!" exclaimed poor deluded Molly, her face lighting up with excitement. "Like you said, I just know you'll be famous one day."

I nearly kissed her for her support, particularly since Dick, whom I had expected to be sympathetic, had been decidedly unenthusiastic after hearing my heavily sanitised version of events. I had expected at the very least a pat on the back from him, followed by 'hard cheese, old boy' or something of the sort. Instead, he said "Time to forget the stage, Bob," followed by a dismissive shrug that really hurt, "Face facts. There are thousands of chaps who can sing as well as you and the entertainment business is all down to luck. If I were you I'd think about settling down in your job and making a career of it."

Dick's response had been so different from what I'd expected of the best friend I had in the world, I very nearly burst into tears. But, on seeing my crestfallen face, he cheered me up by suggesting we go to the Friday night, YC dance at the High Pines.

"Fat chance, but you can try and fix me up with one of the dames who'll be there," he laughed. "Put in a good word for me, you smooth bastard, and then," Dick thumped me on the chest affectionately, "do a few of your one-armed press-ups in the bar and earn a few bob. That'll go some way to repay me the fiver I lent you for the audition, eh, what, what?"

As it happened, the YC dance was a huge success. I might have blown my chances of ever being a professional singer, but after downing several brown ales and listening to a decent swing band I began to feel a lot better about myself. Furthermore, besides extracting a pound from my press-up challengers, I introduced Dick to a sweet-looking girl who was reading history at Oxford. Most unusually for the kind of YC girls who frequented the High Pines, she was immediately smitten by my eccentric older friend.

Dick was so taken by the young woman, who had chosen to dance with him the entire evening, he spluttered and stammered about his good luck all the way back to Willow Cottage.

"Mary's coming to the pictures with me on Wednesday," he said, his voice shrill with excitement. "She's jolly good-looking, don't you agree, Bob?"

"Absolutely, Dick," I replied, truly pleased for his good fortune.

"I've been turned down so often I didn't think I stood a chance," said Dick. "She's clever, too," he added proudly, puffing himself up in his car seat. "I imagine I'll have to bone up on my history or she'll think me a real dum-dum."

Whistling tunelessly, Dick drew up alongside the kitchen window of Willow Cottage. "You go off to bed, young man," he said. "I'll join you in a few minutes after I've drained the radiator."

Some fifteen minutes later Dick slid into his bunk bed below mine. Kicking at the underside of my mattress, he whispered, "Sorry to wake you, old chap, but Mary's a cracking fine girl, isn't she?" As if seeking my blessing, he questioned, "I should ask her to marry me, don't you think?"

"Abso-bloomin'-lutely", Dick.

As the days passed, I buckled down to my job at Lankester Motors and with Molly's help avoided making a pig's ear of it. The pangs of my disappointment gradually receded and then boredom set in. The onset of spring made me feel edgy, too. Dick was dating Mary, sometimes taking her to the theatre, at other times to the High Pines and occasionally, the cinema, too. Whereas I, for the first time in a very long while, had no females I could call on. Perhaps my reputation for dropping a girl the minute I saw someone prettier was the reason. Conceited with a capital C, I fantasised that every girl I met was gagging to sleep with me, yet none ever did, either because I was too scared when it came down to it, or they were. Whichever it was, I was still a virgin in my twenty-first year with no change on the horizon, whereas, judging by the way things Dick's affair was hotting up, he appeared in danger of losing his virginity any time now.

"Unlike you, Robert," he once said to me, quite out of the blue, his facial expression lofty, "I wouldn't dream of trying to seduce a girl without asking for her hand. In my book, a decent chap doesn't do that sort of thing, does he?"

I wanted to say "You are a pompous lying ass", but instead replied with a rueful laugh, "You're damn right, Dick. I'm not a decent bloke. Although I can never stop myself from trying to have a go with girls, it hasn't got me far, has it?"

"You mean you haven't...? Well, you know..." Dick sounded utterly disbelieving. His pale eyes shone; the multitude of freckles on his cheeks merged into one ginger mass as he thrust his face forward to within an inch of my nose.

"Nope, nope and again, nope," I replied, withdrawing hastily.

"Well, I never," he breathed, shaking his head. "I thought there was not a virgin in town because of you."

"Thanks, Dick. You're such a pal."

"You mean to say those late night treks you made back from Waterloo station were for nothing? And what about that Margot, the Bluebell Girl? Didn't you...?"

"No."

"Blimey! Strike me down with a feather."

That, together with other conversations in a similar vein, set me thinking. Perhaps Dick was right. Maybe the thing to do was ask someone to marry me. Others as young as me did it, why not I? I had a steady job of sorts, and if I kept my nose clean I was bound to get promotion. As a couple, we could surely earn enough together to set up house. We could lay off having kids for a while...

This kind of ridiculous daydreaming persisted for a week or two. I even made the mistake of viewing Molly in an amorous light, and asked her out to the Regal Cinema in Walton-on-Thames one Friday night. She knew how little I earned and seemed happy enough to sit with me in the one and ninepenny seats right in front of the cinema organ.

Even before the curtains went up and the organ's monstrous pipes subsided out of sight with a last glimpse of the organist's hands flailing at the keyboard in a grandiose crescendo, Molly had squeezed up close to me. Her head lay on my shoulder, her fingers entwined in mine. As much as I tried, inch by inch, to recoil from a rank odour emanating from her, I failed. Each imperceptible move I made away from her was matched by her pushing up against me with equal pressure, so that eventually I hung over the aisle in the dark and was forced to watch the film from a most unusual angle.

Standing for the National Anthem at the program's end was a delicious respite. Easing the stiffness from my neck, I gained a yard's distance from my co-worker, whose lack of attention to personal hygiene had previously gone unnoticed by me in our open office. In the confines of the overheated cinema, the dense cigarette smoke combined with the dirty linen of the audience in which was trapped the unsavoury reek of flesh bathed just once a week on Mondays, created an atmosphere that stank. I staggered out, with just sufficient grace to hang on to her hand. We emerged into the foyer together, me sucking in the fresh air and Molly gazing at me with her bright eyes.

"'What a lovely film, Bob!" she cried in a rush. "That Dick Haymes—what a beautiful voice," Molly giggled. "Just like yours."

I asked with nauseating coyness, begging for ever more compliments, "Do you really think so? Maybe I'll sing for you one day. How about that?"

"Ooh, will you, Bobby?" said Molly adoringly. "Promise?"

I realised I'd slipped up, at least as far as Molly was concerned. I was now in a terrible bind. It was obvious she had fallen for me, but after the experience of the cinema, I'd already made up my mind I couldn't see Molly again. There had I been, imagining her as a possible bedmate, a cheerful, friendly soul I could nestle up with. Now the very thought of such a thing turned my stomach. Life was terribly unfair.

There was nothing for it. I had to resign my job. Beckoning was another trip to the Labour Exchange and a talk with the weasel behind the counter. Excuses would have to be made to Dick, who thought I had a future with Lankester Motors. I kept putting off the decision, making the pretence to Molly that I couldn't take her out for a while, because I'd been given a part in a Desborough Players production and had to rehearse. She accepted the lie with dogged good grace, saying she'd come and see me in the play. If only she had done the opposite and slated me for being a shit, I'd have felt better. Poor Molly, the proverbial doormat, just lying here for the big boots of Bob Matthews to trample on.

After a couple more weeks of avoiding Molly, I knocked on the door of the works manager's office and offered my resignation. Inviting me in, he heard me out without saying a word. After I'd ended my stammering—the excuse I'd given was I'd been offered a better job elsewhere—he removed the pipe from his mouth and said, "I hope for your sake it doesn't entail any maths. I was about ready to give you the push for all the time sheet cock-ups you've been making, anyway."

Speechless, I only half-heard him add, "I'll arrange for Personnel to have your wages and other stuff ready for you to pick up tomorrow." Replacing his pipe, he gave a thin smile. "No hard feelings and good luck." Even before I had backed out of the office with my tail between my legs, I noticed his eyes had returned to his papers. I was already an ex-employee.

To my great delight and surprise the weasel at the Labour Exchange had sought other pastures. In his place was a keen young fellow hardly older than me, who riffled through a sheaf of job vacancies in the locality.

"Sunbury, too far?" he enquired, selecting one that caught his eye. "Here's a job I think'll fit you. Goldtan, you know, the firm that makes suntan cream. Minimum school cert, it says. Well, you've got that, I see. The job is lab assistant to the head chemist. Pay's good. Six quid. Two weeks hols. Eight-thirty to five. What do you think, shall I phone them and make an appointment?"

I couldn't believe my luck. Sunbury was about ten miles, I guessed. I figured I could get there in about forty-five minutes on my bike. What's more, the pay was marginally more than I had been earning at Lankester Motors. "Yes, please," I replied. "I can go straight down now if they want."

I waited whilst he retreated from his cubbyhole to make the phone call from the office behind. He returned smiling. "Okay, chum, they'll see you now, if you hop along." He scribbled the address on a piece of paper. "Ask for Captain Wooley, he's the guvner. Obviously one of those civvies who hang on to their Army rank. Bloody silly if you ask me. But it's not for us poor chaps to reason why. Oh yeah, the place is down Sunbury High Road, just by the water works on the Middlesex side of the Thames, can't miss it, he says. Good luck, then. Let us know how you get on."

As I thanked him profusely, he gave me a sly wink. “No trouble, chum,” he said, “Fancy going with me to the flicks sometime? Fancy that, do you?” Pretending I’d not heard, I gave him a perfunctory nod and was out of the building in seconds.

Chapter 30

Goldtan's premises consisted of two small ramshackle buildings down a narrow alleyway adjacent to the Victorian waterworks at Sunbury-on-Thames. I rapped timidly on the door marked Entrance, removed my cycle clips and stepped back a pace or two. Hot and sweaty after my bike ride, I eased a finger between my perspiring neck and my detachable plastic collar, one of the two I'd acquired from Woolworths a couple of years before, having learned they could be scrubbed clean each night and be dry by morning. But now, the non-absorbent material felt so wet and clammy, I would have cheerfully sacrificed appearance for comfort. Despite feeling wretched, I pasted a smile on my face I hoped would charm Captain Wooley.

My smile tightening into a rictus, I waited for a response. None came, so I knocked loudly once more. This time the door was slowly opened and a bald man wearing a white laboratory coat peered out.

"Yes?" he enquired carefully, as if I might have been a beggar or someone from the Seventh Day Adventists. Deciding I didn't fit either description, his features visibly relaxed. "Who is it?" he asked.

I was about to acquaint him with my mouthful of a hyphenated surname, which sometimes impressed prospective employers. But taken off guard, I blurted, "Bob Matthews from the Labour Exchange."

"Well, you got here pretty quickly," the man replied, his expression mellowing into a smile of welcome. "Come on in, come in." As he stepped aside to allow me to pass, he stuck his hand out, saying, "I am Captain Wooley. Take a pew in my office, Mr Matthews, won't you? Through the door on the left."

Wooley's office was tiny and sparsely furnished; no files, no paper work anywhere to seen. As if reading my mind, Captain Wooley chuckled, "The paper work is dealt with at our head office in Brixton. We've only recently acquired these premises from a competitor who went bankrupt. While we sort things out, the basic production's done here. I use this place," he tapped the surface of the metal desk, "to meet people, or take a break." Inviting me to sit down, he said, "I guess you've heard of Goldtan?"

"No, sir," I replied, hoping my negative response wouldn't fell me at the first post.

"Lord Almighty!" he exclaimed, in astonishment. "Truly not? My boy, we spend a fortune on advertising, and you've not heard of us?" Seeing how quickly Wooley's face pinked up, I thought he was about to send me packing. Instead, he surprised me by saying, "No matter, no matter, let's just see if you are the answer to our prayers, shall we?"

My job interview, if it could be called that, was over in five minutes flat. No sooner had Captain Wooley read the notes I'd brought with me from the Labour Exchange, than he threw up his hands in delight. With his head bobbing, he mouthed aloud my scant qualifications as if they merited the Nobel prize.

"Assistant scientific officer at the Army Operational Research Group, well, well. And Cambridge School Cert, too, I see. With distinctions." He sat back in his chair and laughed, "Young sir, I am over whelmed by such bounty! My last lab assistant was a dolt. He had more time off than he had on. Now, down to business. When can you start? Monday do you? Pay's six pounds a week with two weeks annual holiday, et cetera, et cetera, eight-thirty to five p.m. Overtime's time and a half." He got up from his chair and pumped my hand. "Follow me," he said, "let's have a shufti at what you have to do."

As he walked me down a short corridor and into an area set about with large stainless steel vats on trestles, all of which looked in need of a good clean, he informed me I was his sole employee. Pointing out the yellowish gooey substance the vats contained, he said, "The stuff in the vats is pure lanolin, in the process of being liquidised by heat. I'll go through the other stages later on, but the resultant cream is just what the Great British public needs to prevent sun burn. It also converts pale freckled Anglo-Saxon flesh to a warm Mediterranean tan. Well, at least, that's the objective."

Captain Wooley swung around, "Your job, Bob, is keeping an eye on the temperature of the ingredients, weighing the materials—". He stopped in mid-sentence to point out stacked barrels marked Pure Lanolin. "You also keep the place clean and tidy. As you can see, it's a bloody mess."

I had to agree, the place was filthy. Wooley continued to witter on as I looked about me.

"The filling machine you see in the corner has broken down. An engineer's coming to fix it next week sometime. So, until then, you'll have to operate it manually. Don't worry," he said, seeing my worried expression, "I'll give you a hand. Well, that about covers it."

As if my job description had fatigued him, Captain Wooley leant against the wall. “If you’ve no questions,” he said, “I’ll stop for a fag now.”

Pulling from his pocket a lighter made from a brass shell case, he lit a cigarette from a pack of full strength Capstan. Inhaling deeply, he allowed his eyes to dwell on my face, “Incidentally,” he said, before exhaling a stream of blue smoke, “if you don’t mind my saying so, you’ve a very nice tan, yourself.”

I said my skin colour was natural. By way of explanation, I informed him my mother was Italian. I always avoided mentioning I’d been born in India, for the response from those who questioned me, was inevitably a relieved “Ah”, as if their conviction I was Indian had been proved right. Furthermore, I’d become both bored and touchy about having constantly to explain where I came from.

“Eyetie, eh?” smiled Captain Wooley. He pulled on his cigarette. “I thought India, myself. No matter, Mr Matthews,” he said, blowing out more smoke, brushing aside the small matter of my racial origin. “Think you can do the job?”

After working with Dr Cosmo Payne at the Army Operational Research Group, the manufacture of Goldtan was a doddle. “Sure,” I replied, “Dead sure.”

“Good-oh,” replied Captain Wooley. “Then Monday it is, at eight-thirty. Welcome aboard.”

After another handshake, I was on my way back to Willow Cottage in Weybridge, bearing my good tidings to Dick, who had a hard time of it keeping up with the number of jobs I’d had in the past couple of years. The worst of it was none of them were getting me anywhere. More depressingly, my ambition to be a professional singer remained as distant as ever.

That weekend, I celebrated my success by accompanying Dick and his new girlfriend, Mary, to the High Pines. For the first time in a long while I had no girlfriend of my own in tow. Now, to my surprise, I found none of the girls present was interested in dancing with me more than just the once.

It was only when I went to the lavatory that I discovered the reason why. Admiring myself in the mirror, I saw to my horror I'd forgotten to stuff my left ear with cotton wool, something I'd always been at great pains to do. The sulfa ointment my GP had prescribed had failed to staunch the suppuration and there was a nasty odour coming from my ear. Blushing with shame, I pictured myself dancing cheek to cheek with my erstwhile partners, and them recoiling from me as I tried to pull them close. By now hugely embarrassed, I shrank into a chair in the corner of an anteroom by the bar. Nursing a beer, I tried to merge with the wallpaper until Dick was ready to go home.

I didn't feel any better about myself when I awoke the next morning and spent the rest of the day in a state of self-disgust, convinced my days of being attractive to girls were over. By now I was certain the news of my smelly ear was known to every girl in town. I was sure to be shunned, never to be invited to parties or functions again, and worst of all, to remain girlfriendless until the damned ear either fell off or a miracle cure was found.

Dick told me brusquely to grow up, take a bike ride, get some fresh air, allow the breeze to dry out my ear. I figured it was good advice, so, as the evening drew in I decided to see how long it would take me to cycle to Sunbury at racing speed. The experiment would be useful, if I was ever to be late getting to work at Goldtan.

By the time I crossed Walton Bridge, I had already shaved a full five minutes from my previous ride. Head down over the handlebars and pedalling furiously, I managed to reduce the time to the waterworks at Sunbury by another five. Satisfied with my performance, I dismounted by the alleyway leading to Goldtan. At that moment, I thought I saw someone resembling Captain Wooley, weighed down by containers in both hands crossing the narrow passage. I wondered whether I should pop in and say hello, but deciding against it, I turned about and cycled home again, this time at a more leisurely pace.

At six-thirty on Monday morning I did my usual chores and, since it was my turn, fed the chickens as well. I brought Dick a cup of tea and scoffed down a plate of rough porridge oats before leaving in good time to cycle to work. I'd thrown off the doom and gloom of the weekend and was looking forward to sorting out the mess at Goldtan, better by far than spending my days calculating time sheets, as I'd done so poorly in my last job.

As I slowed to take the turn past the waterworks, my approach was halted by a fire engine blocking my path. All that remained of Goldtan as a going concern was a roofless blackened hulk. Firemen stood about picking at debris. By what had once been the front door, a policeman stood in deep conversation with an agitated Captain Wooley. I stood gaping, my mind refusing to take it all in, until I saw him wave to me to come across.

"Matthews," he choked, "don't know what to say." Clasping his head between his hands, he said, "As you can see, we had a fire last night. Obviously, there can be no job for you now." Then, gripping me by the arm he pulled a five-pound note from his pocket and gave it to me. "Take this, lad. I hope you find another job soon."

Was it Captain Wooley I'd seen acting suspiciously the previous evening, or just someone who looked similar? Seeing how distraught he appeared and considering how generous he'd been to me, I decided I'd been tricked by the light and put it down to some sort of aberration. But now I was faced with a wholly unexpected problem. I had no job and no idea where I could find one.

Over the last couple of years, I'd entered several talent competitions at the Odeon cinema in Kingston-on-Thames and often passed the Alfred Marks and Brook Street Bureaux on the way. Since Kingston was a mere ten-minute bike ride away, I decided to see what the agencies had to offer.

I headed for the nearest of the two, the Brook Street Bureau in Eden Street. Since I had dressed with some care for my first day at Goldtan, I looked respectable enough to be interviewed. However, it was with some trepidation that I parked my bike outside their premises and took a flight of stairs to the office, where I was confronted by a notice stating opening time was nine o'clock. It was still only eight-thirty, so I absently wandered up and down Eden Street to while away the time.

Down by a church on the right, I came across a recruiting office, whose windows were plastered with posters extolling the virtues of the Army, the Royal Navy and the Royal Air Force as careers for young men. The temptation to enter and sign up on the spot almost overwhelmed me. There would be no more looking for work. I'd never again want for anything. Since everything was provided, I would no longer worry about enough spare cash for cigarettes, pipe tobacco and the odd beer. I stood there convincing myself I'd never make it as a professional singer, so why waste my time pursuing a forlorn dream? My future was right there in front of me.

It had briefly been my intention to join the Air Force, and I'd only been deflected from doing so because of the competing attraction of the numerous pretty girls I met soon after arriving in England. I stood outside the recruiting office castigating myself for having been such a fool. After all, I'd learned to recognise every single fighter plane flown by the

British, the Germans and the Japanese during the war from a *Jane's* encyclopaedia. I could answer any question on the subject thrown at me. In my mind, I out-Biggled Biggles as a fighter ace and had notched up hundreds of kills in my Spitfire Mark 9. That I'd probably be despatched to Korea after passing out never occurred. Even if it had, I'd have relished the prospect of my Vampire jet taking on Korean MiGs in mortal combat. My mind in the clouds, my body nudged, shoved by pedestrians hurrying on their way to work, I decided the Royal Air Force was the life for me. But I was abruptly brought down to earth by the sound of bells from the nearby church chiming nine o'clock.

A few minutes later I found myself pushing open the office door of the Brook Street employment agency. Facing me across a large desk was a formidable-looking harridan. About forty, she had flaming red hair, a coarse complexion nearly as florid, and a disagreeable expression on her face, suggesting she was not as yet ready for business. Waving a cigarette, she heaved her bulky form up from her chair to confront me. As she barked "What can I do for you?" she hacked several times into a handkerchief drawn from her sleeve.

"I'm looking for job," I quavered, ready to cut and run.

"What sort of a job?" the woman enquired icily. She looked at me as if I might have been something the cat had dragged in. "You do know the Brook Street Bureau specialises in management and office situations," she continued, with a cold stare. "Since you are here, I imagine you have the appropriate educational qualifications?"

Swallowing, I replied nervously, "Er, yes, I've a Cambridge School Cert."

"Cambridge School Certificate!" she shrieked, as if its worth was no more than coming third in a three-legged race. "Let me tell you, young man, most of our clients are graduates." Fixing me with gimlet eyes, she sighed heavily. "I suppose, since you are here I could see if we've some junior position that might suit."

She fetched a thin file from her desk drawer and consulted it. As she lifted the receiver of her telephone, she added, "It is difficult these days to find positions for coloured people like you." I digested her remark (coloured people like me?) as she dialled and I was just about to speak up when she silenced me with an imperious hand. "Is that the Witwatersrand Gold Mining Company?" she asked. "Oh, good. Kindly put me through to Mr De Kloop, will you please?" After a fractional pause, I heard her say, "Ah, it is Mr De Kloop I'm speaking to. Well, this is Mrs Weatherall from the Brook Street Bureau here. I'm calling about the vacancy in your post room for a post boy. I have here a young coloured gentleman who I think might suit you admirably."

Even though I stood more than half a dozen paces away from her, I was treated to an unintelligible roar coming from the receiver. One hand covering her mouth, Mrs Weatherall reeled from the sound. I stood slack-jawed with astonishment, trying to absorb Mrs Weatherall's description of me.

Having been brought up in the subcontinent of India and taught to believe I was superior to the locals, the Anglo-Indians and the Eurasian community, it was a salutary experience to find myself with the boot on the other foot. I'd been called a wog before, but I'd always shrugged it off as a joke. The revelation that Mrs Weatherall considered me an inferior was shocking, but it made me realise, ultimately, that I'd also been guilty of bigotry and racial discrimination all my life.

Nevertheless, I retaliated by shaking my fist and shouting, "How dare you? I am not bloody coloured. You don't even know a damn thing about me, do you?" Mrs Weatherall shrank visibly. "May I inform you, Madam, although you think of me as being coloured, this dark skin I have comes from my being suntanned. Suntanned, I tell you. Guess from where? Go on, guess." Before I could stop myself, I sneered, "From service in Korea, that's where."

My imagination was running riot now. I was Biggles the famous aviator again. On a roll, I said through gritted teeth, "You never gave me the chance to say who I am, or what I am, did you?" I took a deep breath. "Well, let me tell you, missus, I served in the RAF as a pilot officer in Korea. I've just completed my short-service commission and I was here hoping to find a decent job. Do you always treat ex-officers so shabbily?" Sniffing dismissively, I growled, "Coloured, huh?" I was enjoying the spectacle of Mrs Weatherall flinching behind her desk under my withering onslaught. Walking over to the front door, I called out, "Stuff your bloody job," and left the room.

I caught my breath at the bottom of the stairs and, as I calmed myself down, felt almost sorry for ruining Mrs Weatherall's day. Although I had hated her description of me, I realised her racism simply came from pig-ignorance. Compounding her rank stupidity, it was foolishness in the extreme to have offered an Afrikaaner the services of a coloured gentleman.

As I left the building the sun came out and lifted my spirits. Destiny called. Nothing now was going to stop me joining the RAF. Almost of its own volition, my bike wove in and out of the desultory traffic and led me to the recruiting office. I leaned my bike against a wall, swung the main door open and entered in a rush. Just inside, on the left, there were three tables. Seated behind the first of them was a naval petty officer. As a representative of the Senior Service, he presumably took precedence over the Army sergeant who sat alongside him. The last in line was a senior aircraftsman of the Royal Air Force. All three brightened visibly as I approached; I might well have been their first capture of the morning.

Smiling at the senior aircraftsman, I said, "I've come to join the RAF."

I was corrected instantly. "The Royal Air Force, sir," he admonished. "It is the Royal Air Force."

Abashed, I muttered my apologies and asked, "What do I have to do now?"

In his early twenties, with eyes as blue as the sky in which I was soon to learn how to fly, he replied, "Take a seat." Handing me a buff-coloured piece of paper, he said, "Just fill in the form. Name, address, age, that's all. He looked me straight in the eye, saying, "No offence, I have to ask this of everyone. But you can read, can't you? You'd be surprised how many who try to enlist can't."

"Yes, I can," I answered, which seemed to please him.

"Let me know when you are done filling in the form and I'll take you for your medical. That won't take long. Then we'll have a good chat afterwards and I'll fill you in. Okay?"

Completing the form took no more than a couple of minutes. Before I knew it, I was being led to a door at the far end of the room. The senior aircraftsman rapped on the door and took two paces back. A voice from within called "Come", at which the senior aircraftsman snapped his heels together. "Sah," he replied, "one for a medical, sah."

With that, he opened the door and urged me in. Facing me was a man wearing a loose white jacket with a stethoscope hanging from a pocket. Beside him stood an orderly, who came forward and asked politely if I would remove all my clothes.

Everything was moving so fast, I had no time to take in what was happening.

"All of my kit?" I asked nervously.

"Yus, chum, all of it, underpants an' all," he said, going over to stand by a weighing machine in the corner.

Meanwhile the doctor circled me with an amused expression on his face, as I divested myself of my Burberry, jacket and shirt, followed by my shoes and socks.

"And your trousers and underpants," he murmured softly.

Blushing red, for as usual I wore no underpants, I dropped my trousers and stood naked in front of him.

"No underpants?" questioned the doctor. "Bit bloody chilly for that if you ask me."

Beyond that, he made no mention and got on with the business of checking my lungs with his stethoscope. Now feeling hopelessly uncomfortable, I caught sight of the orderly giggling as the doctor turned me about. Shivering, I covered my nether regions with my hands.

"Needn't bother, young man," smiled the doctor, brushing away my hands. "I've seen more todgers than I've had hot dinners. Now let's have you." Stooping down, he ordered: "Cough. Now, again. Cough." Gulping, I did as he asked. Apparently satisfied with the outcome, he requested I sit on a chair, cross my legs and have my reflexes checked by banging a gavel on my knee caps. "You are a healthy enough specimen," he said finally. "Now open your mouth and let me have a look-see." After which he came round to peer into my left ear. "How long have you suffered from this otitis externa?" he asked grimly, standing back. "Young fella, your ear's a bloody mess."

I replied, "I've had it for about two years."

"Two years?" he exclaimed. "Well, that puts the lid on it. Sorry, but we can't take you. Get your ear fixed and try again.

As it is, it's no go." Summoning the orderly, he said sadly, "Show this man out, will you?"

Bundled out of the recruiting office and onto the street once more, my dreams of flying fighter planes shattered, I gazed about me in a state of bewilderment. Blindly, I retrieved my bike and rode off in a daze down Kingston's High Street. Baulked by pedestrians spilling off the pavement and onto the roadway, I slowed to a stop outside Bentalls, Kingston's flagship store, where I spotted a placard in a window announcing part-time vacancies for sales staff.

Pushing my nose to the glass, I read that the hours were Mondays through Fridays, mornings only, with a full day on Saturday. Noting my interest, the uniformed commissionaire standing by the main entrance sauntered over. To my surprise, he offered to look after my bike if I wished to visit the Personnel Department. As I thanked him for his kind, unexpected gesture, he wished me good luck and told me to head for the third floor, where I was sure to find Personnel.

I emerged half an hour later, having accepted a position in the sanitary ware department. My job was to sell the latest plastic toilet seats, of which the store had received a huge inventory it needed to shift quickly. "Not as warm to the bum as wooden ones," my manager-to-be had said, "but they are much more hygienic, so I am told." I was not about to question his opinion, happy enough I'd found work of some description after all. It would take me the best part of an hour to cycle to Kingston, but since opening time of eighty-forty was later than I was used to, I didn't see it as a problem. Anyway, I had afternoons off, which gave me time to look around for something more worthwhile.

It was a morning to savour. A putative lab technician at eight o'clock. Fired before eight-thirty. At nine, refused a job with a South African gold mining company on account of my skin colour. After which, even before it was ten, rejected by the Royal Air Force because of an infected ear. Finally, a part-time purveyor of plastic toilet seats, and it was not yet midday.

Chapter 31

As yet I didn't know it, but there were more surprises in store for me when I returned to Willow Cottage. Opening the door, I discovered a telegram from my mother lying on the mat. I sensed, even as my eyes lit on the envelope, that it was the harbinger of unwelcome news.

On average, I received a letter from my mother every three months. Prior to the messy divorce from my stepfather, her news was mostly gossip about her friends at the Attock Oil Refinery. She mentioned the Hurds, whom I recalled, the MacGiverns and the rest, with whom she filled her days indulging in mah-jong and bridge.

I pictured them lolling in their cane chairs on the verandah, sipping iced gin and lime, fanning their playing cards, bemoaning the changes in their lives since the British had left. Wailing about how things had gone to pot after Pakistan gained independence, they fantasised about the rolling green fields of home, snug country cottages in Devon where they planned to retire, cream teas, strawberry jam and the like. Most of the company's British employees had come out to India well before the war and had lived in a gilded bubble ever since. With no home leave during the war years, they had been unable to see for themselves how things had changed. Their minds refused to accept that the England they'd left so many years before was, post-war, a drab, dreary place in which to see out their days. No more would there be servants at their beck and call, nor pensions adequate to match the quality of life they'd enjoyed on the subcontinent. As they sweated in the heat of the plains, dreaming their dreams of home, they wallowed in a state of hopeless self-delusion.

After Maurice Cuell divorced my mother, the managing director of the Attock Oil Refinery had forced my mother to move out of her company bungalow. She was now holed up with Colonel Nick Grahame-Carter in a Rawalpindi hotel, together with my three brothers: seventeen year-old Richard, David who was thirteen and Ronald, aged four.

Of late, my mother's letters to me were hastily scribbled, each on a single page of notepaper. She now never mentioned her social life. I surmised this was because Nick Graham-Carter might have been blackballed from the Rawalpindi Club after their affair became public knowledge. Now that her social life had been seriously curtailed, my mother had little to write about, other than to comment on how boring life was in the cantonment. She longed for the day Nick's contract with the Pakistan Army would end and they could all come home.

I ripped open the telegram. The terse sentences ballooned up before my eyes as I read and re-read them.

Sailing SS Strathclyde on 15 Aug. Plse meet boat-train est. arr Kings Cross 3 pm 25 Sept. Plse book suitable accomm in local hostelry for the five of us near you. Love Mummy.

I continued staring at the telegram for a long time. The news was the last thing I expected. On one hand, I was excited by the prospect of seeing my mother and my three brothers. But on the other, my nemesis, Colonel Nick

Grahame-Carter, would also be in tow. The thought of encountering him again was horrifying. I allowed the telegram to flutter to the floor as I sat down at the kitchen table. As I reflected on what lay ahead, I noticed that Dick had left a folded note on the sideboard addressed to me. Flipping it open, I read:

Bob, old boy, you'll be delighted to know that Mary has agreed to marry me. Can't wait to tell you all about it when I get home about around seven. Don't wait supper for me. I've left some stuff in the cold box for you and a piece of Cheddar, which I know you like. Hey ho, Dick.

I reached down for the telegram and placed it together with Dick's note. It was ironic how one filled me with a sense of doom and the other delight. My dear friend Dick, the perennial virgin, thirty-three years old, inordinately awkward in women's company, who I thought would always remain a bachelor, had finally found someone who loved him.

I did as Dick suggested and by six o'clock had polished off the contents of the cold box. Replete, with a cup of tea at my side, I lolled in front of Dick's nine-inch black and white television set and watched the BBC news. Hazy film footage showing the Viet Minh mauling the French Army in Indochina preceded clips of a smiling Princess Elizabeth whose coronation was to take place on June 2, in two weeks' time. I wished the BBC had shown something of Princess Margaret, whom I'd always fancied. As I dozed off, I pictured myself on one knee asking her to marry me and being rejected because of my smelly ear.

Dick bounced into the room just after seven and shook me wake.

"Aren't you going to congratulate me?" he asked, sticking his hand out for me to shake. I leapt from my chair and pumped his hand up and down.

"That's terrific news, Dick!" I shouted. "When's the happy day?"

At the question, Dick's face sobered up. "Ah," he said, "there's the rub, old boy. The wedding's in early September at St Mary's Church in Walton. I'm afraid you'll have to move out before then, chum. Find somewhere else to live."

Stunned, I replied, with a laugh, "Naturally, Dick. Three's a crowd, eh? I'll start looking around for digs in Weybridge right away." The timing was uncanny. I'd have to move out just about the same time as my mother arrived.

"I'm truly sorry Bob," said Dick, sounding concerned. "I'll miss having you around, but I'll give you a hand finding somewhere decent, don't you worry."

I was seriously worried. All I had was a part-time job selling lavatory seats in Bentalls, no regular work in sight and the added concern of dealing with the problems my mother and Colonel Nick Grahame-Carter would surely bring to the equation.

Dick's insistent voice interrupted my grim musings. "Got to celebrate, old boy! What say we break open that bottle of sherry in the kitchen and have a noggin or two? Then we can start on the sloe gin, eh?" Slapping me on the back, he said, "Come on, old bean. Cheer up and wish me good luck." Infected by Dick's enthusiasm, I momentarily forgot my woes. Together, we finished the sherry and a bottle of three-year-old sloe gin and by midnight we'd both passed out in the sitting room.

I was woken by the postman on his rounds early the following morning. Bleary-eyed and with a thundering hangover, I pushed open the kitchen door and retrieved from him a thin foolscap-sized package too large for our letter box. I saw that it was addressed to me and printed with "Photographs Do not Bend". Intrigued, I lifted the flap and removed two photographs of myself I'd had taken by a friend, together with a letter from the *Surrey Herald*. My heart sank. I'd entered the photographs into a competition run by the newspaper, entitled *Stars of the Future*. My immediate reaction was that my entry had been rejected.

But the letter, signed by the editor, stated I'd been selected, together with two other men and three women, for a film test at Nettlefold Studios at Walton-on-Thames in a couple of weeks' time. The enterprising owner of the Palace Cinema in Church Street, a small independent picture house, planned to screen the film test for one night, with the audience selecting two winners, one of each sex. The prize to be an audition with the Italian film director Renato Castellani, who was casting newcomers as Romeo and Juliet for his new film version of the play to be shot in Verona in early 1954.

I called out to Dick, who had set about making some tea for us. "Listen to this! I've been chosen to make a film test at Nettlefold studios." I showed him the letter.

Rubbing a hand over his unshaven chin, he turned his bloodshot eyes in my direction and croaked, "Bloody film star, are you now?" Groaning, he mumbled, "Good luck, chum," and picking up his cup of tea, vanished into the bathroom.

I wished he'd been more responsive and pleased for me, but then, after the debacle at The Windmill Theatre, the numerous talent competitions I'd won without getting anywhere in show business, who could blame him for his lack of enthusiasm? Still, I was over the moon with excitement, and the announcement of the film test augured a better start to the day than I'd had the day before.

Dick emerged from his ablutions still looking the worse for wear. Cocking his thumb, he muttered, "Your turn. 'Fraid the water's cold. The meter's run out, you'll have to find sixpence if you want it hot."

The mirror in the bathroom had steamed over. I cleared it with a damp towel and peered at my image. Romeo stared back at me.

Chapter 32

I hardly saw Dick over the ensuing days. He now spent most of his evenings with his fiancée, at her parent's home in St George's Hill, and came home just as I was about to turn in for the night. Apart from small talk about the impending coronation, about which he enthused, we now shared little conversation except discussing whose turn it was to feed the chickens or pick the raspberries and such like.

Dick's mind was utterly occupied with his forthcoming nuptials. Besides, our relationship had changed in all kinds of subtle ways. I was simply the lodger now, and in the way. Since I treasured our friendship, it was imperative I find a proper job and also somewhere else to live.

Notwithstanding those problems, my first priority was finding a hotel for my mother, her lover and my three brothers. The only one in the area that had rooms available for such a large brood was the Oatlands Park Hotel, an Edwardian pile set in acres of landscaped parkland midway between Weybridge and Walton.

I visited the place as soon as I was able, with the view to making a reservation. The hotel manager, clad in a black frock coat looked like Frankenstein's monster. Tall, with waxen features, he stood behind a desk at Reception, licking his lips.

After a few words of welcome, the manager informed me that no alcohol was allowed on the premises, explaining the hotel was owned by Quakers. Just the thing to fix Colonel Nick Grahame-Carter, who likes his tipple, I thought.

The manager, who eyed me up and down as if I was a tasty tidbit he'd enjoy devouring, fell over himself to show me around the hotel's enormous bedrooms. Pirouetting about, his arms outstretched to emphasise the size of the rooms, his coat tails flapping against his skinny thighs, he assured me everyone could easily be accommodated within two double bedrooms. We then traipsed around the vast galleried drawing room. Pointing out the expanse of tatty carpet and the huge sagging sofas resembling mournful buffalos at a waterhole, he explained apologetically that the hotel was in dire need of refurbishing, having been requisitioned by the Army during the war.

"Therefore," he said, "we are able to offer a reduced rate for the rooms, inclusive of full board for your family of five persons. Making a small allowance for the little one, our rates will be... Er, let me see." He coughed lightly into his cupped fist, before continuing, "Five pounds and twelve shillings per week." His sunken eyes wavered over me momentarily. "Is sir also likely to be our guest at any time?"

Ignoring the question, I said, "Okay, that seems fine. Now do you want me to sign anything, or is that it?"

"No, no, sir, not necessary sir," the manager simpered. "However we would appreciate written confirmation from your relatives, when convenient. A telegram will do. Let me give you our telegraphic address, if I may." He pulled a card from his top pocket. "It's all there, sir."

Making a mental note to send off a postcard to my mother requesting Nick confirm the reservation by telegram, I left the hotel's premises feeling inordinately pleased with myself Never before had I been called upon to negotiate matters of such importance or been treated with such forelock-tugging deference. I fastened my cycle clips around the turn-ups of my flannel trousers and pulled my hat down firmly on my head. Giving the hotel manager a cheery wave, I set off on my bike, Dunhill pipe gripped firmly between my teeth. As I turned for a last look at the hotel, I saw the manager wave a limp white hand in my direction. I took this to mean he was enchanted by the magnificent sight I made.

When I told Dick of the outcome of my visit, he was enraged by what he considered to be profiteering by the Oatlands Park Hotel. Huffing and puffing, he protested he'd not been fighting the war for crooks and scoundrels and that I should return and renegotiate the price. Privately I thought the cost to be fair, though I agreed with Dick just to keep the peace.

Meantime, the days inched toward the coronation. The nation was gripped with so much nationalistic fervour that there was talk of nothing else. Caught up in the excitement of it all, I was unable to summon any enthusiasm for selling toilet seats in Bentalls' emporium. As I was heartily sick of the place, it was something of a relief when the manager of the sanitary ware department made it plain my days were numbered unless I pulled up my socks. Apparently, he'd overheard me joking with a customer that plastic seats induced more satisfactory motions than wooden ones.

"I was informed the lady took umbrage at your crass remark," said the manager. "And if, Mr Matthews"—it was all very formal in Bentalls—"you do it again, I shall have to sack you."

"She took umbrage?" I asked, with mock incredulity, repeating the question for the second time, "Umbrage? Surely, you mean bum rage?"

Mr Waller was unamused by my witty riposte and, sniffing dismissively, told me to be about my business or else.

Deciding it was sensible to keep my head down until I found a regular job, I counted off the days towards my film test.

On June 2, 1953 I watched the entire BBC TV transmission of Queen Elizabeth II's coronation, lasting a full seven hours. When it came to having the crown placed on the new queen's head, Dick was hugely offended by an innocuous comment I made about the damn thing being too weighty for the poor woman. As we sat side by side, riveted to his tiny television, he claimed I was a bloody republican and should be ashamed of myself for being critical of the queen. He genuinely believed that, after God, the new Queen and Defender of the Faith should be revered more than anything or anyone in the entire civilised world. His face stayed puce even though I protested vigorously I wasn't criticising Her Majesty at all, just stating a fact. He huffed and puffed as he sipped his sloe gin. He hadn't lost his wits, he was just being Dick. Crusty, old beyond his years, Dick was a throwback to the times when men doffed their caps at the mere mention of the monarch.

Chapter 33

My film test was fixed for the week following the coronation. To my surprise, I learned that the unremarkable buildings housing Nettlefold Film Studios in Hurst Grove, Walton-on-Thames, disguised one of the world's earliest movie lots. Created by a Mr Cecil Hepworth in 1899 to shoot one-reelers, the studios found initial success after filming Queen Victoria's funeral in 1901. With the increase in the number of picture palaces, as they came to be known, Nettlefold Film Studios continued to flourish throughout the thirties, forties and fifties. The 1951 film *Scrooge* was the studio's latest production. Featuring the youthful Alastair Sim, it presaged his illustrious film career, which a certain Mr Bob Matthews hoped to emulate, perhaps even surpass.

I was to be at the movie lot by eight sharp on the day of shooting. Up bright and early, with my face scrubbed pink and teeth well brushed, I joined the other five hopefuls at the wrought iron gates fronting the entrance to the studios. All three of the girls were very attractive, but one in particular, a pert brunette with enormous brown eyes and dark curly hair, caught my attention. There were two other men who, to my eyes, looked very ordinary, tweedy sorts, almost middle-aged and, I thought, standing no chance of winning against me.

As we stood, nervously avoiding each other's eyes, a cheerful-looking fellow emerged from a doorway. After calling out our names, he led us into the building. I picked up on the brunette's name, Susan Kenyon. My heart a-flutter, I followed closely behind her, enjoying the spectacle of her hips swinging under her yellow summer frock. We entered a hangar-like space hung with cables and lighting equipment, where we were all introduced to one another before meeting the film director. His name escaped me, since I was more engaged in drinking in the beauty of the delectable Sue Kenyon than in listening to our guide. Nevertheless, I gathered we were to take tea in the canteen before being handed our scripts to learn, after which would come the serious business of filming *Stars of the Future*.

"We will have to get a move on and be off the lot by mid-afternoon" said the director. "We're shooting *Krakatoa* later on. It's a new film with George Raft."

In the canteen, I offered to fetch Sue Kenyon's tea. "Why not sit down here?" I said, patting a folding wooden chair. "One lump, or two?"

"None," she replied. "Thank you, Bob."

Overjoyed she'd remembered my name, basking in her incandescent smile, I hastened away to the service counter, where I stood alongside a short, lean man with a swarthy face who looked familiar.

"How ya doin'?" the man said in a slow, deep, gravelly American accent and a voice I instantly recognised as George Raft's. I had seen too many of his gangster films to have any doubt. Thrilled to be conversing with such a famous man, I muttered I was fine, and thanked him for asking.

"You an actor?" asked George, stroking his head of slicked-down black hair, shiny as patent leather.

I quickly explained why I was present at the studios, admitting I wasn't really an actor, just a contestant in a competition for film hopefuls. Smiling his trademark menacing smile, he asked politely to be introduced to them. Staggered that George Raft could bring himself to show interest in us, I carried my tray of tea over to my table with him following on his built-up shoes. Shaking all of our hands in turn, George Raft graciously wished us all well, repeating each of our names before excusing himself.

"Gotta go and get made up," he said, showing his teeth. "Gotta look beautiful."

We all sighed as he sauntered off with an easy gait, leaving us stupefied that George Raft had bestowed his blessings on us.

Meeting such a big-time film actor in the flesh broke the ice and got all of us talking and laughing. Earlier, we had all been nervous of each other and shy of opening up. Now we couldn't wait to talk about ourselves. I didn't listen to what anyone else was saying, other than Sue Kenyon, who I discovered was twenty-one and, like me, lived in Weybridge. She was so sophisticated, so charming, so much in command, I prayed she didn't think me gauche for staring into her eyes like some captivated idiot.

As the time passed, we sat, feverishly excited, wondering what was to come next. Eventually a young female assistant turned up and handed each of us a single sheet of paper.

"It's your dialogue," she said. "Get stuck in and learn it. You've got ten minutes." So saying, she divided the group into mixed couples. "There's just one short scene," she said. "Each couple will play the same role as the others, so the audience can compare performances. All the boys will speak the same dialogue, same goes for the girls."

To my delight, I was partnered with Sue Kenyon who, within minutes of being handed her script, got her few lines of dialogue off pat. Mine was more of a struggle. I found the banality of the script so astonishing, I felt like throwing it away.

FADE IN.

Ext. Tennis court. Day

(A tennis court, overlooked by a mock-Tudor house. Diana, a pretty girl, swings a racquet, waiting impatiently for her partner, Brian, to emerge on court.)

DIANA Oh, do hurry up, Brian. It's cold out here.

BRIAN (off-set)

Be with you in a sec, Diana.

DIANA Oh, botheration. Why can't you be on time just the once?

(Brian hurries on set, a racquet tucked under his arm.)

BRIAN Here I am. Will you serve first, Diana, or will I?

DIANA Let's toss for it. Have you a coin?

(Brian fumbles in his pocket.)

BRIAN Sorry, no. Okay, then. Gels first.

DIANA You know you're pretty useless don't you, Brian?

BRIAN

I say, that's a bit rich, Diana, coming from you.

DIANA Well, you are. And that's that. Now, shall we play?

FADE OUT:

That was it. Each couple would appear on screen for at most a minute. I asked myself how any audience could possibly select a winner from such drivel. The whole thing was a charade obviously designed to publicise the Palace Cinema and had nothing to do with auditioning for *Romeo and Juliet*. I figured the owner of the cinema must have come up with a whole bundle of cash to cover the cost of studio time, money he'd never recoup, even with a full house. More puzzling, however, was this: how had Renato Castellani, the Italian director, been persuaded to be involved, other than for publicising his film on the cheap?

Sue laughed aloud as she read her part. "Can you believe this rubbish?" she chortled. "The whole thingy's a bit of a put on, don't you agree?" She paused for thought. "But then again, it would have cost the Palace Cinema a fortune to make a film of anything longer. Imagine—if we had a proper script, with rehearsals and all, the studio time taken up would be astronomical."

I had to agree with Sue. "What the hell?" I laughed. "*Romeo and Juliet* or not, let's give it a bash and have some fun, shall we? But hang on a mo', let's ask that chap standing there with a clipboard. Who knows? He might tell us the truth about the audition with Renato Castellani."

"Excuse me, sir," I said, approaching the man, who by now was giving instructions to a cameraman perched on a gantry. "Have you a second to answer a question?"

"Yes," he replied with some irritation, "but hurry up, will you? We've only got half an hour to do this job."

"Sorry to bother you, sir, but is it really true that winner of the competition is going to be auditioned by Renaldo Castellani for his film?"

"It seems so. Why do you ask?"

"Well, we are all supposed to playing tennis, but we are still in our normal clothes. It doesn't seem right somehow. And, as for the script—"

"Listen, cock," the man grinned, "I'm just the director. Mine's not to reason why. My instructions are to work with that script, diabolical or not, tennis kit or no, and shoot you guys playing your parts, as is. And as for Renato, well, yeah, I believe he's seriously looking for unknowns for his movie. Answer your question?"

I mumbled in assent.

"Okay, then, all of you," he called out, "pay attention and we'll get the show on the road."

The filming commenced under his direction almost immediately. There was nothing of the glamour I'd expected, and it was surreal for the men to be playing tennis in grey flannels and their partners to be still wearing frocks. I'd anticipated a huge set kitted out with props, with cameras all around and make-up artists dashing about dabbing at our faces. Instead we followed the director to a tiny sound stage, set apart in a wing of the main building, and huddled there like lost sheep, awaiting instructions.

The director selected one of the couples at random, giving them terse orders to take their places on chalk marks drawn on the dusty floor, before shouting "Action!" The remaining couples followed one another, to be filmed brandishing tennis racquets and saying their lines with varying degrees of audibility.

A dolly cameraman whose seat was fitted with a boom microphone filmed each couple's performance in a single take. The entire process of filming all of us took no more than fifteen minutes. However, that was not quite the end of it, for the director had a small surprise in store. Each contestant was coached in how to smile looking directly at the camera, before being shot in close up.

"That shot's for the cinema audience," the director said, "to remind them who to vote for in case they forget who is who."

Unaware that my performance had been under any kind of scrutiny, I noticed a dusky gentleman standing behind the camera advance towards me.

"Excuse me," he said in an accent unquestionably from the subcontinent, "you are a professional actor, are you not? I was observing you in that dreadful part and thought you really made the best of a truly bad script, if you can call it that. Let me introduce myself. I am Hanif Khan, film director from Bombay. I make many musicals there and I think you could be very good working with me. No need to learn to learn Hindi or Urdu. Please, take my card." Hanif drew an embossed card from a slim silver case and passed it to me.

"If you are interested, perhaps you could visit me in London to discuss matters? I am only here for another week, at the Ritz."

Sue Kenyon, who stood at my side, said quietly, "You should go, Bob. None of my business really, but you should take up Mr Khan's offer."

Sue did not know then that I had left the subcontinent to make a future for myself in England, or that for me to consider the proposition was ironic, all things considered. India was not where I wanted to be, however tempting the proposition.

Thanking Mr Khan for his kind offer, I said goodbye to my new friends from the *Stars of the Future* competition, and left the studio with Sue Kenyon. I'd promised to see her home on the bus, even though it meant leaving my precious racing bike padlocked to a railing.

I had started out on that sunny morning in June utterly convinced my destiny was to be in films. I would bring my talent as a singer to Hollywood musicals, just like Mario Lanza, but without turning as elephantine in the process. I would be famous, own a yacht, be lionised by pretty women, be someone. But the truth I had learned that day was show business was all smoke and mirrors.

Not everything was lost, however, for as compensation, I had at my side the beautiful Sue Kenyon, which made up for almost everything. But I knew I stood no chance with her unless my infected ear was cured. I decided there was nothing like the present to make a start; I would immediately cease tearing inside my ear with paper clips, matches, anything that came to hand, and put up with the persistent, excruciating itch that drove me mad. I would apply oodles of sulfonamide ointment as prescribed by my doctor and even visit Doctor Schwartz, the psychiatrist who thought me to be a homosexual and a psychopath, if it helped. I'd do anything if my ear could heal at last, cease stinking and be free of being plugged with cotton wool. I would do all of this for the sake of the heart-wrenchingly lovely, the wonderful Susan Kenyon of Weybridge, Surrey.

Sue said I was a real gentleman for seeing her home. "Not many people have such good manners these days. It's good to meet one who has."

Having dropped her off at the bus stop a few yards from her detached house in Oatlands Chase, I had a good half-hour to wait for a bus going in the opposite direction.

Glancing at the gold and diamond studded watch she wore, Sue said, "Why not come in? I know Mummy would love to meet you. Come on, you've plenty of time."

"Are you sure?" I asked, curious to see the kind of house Sue lived in. It was obvious the Kenyons were not hurting financially. Speculating on what her father did for a living, I said, "Well, okay, just for a few minutes. Your mother might not like to have a stranger turning up out of the blue."

"Nonsense," laughed Sue. "My friends are always welcome." With that, she took my hand and we walked to her front door together.

Apparently Sue's mother had seen us approach, for I saw her already standing in the open doorway. A stout motherly figure with grey hair, she had the same smiley dark eyes as her daughter and a grin equally as broad.

"So, how did it go, darling?" she asked, pecking her daughter on the cheek, before turning to me to say, "I'm Susan's mother, Helen. And you are...?"

Sue cut in quickly. "This is my friend, Bob Matthews, mother. He brought me home from the studios on the bus."

"Oh, how kind," Helen murmured. "You must come in for a spot of tea. You've got time, I'm sure. I absolutely insist."

"Well, okay, just for a minute or two. Then I have to be off. You see, I've left my bike back at the studio and I'm scared someone might steal it."

"Oh, you poor, poor dear. You truly are a knight in shining armour."

"A touch tarnished, some might say."

"Oh, no, no, no," Helen cried, "certainly not."

My attempt at a joke had gone over Helen's head. Sue laughed, "Come on, Bob, let's go inside."

I was led into a large, comfortably furnished drawing room with leaded windows and floral carpets. Oil paintings, mostly scenes of Scotland, although thankfully none of the Stag at Bay variety, hung on all four panelled walls. Beneath were bookcases lined with yards of classics, their pristine leather bindings implying they'd not been often opened.

As my eyes continued to sweep over the room, they were caught by a beautiful Bechstein grand piano standing in one corner. Since Sue and her mother had already disappeared into the kitchen to drum up tea, doubtless also for Helen to ask about the foreign-looking chap her daughter had brought to the house, I went over to investigate. On the music stand, sheet music from my favourite film, South Pacific, lay open at Bali Hai, one of its most memorable tunes. I was already humming it to myself when the two women re-entered. Helen bore a tray with a silver teapot, bone china cups and saucers, and Sue carried a large plate of yellow Madeira cake.

"Come, tuck in, dear," said Helen, laying down her tray before collapsing onto a damask covered sofa.

Now short of time, I wolfed down my cake and polished off two cups of tea even before Helen, one little finger sticking out delicately from her cup handle, had taken more than a sip of hers.

Sue sat on the arm of a sofa looking amused, saying little, her eyes taking in everything. Eventually, she looked at her watch. "Time to go, Bob," she said, "Bus will be here in two minutes."

"Bye-bye, Bob," Helen called. "Do come again."

Fleeing from the house, I shouted, "Thank your mum for me, Sue."

"I'm right behind you," Sue laughed, breathlessly, as I heard her footsteps. "You doing anything tonight? I'd love to see you, if you can make it."

"Where?"

"Here," she replied. "Come for supper and meet Daddy."

Dying to say "yes, please", I hesitated as I saw my bus round the corner.

"Seven o'clock," Sue shouted. "Please come!"

Jumping on the open platform at the rear of the bus as it moved off, I gave Sue the thumbs up.

"See ya, then."

The moment I got home, Dick asked how I'd got on at the studios. "How was it? Meet any stars?"

I told him of my encounter with George Raft, which made his eyes roll with wonder.

"Woweee! Truly? You actually met *the* George Raft?"

I responded airily, as if I associated with film stars every day. "Yeah, I did. Nice guy. No side. Spoke to all of us. Looked like a gangster, talked like a toff."

"So what happens now?" Dick probed. "You've had your film test. So what? Even if you win and get an audition with that Italian director chappie, what chance have you got of getting a part in *Romeo and Juliet*?"

After being so casually treated at the studios, I answered that the possibility was slim to none. I went on to say that I wouldn't have missed the experience for the world, even though the actual filming and the people I met at the studio were nothing like as glamorous as I had expected. I told him filming had been a quick-fire affair, the director hurrying us onto the sound stage to deliver the appalling lines and then off again like a dose of salts.

"The bloody dialogue we were dished up was obviously cobbled together by an illiterate tea boy in the canteen at the very last moment," I said. "I really can't describe how awful the script was." I stood waving my arms about theatrically, "Dick, I could have written something better in no time." As my words spilled out, I was struck by a brilliant thought. "Hey, Dick," I said, "what do you think? Maybe that's what I should do? Become a scriptwriter and forget about acting and singing."

"How many times have I told you that, old bean?" Dick fastened his eyes on me. "Come, sit down and let's have a chat, shall we?" His freckled face was usually kindly. Now it looked as stern as his voice sounded. "You arrived in England, let's see, three years ago this coming August. You've been living with me at Willow Cottage for two of those. I have enjoyed having you with me. You've been like a younger brother to me. And you must be aware how fond I am of you." He sighed heavily. "Listen to me for once. First off, you're much brighter than me, yet you can't hold down a job. I mean, how many have you had? Seven, eight, more? All of them shitty, poorly paid. You may fancy yourself being on the boards, but you blew any chances of that happening at The Windmill. Face facts, Bob, you've no hope of making it in showbiz, as you call it. Winning the odd fiver in talent competitions won't get you anywhere."

Dick went silent as I contemplated my fingernails in dismay. After what seemed an age, he said, "All right, chum. For instance, take *moi*. I may only be a commercial traveller flogging Christmas cards and what not, but I own this house, a car, and have cash in the bank. Now, I am in a position to get married and start a family. That could be you in ten or eleven years, when you are the same age."

Having finished with giving me a terrific wigging, Dick came and placed an arm about my sagging shoulders. "You'll soon be on your own, Bob," he said, concern writ large on his face. "Seriously, I mean seriously, think about getting yourself a steady office situation. Keep your nose clean and you'll get there, chum. You see, there's time for dreams and there's time for dreaming."

Tears welled up in my eyes. Brushing them away, I shook Dick's hand.

"Thanks for the lecture," I said. "I needed that. But even before you'd told me off, I'd already decided to make something of my life. You see, I met a girl on the set this morning. I have fallen for her hook, line and sinker. Please, Dick, just a mo'," I protested, gripping his hand as it was about to shake in irritation. "Listen to me. She's the incentive I needed. I've got three days free this week, a fiver in my pocket and I'll be damned if I don't find a decent job in that time. As of tomorrow, I'm back to the Labour Exchange to see what they've got. There's a bloke there who'll help me. If he can't, I'll trawl round the factory estates. Then, when I've got a job, I'll find digs near Sue.

"She lives with her parents in Oatlands Chase. I took her home on the bus this afternoon. Smashing looking dame. I get the feeling she likes me, too. She's asked me over to her house this evening, so if you'll excuse me, I'd better get on with ironing my shirt and trousers."

Dick groaned. "Girls, girls, girls. All you bloody think about. Well, that's your problem. I've said my piece. You makes your own bed..."

Chapter 34

By six, I was already dressed up for my date in my blazer and flannels. I'd inserted cardboard insoles into my polished black brogues to stop the wet coming through. The soles were holed in two places. I never had money enough to acquire a new pair, so I had to make do with these. I dare say, if I'd sucked up to Mr Waller, the manager of Bentalls' sanitary ware department, the store might have loaned me the cash to buy some shoes at a staff discount. Since my position with the company was tenuous to say the least, the idea was impossible.

I figured the Kenyons were too well bred to comment if I happened to cross a knee and they saw my gaping soles. On the off-chance they did, I practised an excuse they were sure to accept. I'd say, looking directly at Mr Kenyon, "Sir, I wear these worn shoes because I damaged my feet triple-jumping at school. So, from time to time, I am forced to put them on. You see, they don't hurt my toes like my others." An excuse of that sort was bound to stop Mr Kenyon in his tracks. He was sure to express deep sympathy for my sporting injury and ask if he could be of any help. I'd provide a sad shake of the head and show a stiff upper lip.

Aside from my footwear, I was also in desperate need of a haircut, but since a haircut cost a shilling, my visits to the barber down the road were infrequent. Only when my dense, wavy black hair encroached on my collar did I go, at which time I requested the barber give me a crew cut, shorn down enough to make an American Marine proud.

As I brushed my teeth, I asked of my image in the mirror if Sue Kenyon would be the first girl to sleep with me? My reflection shook its head, so I got on with winding my navy-blue and gold striped school tie around my plastic collar. I decided on a Windsor knot to impress Sue's father, who, being the owner of such a large house and obviously someone of importance, he was certain to recognise that the visitor to his home was truly an arbiter of fashion.

Finally satisfied with my appearance, I cycled off to see the Kenyons. Whistling tunes from *South Pacific*, I pedalled away slowly, so I wouldn't look too dishevelled when I arrived. As I approached her house, I wondered if it was Sue who played the piano. It would be great if she did. Perhaps then I would not have to learn songs from records or the radio. I'd be a real professional at last, with a proper accompanist onstage with me. With these thoughts floating aimlessly in my mind, Dick's sermons about making a career in business receded the closer I got to the Kenyon's. His talk about owning a house and car in ten or eleven years evaporated like so much hot air.

Of all the resolutions I'd made that day, the one I most intended to keep was to have my ear cured. As I pictured Sue flinching from me each time she came near, my ear started to itch again. The horrid sensation was like having an earwig or a caterpillar wriggling about in the middle ear so that the surrounding area cried out to be scratched. Struggling to control the unbearable desire to tear at it, I recalled my doctor's advice on how to cope with the irritation. "Use your elbow when you feel the itch coming on." I laughed aloud at the cartoon image of a bendy elbow wedged in my ear hole. Guffawing as I rode, my ear ceased to itch.

Dismounting outside the Kenyon's house, I smoothed out saddle creases from my jacket and trousers and patted down my Brylcreemed hair before rapping on their front door.

There was an interminable delay before my knock was answered. I stood scratching my head wondering if I had misconstrued Sue's invitation, when she emerged from somewhere behind the house.

"Oh, sorry, Bob, we were all in the garden at the back," she explained in a rush. "Bring your bike round. It's such a warm evening, Daddy's got a fire going to cook some wood pigeons he shot for supper." Pausing, she asked, "I do hope you like pigeon. There's one for each of us. Mum was plucking them when you knocked." Touching her nose, she whispered, "Not a word to anyone. Daddy shot them with his air gun in next door's vegetable garden. Our neighbours would go potty if they knew."

"Oh, I used to shoot partridge when I was in India," I replied. "Well, what's Pakistan now. I imagine pigeon tastes as good."

"India? Pakistan? I had no idea you'd lived there."

"Well, actually, we haven't had much chance to talk, have we? There's a lot you don't know about me. On the other hand, I don't know anything about you either."

"Ask me over supper," Sue smiled, "but first, leave your bike there and come and meet my lovely daddy."

Sue's father, Bill, appeared to have been trying to get a fire going in an old oil drum stuffed with dried sticks, but as soon as I appeared he bounded up to greet me.

Wiping his hands on his trousers, he shook my hand, saying, "How do you do, how do you?" Red in the face from his labours, he said in a voice full of good cheer, "Ah, so you're the chap who brought Sue home from the film studios. I gathered from her the film test was a bit of a nonsense. But never mind, eh?" A big smile wreathed his broad features, instantly putting me at my ease. "Come on, Sue," he said, putting an arm around his daughter's shoulder, "you look after Bob. Fetch him a drink. Poor chap must be dying of thirst." Giving me a wink, followed by a dig in the ribs, he asked, "Fancy a glass of my home-made brew? Go on, give it a try while I get that bloomin' fire going."

Sue made a face. "Would you really like some, Bob? I warn you, two glasses and you'll be flat on your back."

Puffing out my chest in mock bravado, I answered untruthfully, "Sure, thanks. I can handle anything you dish up."

Sue eyed me up and down. "Oh, yeah," she replied, with one of her beguiling smiles that made me go weak at the knees. "We'll see."

By dusk, with the mingled smells of wood smoke and grilled meat lingering in the air, I sat stuffing myself in the Kenyon's garden. Sue's father and mother waited on me hand and foot, insisting I devour more and more of the grilled pigeon than my stomach could handle.

Sue had edged her folding chair closer to mine, so she could pile my plate with mounds of salad, while Bill plied me with his powerful home-made beer, making my head spin after a single pint.

I had expected to be questioned about my background during the course of the meal. But Bill Kenyon's gentle enquiries were so casually put that I did not feel in any way interrogated. On the contrary, it was I who volunteered a deal of information about my life, which appeared to interest the family greatly, most particularly the bits about my schooling in the Himalayas.

When I'd finished describing the beauty of the mountains, Helen cried, "I've never been anywhere, Bob. You are so lucky to have lived out there." She gave her husband a nudge, saying, "Bill saw a bit of the world during the war, didn't you, Bill?

Bill smiled at his wife. "Too much, luv. Mostly desert, a bit of Burma and not much else." Turning to gaze proudly at his daughter, he said, "Sue's the one who has travelled. Twenty-one years old, she's already spent a year in Paris, studying piano at a *conservatoire*. Haven't you darling?" He patted Sue's knee affectionately. "You're quite the traveller, aren't you gel?"

"So it's you who plays that beautiful grand piano," I said. "Please play something, Sue. If you do, maybe I can sing along."

"Sing? You can sing? You never said."

"You never asked."

"Baritone or tenor?"

"Baritone."

"Thought so. What kind of music do you like?"

"Oh, stuff from musicals. Standards, ballads, Bing, Sinatra."

"Oh, good. Me, too. And jazz, the blues, Beethoven, Bach. All kinds of music." I go to the Royal College of Music in September. I'm training to be a concert pianist."

"What about now? What are you doing until then?"

"Oh, I'm filling in time at the family's printing works in Chertsey. Just during the summer." Sue stretched lazily, before levering herself up from her chair. "Come on, Sir Lancelot, let's go inside."

Whilst I was aware of Bill keeping an eye on Sue and me as we chatted, I noticed Helen had fallen asleep in her chair.

"Don't wake Mum," Bill said. "You chaps go into the lounge. I'll clear up and be with you in two ticks. When Mum wakes we'll look forward to being entertained by," he slapped his thigh, "the stars of the future."

Passing through the Kenyon's kitchen on the way to their drawing room, I noticed they owned a refrigerator and also a machine for washing clothes, such as I'd not seen before.

"Gosh, Sue," I said admiringly, "you are so lucky to be well off. Maybe one day I'll be rich, too. Where I live at present, we've just a cold box to keep food in. Dick and I wash our clothes in the bath tub and wring them out with a mangle. Can you imagine?"

"Yes, I can," Sue smiled, "because my tiny flat in Paris wasn't much different. Very basic, had to send out my washing. But none of that mattered, I was mad about Paris—the food, the freedom, the life. Oh, everything, really." She gave me a wistful look. "Mummy and Daddy were very generous to send me to the *conservatoire*."

I did not know exactly what a *conservatoire* was, so I avoided asking in case she would think me an ignoramus. Instead, I questioned her about Paris. "Was Paris as nice as it's kicked up to be?" I asked. "A Bluebell Girl I knew told me she absolutely loved living in Paris."

"What were you doing with a Bluebell Girl?" Sue looked at me, astonished.

"Long story, Sue. I'll tell you about her one day, when I know you better."

"I feel I know you already, Bob," Sue replied. "Funny that, because we've only just met."

I gave Sue a sly grin. "Shall we elope and run off to Paris, then?"

"I'd go and live there like a shot," replied Sue, brushing my cheek lightly with her fingers. She sat herself down at the piano and, blowing me a kiss, began to play. Even I, the uncultured clod, recognised Chopin when I heard it. I fell into a nearby arm chair to listen with my eyes shut. I had never heard anyone play the piano so well, or so effortlessly. Neither had I been as happy in my entire life.

The last notes of the sonata faded away. Poised above the piano keys, Sue's fingers flexed and stretched. She raised her head to look at me, her eyes all misty.

"Did you like that?" she asked in a soft voice. "That was Chopin's Piano Sonata No. 8 in C minor. Now, Robert, your turn, let's see how well you can sing." She gave a laugh. "If you're any good, maybe we could do cabaret together in *Gay Paree*. I heard you humming *Bali Hai* earlier—let's try *Some Enchanted Evening*." Her expression now serious, she tapped middle C with one finger. "Come on, give me your key."

Getting to my feet, I sang the opening bars of the song.

Sue nodded appreciatively, "Not bad Lancelot. You happy in C?"

Sue and I finished a second run through of the song just as her parents entered the room arm in arm. "Now, go on, Bob, give it some real wellie," Bill said, releasing Helen. They both sank down on a sofa and waited for me to start.

I sang my heart out for a full hour. Sue as well as her parents egged me on and on, clapping until I'd had enough. I'd sung pretty much the entire score from *South Pacific*, then some Mario Lanza stuff, finishing off with Sinatra's *Foggy Day in London Town*, before begging a cigarette from Bill as an excuse to stop.

"Lancelot, you really are quite good, you know," said Sue from her piano stool. "Range two and a bit octaves, nice vibrato, but the trouble is you don't keep time to the music. Plus your breathing's all to hell. The fags I suppose. Fancy rehearsing your timing with me sometime? I could manage twice a week if you'd like."

"You're kidding? You'd do that for me?" I was genuinely surprised. Call it conceit, but since I was more used to praise than criticism I was somewhat miffed I wasn't going to let a trifle like that stop me from seeing Sue. I'd have leapt at her offer even if she'd said I couldn't sing at all. "Like when?"

"How about tomorrow and the day after, until you get your timing right?"

From his position on the sofa, I heard Bill chortle. "Bob, watch out. She's a helluva taskmaster, that daughter of mine. Anyway, m'lad, I imagine your throat's dry by now, so have another beer. Then you can tell me what you do for a living."

The question had come out of the blue and it took me by surprise. It was quite out of context with what we'd previously been talking about. I figured Bill had just spotted the holes in my shoes and concluded he'd better find out a bit more about me if I was to be a regular visitor. Buying time, I took a swig, then another, before replying.

"Er, I am a sort of salesman," I stammered lamely, looking deep into my glass. "I've a temp job with Bentalls."

"Which department?" Bill enquired.

Squirming in my seat, I answered, "Sanitary ware." My eyes went everywhere but at Bill. "The firm I was going to work for burnt down, so I took the Bentalls job while I look around for another."

Bill gave me a look of sympathy. “That was bad luck, son,” he said. Leaning forward in his seat, he continued, “Forgive me for being so rude, but I guessed you might have been having a hard time of it, judging by the state of your shoes. I just wondered, if maybe, just maybe, I could somehow be of help?”

I felt for my ear, which had started itching of its own volition. Uncomfortable and embarrassed, I forgot my story of triple jumping and damaged feet being the reason for my wearing old shoes. I was aware of a burning sensation as my cheeks went scarlet under Bill’s steady eyes. Sue sat silent on her piano stool, her features softening with sympathy as I turned to face her. Helen, I noticed, had developed an intense interest in the hem of her dress.

I muttered, “I don’t know what to say, sir. I really don’t. But yes, I’d be grateful for any help right now.” My brain raced. Surely such kindness didn’t exist in the world? Were these people real, or was I dreaming?

“Come on, son,” said Bill, coughing awkwardly, “we’ve all been to the school of hard knocks at some or another. Now, maybe, that is if you don’t mind telling me, do you have any qualifications?”

I told Bill that all I had to my name was a Cambridge School Certificate, to which he replied it was more than he had. No matter, he said, that was plenty good enough for lots of jobs. He then went silent, his thumb to his mouth as he pondered. The only sound in the room was the tapping of his thumbnail on his front teeth. Then, as if struck by some divine revelation, he sat upright with a jerk, smacked his lips, and cried, “Helen, that bloke… What’s his name? You know, the chap who came to the firm asking for that complicated dyeline printing job?”

"Oh, you mean, my friend Charlie," replied Helen, quickly coming to her husband's assistance. "Charlie Hunt from Midland Gypsum. What about him?"

"Didn't he tell you his office supervisor had just upped and left?" asked Bill, his voice now full of excitement. "Wasn't he complaining he couldn't find anyone suitable to fill the job? Didn't he?"

"So he did, Bill, so he did."

"Midland, good company, that," said Bill. "Now, Bob, with your permission old chap, Helen will give this Charlie Hunt bloke a ring tomorrow to see if he'd be interested in meeting you. How's that suit you?"

"I feel very humble, sir," I replied, with feeling. "Don't know what to say. Or how to thank you. I met Sue just this morning, and the both of you only this evening." Pulling a handkerchief from my breast pocket, I blew hard into it. "It's all too much, too much. Nobody has ever been so kind to me in all my life."

Sue got up from her stool and went to her father's side. Giving him a kiss on the cheek, she said, "I told you I had a wonderful daddy, didn't I, Bob?"

Bill gave a snort, before blowing his nose into a cleaner handkerchief than mine.

I decided to keep the details of the evening from Dick, who was bound to scoff at the romantic views I had about the Kenyon family. Although he himself had come to my rescue when I was down and almost out three years before, he was cynical about others being as altruistic. "There's always a catch, chum," he said, whenever I waxed lyrical about someone or something.

So the following morning, when he asked how the evening with the Kenyon had gone, I merely said, "I had a super time. They were very kind and gave me a nice supper," avoiding any mention of the pigeon or of Sue's offer to help with my singing. He'd not have taken kindly to that, for hadn't I promised to look for a proper job and forget showbiz?

Although there was the faint possibility that Helen Kenyon might come up with an interview for me, I decided it prudent to trek around the Addlestone Factory Estate to see if any of the firms that littered it—some of which, like Remington Rand, I'd previously worked for—had vacancies. I did not relish the idea of working there again, because it felt as if I was going backwards.

It was a dispiriting, grim business going from factory to factory, seeking out personnel managers, and being turned away with words like "sorry, chum, full up" or "we've nothing at the moment", but I persisted until I'd visited all of them without success. If I had been sensible I'd have gone straight to the Labour Exchange for a job. They might have helped, but I was fed up with sticking my head through the small window in the passageway of the Exchange and asking if they had anything suitable for me. They were a last resort now; it was not much fun always to be on the receiving end of sarcastic jibes such as "Not you again Mr Matthews" or "Anything we can do for you, m'lord?"

The pointless cycling about on the factory estate had the merit of using up time. By mid-afternoon I could hardly contain myself, and so, taking a chance on Sue and Helen being at home, I made my way over to their house.

Sue greeted me at the door. "Bob! What a nice surprise! We didn't expect you this early." It must have been a habit she'd learned in Paris, for she kissed me on both cheeks, which I rather enjoyed. "Mummy's got good news for you. Her friend wants to see you. Come in, come in, Mum's in the kitchen as usual."

Hearing the sound of our voices, Helen appeared, wiping her hands on her apron. She welcomed me as if I'd been a long-lost son, enquiring anxiously if I'd had a good day. "From the expression on your face, I think Sue's already told you the news," she said. "Good thing you came early. I rang Charlie Hunt this morning and he really would like to meet you. The job's still open. You should ring him back right away." Seeing I was flummoxed, she quickly added, "Phone from here. We do have such a thing as a phone, you know. Come on, follow me, I've his number written down."

I was unused to phoning anyone, so I misdialled twice before finally getting through to Mr Hunt, who said he'd heard good things about me and looked forward to meeting me, the sooner the better.

"If you can make it down us by ten tomorrow morning, that would be terrific," he said in a Scottish burr. "Helen can tell you how to find us. It's not far from Murrells."

I told him I'd be there at ten sharp. 'Sharp' had a business-sounding ring to it. I fondly imagined my use of the word was certain to impress Mr Hunt.

"I can't believe you did all this for me, Helen," I said, extracting my person from the small, dark cubbyhole in the hallway, where the phone sat hidden from view. "I'm seeing Mr Hunt tomorrow morning. He said you'd show me how to get to his office."

Sue flounced into view, showing a lot of leg and looking ravishing as usual. "Mum's making some tea. Come into the drawing room, Lancelot, and I'll draw you a map" she said. "Midland Gypsum's just round the corner from Murrells. When you've done, promise you'll pop in and see me, okay?"

I promised, of course, and by the time we had finished with tea and sandwiches, cake and biscuits, Bill had pulled up outside the house in his Morris Eight saloon car. I learned later it was owned by the company for which he worked as a commercial traveller. The company sold engineering equipment up and down the country and had no connection with Murrells printing works, which belonged to Helen's side of the family.

Bill was as delighted as everybody when he heard of my appointment. He brushed away my thanks and, with Sue vouchsafing I was terribly skinny and needed building up, insisted I stay for supper. And so I stayed, being thoroughly spoiled, stuffing myself for the second night running with Helen's wonderful cooking. Not since dining on one of Mrs Beeton's recipes prepared for me by my old cook, Booloo, in Pakistan had I enjoyed such a meal.

After supper Bill and Helen retreated to their telly parlour, as they called it, where the latest combined Bush radiogram and television set with a monstrous 12-inch screen resided, leaving Sue to teach me the mysteries of singing in time. For myself, I'd rather have spent the next hour or so petting. Of late there had not been much of that with any girl, what with my bad ear and all. But I recognised that, until my ear was better, the sort of heavy petting I envisaged would have to be put on hold.

Sue had other ideas. No sooner had we stepped inside the drawing room than she flung her arms around my neck and kissed me passionately, full on the lips. She'd obviously been taught more than music in Paris, for her searching tongue set my nerve ends tingling, as it delved and flicked inside of my mouth, turning my legs to jelly as I stiffened up against her. She was moaning and groaning as she pressed herself against me. I tried to turn my head away to distance my ear from Sue, and in this curious, unnatural position, not seen since the Kama Sutra discarded the posture as being too difficult to maintain, tried to keep her open mouth in contact with mine.

Sue, breathing heavily, drew herself away from me at last. "Why do you keep pulling away from me?" she asked, her full breasts heaving with each breath. "Don't you like kissing me?"

"Oh, Christ, Sue! 'Course I do, more than anything else in the world."

"Then why?"

I decided there was no point in my avoiding telling the truth. I could not hide my embarrassment forever.

"Well, it's this bad ear I have," I said, pointing to the barely discernable plug of cotton wool I'd inserted deep with my ear.

"What of it?" Sue accused almost fiercely. She giggled, "I shan't bite it you know."

I shifted nervously from one leg to another as I looked at the beautiful creature in front of me. Eventually, I dredged up the courage to tell her I was afraid of losing her because of it.

"You are a bloody fool, you know," Sue said, sounding relieved. "I thought it was something about me." Tipping her face up for me to kiss, she said, "I could tell you had some sort of infection there. Why else would you have cotton wool in your ear? Makes no difference to me."

"Cheeky girl," I said, taking her in my arms again. "Sure the smell doesn't put you off?"

It was when I heard her reply "What are you talking about? What smell?" that I knew I loved Sue. My confidence now fully restored, I began to kiss her all over again, and then some more, before Sue pushed me away. "We'd better stop, now," she whispered, "Mum and Dad might come in. 'Specially if they don't hear you singing and me playing the piano."

Sue was a martinet when it came to getting me sing in time. She suggested I try *Some Enchanted Evening* once again, now using a metronome to help keep time. I soon realised that, although I'd sung in the school choir for all of nine years and had won all kinds of talent competitions since then, Sue was of the opinion that, although possessed of a decent voice, I was still a rank amateur. Needled by this, convinced I was better than she gave me credit for, I sulked like a child when she asked to me to sing the song over and over again.

Finally, she threw up her hands in triumph. "At last, my Lancelot! At last!" She sat back on her stool and looked at me. "Thank you," she said, a smile playing around her lips. "I think that's enough for tonight, don't you?" Her smile widening, she said, sounding astonishingly like a mother calling for her child, "Come, Lancelot, give Sue a kiss before you say goodnight."

"Only if you promise to stop calling me Lancelot."

"All right, if you insist, but Bob is a funny name for a knight in shining armour."

"Even if he has a bad ear?"

Sue's response was to throw her arms around my neck once more and say, "I'll see you tomorrow, then. But, before you go, I've a present for you from Daddy." She dug about the base of the coat rack standing in the hallway and withdrew a brown paper package, which she thrust in my hands.

"What this?" I asked, immediately aware from its shape and size that it was a shoe box. "Is it what I think it is?"

"It's for me to know and for you to find out," Sue replied, grinning.

"I can't take this."

"You can, and you must," replied Sue firmly. "Daddy would be terribly hurt if you refuse. He told me he never wears them. They are a bit on the tight side for him. You'd being doing him a favour by having them. They are size eight black brogues which Dad thinks will fit you."

"Oh, Sue..." I tried to speak, but the words choked in my throat.

"Don't say another word please, Bob," Sue sniffed into a handkerchief, "just go home."

Chapter 35

I'd been interviewed for jobs by a multitude of companies over the past three years. To name but a few, Remington Rand, Peto-Scott, AORG, Panelite, Woolworths, Lankester Motors, Goldtan and Bentalls had all interviewed me before hiring me. I'd become expert at telling employers what they wanted to hear, guessing from their body language what my response should be. So being subjected to yet another grilling, such as the one I faced from Mr Hunt of Midland Gypsum Industries, held no fears for me. Nevertheless, I was to find Mr Hunt had a supremely novel interviewing technique, quite different from any other I'd previously encountered.

I'd woken early to find a note from Dick saying he was going up north for a few days to meet some of his fiancée's relatives. He apologised for not having told me earlier, scribbling that we had been rather like ships in the night of late. I was pleased to have the house to myself, thinking that Sue might like to visit now that Dick was away.

Leaving plenty of time to make myself as presentable as possible, I sat for a long time looking at the shoes Bill had given me. In the past, particularly when clothes rationing was in force, I'd gratefully accepted hand-me-downs from others, for instance, Dick's Burberry, which still had years of service left in it. But Bill's gift smacked of charity and made me feel uncomfortable. Doubtless he'd thought he was doing me a kindness. Nonetheless, it depressed me to be again beholden to someone else for my welfare.

Continuing to beat myself up for having accepted Bill's gift, I tried on the shoes. Amazingly, they fitted perfectly. After I tested them out by walking across the floor a couple of times, finding them more comfortable than any shoes I'd previously owned, my disquiet faded and I went from the house whistling happily.

By following Sue's directions I made it to Midland Gypsum Industries in twenty minutes, where I was shown into Mr Hunt's office by a pretty receptionist. I refused her kind offer of tea whilst I waited for her boss to make an appearance.

The four walls were covered with faded photographs of cricketers, test and county players, cricket grounds and other ephemera relating to the game. Having been captain of the first eleven at school, I had a real interest in everything I saw there. As I took a closer look, the door behind me opened and Mr Hunt burst in. "Sorry to have kept you waiting, old boy," he said, "Bloody car packed up. Please sit down, we don't wait on ceremony here."

He circled the office at speed before coming to a stop in front of me. Smiling from ear to ear, he said "So, you are Bob Matthews? Helen Kenyon, nice woman that, said you were looking for a job. Now," he paused, as he went to sit behind his desk, "let's get down to business. I'm Charlie, just call me Charlie, everyone else does." He gave a laugh, before asking, "Know anything about cricket?"

I nodded uncertainly. "Used to play a bit, sir..."

"Charlie, dear boy, Charlie. Good, good. Bowler? Batsman?"

"Bowler, medium pace," I replied, mystified by the direction my so-called interview was taking.

"Mind if I test your knowledge, pop a question?" enquired Charlie, brushing a hand over his unruly mop of red hair. Narrowing his eyes to slits, he asked, "On a cricket field what position is short leg?"

My answer satisfied him,.but he wasn't done yet. "Now, point and cover?"

This went on for about five minutes, with me thinking this was the oddest interview for a job I'd ever had, when he said, "Right, Bob, I see you know your stuff about cricket. Tell you why I asked. We've got a little challenge competition going on between a few of the other companies in this building of ours. Just a bit of fun in the lunch hour, a few overs with the ball and a bit of a slog with the bat, that's all. However, the fellow who just left was our star bowler. I just wondered if you'd do in his place. Perhaps you think me daft?"

Charlie picked up a pencil and rapped the top of his desk, "My belief is that teamwork can make work fun. Ergo, a happy work place results. Obviously, there's a serious side, too. Brass tacks now, tell me if you know what gypsum is?"

Shrugging, I said I knew nothing at all about gypsum.

"Not exactly surprised," commented Charlie, who went on to explain in some detail that gypsum, or hydrated calcium sulphate, was used in the manufacture of plasterboard and that Midland had a major share of the market in Southern England. "This office is purely for local sales," said Charlie, "Head Office is in London, the quarries are all over the UK." Leaning back in his chair, Charlie's eyes swept over me, "Now, young fellow-me-lad, tell what you've been up to since you left school?"

Ashamed to admit I'd not held down any job for more than a few months, I disclosed only half the number to Charlie, whose eyebrows reached up towards the ceiling as I described the kind of work I'd done. Instead of sending me packing as I half-expected, an expression of sympathy came over his face.

"Seems you've had a rough time since you came to this country," he said. "I think you deserve a chance. So tell me, think you'd like to work with us?"

I replied I didn't know enough about the job or the prospects or the weekly wage to answer him truly. My candour seemed to please Charlie for, without further ado, he got up from his desk, shook my hand and then showed me around the rest of the offices. Introducing me to the staff as we went, he explained what would be required of me.

"You'll take orders over the phone, handle and process enquiries, contact potential customers, mostly deal with sales. How does it sound to you? Think you can do it?"

I replied I liked what I'd heard and was confident I could. "Well then, Bob, let's discuss the nitty gritty in my office and see if you accept our terms."

I was delighted when Charlie offered me six pounds ten shillings a week for a forty-hour week, starting at nine in the morning and finishing at five-thirty, with a week's paid holiday. My job title : Sales Supervisor. I shook hands with Charlie, agreeing to start on Monday, and left Midland's premises, fizzing with delight.

Ahead lay the entire weekend for me to enjoy. Besides the prospect of meeting Sue and her family, there was the screening of *Stars of the Future* at the Palace Cinema to which I looked forward. All was well with the world, with no impediment in sight other than the arrival of my mother and the dreaded Nick Grahame-Carter.

I cycled off to Murrells, where a receptionist sent for Sue, who appeared wearing a fetching cotton skirt and blouse. Whereas I was hot, she looked cool, her complexion clear, dark eyes sparkling. She was a vision. Taking my arm, she walked me outside, so we could talk in private.

"I got the job. I'm starting Monday," I said. "I liked Charlie and I think I'm going to enjoy working with him."

She giggled helplessly when I told her about the bizarre preamble to the interview. Casting a sidelong look at my newly shod feet, she joked, "It was Daddy's shoes that did it."

Blushing, I replied I still felt bad about accepting them. What was worse, I hadn't as yet thanked him, either.

Digging me in the ribs, Sue said, "If you come up the house this evening, you could thank him then."

"That's three days in a row, Sue. Surely, they'll get fed up with seeing me?"

"Pish, posh," she said, wrinkling her nose. "Tell you what. Come after supper at eight and we can go through a few songs. That way you can tell Mummy and Daddy in person about the job. They'll be awfully pleased, you know. Please, oh please, say you'll come, Lancelot."

Giving me a kiss on the lips that made my head spin, she said, "Must dash and do some work or else I'll be sacked."

As she retreated towards the main door, I called out, "How can they sack you when your family owns the joint?"

Sue's response was to stick her tongue out at me.

Since I did not have the wherewithal to buy even the smallest posy of flowers for Sue's mother, I scoured Willow Cottage's garden for some wild specimens. Selecting some poppies, daisies and cornflowers from the profusion growing in the vicinity of the compost heap, I made up a bouquet of sorts. In an attempt to give my handiwork a more professional appearance I added a spray of fern, but the net effect was still amateurish. Debating whether to discard the whole idea and turn up empty handed at the Kenyon's house, I decided I'd take what I'd collected. Helen was such a good-natured person she was sure to think it was the thought that mattered.

Standing by the Kenyon's front door at eight that evening with my bunch of wild flowers held stiffly in hand, I caught sight of Helen's face peering through a side window. She opened the door to me with her usual welcoming smile.

"These are for you, Helen," I said, hurriedly presenting the flowers like a guardsman offering his rifle for inspection.

"For me? How sweet of you, Bob. What a lovely bunch." Helen stood stroking the tissue paper I'd wrapped them in, as if the flowers were prize blooms. "Come," she said, "give me a kiss and then let's go in." I watched her bustle into the house ahead of me, wishing my own mother might have been like her.

Now shod in Bill's shoes, I felt more than awkward about meeting him. However, the moment he spotted me, he gripped my hand saying how pleased he was the shoes fitted me and glad he'd found a home for them at last. Overwhelmed by his kindness, I declared that they were brilliant, the best shoes I'd ever worn.

"That's enough of that my boy," said Bill gruffly, "now let's have a beer to celebrate your new job. I daresay Sue can find room for a glass of sherry, too."

"Darn right, Daddy, I'd love one, please," Sue agreed, greeting me with a kiss. I was surprised that Bill wasn't fazed by his daughter's display of affection. If Sue had been my daughter and she'd only just met a young fellow who clearly had designs on her, I'd have had a thing or two to say. I kept reminding myself that it had only been three days since I'd met the Kenyons. They were altogether extraordinary people and if it kept on like this, they'd have me moving in.

My thoughts about moving in with the Kenyons proved uncannily prophetic. Barely a month on, as Sue and I strolled by the Thames early one evening, she suddenly burst out with "Mummy and Daddy think you should come and stay with us. After all, you'll soon have nowhere to live after Dick gets married. At least with us you'll have a home."

Taken off balance, I blustered, "That's impossible, I couldn't do that."

The idea germinated in my mind, becoming more and more appealing. It invited all sorts of enticing possibilities. At the same time, I found it incredibly naïve of the Kenyons not to have given a thought to what might follow. That I was being trusted not to seduce their daughter, after promoting the ideal conditions for seduction, suggested a degree of myopia about what young people got up to. Were they mad? Wasn't it obvious Sue and I had the serious hots for each other?

"Why impossible?" Sue asked, in a calm voice, stooping to throw a stone into the dark waters. "To my way of thinking"—I was about to interrupt when she put a finger to my lips to silence me—"it makes absolute sense. Just think about it for a minute. You spend most evenings with us. You take your meals with us. We have fun together, you and I, and anyway, you silly dope, don't you know I'm in love with you?"

Astonished, I cried out in disbelief, "You love me? Me? Oh, my God, Sue! I love you, too. I have from the first moment I saw you." Pulling Sue to me, I kissed her fiercely on the lips, again and again.

We appeared to be of great interest to people out walking their dogs, who looked at us curiously before going on their way tittering. But we were unconcerned, and sank to the grass beside the towpath. Clinging together, we whispered how much we loved each other. Then I heard myself asking Sue if she'd marry me. Her response was a softly murmured, "Yes, I will," before she buried her head in my chest and repeated, almost defiantly, "Of course I will, silly."

The full import of what we'd done struck us both at the same moment. Silent now, we faced one another. My eyes wavered over Sue's face, searching for signs of doubt. Instead of which, I saw only love in her eyes.

After a time, I asked, "Are you sure, darling? After all, I've got nothing to offer you."

"I don't care. We'll manage," Sue replied, gripping my hand firmly to emphasise her point. "You've got a nice job now. Mummy says Charlie Hunt already thinks the world of you. And, anyway, we'll live with Mummy and Daddy until we can afford to find our own place. Then after I've finished with my studies I'll get a job with an orchestra to help out."

Sue's phrase—'our own place', 'our own place'—spun like a top inside my head. I was only twenty-two; she, twenty-one. Suddenly the whole idea seemed crazy, unthinkable. Swallowing hard, I asked, "What will your parents say?"

Sue tossed her head, her eyes fixed on D'Oyly Carte Island out in the Thames, bathed in pale yellow sunlight. "Oh, they'll say we should wait, of course," she replied at last.

"How long do you think?" I asked, knowing I was bound to accept whatever conditions Sue's parents proposed. "It's sure as hell going to be hard, living as an engaged couple in the same house if we have to wait for too long." I gave a weak laugh. "Know what I mean? Really hard."

"We'll manage." Sue said firmly, getting to her feet. Giving me a kiss, she said, "Let's go home now and give Mummy and Daddy the good news, shall we?"

Sue's parents took the news of our engagement with surprising equanimity. Congratulating me, Bill laughed, "It's customary for the bloke to ask the father for his daughter's hand in marriage. After which, the Dad enquires about their future son-in-law's prospects. But since Charlie Hunt tells me you've a good future with the firm, you have my blessing, son."

Helen then kissed me on the cheek and said how happy she was for both of us. Holding her daughter's hand, she said, "I've heard good things from Charlie, too."

Actually I very much enjoyed working at Midland Gypsum Industries. For the first time in my life I had actually managed to save a few pounds, which I asked Dick to put by for me. I found working in sales very satisfying, finding it easy to lay on the charm to obtain orders. Then there was the cricket competition, which had got me the job in the first place. On my first day out with the team, playing against another firm, I got their star batsman out with my first ball and then took another three wickets in the next four overs. Our opponents were probably the worst team I'd ever played against, although in Charlie's eyes I was the best thing since Denis Compton.

Bill Kenyon insisted on opening a dusty bottle of champagne to celebrate our engagement. Helen, Sue and I downed a glass each. Bill polished off the remainder of the bottle, his face more flushed by the minute as he sat beaming at Sue and me. Slurring his words, he asked when the two love birds intended getting married? I hummed and hawed because, an hour or so before, any thought of marriage was far from my mind.

Sue answered her father. “In three months’ time,” she said, which made me shiver nervously. Helen insisted we wait at least six months. Bill agreed, so we finally settled on the following January.

As I sat wondering what was to come next, Helen patted me on the knee and said, “Sue’s told you about moving into our spare room, hasn’t she? We’d love you staying here. I can fatten you up then. You are much too skinny, you know.”

I was surprised Helen considered me thin. Out of vanity, I’d always thought of myself as being rather muscular. However, I decided not to contest the issue, when Helen was being so kind to me.

“So, Bob, move in whenever you like,” Helen continued earnestly. “You don’t have to wait until your friend Dick gets married.”

Overwhelmed by the Kenyon’s beneficence, defeated by their unrelenting charity, I replied, “If I accept your kind offer, I insist on paying rent and for my food, too,” hoping against hope she’d ask for no more than I could afford.

Bill intervened quickly. “Don’t be a silly chump! We don’t want your money, do we, Mum?”

Helen shook her head vigorously. “Of course not. We wouldn’t think of it.”

That was the end of the discussion. Sue and I cycled down to Willow Cottage to inform Dick we were getting married and that I’d be moving out in a week’s time. He’d already met Sue, of whom he approved as the right sort of girlfriend for me, better than my more usual ones, he said, possibly because she came from a wealthy family and had the right sort of accent. Dick was proud of being a snob, as if being a snob was something to be admired.

Dick's jaw fell open. "Both of you are too bloody young!" he exploded, incredulous at the very idea. Sue looked on, bewildered, as he continued in a sharp voice, "Do either of you know what you are doing? Bob, you don't have a bean." He ceased for a moment, then stuttered, as he did when agitated, "Sue, Sue, Bob, Bob, Bob, I wish you both all the luck in the world, but are you sure you know what you are getting into?"

"Yes," replied Sue, finding my hand, "we are."

I could have kissed my beautiful Sue for her absolute certainty. Nevertheless, Dick's words had insinuated a worm of doubt inside me, one that niggled and niggled.

"Well then," said Dick, his old cheerful self at last, "I think a glass of my infamous sloe gin is called for."

Chapter 36

A week later, I was installed in the Kenyon's spare bedroom with my few belongings in my old tin trunk shoved under the bed. Dick, bless him, forgave the week's rent I owed, saying I should put it towards an engagement ring for Sue. I'd forgotten that girls required such things, so hurried off to look in the window of the jewellers in Baker Street to see what kind of ring I could afford. The jeweller, recognising a pauper when he saw one, showed me a tray of rings ranging in price from five to ten pounds. Pointing to the most expensive one, a thin gold band with a tiny speck of diamond, he asked if sir liked it. I gulped nervously, my eyes going to others costing five pounds, which was all I could run to.

"What about this one?" I asked, indicating a ring set with a miniscule blue sapphire.

"How perspicacious of you. What a splendid choice sir has made," the jeweller replied, appearing awestruck. "That particular one is indeed remarkable value. Confidentially," hiding his mouth behind his hand, he smarmed, "the ring was recently returned by the betrothed of one sadly deceased, which is why we have reduced it in price. It is a nine-carat gold ring with a genuine sapphire. Normally, this ring would be nearer six pounds, but to you, sir, we'll let it go for four pounds, nineteen shillings and sixpence."

"I'll have it," I replied without hesitation. "Can you please put it in a nice box for me?"

"All our rings come in nice boxes, sir," he admonished gently.

A faint look of disappointment flickered briefly in Sue's eyes when she opened the box I handed her, replaced by one of delight almost immediately.

"Oh, Bob, what a sweet little ring," she cried, slipping the ring on her finger, "and with a sapphire, too. My favourite. Oh, Lancelot, thank you, thank you." Finger raised high in the air, she went running to her mother. "Mummy, look, Bob's got me an engagement ring!"

Helen commented sweetly that it was nice of me to have bought one. Accompanying Sue to the window, she held the ring up to the light. "That must have cost a pretty penny," she smiled.

"Aw, shucks," I replied, shuffling my feet with embarrassment, taking off George Raft's accent, "nuttin's too much for my Susie."

The next evening Bill drove us to the Palace Cinema, where we had four complimentary tickets for the screening of our film test. To our surprise, we found a long queue already waiting outside.

"Obviously the other contestants have brought their friends and family to vote for them," commented Bill sourly. "If only we'd thought to do the same."

Judy Garland and James Mason's *A Star is Born* preceded the showing of our film test footage, billed as *Stars of the Future*. I figured the owner of the picture house had a wry sense of humour, for the movie's last scene was of Judy

Garland walking out to sea to drown herself. Following her demise, the curtains closed. Reopening immediately, the title *Stars of the Future* flashed on the screen, followed by the first of the contestants performing their dire scene.

As bad as I thought we all were, I was still fascinated to see myself on the silver screen. Sue had made the most of her script and looked ravishing, whereas I overacted horrendously, grimacing at the camera, moving awkwardly. As a finale, there followed quick-fire shots of all the contestants' faces with a voice-over exhorting the audience to note down their choice of best actor and actress. The winner was to be announced in the *Surrey Herald* newspaper in about a month, after a panel of film directors had also deliberated.

In the meantime, the first sign that I might have been wrong to have moved in with the Kenyons appeared. Not that I wasn't having a good time of it. Actually, I was happier than I'd ever been since coming to England. The problem simply revolved around my lack of underpants. The only pair I'd ever owned were those Beryl, the flatter, had persuaded me to buy, and they'd long since worn out and been discarded.

When Helen asked for my dirty washing, she was sympathetic when she found I only owned two shirts, but scandalized when she discovered I didn't wear underpants.

"I don't think I like the idea of people going about without underwear. It's not civilised," she said, and then, "Does Sue know?"

Sue did, but I wasn't going to admit that to anyone, least of all her mother.

"Of course not," I replied, my expression one of outrage at the very suggestion.

"Just as well then," said Helen, stomping from the room.

Helen and Bill turned cool towards me from that moment, and dinners became frosty affairs, even though Sue remained her usual cheerful self. Outside of her parents' hearing, I promised to buy some underpants, but when I said I couldn't afford more than three pairs because they cost over five shillings each, she protested, "No, no. You're talking nonsense, Lancelot. You've forgotten the talent competition at the village fete in Chertsey. It's this Friday night." Looking directly into my eyes, she added, with utter confidence, "You fool, we're sure to win first prize. Five pounds will buy you any number of underpants, enough for a fresh pair every day of the week."

So that was it. To be rehabilitated in the Kenyon's household all I had to do was to find a suitable song and win the forthcoming talent competition. I decided on a cloying Frankie Laine number entitled *Darling Be Mine*, which was currently on everyone's lips. Sue got me to sing it over and over again, until she was satisfied and I was sick to death of it.

The competition on Friday night was almost called off due to the weather. Heavy rain short-circuited the electrics and so brought the Ferris wheel and Dodgem cars to a standstill. Damp children picked at soggy candy floss and bedraggled adults browsed goods displayed by sodden stalls; we joined them until time to report.

The so-called stage, more accurately a wooden platform with a canvas awning, was strung with fairy lights, and a banner reading "*Grand Talent Contest 1953*" flapping in the breeze. A large woman with a booming voice announced in which order we were to perform. I felt Sue nudge me. "Lancelot," she whispered, "I'm glad we're last on. What an odd bunch the others are."

When it came to my turn, Sue went onstage ahead of me. Taking her place at the piano, she played the opening bars of my song like a professional. The judges stiffened in their seats with surprise and, even before I had finished singing, were clapping enthusiastically along with the crowd. When the applause subsided, the judges immediately announced me the winner and handed me an envelope containing five pounds.

When I handed Helen several pairs of newly acquired jockey shorts for washing, she simply remarked, "Oh, good," as if the subject of my nether apparel had never, ever been broached. Bill and Helen returned to being as kind and friendly as before. However, the experience had been a bruising one, and it left me wary of upsetting them again.

Now that I had enough money, what was left over from the singing competition plus a little extra I'd saved up, I decided to take Sue to see Lerner and Loewe's *Brigadoon* in London. After the show, Sue suggested we dine at the Hong Kong Restaurant in Piccadilly Circus, which she said she loved. Since I'd never before tasted Chinese food, and had only seen the inside of one other restaurant in my life, I felt a touch nervous as we were shown to our table by a waiter in Chinese dress.

Sanguine about affording the meal on account of the crisp ten-shilling note in my pocket, I set about my food with gusto, relishing each and every one of strange looking dishes put before me. When I was finally presented with the bill on a silver tray, my heart missed a couple of beats, for it came to precisely ten shillings. In my naïveté, I'd expected to receive some change after paying for the meal. Now I had nothing left for a tip, which I'd heard was the done thing.

Unsure as to what the waiter's reaction would be if I didn't leave one, I desperately searched my trousers pockets for any stray coins. Not finding any, I vainly dug around in my jacket pocket. I saw a look of concern pass over Sue's face as she watched me.

"I've cash, if you're a bit short, Lancelot," she said. Reaching out a hand she took the bill from the tray and scanned it quickly. "You've left the correct amount," she pronounced, with the air of one well-used to dining in expensive restaurants. "See, it says here," she pointed with a manicured scarlet fingernail, "*service compris.* That's French, for service included."

"Ah, so it does, so it does," I replied, at the same time making a mental note of the vital phrase.

As we left the restaurant, Sue squeezed my hand. "Thank you, darling, for a lovely meal. Next time, my treat, okay?" She gave a wicked laugh. "Since I see you're now a linguist, how about a French restaurant?"

On the journey home to Weybridge, Sue only spoke of how wonderful it would be to make a home together. Then, just before we finally arrived at the station, she whispered in my ear, "I'd like lots of children. Wouldn't you?"

Sue's words stunned me. I felt as if I'd been shot. My juvenile perception of wedlock was of a cosy, romantic state of bliss in which Sue and I would live forever and ever, with children never in the equation. As I dwelt on the enormity of Sue's proposal, I was left quailing inside. Suddenly irresolute, it came to me we'd been rash to consider marriage and we should put off the idea until much later. I convinced myself we were really far too young after all, and neither of us was prepared for the responsibilities marriage entailed.

As I bided my time to answer Sue, I speculated whether it was true love I felt for her, and not just infatuation. I asked myself if I was blinded by an overwhelming desire to make love to her and nothing else. If so, I was honour-bound to break off the engagement, for it was unfair to allow Sue to dream on. Laughing off Sue's question, I evaded the truth like a coward.

"Sue, darling, let's talk about it later, yeah?" I answered, smiling at her.

She gave me a curious, hurt look. "You are not having second thoughts are you, Lancelot?" she asked.

"No, of course not, darling. You know I love you more than anything."

"Me, too, she said." Ignoring the other passengers in the compartment, she gave me kiss and nestled up to me.

Sue's parents had gone to bed by the time we got home. They had left a note in the kitchen which Sue read out to me.

Hope you two had a nice evening. If you're hungry, you'll find cheese sandwiches in the bread bin. There's cocoa in the cups. Just add some hot water. See you in the morning. Love Mummy.

PS. Bob, there's a letter from your mother in the hall.

"I don't fancy anything to eat, do you?" said Sue.

I shook my head. "No, but I'll have a quick shufti at my Mum's letter though."

I had written to my mother informing her of my engagement, so I was interested to see if she'd received the news. Hurrying to the hall, I found a blue airmail letter addressed in my mother's familiar handwriting. As I scanned the letter's contents, I became aware of my left ear itching unbearably. My ear had healed completely since I'd ceased scratching at it and hardly tormented me now. However, as my eyes searched for Nick Grahame-Carter's name, only with the greatest difficulty did I restrain my fingers from digging in my ear again.

My darling Bobby,

Thank you for letting me know about your engagement to Sue Kenyon. She sounds like a very nice girl. But I am forced to ask, aren't you both too young to think about marriage? You are only twenty-two, Bob, and just getting on your feet. Give it a year or two more. Sue will understand I'm sure, if she's the kind of girl you say.

I'm not preaching darling, but getting married is a big step and I worry, what with you being so far away, whether you are doing the right thing.

The rest confirmed the date and time of her arrival at Kings Cross station in September, and warned that my brother Dick had broken his leg in a motorcycle accident, and would be on crutches when I saw him. Surprisingly, she'd not mentioned Nick Grahame-Carter, which made my ear feel as good as new again. I folded my Mother's letter and put in my pocket, just as Sue entered the hall.

"Good news?" she enquired.

"Usual guff," I replied noncommittally, taking her hand. "She sends her congratulations and says she can't wait to meet you. That sort of thing." I looked at Sue hopefully, "If you're not too tired, why don't we sit and chat for a while?"

"Oh, yeah, chat. Pull the other one, Lancelot," Sue said, taking my hand and leading me through the door to the drawing room. "We'll have to be quiet as mice. Daddy sleeps awfully lightly."

The instant we entered, we fell onto the bigger of the two sofas in the room. Sue gave a moan of pleasure as our mouths engaged in a frantic bout of kissing. Undoing her brassiere, my hands cupped her breasts and found her nipples hardening under my fingers. This was as far our necking had previously gone, but now I felt her fingers unbuttoning my shirt, before reaching down to unfasten my belt and loosen my trousers. Her mouth on mine, she ground her hips up against me. By now almost out of my head with lust, I traced over the smooth, firm flesh of her thighs, which parted at my touch. Feverishly, I eased my trousers down over my hips. As I railed inwardly at my accursed new underpants, which were impeding my progress to the certainty of the nirvana I had dreamt of, Sue suddenly squirmed away from under me.

"We can't go any further!" she cried, sitting up. "Not until we're married."

"What?" I asked, unable to believe my ears. "You can't mean it, Sue?" Frustrated beyond belief, I gripped her by the shoulders. With barely suppressed anger, I sneered, "I didn't think you were a bloody prick teaser."

Sue burst into tears. I was so distressed by the sight, for I'd not seen her cry before, my lungs deflated audibly and all my pent-up emotion was expelled in a rush. Utterly confused by the turn of events, I asked Sue gently, "Why not, Sue? Why ever not?"

Sobbing uncontrollably, she shook her head, "I just can't do it Bob. I'm sorry for leading you on, darling. Really, I am. I wanted you so much. It's just that I promised myself I'd wait until we are married." Sue wiped the tears from her eyes on the sleeve of her blouse. "And Mummy said she trusted both of us not to get up to anything under her roof. So, you see, I can't. I mustn't. I want to save myself for our wedding night. I'm so, so sorry for what I did. Can you ever forgive me?"

Naturally, I forgave her. What else could I do, given the circumstances? Nevertheless, I was distraught at having to wait until after we married to discover the joys of sex, when I had been so close a few moments before. So getting a grip on my emotions, I consoled myself that Sue was one in a million. How many others could have been as true to themselves as she'd been? I convinced myself that such constancy, her purity, augured well for our married life.

What I had not bargained for was her desire to bear lots of children, the subject of which was again raised a few days later in the back row of the Regal Cinema in Walton, as we watched a film musical featuring the baritone Dick Haymes. Having whispered in my ear that I sounded just like him, Sue followed up with, "I've heard he has lots of kids." After a short pause, she said even more softly, "Lancelot, you've never told me how many children you want. It's important to me, because you know I'd like several."

I removed my arm from around Sue's shoulders, sat back in my seat and gibbered silently to myself.

"Anything the matter, Lancelot?" Sue asked innocently.

I managed to gulp, "No, nothing darling." Replacing my arm, I muttered, "A bit of heartburn, that's all." Heartburn was nothing as painful to me as what I'd heard Sue say. To keep my mind off it, I hummed along with Dick Haymes singing *Spring Fever*, a song I thought would be perfect for me to sing at the forthcoming talent competition at the Odeon, Kingston, a week or so away. But Sue was like a dog with a bone, not satisfied until she had received the answer she wanted.

On the bus home, she dug me in the ribs, demanding, "You haven't told me how many children you'd like."

To that fatuous remark I gave an equally fatuous reply. "How about sixteen?" I said.

"Silly Billy," Sue grinned, evidently pleased by my response which, for the time being, she thought satisfactory.

Chapter 37

In September there would be Dick's wedding, which I was looking forward to, followed a week later by the arrival of my mother and three young brothers. I was excited at the prospect, but the presence of Nick Grahame-Carter put a pall on it. In between times, Sue was to commence her studies at the Royal College of Music in London, so we had a busy time of it ahead.

Dick had recently come up to see Sue and me in his car, which, unusually for him, he'd recently polished. "Would have loved you to be my best man, old chum," he said, grimacing, "but my cousin Bill Tovey, the *News of the World* photographer, insisted I ask him. He's fixed up for a pal of his to take the photographs of the wedding at no cost, so what could I say?" Pausing, he continued, "So, Bob, I would deem it a great honour if you'd act as one of my ushers instead."

"What's an usher, Dick?" I asked. The only wedding I'd ever attended was that of my mother, when she married my stepfather in the hill station of Murree in the Himalayas. It had been a simple church ceremony, attended by about sixty guests who'd driven up from the Attock Oil Refinery in Rawalpindi. From memory, I could not recall anyone present called an usher.

"An usher, dear boy," replied Dick patiently, his freckled face smoothed with a paternal smile, "is just that. He's a chum of the groom and he ushers guests to their pews, hands out the order of service and whatnot, generally keeps an eye on things. I've asked John Greenwood to be the other one. There's to be a rehearsal the day before to fill you in. So what say, old bean?"

"Of course, Dick. I'd be delighted."

About to take his leave, Dick fingered his chin thoughtfully, "One other thing, Bob," he said. "Push off down to Walton. Go see Moss Bros in the High Street as soon as you can. Get yourself measured up for a morning suit, top hat, gloves, and all that palaver. Now, before you ask, I've settled up with them in advance. So just say it's the Purkis order when you go. You've nothing to pay." Bowing like a courtier, he addressed Sue, "You'll be the most gorgeous girl at my wedding, apart from," he coughed into his hand, his eyes twinkling, "Mary, my wife to be."

Dick waved us goodbye, before climbing stiffly into his car. Always the gentleman, he drew down his window and doffed his hat in Sue's direction, before proceeding sedately down the road.

"He's a lovely chap, that Dick," remarked Sue, as she stood waving. "So sweet of him to pay for your morning suit, isn't it? It's about thirty shillings a day to rent, did you know?" She reached up to give me a peck on the cheek, saying, "Lancelot, you're going to miss him awfully, now he's moving to Selsdon."

"Never a truer word, Sue," I replied sadly. My life would have been much the poorer had I not met Dick Purkis. He'd been a father to me through thick and thin, the kindest man I'd ever known.

Having seen photographs of society weddings in the *Tatler* magazine, where the bridegroom and guests were dolled up in morning suits, I could not wait to try on mine. So, it being a Saturday afternoon, I cycled over to Walton-on-Thames and ventured into the portals of Moss Bros.

I stepped across the threshold and was immediately confronted by an elderly man who wore a black suit and had a tape measure around his neck. I was eyed up and down and had my financial status assessed in a flash. His face remained expressionless as he enquired with studied politeness, "And what I can do for sir this morning?"

"Oh, I've come to be measured for a morning suit," I replied brightly.

In response to this, there emerged from the man's throat a delicate stretched-out "Ah" followed by "Measured for a morning suit, sir?" asked with a barely disguised note of surprise. Seeing my nod of assent, his manner changed instantly, concluding incorrectly that his young customer had money to burn. For why else would he choose to have a suit made for him when he could hire one? He ushered me into a rear sanctum.

The tailor removed the tape measure from around his neck with a practised flick. Making a curious zizzing noise, its entire length slid over his collar to end up dangling loosely in his fingers. "Now, sir," he said, "let's take your inside leg measurement, shall we?"

I was taken aback. The last time I'd had clothes made for me was by a tailor who sat on the verandah of my house in Pakistan, a man who relied on his eye rather than a tape measure.

"Inside leg?" I asked. "Inside what?"

Thinking I was making some sort of joke, the man replied wearily, "Very humorous. Oh, yes, sir, very. Now if sir would kindly place his legs apart, I shall take his inside leg measurement."

Mystified, I did what was asked of me and became even more puzzled, when I heard him question, "On which side does sir dress?"

"Dress? Dress? The usual side I suppose," I answered, making a face. "I really don't know."

"Well, let's go for the middle then, shall we?" The assistant was now on his knees, his tape measure fetching up in my crotch.

"I say, I say," I muttered through gritted teeth, "steady on there." The old boy ignored me and got on with his business, making notes as he went. Finally, he got to his feet. "Now, when does sir require his suit?"

"Oh, I'll come down and collect it tomorrow," I replied blithely.

"Tomorrow!" he screeched. "We can't make a suit by tomorrow."

"No, I know that," I said, suddenly unsure of myself. "It's just that I understood I could hire a morning suit and pick it up immediately. My friend Mr Purkis has already settled up with you."

A look of disbelief came over the man's face. "Hire?" he asked, appearing more put out by the second. "You asked to be measured for a suit, didn't you? By that, I assumed you wanted one made."

"I'm sorry you feel I've misled you," I replied. "It's just that Mr Purkis said I should go and get myself measured up for a morning suit, which is exactly what I did."

"Argh," the man gurgled, trying to control himself, "clearly my mistake. Now, if you'll follow me, I shall take you to the hire department."

I left Moss Bros some half an hour later having been fully kitted out with a black tail coat, striped waistcoat, dress shirt, grey tie, black and white striped trousers a touch too long for me, a shiny black top hat a mite too large, and grey gloves that fitted snugly. I'd admired my reflection in the mirror with my top hat on. Then again, without it. Revolving on my heels, arching my back like Fred Astaire gliding in a foxtrot, I fell absolutely in love with myself, itching to get home to show off to Sue.

As I expected, Sue was impressed, as were Helen and Bill, in front of whom I strutted around the drawing room like a peacock.

"Ooh, you do look so handsome, Lancelot," Sue breathed, viewing me from every possible angle.

"Right tailor's dummy," Bill remarked, slapping me on the back.

"Wish we could come to the wedding," sighed Helen, to which Sue and I replied, "'Course you can. Come to the church and see us both."

"That'll be nice," Helen said, brightening. "You'll make a lovely couple, what with Sue in her beautiful new dress and that little cloche hat and Bob in his get-up. Oh, yes, lovely."

Ahead of Dick's wedding, The Odeon Cinema talent competition in Kingston had attracted a large number of entrants from a wide area, which meant auditions were called for. All the contestants, the jugglers, mime artists, singers who turned up and did their bits onstage were judged by professionals. After weeding out those who had no business being there, a dozen hopefuls, of whom I was one, were left to perform the following day.

Sue had prepared me as thoroughly as ever, saying the Dick Haymes number *Spring Fever* suited my voice perfectly. As I stood with Sue in the wings, smoking cigarette after cigarette, awaiting my turn with the usual nervous tightening in my stomach, I suddenly found difficulty in swallowing. I rubbed, massaged, eased and contorted my facial muscles but nothing I did relieved the stricture in my throat. Holding my neck, I managed to croak helplessly, "Sue, Sue, I don't know what's happened to me. It feels as if I've got a hot boulder stuck in my throat. What can I do? I can't go on. You'd better get the call boy and let him know."

"Open your mouth, let's have a look," Sue replied, stern as any hospital matron. "My God! Bob, why didn't you say something about this, earlier?" she exclaimed, inspecting my throat. "It's scarlet, terribly inflamed." Sympathy replaced severity as she soothed, "Poor, poor Lancelot. I know Mummy and Daddy will be disappointed not to hear you sing. But it's better Daddy takes us home and you go right to bed."

Hopelessly disappointed, I allowed myself to be driven home, where Helen daubed my throat with foul-tasting Mandell's throat paint before taking my temperature.

"It's a hundred and two!" she exclaimed. "Bed for you, my boy. If you're not better by morning I'll call the doctor."

Helen was at my bedside at eight the following morning to take my temperature again. I'd had a sleepless night and could hardly swallow.

"It's still up," said Helen shaking the thermometer. "Right," she said briskly, "I'll call the doctor. He starts surgery about now. Then I'll phone Charlie Hunt and tell him you won't be in today and, by the looks of you, not for the rest of the week, either."

Unable to respond because of the pain, I meekly nodded my thanks. I was in and out of a fitful sleep until the doctor called. Sue and her mother showed him to my bedroom, before leaving him to examine to me.

"You've a bad dose of tonsillitis, young man," he said, when he'd finished. "How long has this been going on?"

When I replied I'd no problems with my throat before, he looked amazed at first. Then, spotting the open packet of Capstan Full Strength Navy Cut cigarettes lying on my bedside table, he tut-tutted disapprovingly. "I see the culprits. Too many fags that's what. Nevertheless, your tonsils are seriously enlarged and should be removed. You really must stop smoking, or else this infection will occur time and time again."

I felt a sense of doom approaching as he droned on.

"I'll write out a sick note for your employer. You're to stay in bed for a week. I shall leave Mrs Kenyon a prescription for some medicine, which should settle the infection and get your temperature down. I'll call again before the weekend and see how you are getting on. If you're not better by then, I'll see if the cottage hospital can find you a bed and we'll have your tonsils out." Pulling his stethoscope from his ears, he wagged an admonishing finger. "Bed rest, no fags, and drink lots of liquid, d'you hear?"

It was only after the doctor had left my room that I realised that if I was to stay in bed as he'd ordered, I would miss Dick's wedding. My dreams of being Fred Astaire, with Sue on my arm looking even more spectacular than Ginger Rogers, were to be dashed. My eyes filled with tears at the thought of not being able to attend.

Sue, always loyal, said she wouldn't think of going to the wedding without me, but in the end I persuaded her that she must. In the new pale blue satin dress, she'd bought specially for Dick's wedding, with matching shoes and a small feathered hat, Sue looked absolutely stunning. Choked, I watched from a window in the drawing room as she drove off with her father and mother to St Mary's Church in Walton, feeling utterly depressed on that beautiful sunny day, wishing I could have been with Sue to see my dear friend married.

On Bill and Helen's return from the wedding—Sue had stayed for the reception—Helen sat down by me in the drawing room and described the scene at the church. Enthusiastic words spewing from her in a rush, she rattled away, hardly taking a breath between sentences. "The bridegroom and the gentlemen in morning dress, all the beautiful dresses—oh, it was lovely, simply lovely. Very posh, you know, but our Sue looked the most beautiful of all of them. Absolutely the best. Oh, dear, I wish you could have been there. And the bride, all in white, with six bridesmaids to hold the train. Dear little things they were. And the bouquets, they must have cost a fortune."

She looked into my face, perhaps expecting to find a hint of jealousy there and added, hurriedly, "Bob, dear, Bill and I will give you both a lovely wedding, too, just you wait. Won't we, Bill?"

Bill gave me a wink, as Helen continued on a path from which she would not be deviated, "I've got everything planned already..."

My heart sank when I heard Helen say 'planned'. Over the past week, while I was bed, I'd been turning over and over in my mind the question of whether Sue and I were truly ready for marriage.

"Gosh, Helen," I replied, shifting uneasily in my chair, "how clever of you to think so far ahead."

"Well, one has to these days, doesn't one?"

My mind drifted to Dick's wedding. I imagined Sue standing in a swirling cloud of confetti cast by the guests, with Dick and his bride ducking and laughing. I visualised a photographer dashing about with his plate camera and tripod, vainly attempting to get everyone in line to pose for a picture, before being drawn to my beautiful Sue, to take a close up shot of her just for me. Then I projected a gleaming Rolls Royce gliding to a stop outside the church, ready to sweep the happy couple off to a grand reception in a fairy-tale mansion.

My stomach tightened. All Sue's hopes and longing for our future were present in my daydreaming. The Rolls Royce, the mansion, the conspicuous wealth were all there. At twenty-two, I thought the probability of my attaining any of those things was as distant as the Himalayas. I dismissed the depressing thought and continued with my fantasies of Dick's wedding reception. I pictured Sue with lots of young, handsome, rich fellows from St George's Hill, each vying to give her a lift until she accepted one from the best looking chap of all.

The hours dragged as we waited for Sue to telephone to ask Bill to collect her, but she never did. Instead, at a few minutes past seven o'clock, I saw a blue Triumph saloon pull up outside the house. Sue got out and waved to the driver as he drove off. Flushed in the face, she burst into the drawing room, bent down to give me a kiss and then kicked off her shoes before flopping down on a sofa with her arms spread out wide.

"Oh, I've had a lovely time of it," she exulted.

"And doing a bit of drinking too, I see," said Bill, adding caustically, "I thought you were going to ring me. We've been waiting here for hours. Then you turn up in some bloke's flash car, pissed."

Helen interrupted Bill in a voice full of reproof. "Such language, Bill," she admonished. "Anyway, Sue's here now. And of course she's had a drink or two. She's been to a wedding reception. Or didn't you know?"

"How was it, Sue?" I asked quickly, defusing the situation. "Who was the bloke?"

"Your pal John Greenwood from the YCs," Sue replied. "He offered to give me a lift home." She gave Bill an apologetic look. "Sorry, Daddy, I was having such a good time, I forgot to ring. I'm sorry."

John Greenwood was no friend of mine. Chairman of the Young Conservatives, he was from a very rich family. Besides living in an enormous house, they also owned a snazzy yacht. Imbued with the charm of the devil, John always had a beautiful girl in tow. I was inordinately envious of him.

"John Greenwood?" I asked, casually, "Nice chap, you think?"

"Lancelot, you're jealous," laughed Sue, instantly divining my thoughts. "Of course he's nice. What's more, he said he likes you very much. He's asked us both up to his house for supper, soon as you're better."

Seething inwardly, for I knew all about John Greenwood's technique with women, I retorted acidly, "How nice," before changing tack. "Come on, tell us all about the wedding and who else was there."

"Oh, the wedding service was lovely. The vicar read a lovely passage from Corinthians, which we should have for ours, too. Dick's father was there, lovely old buffer, didn't look a bit like Dick, all pink cheeks and a roly-poly tummy. Mary's father gave her away. They arrived at the church in his Rolls. And the reception. What a do. What a garden. What a house. Someone said seven bedrooms. At a guess, I'd say there were a hundred and fifty guests. Where Mary's father managed to get all that lovely food and champagne from I'll never know. All I can say is he must be very rich, and have contacts with lots of farmers to get all that ham and stuff."

Sue giggled and began to wave her hands about. Slurring her words slightly, a sure sign she'd had too much to drink, she continued, "I also met poor Mary's mother, who was awfully biffed. She was sozzled most of the time. As for me, I stuffed myself all afternoon and swanned about chatting to a load of your friends. Darling, it was such a shame you weren't there. Everyone was asking after you and sending their regards."

"Well, if you'll all excuse me," I said, tight lipped, "I'm off to bed."

Chapter 38

The doctor signed me off the sick list on the Monday. As he scribbled a note to my firm, he asked if I'd been successful in kicking the tobacco habit. Lying, for I was in no mood to receive a lecture from him, I said I'd forsworn cigarettes and my pipe forever. Immediately after leaving his surgery, I lit up and cycled off to work.

Although I was not as yet feeling a hundred per cent fit, I'd decided going to the office was preferable to spending another day mooching about the house being fussed over by Helen. Besides which I was depressed and still sulking over Sue's enthusiasm for John Greenwood, whose name had cropped up several times the following day. She'd mentioned 'John Greenwood has this' and 'John Greenwood's family have that' to the point I asked her to play a different record. This provoked the furious response that I was just being jealous. This resulted in me excusing myself from joining the family for Sunday's high tea in the garden, saying a walk would do me good.

Ignoring Sue's distinct lack of interest and the perplexed looks passed between Bill and Helen, I strode off to the Oatlands Park Hotel. Pottering about, absently sniffing at the odd bloom that caught my eye, I spent an hour in the hotel grounds. As I pondered how my life would change after my mother's arrival in less than a week, it came to me that I had no idea where my brother Geoff lived or what he did for a living. We'd had no contact with each other since he'd gone his own way three years before. Even though I wasn't close to Geoff, I hoped for my mother's sake he'd kept in touch with her.

Sue had said she wanted to accompany me to Kings Cross station to meet my family. However, a letter from the Royal College of Music requesting her attendance at a pre-term meeting of students on the same day forced her to cry off.

"I'm sorry darling, but I can't possibly duck out," she said to me. "Next Monday's the first day of term." Seeing my look of disappointment, she gave me one of her most dazzling smiles. "Come on, cheer up. I'll meet your mother and that chap, Nick Whatsit, on Saturday instead."

At the office, I got stuck into work the minute I arrived in an effort to make the time pass more quickly. Charlie Hunt poked his head around the door and asked after my health, at the same time enquiring if I was up for the cricket fixture against our main rivals on the Thursday evening. There was nothing said about catching up with my work and making up for lost time, and as luck would have it, Thursday's cricket match was postponed because of heavy rain anyway.

Charlie kindly allowed me to leave work early on the Friday. Even so, the few hours I spent in the office felt like an eternity. When I finally left to catch my train to Waterloo, I was in a seriously jittery state.

Although my mother was indubitably short in the maternal instincts department, I still loved her and longed to see her again. I was also looking forward to seeing my three young brothers, but encountering Nick was a prospect I did not relish in the least. I wondered how he'd react when we met, and for that matter, how would I?

I took the Tube to Kings Cross station, and bought a platform ticket for a penny. By now perspiring heavily in the heat, I decided I had enough time to chain smoke two cigarettes as I waited. Puffing away, I leant against a wrought-iron pillar by the entrance to the platform, reeling from the rank odour of stale sweat coming from the press of humanity hurrying by. The noise, too, was deafening, the screech of steel on steel as engines shunted trains in the yard, their wheels slip-sliding as they braked. Drowned out by hoots and whistles and the hiss of steam, announcements bawled over the Tannoy were unintelligible. So, instead of concentrating on what was being said, I turned my attention to the huge station clock, whose minute hand clunked audibly as it moved inch by inch towards the quarter hour, as if some force was restraining it from ever reaching there. I was just about to light my third cigarette when I saw the boat-train suddenly emerge from the gloom of a tunnel ahead. The locomotive squealed to a stop a few yards down the line from where I stood. Carriage doors were flung open and passengers spilled out onto the platform. My eyes searched the length of the platform before I finally caught sight of my mother. She stood beside my brother Richard, whose leg was in plaster. Nick stood holding the hands of David and Ronald at the very rear of the train.

As I threaded my way through the throng in their direction, I heard my mother shrill as she caught sight of me, "Bobby! Bobby!" She bounded forward and embraced me. Forever onstage, she stood poised on her right leg, her left leg hoisted buttock-high behind her. Puckering up, she embarrassed me by kissing me full on the lips. At forty-five she was still beautiful, her face remarkably unravaged despite many years spent under the Indian sun.

"Dahling, Bobby, we're home! Home!" she cried. Tears ran down her cheeks. "My, you look sooh well, sooh grown up. Oh, dahling, your being here has made Mummy sooh happy."

Even though her gushing sounded insincere, I knew she meant every word. Ignoring Nick Grahame-Carter looming behind her, I pulled her to me and held her tight.

Richard hobbled forward on crutches. "Hello, Bob", he said, smiling broadly. Releasing a crutch, he gripped my hand and shook it.

Four years my junior, he'd done much better than I had at our boarding school. Academically, he was brilliant and had never been below top of his class. No swot, he'd also been good at games, a proper all-rounder. Throughout our school years in the hills, I had shielded him from the kind of unholy bullying to which I'd been subjected. In the process, we had grown very close. But he was no longer the small boy I remembered. At eighteen, he was now as tall as me. Heavily tanned from his journey by sea, he looked fit despite his injured leg.

Squeezing his hand, I choked back my tears. "You silly bugger," I said.

I turned away from him to greet thirteen year-old David, who'd disentangled himself from Nick and now stood grinning at me.

"Hello, David," I said, giving him a hug. "How are you?"

"Fine, thank you," he replied, sounding older than his years: a proper little gentleman.

Meanwhile, my five-year-old stepbrother, Ronald, had struggled out of Nick's grasp to reach me. His vivid blue eyes widened as he gazed at me.

"Hello, Bobby," he said in a baby voice. "Who are you?

Even though I was exhilarated at meeting my family, I knew I had to eventually confront Nick who, thus far, had stood apart, a silent bystander to the effusive family reunion. But the stand-off I'd expected never occurred, for he came forward then, hand outstretched, surprising me with a disarming smile of genuine welcome. Dressed now in a creased grey wool suit instead of his Intelligence Corps uniform, he looked an altogether different person than the one I'd been nervous about meeting again.

"Good to see you, Bob," he said formally, stroking his thin black moustache. "How are you? Well, I hope."

Although I had long conjectured about how I'd respond to seeing Nick, hoping I would steel myself and face up to him, Nick's affability caught me off balance.

I took his hand reluctantly. "Fine, thanks," I replied, with similar formality. "And you?"

"A touch tired, old chap," he answered. "Nothing a double whisky won't fix when we get to the hotel."

I did not let on that the Oatlands Park Hotel was dry. Instead, I said we'd better get on with it. Our train from Waterloo left in an hour.

"Righto, old boy," said Nick, galvanised into hailing a porter to load their five small pieces of luggage. "The rest of our stuff's being forwarded to the hotel by Cox and Kings. Should arrive in a couple of days I expect. Meantime, we'll make do, eh, what?"

The porter carted the luggage directly to the taxi rank outside the station, where Nick paid him off. The driver of the first taxi Nick approached baulked when he saw there were six passengers "Nah, guv," he said, "you'll need two cabs for this lot. Sorry, but can't squeeze you all in." There was nothing for it, we set off in two taxis—my mother, Richard and I in one, the others in the second—and arrived at Waterloo in good time to acquire seats on the 5.15 p.m. train.

On the thirty-minute train journey to Oatlands station, my mother plied me with questions about Sue, my work, what I'd achieved so far, and just about everything, before surprising me with the news my brother Geoff was coming to visit the next day.

"I'm glad he's been in touch with you, Mops," I said, using the nickname I'd given her when I was small, "because I haven't seen or heard from him for years. How's he doing?"

"Apparently, quite well," she replied. "He works in a magazine office in London somewhere. Something to do with holiday travel, as I recall. He has a room in, lives in, er, let me see," her brow furrowed, "in Clapham, I think. That's it, Clapham."

So Geoff was working for a magazine. Good for him, I thought, envying his success, jealous he was earning a living doing something I should have liked to do myself. I looked across the aisle to Richard, who'd had his face pressed to the carriage window throughout the journey.

"I didn't know there were so many bombed out buildings still left in London," he remarked, shaking his head. "Everything looks so bloody drab, doesn't it? I had no idea London was like this. No idea at all."

"It's different in Surrey," I said, trying to cheer him up. "Lots of greenery, nice houses, et cetera, et cetera. I suppose when your leg's fixed, you'll be looking for a job of some sort?"

"Yeah, well, I'm thinking of joining the Army," Richard replied. "Hopefully, the plaster will be off in a week or so. Maybe then I can find some sort of work until my leg is stronger and then I'll be off.

"How did you break it, Richard?"

"Bloody motor bike. Going too fast. Skidded, hit a wall, shattered the femur in several places. In the military hospital in Rawalpindi for three months."

Nick, who thus far had been silent, removed the cigarette holder from his mouth. Exhaling a cloud of smoke, he said, "This Oatlands Park Hotel we are staying at sounds a decent sort of place. Good of you to have fixed us up there, Bob. Before the war I knew Surrey quite well. I imagine we'll stay at the hotel for a week or so, get our bearings, then look around for a house nearby to rent."

My heart sank at the idea of Nick living on my doorstep, for the hotel was no more than a quarter of a mile away from the Kenyon's house.

There were no taxis to be had outside Oatlands station, so I set off to the hotel on foot and arranged with the manager to send a car to pick up the family. After all the formalities of registration, Nick, my mother and the boys were shown to their rooms. By now it was nearly seven in the evening, time for them to have an early supper and for me to disappear before Nick realised he couldn't buy a drink at the Oatlands Park Hotel at any price. I made the excuse I had to get back to have my evening meal with the Kenyons, who were expecting me. Saying I'd return the following morning, no earlier than eleven because no doubt they were all tired out, I escaped from the place as fast as I could.

Bill and Helen greeted me on the doorstep the moment I got home. "Did your family arrive all right?" asked Bill. "Can we be of help?"

Dear Bill Kenyon, kindness itself.

"They're all fine," I said. "They were tired, of course, after their long journey. "I'm sure they'll tell me their plans when Sue and I visit them tomorrow."

"From what you told me about your stepfather, he won't be too happy when he discovers there's no bar at the hotel," Bill chuckled.

"He's not my stepfather, Bill!" I replied, sharply. "I hate the swine. I don't know what my mother sees in him. Serves the chap right if he can't have a drink there."

"Well *you* can, here, my boy," soothed Bill, taking my arm. "Thought you'd be thirsty by now. So, come along, I've got some Watneys bitter waiting.

As Bill and I sat drinking our beer in the drawing room and Helen sipped at a sweet sherry, I went over the day's events with them. Helen said she'd love to meet my mother at the very earliest, because she sounded sweet and besides they'd soon be related by marriage.

I wondered how the two of them would get on. On one hand, there was Helen, a staid suburban housewife, and on the other, my mother, outrageous and overwhelmingly dramatic. Then there was the question of how Bill, the bluff, kindly salesman of widgets, would take to the glaringly upper-class Nick Grahame-Carter, with his ivory cigarette holder and superior air. I didn't have time to dwell on the issue, for Sue entered the drawing room in a rush and flung a newspaper in my lap.

"Lancelot, we won the film test competition!" she cried, bending down to plant a kiss on my cheek. "That's today's *Surrey Herald*. It's all in there."

I picked up the newspaper and began to flip through the pages. Sue grabbed it from my hands.

"We are on the front page, silly," she said. "See? Here!" She jabbed a finger at the front-page article. "It's a lousy picture of us, but there it is. 'Robert Monteath-Matthews and—'" She stopped short, then added, "Bit flashy of you, that. I didn't know you'd told them your surname was hyphenated. Makes 'Sue Kenyon' sound awfully ordinary."

Blushing, I replied I'd given it out as a laugh. "But, darling, just think of it," I said, trying to humour her, "'Susan Kenyon' will look great as a screen credit. Better than 'Bob Matthews' by far."

Sue's response was a dismissive "humph", before reading aloud the caption.

As winners of the recent Stars of the Future competition, Mr Robert Monteath-Matthews and Miss Susan Kenyon will be auditioned by the Italian film director Renato Castellani for the roles of Romeo and Juliet in his forthcoming film to be shot in Verona. As runners up, Diana Dove, John Murtough, Sheila Wilson and Henry Lane will each receive free admission to the Palace Cinema for a period of six months.

Helen beamed, "We always knew you'd both win. Didn't we, Bill?"

"Without a shadow," agreed Bill, looking as pleased as his wife. "But that poor Diana Dove, her nose will be put out of joint won't it? I remember you saying she was at an acting school in London. Nice girl. She'll be so disappointed. Free seats in that flea pit of a picture house," he laughed, "can't say that's much of a prize."

"I wonder when we'll hear from this Renato Castellani bloke?" I said, already warming to the prospect of playing Romeo. "I imagine it'll be soon."

"I've rather gone off the idea," remarked Susan gloomily. "I can't help thinking the competition is all about promoting his film."

"Oh, no, darling," said Helen stoutly, "they wouldn't do that, would they, Bill?"

Bill replied instantly, giving me a wink, "No, not at all."

"Well, I don't know about you lot, I fancy an early night," said Sue, getting to her feet. "It's been a long day."

"Sue, aren't you even going to ask Bob about how he got on with meeting his family today?" asked Helen, disapprovingly. "I am surprised at you, girl. There's Bob on tenterhooks waiting to tell you about it, and you haven't even bothered to ask."

"Oh, Lancelot, I am sorry," replied Sue, falling to her knees in front of me. "That was awfully selfish of me. Come on, darling, tell me all about it."

"No, you're tired out. It'll wait 'til morning," I said, tight-lipped. "What with your being held up in London and getting back late and all, it'll keep."

"It was nothing," protested Sue, "I met John Greenwood at Waterloo station by chance—" At the slip of her tongue, her hands went to her mouth. "He asked me to join him for a drink and we missed the train. That's all." She sat on the floor looking up at me, her expression abject. "Honest. That's all there was to it, and then John gave me a lift home."

Helen called across to Bill, whose expression was blank, "Come on, Bill, time for bed." Her face grim, she said, "Goodnight, Susan." Then, in a more sympathetic tone of voice, she blew me a kiss, saying, "Nighty-night, Bob." Taking Bill's arm they both silently left.

Alone now, I turned to Sue. "What's this with John Greenwood?" I can't believe you met him by chance. You always seem to be meeting him *by chance*."

But it's true," Sue protested vehemently. "I was very early for my train and he just happened to be waiting on the platform, as well. So, when he suggested we go for a drink at the station bar, I thought, 'oh, why not?' Then we got chatting and, well, you know the rest." She put out a hand to touch my knee, "It was nothing, darling, nothing."

I wasn't sure whether Sue was telling the truth or not, but I was so consumed with jealousy, I chose not to believe her. "Look, Sue, if you want to call it off—us, I mean—just say so."

"Don't be so bloody ridiculous, Bob!" Sue seethed. "If you are so jealous of John, I promise never to speak to him again. How's that? I was telling you the truth, and if you really want to know, he doesn't hold a candle to you." Her voice softening, she gazed at me and said, "I love you. Only you, you dope."

All my rage deserted me. I pulled her to me and we clung together for a long time, with me whispering over and over again how sorry I was. And, when all the recriminations were done, I told her about my day: my mother, Nick, my brothers and my fears about them living close at hand. She responded by saying how nice that would be, showing she did not understand at all.

Chapter 39

Sue and I figured that by eleven o'clock in the morning, my family would have done with breakfast and be ready to welcome us. Instead, when we arrived at the hotel, we were directed to the dining room where my mother and Nick were still sitting a table tucking into toast and tea. Of the boys there was no sign.

My mother greeted me in her usual effusive way. She embraced Sue, then pushed her away an arm's length to view her from every possible angle.

"My, you are even prettier than Bob said," she said.

Sue, flushing with embarrassment, detached herself from my mother's grasp and found herself facing Nick, who had got out of his seat and come round to be introduced. He stood observing Sue, stroking his moustache, before taking Sue's outstretched hand.

"How do you do?" he said, shaking Sue's hand. "Would you care to join us?"

"No thanks, Nick," I interrupted. "We didn't mean to disturb you. Come, Sue, we'll wait in the lounge, shall we?" With that, I hustled Sue out and found a sofa on which to sit.

"Sorry about Mum," I said to her. "She's a bit dramatic, and Nick's, well—"

Surprising me, Sue interjected, "Oh, I thought she was terrific, actually. I was just taken off balance that's all. As for Nick, he's much nicer than you described."

Put in my place, I grunted something noncommittal in response before suggesting we look for my brothers. We discovered them in the garden just outside the hotel, sitting on a bench facing the entrance. Sue immediately bent down and picked up Ronald in her arms.

"Who you?" the little boy asked.

"I'm Sue," she replied, "and you who?"

"Wonald."

Sue charmed them all, promising to play with "Wonald", telling David he was better looking than I was, resulting in him blushing, and saying to Richard that she'd heard he was cleverer than I was, making him squirm.

"I think Geoff's coming down this morning," said Richard, addressing Sue. "So, with the exception of my sister, you'll then have met all the family." Pausing, a grave expression suddenly came over his face, betrayed by eyes filled with humour. "Sue, you don't know what you're getting yourself into with Bob," he warned. "Bob's always had an eye for the dames."

Having finished with breakfast, Nick and my mother came to join us in the garden. "I say, Bob," said Nick, "good job I had a bottle of whisky in my case. Can't get a drink here. This damn place hasn't got a bar. Owned by Quakers, did you know?"

"Oh, I am sorry, Nick," I replied, feigning innocence, "I never thought to ask." I sulked inwardly. All my scheming to deprive Nick of a drink had come to nothing.

"Good job the pub's just down the road," Nick smiled. "I think when Geoff finally gets here, we'll all poodle off there, don't you agree? Haven't been inside a pub for years."

It was nearly one o'clock before Geoff made an appearance. Appearing harassed, he went round greeting each of us, apologising for being late, explaining the trains were not running on time. My mother did her usual turn, kissing him on both cheeks. I saw that Geoff had not changed; introduced to Sue, he lifted an eyebrow and drawled in his fake American accent, "Gee, Sue, that bro of mine gets all the pretty dames."

Dressed in a too-large drape jacket with wide shoulders he was as skinny as I remembered. "How ya doin', Bob? Long time no see," he said, surprising me with the genuine warmth in his voice.

"Now, come on, chaps," said Nick, cutting in. "Don't know about you, but I want a couple of pints before the pubs shut. Richard, you stay behind. Have some lunch and look after the boys. We'll be about an hour at the most. Righto?"

Richard looked disappointed at first, but then realised that he could not trek to the pub on his crutches, so giving me the thumbs up, he took David and Ronald inside the hotel. Poor Richard, I thought. The sooner the plaster came off his leg the better off he'd be. He could then be independent, join the Army and get well away from Nick and my mother.

The regulars inside the *Flintgate* pub on Oatlands Drive could have been forgiven for looking startled when our motley-looking crew made an entrance in the smoke-filled bar. My mother, wearing a floral dress copied from *Vogue* and run up by a tailor in Pakistan, sat down on a bench beside Sue, glamorous in a filmy white skirt cinched tight at the waist by a shiny black belt. Geoff, incongruous in his Hollywood-style get-up inched up close to her, leaving me to pull up a stool for myself. Nick, louche with his thin black moustache and cigarette holder jutting from his mouth, asked the ladies what they'd like to drink, ordaining beers in straight glasses for the men.

I shrank when I heard Nick address the barman, a corpulent red-faced chap with ginger whiskers sprouting from his cheeks, as if he was a private in the Army, "Two Babychams, whatever they may be," he ordered in a loud voice. He stood tall, stroking his moustache as he rapped loudly on the counter. "And, ah, let me see, what kind of beer do you have, my man?" He appeared oblivious to the barman's bridling at being treated like a serf. "Ah, I see you've Watneys," Nick continued, in his frightfully upper-class accent. "Well, that'll do. Three pints, straight glasses. Now how much is all that?"

The barman sucked in his cheeks before replying through compressed lips. "That will be four and six, sir." His angry eyes went to a couple of men at the bar, who nodded imperceptibly, their expression implying it takes all sorts.

"How much did you say?" exclaimed Nick, expressing a long stream of smoke. "My word, things have jolly well gone up since I was last in Blighty. That lot would have been about half the price before the war."

"I dare say, sir," remarked the barman, sounding bored now, taking the one-pound note Nick proffered, then scattering the change all over the counter.

I noticed my mother looked embarrassed as she turned to Sue to talk about our impending wedding.

"We must meet your parents, Sue," she said, "see if we can be of help. That sort of thing."

"Absolutely," interjected Nick as he sat himself down at the table. "Do our bit, doncha know?"

I was not enjoying the direction in which the conversation was going. The idea of Nick and my mother getting involved in the wedding arrangements was positively frightening. I feared my mother taking centre stage, with toffee-nosed Nick putting the guests off.

Possibly because she sensed what I was thinking, Sue took my mother's arm, saying, "Mrs Carter—"

"Alys, please call me Alys."

"Well, Alys, I was about to ask you if Bob's told you about our film test—"

"No. Film test! What film test?"

"Oh, we both had a film test at Nettlefold studios and the prize was an audition with the Italian film director, Renato Castellani—"

"My father was Italian. My maiden name was Belletti, you know," my mother interrupted. Catching herself, my mother apologised, "Sorry. Sorry, Sue, do go on."

"Well, Renato Castellani is making a film of *Romeo and Juliet* in Verona. We won the competition, Alys! We're auditioning for the part of Romeo and Juliet."

"How marvellous! How exciting. How absolutely wonderful. Oh, m'dears, I'm so happy for you both."

Sue and my mother were talking so loudly now, we had the rapt attention of all the drinkers at the bar.

Annoyed, I said, "Oh, do let's change the subject."

Geoff was having none of it. "Gee whizz, Baab. My bro is going to be a Hollywood film star. Ain't that great?"

To my relief, the publican called "Time gentlemen, please" at two o'clock on the dot.

As we ambled back to the hotel, my mother and Sue leading the way, talking animatedly, I hung back with Geoff, who told me about his life in London. He said he'd got a job with a magazine as a junior office boy, but that he hoped to become a journalist. I was happy for him. He was heading in a direction I'd have wished for myself.

"How did you get the job Geoff?" I asked, with a twinge of jealousy. "I never had such luck." And, I might have added, I had more qualifications than he had.

"Oh, I never admitted I came from India. At all my interviews, I guess, with my accent, they thought I was either American or Canadian. It seemed to impress them. Surely you didn't admit to coming from Pakistan or India, did you?"

"'Course I did, and I was often called a wog. The chap at the Labour Exchange put me down as an Indian on the form. I told him I wasn't. I said Mum was Italian. He wouldn't have any of it, though. He said since I was born in India, I was Indian. I said 'if I'd been born on a ship, it wouldn't have made me a lifeboat, would it?'"

Geoff laughed, "I bet that fixed him."

"Anyway, Geoff, I could never pass for an American. I can't do the accent and what's more, the rest of you are white, unlike muggins here. So the Labour Exchange dished me out the kind of work nobody else wanted. But so what? I'm okay now."

As we walked, I mused about our strange upbringing, until Nick, who'd come up alongside, brought me abruptly into the present.

"Bob, my boy," he said, coming to a halt on the pavement, forcing me to stop, so that Geoff went on ahead. "I've been meaning to say this since we arrived. I am prepared to forget our little contretemps if you are. What say, we let bygones be bygones and start afresh, eh?" He held out his hand. "Shall we shake on it? It was wrong of me to give you a slap. I deserved what you dished out." Nick smiled, rubbing his jaw. "You certainly pack a punch."

I was more than relieved to accept Nick's offer of an olive branch, for although I would always remain wary of him, harbouring hatred for him was pointless and self-defeating.

"I am shortly to be demobbed, you know," Nick continued. Searching my face for approval, he said, "I plan to marry your mother as soon as my demob comes through. That all right by you, my boy?"

Not quite knowing how to respond, I merely shrugged, signifying neither approval nor disapproval, as if to indicate their business had nothing to do with me. Apparently satisfied with my non-answer, he recommenced walking before pausing once again, his brow furrowed as he looked up into the trees overhead. It was as if he was searching through the skein of oak branches, burdened with yellowing leaves presaging an early autumn, for the right words. Finally, after an interminable wait, he swallowed and, hunching his shoulders up, his arms tight to his chest, he showed me the palms of his hands.

"I love your mother and the boys," he said, his voice breaking. "I shall always care for them."

Nick sounded so sincere I could not help being touched. But my heart hardened as I recalled how he had cuckolded his best friend, my stepfather. Maurice had been so good to us and had not deserved having his life ruined by Nick and my mother. Poor Maurice, driven to alcoholism out of despair, now seemed destined to live out his life alone at the oil refinery at Morgah. The fact that my mother was also responsible didn't alter my feelings for Nick.

"I'll start looking around on Monday for a place to rent in Weybridge," said Nick, collecting himself as he got into his stride once more. "Can't afford to stay at Oatlands Park for too long. It was deucedly expensive bringing the family over to the UK, you know. The Army wouldn't pay for them, because as yet they're not my dependents. As a result money's pretty tight." He hesitated momentarily. "Bob, what do you think about my asking Sue's father if he knows of any properties for rent in the area?"

My heart missed a beat, hoping Nick would not approach the Kenyons. Being the sort of people they were, they'd offer to help, I knew, but I was reluctant to put them to any trouble after the kindness they'd shown me. But having already witnessed Sue's enthusiasm for my family, I knew it was a forlorn hope.

My fears were soon borne out, for no sooner had we sat down for afternoon tea on the lawn outside the hotel, then Sue rushed off to phone her mother. Returning almost immediately, she burst out with: "Mummy won't take no for answer! She'd dying to meet you, and you are all to have lunch with us tomorrow."

I decided to make no comment and went off with Geoff, Richard and the two young ones to try our hand at croquet, while Sue and my mother continued chirping on about our wedding and the audition. They were still at it an hour later when we returned. Nick had gone up to his bedroom to rest, presumably bored out of his mind. At four o'clock Geoff left to catch his train to London, and only then could I finally interrupt the two women and persuade Sue it was time to leave.

Chapter 40

When the family turned up for lunch the next day, Bill and Nick appeared to get on very well. Initially, I thought Nick would play the senior intelligence officer to Bill's corporal in the Signal Corps, but he never did. Instead, they discovered they had served in Burma at roughly the same time, and were soon exchanging reminiscences about Rangoon and what they had got up to fighting the Japanese in the Irrawaddy Delta. I was surprised too, that my mother and Helen Kenyon were immediately at ease with one another, their common bond presumably the forthcoming wedding of their offspring.

Meanwhile Sue fussed around Richard, ensuring he was comfortable in his lounging chair in the garden, not forgetting David and Ronald, for whom she'd prepared a jug full of home-made lemonade.

It was a sunny day, unusually warm for late September. Jackets and coats were soon discarded and everyone relaxed in the Kenyon's carefully tended garden. I smiled when I saw my mother grimace as she sipped at a gin and tonic without ice. She hated drinks which weren't laden with it. Nick and Bill, jugs of beer in hand, sauntered about the garden throwing balls for the boys, who scampered about whooping with laughter.

Everybody else was enjoying themselves, but I became more and more despondent as I listened to the women banging on about the wedding arrangements. I felt as though I were being pushed into a marriage about which I was becoming increasingly nervous. The thrill, the initial excitement of marrying Sue, had been replaced by terror at the very idea. Furthermore, I was no longer certain I was in love with Sue or indeed if she was with me.

John Greenwood's name kept intruding in my thoughts, reminding me that he could give Sue everything she desired. Despite her protestations that she loved me, and her starry-eyed plans for our future, I asked myself if we weren't simply digging a hole for ourselves because neither of us had the courage to withdraw at such a late stage. The effect of these depressing thoughts must have shown on my face, for Richard leaned across to dig me in the ribs.

"Can't be as bad as all that, Bob," he said. "Your face looked as though you were at a funeral."

"Was it, really? I can't imagine why. I'm fine."

"You sure?"

"Sure, I'm sure. Absolutely."

Fortunately, I was saved from Richard questioning me further by Helen calling on the men to help bring chairs out. No sooner had the chairs been arranged than Helen, Sue and my mother came out from the kitchen, each bearing a tray with cold chicken, mounds of salad, boiled new potatoes and a variety of puddings.

Bill rented an allotment where he grew vegetables, which accounted for the salad. He also had relations who kept chickens. However, a deal of bargaining must have gone on to procure what I figured must be four decent-sized chickens.

My mother would have been ignorant of how much trouble the Kenyons had gone to in providing us with such a fine meal. In Pakistan lamb, beef, chicken, vegetables and fruit were always readily available in the bazaars. Mother would shortly learn what rationing was all about, a difficult lesson for one who had employed a cook all her life.

At that instant, almost as if my mind had been read, I heard Helen ask my mother, "Alys, do you like to cook? I love it. But these days we can't even roast a joint with Yorkshire pudding, you know, like we used to have every Sunday before rationing came in."

I saw my mother swallow hard as she answered, "'Fraid I'm not much of a hand in the kitchen, Helen. In India, we had a cook and servants, you see." She gave an embarrassed half-smile, "I imagine I could just about cope with an egg." I felt a twinge of sympathy for my mother as she continued lamely, "I'll just have to learn, I suppose."

"Well, Alys, my dear, you've come to just the right place," said Helen bustling about, handing out plates. "I'll be more than happy to show you."

"Oh, will you, really?"

"Yes, of course, I will. Starting tomorrow."

"Oh, Helen, you are a dear," my mother enthused.

It was not long before the main course was disposed of, and the boys set about demolishing a sponge pudding and custard, followed by orange trifle. "Not eating much, Lancelot?" asked Sue, coming up behind me to give me a peck on the cheek.

"I'm stuffed," I replied. "Lovely lunch. Don't know how Helen did it at such short notice. She's amazing."

"Yes, isn't she just? Mummy's talking about doing all the catering for our wedding. We're going to have the reception in the garden. And, oh, yes, Mummy's had a word with the vicar of St Mary's Church, to hold the service there."

I felt iron bands tighten around my heart. "Did she say when?" I squirmed, hoping that the wedding, if it was to be in January as planned, would be pushed back to the last possible day.

"We both thought Saturday the twentieth of February. Only because the vicar can't do us before then."

"If that's the case, why can't we be married in March or something?" I asked, suppressing my relief. "Another month won't matter." Hoping against hope that Sue might agree, I suggested, "What's more it'll be warmer then."

"Don't be ridiculous, Bob. Daddy's getting a marquee and with all the guests inside it'll soon warm up." She gave me a curious look. "You do still want us to be married, don't you?"

I wanted to tell Sue the truth that I really didn't know. I wanted to ask for time to think, anything to avoid answering her directly, instead of which I blurted, "Don't be silly, of course I do." As Sue levelled her eyes on mine, I said, with more certainty than I felt, "We'll get married whenever you like." Cursing myself for being so lily-livered, I squeezed Sue's hand and propelled her to where Richard was sitting.

"Come on, chaps," I said; now brightness itself, "you talk amongst yourselves. I'm off to help Helen clear the dishes. It won't enter Mum's mind do it." I glanced at my mother, contentedly lounging in her chair, eyes closed, pulling on a cigarette.

My family stayed on until well after teatime. When they'd gone, I sat with Sue in the drawing room, our hands clasped. Helen had crept out, thinking to leave the lovebirds alone, but Sue fell asleep with her head on my shoulder, while I allowed my mind to drift over the events of the day.

Nick and my mother had certainly made a hit with Sue's parents. I'd overheard Helen telling Bill that she found my mother scatty, but sweet. Whereas, Nick's old pals act with Bill made me suspicious. Although I hardly knew Nick, I felt sure he was after something. But what?

A strand of Sue's hair tickled my nose. I was about to remove it when she awoke. Stretching, she sighed, "That was the most delicious sleep, Lancelot." Nuzzling up to give me a kiss, she asked, "Where's Mummy and Daddy?"

"I think they've gone to bed."

"Oh, good," she said, kissing me.

I assumed from Sue's enthusiastic response, she was at last giving me the signal I'd been waiting for so long, and she was now ready for me to make love to her. I started kissing her long and hard, while my hands searched over her breasts. Pushing her down on the sofa I drew her skirt up, exposing her thighs. She sighed and moaned with pleasure as my hands explored, but then suddenly, abruptly, she forced me away. I watched helplessly as she adjusted her clothing.

"Oh, Bob, I just can't," she pleaded, her eyes brimming with tears. "Darling Lancelot, I want you to so much. So much. But we mustn't. " Sue wiped her eyes dry with a sleeve. "You think I'm a tease, don't you? But I'm not. Really, not. We've got to wait until after we're married."

I should have known. Once again, I had completely misjudged the situation. Having previously been through the same scenario, how could I possibly be angry with Sue, even though she'd left me feeling utterly frustrated?

Later on that night, unsettled by what had occurred, I twisted and turned in bed, wondering when I'd grow up and realise how fortunate I was to have a girl like Sue to love me. I kept repeating to myself, "She's beautiful, she's kind, she's fun. A chap couldn't want for more. For God's sake stop whining, Matthews. Marry Sue and live happy ever after."

Chapter 41

Three weeks later my family moved into rented accommodation: a small three- bedroomed semi in Weybridge that Bill and Helen had found for them. Once they had settled into their cramped, furnished quarters, Helen came over to show my mother how to light the stove and prepare a few simple dishes. It was just as well, because my mother had nearly blown up the house, experimenting with matches and scraps of paper to light the gas.

In case she had a similar scare in the bathroom, I instructed her in the mysteries of the coin-operated gas boiler located there. Similar to the one in Willow Cottage, it required a threepenny piece to turn it on. From past experience, I found it useful to have a few more coins handy, for all the hot water threepence produced was barely sufficient to bathe a baby.

Most people I knew got by with one bath a week, usually taken on Mondays, whereas my mother insisted on bathing every day. Clearly, if she continued with her habit of wallowing in water up to her chin, the extravagance was bound to make a hefty dent in the family budget. I pointed out that if the rest of the family followed her example, they'd be bankrupt in no time at all. Still she refused, absolutely refused, to lower her standards, as she put it.

Helen had the family registered with her doctor, who immediately arranged for Richard to have the plaster removed from his leg at the cottage hospital. Happily, his femur had knitted perfectly and after a few sessions of physiotherapy to strengthen his muscles he was able to walk with barely a limp. Assured by the doctor that he'd be fit enough to join the Army by January, Richard took to walking long distances just to make certain. "I'm peed off with doing nothing all day," he told me, "I just can't wait to join up."

David was found a place in the local secondary school, whilst my mother looked after Ronald at home. Meanwhile Nick spent his days searching the situations vacant columns in all the local newspapers. When I commented that Nick appeared increasingly tired and disconsolate, my mother confided that he'd written to all the schools in the area, asking if they had a vacancy for a French teacher, as he'd taught French in a public school before the war, but without success.

"Nick must find a job soon," my mother said. "He's been in touch with the Ministry to speed up the demob pay he's due, but so far he's only received a piffling amount. I really don't know how we are to manage if they don't come up with more."

I called in every few days on my way home from work, which gave Richard the opportunity to ride my bike up and down the towpath to help exercise his leg. Meanwhile, I sat in the kitchen itching to be away, listening to my mother bemoaning her fate whilst Nick remained closeted in the sitting room writing applications for jobs.

"You'd think" I said, to my mother one day, "that with all Nick's contacts, his connections from before the war, some of them would help out."

"Yes, you would think so," she replied, "but only one chap, can't think of his first name, but his surname's Silk, someone Nick knew at Wellington, replied to Nick's letter. He's the Attorney General, as I recall. The bloody man sent a scribbled note, wishing Nick well in the future and enclosed a five pound note in the envelope. Can you imagine the cheek of it, after Nick had once helped the beggar out when he was in trouble? Nick's absolutely fed up and considering writing to Winnie now—"

"Churchill? Winston Churchill?"

"Yes, of course, why ever not?" my mother replied airily, as if the great man was a bosom friend. "Did you know that he once personally congratulated Nick? It was after a private intelligence briefing Nick gave on how the French Army was faring against the Viet Minh in Indochina. So Winston's bound to remember him, isn't he?"

"But why is Nick writing to Churchill, Mops?" I persisted.

"To complain about his treatment by the MoD. After all, he did his bit in the war and deserves better."

Convinced my mother had lost all sense of reality, I kissed her goodbye and left the house wondering what other foolishness she and Nick were about to indulge in next. I had not long to wait, for when I dropped in a couple of days later she told me, "Nick's got a job with the *Encyclopaedia Britannica* company as a salesman."

Sounding as if she'd just won the pools, she cupped my face in her hands and chortled, "Isn't it simply marvellous news?"

I was aghast. "Christ, Mops! Door to door selling is the toughest job in the world. It's commission only. There's no salary!"

"It's not door to door. It's all done by appointment," my mother insisted, puffing wildly on a menthol cigarette. "I'm sure Nick can persuade customers to buy. Just you see, Bob."

Defeated, I asked her to pass on my good wishes to Nick and headed off in the dark for the haven of the Kenyon household. I had a moment of guilt, reflecting that I was certain of a substantial supper there, whereas, judging by the meagre fare sitting on my mother's kitchen table, my brothers would not do half as well as me.

Ultimately, and to Nick's credit, he confounded us all. I gathered from my mother that the company had only given him a day's training in the arcane art of selling encyclopaedias to the public. Amazingly, Nick made a sale in his first week and was paid a handsome commission immediately. Spurred on by this, Nick bussed and trudged his way around his sales patch in Surrey from morning 'til night. Unfortunately, his early success was something of a flash in the pan, because it was another two weeks before he achieved another sale. Nonetheless, he stuck at it. A heavy valise in hand, containing bulky volumes of encyclopaedias, he made his way from prospect to prospect in the cold and the rain with a determination that deserved respect.

In mid-November he asked me to join him for a drink to celebrate making two sales in one day. Beaming, as he thrust a pint of mild and brown beer into my hand, he told me he'd been paid ten pounds commission that week.

"My luck's changed, Bob, old chum," he said, as I quickly calculated that it took me two weeks to earn the same amount. "I've also had an interview with the headmaster of a grammar school in Shepperton," he continued, "so I shan't be doing this for much longer." Putting a finger to his lips, he said, "Mum's the word, eh? Don't tell Alys, just in case I'm not selected. Anyway, I'll know by next week. From the impression I received, I think I've a good chance of getting the job. I'll be teaching French to sixth formers, commencing January. So, at least, we can all look forward to having a decent Christmas. After which, we'll move to Shepperton."

I returned to the Kenyon's house in a good frame of mind. If Nick got the job and the family settled in Shepperton, I could finally get on with my own life and not be too concerned about theirs.

Sue opened the front door before I could knock. She stood waving at me as I came up the path to the house. "Lancelot, I think we've both got auditions next week!" she cried. "I've just got a letter from Renato Castellani. Says he wants me to see him at eleven next Monday." She offered me an envelope. "This one's for you. I imagine it's also from him."

"Seriously? It's actually happening?" I opened the letter. "Yeah, it's from him. I'm seeing him on Monday, too, at a quarter past eleven." I had imagined myself reading from a script, with a photographer at hand taking pictures. "Fifteen minutes each doesn't seem much time for a proper audition, does it?" I said. "What's more, it's terribly short notice for me to ask Charlie Hunt for the day off."

"Don't be such a bore, darling. Charlie will understand. It's all so exciting, isn't it?" Sue took my arm. "Who knows? He might even pick you."

"He'll be an idiot if he doesn't choose you."

Bill and Helen insisted on drinking a toast to the film *Stars of the Future*, while Sue and I stood awkwardly in front of them. With our glasses of sherry in hand, we kissed like the Romeo and Juliet we were destined to be.

Chapter 42

As soon as I got to work the next day, I knocked on Charlie Hunt's office door. Stuttering, stammering, I told him about my audition, explaining how much it meant to me and so on, and asked if I could please have Monday off.

He listened quietly until I had quite finished, then got up from behind his desk and came over to me. Putting a fatherly arm around my shoulder, he said, "Yes, you can have the day off. But before you dash away there's something I've been meaning to say to you." Seeing my startled expression, he quickly added, "nothing to worry about, son. Just listen carefully to me. What I am about to tell you, you must keep to yourself. In view of your imminent marriage, I've decided to let you into something. But you must promise never to speak to anyone in the office about it. Do I have your word?"

I nodded.

"Well then," he said. "The company is moving to High Wycombe in March." My eyes popped wide in surprise as I heard him add, "I'm offering you a job in sales, based at Head Office. If you accept, we'll assist in finding you somewhere to live nearby. After six months training, you'll go on the road. You'll be given a company car, so you'd better learn how to drive soon. The starting salary's four fifty a year. Keep your nose clean and you'll be on five hundred the next."

He took a deep breath. "The problem is, if you pursue this singing and acting lark, you are obviously no good to us and you should look for another job right away. My advice is to have a good think about making a career with us. Talk it over with Susan and let me know on Tuesday what you decide, after you've been to this... this..., audition of yours. That's all I have to say for the moment. With Midland Gypsum Industries, you have the chance of making a great start to your married life. You'll have a good steady job with excellent prospects of promotion, far more stable than being on the stage."

I knew right away that Susan would not be pleased by the news. My initial reaction, after I had gathered my wits, was to immediately accept the position I had been offered and hang the consequences. Where would I get another opportunity as good? If it meant moving to High Wycombe, well, so be it. Charlie was right on all counts: I should forget show business and concentrate on making a home for Sue and myself.

"Thanks Charlie," I replied. "I promise to give you a definite answer on Tuesday after I've had a chat with Sue. It's a terrific offer."

"Off you go then," said Charlie, "remember, Mum's the word, eh?"

I left Charlie's office in a state of high elation and went straight to my desk, where I sat considering all the ramifications of Charlie's offer. I soon realised just how difficult it was going to be to face Sue. She had said many times that she wished to live in London and would consider nowhere else. What would she make of High Wycombe as an alternative? I knew the answer, of course. But convincing myself of the possibility that Renato Castellani might yet cast us both in his film, I decided to delay discussing the subject with her until after we'd auditioned.

On my way home after work, I called in on my mother, whom I found half-asleep in an armchair in front of the small bay window overlooking the street, an open copy of *Vogue* magazine by her side. Even before I'd finished telling her the news about the audition, she exclaimed, "My, that's just wonderful," her voice thrilling with excitement. "You'll be a star. I've always known it. Now, have you done anything about your fingernails?"

"Fingernails?"

"Yes, your fingernails. Let me see them, darling."

I held out my hands for inspection. "As I suspected," my mother scathed, "not cared for at all. You can't possibly go the audition with fingernails looking like that."

"Why not?" I replied, examining my fingernails, which seemed to me clean, unchewed, and to all intents and purposes in pretty good shape.

"Bob, don't you know that fingernails are the first thing film directors look at?"

"That's nonsense, Mops. I would have thought it was the last thing."

"No, no, Bobby, you are so wrong. I remember very well Madam Rambert examining my fingernails each time I went onstage. She did it with all the dancers."

"For Chrissake, Mops, I'm not a bloody ballet dancer!"

"Well, humour me this once," said my mother, quite unperturbed, glancing at her own long, scarlet-tipped fingers, "and let me do them for you, please. Just sit there while I fetch my manicure kit."

Defeated, I sighed, "Oh, well, if it makes you happy."

Getting to work on my left hand, she dabbed a damp piece of cotton wool over each nail, before working the cuticle of each finger down to the quick with acetone. Murmuring and sighing over her tokens of affection, she trimmed each fingernail into a perfect oval shape before filing it smooth. I had to admit, she had made a significant improvement. She proceeded to do the same with the other hand and, before I could stop her, produced a bottle of clear nail varnish, which she began to apply deftly with a tiny brush.

I cried out, pulling my hands away from her grasp, “Stop! Girls use nail varnish, Mum. I’m your son. A bloke. Can’t you tell? That’s it! No more of this!”

“Dahling, please stop being so silly,” my mother protested. “Varnish is just to finish the nails off. All manicurists use it, even on men. It gives the nails a lovely sheen.”

Seeing how determined my mother looked, I allowed her to complete her mission, thinking I’d remove the varnish the minute I got home.

““There,” she said, re-capping the bottle with a flourish, “isn’t that better? Your film director is bound to be impressed.”

“I feel like a cissy,” I replied. But seeing the hurt in my mother’s eyes, I said hastily, “I didn’t really mean that, Mops. My nails do look good. Thanks so much. I must show them off to Sue.”

“Yes, dear, do,” she said, sniffing into her lace handkerchief, making me feel a heel. “I’m sure she’ll appreciate how good they look, even if you don’t.”

Wishing me all the luck in the world, my mother stood at her front door, tears streaming down her face, waving her handkerchief as I left. I beat a rapid retreat, not daring to look back at her. She was again playing the role of the tragic mother. I'd witnessed it often enough before and by now she'd honed the part to perfection. As much as she embarrassed me, I still loved her, knowing she could no more cease being dramatic than fly.

The weekend passed infinitely slowly. Sue and I were edgy with one another: I, because I was bursting to discuss the job offer Charlie had made and she, with a woman's intuition, was aware I was hiding something from her.

"What's wrong with you, Lancelot?" she asked more than once. The more I replied, "Nothing's wrong. Why do you ask?" the more she insisted.

I watched Helen and Bill eye each other over supper as Sue and I silently ate our meal. Not helping our mood, it had been raining all day, cold November rain sheeting down from black clouds, with the following day forecast to be as bad.

"You'll both need brollies tomorrow," said Helen. She put an arm around her daughter's shoulder, "Can't risk ruining that lovely frock you bought for the audition."

Bill, who had been sitting quietly throughout suddenly intruded: "C'mon, Mother, we'll treat them to a taxi. That'll solve the problem won't it? Now, if you'll excuse me I'm going to watch the news on telly." Giving me a mischievous grin, he asked, "Had a manicure, have you?"

"Oh Christ!" I blurted, burying my hands in my trouser pockets. "I'd forgotten. I meant to clean that stuff off. My mother cut my nails and put varnish on them." I gave a lame laugh. "It's all her fault."

By this time, Helen was trying to stifle her giggles with a napkin stuffed in her mouth and Sue was scarlet in the face with suppressed laughter. The general hilarity at my expense was so infectious; I caught the disease, too. Although I felt a fool, the joke had the effect of improving the general mood.

Susan led the way to the bathroom, where she removed the offending varnish with acetone. "There, that's done," she said finally. "What a daft idea of your mother's." Placing her arms around me, she whispered softly, her glossy dark hair loose about her face, her eyes searching mine, "Tell me, darling, what's up? You've been like a bear with a sore head these past two days. Is it because you don't love me anymore?"

"'Course I do," I mumbled. "Of course I do, darling." My mind raced as I tried to find some kind of excuse for my boorish behaviour other than the truth. "It's the audition. I'm really nervous about it. You're bound to be chosen and I won't be. What'll happen then? You'll go off to Italy to play Juliet, and I'll be left here on the shelf."

"Oh, Lancelot," replied Sue, lifting my head to kiss me gently on the lips, "you are such a bloody idiot sometimes. Is that all? You really had me worried."

"Yeah, that's it," I lied, clutching her close in case my eyes betrayed me. "I've been feeling sick over it."

"Did it ever occur to you that you might get chosen and not me?" asked Sue. "What would you do then? Darling, stop being so ridiculous. I just know in my heart Renato Castellani will choose us both, and that's all that matters. Now come on downstairs, otherwise Mum and Dad'll think we're getting up to something here."

"Chance would be a fine thing," I laughed.

Once downstairs, Sue surprised me by handing me a copy of *Romeo and Juliet*. "I've got one, too," she said, "from the library. Just thought it would be a good idea to familiarise ourselves with the play. Can't do any harm. At the very least, it'll show we're interested."

To please Susan, but without much enthusiasm, I curled up at one end of a sofa and began to read the play. I had studied it for my final exams and was able to recall much of it. However, what Charlie Hunt had said to me kept intruding, making me feel it was a waste of time to study the play when I had already made up my mind to accept the position he'd offered. Besides, I had already convinced myself I had little chance of succeeding at the audition.

But I had not reckoned on Sue's newly discovered belief that we were both destined to be stars. "I had a dream last night, Lancelot," she said, coming to sit close by me. "It was so real. Almost scary. We'd both been chosen. We were on set, all dressed up in medieval costume with the director shouting, 'Action!' Honest, darling, it's an omen. It's why I went to the library this morning to get the copies of the play."

Rather than challenge Susan, I murmured something anodyne about dreams sometimes coming true and left it at that. She was not to be denied and turned on me fiercely, saying, "You think I'm mad, don't you? I'm not, you know. I've got this feeling, here," she pounded her heart. "We are going to be chosen. Definitely. So come on, you read out Romeo's part and I'll do Juliet's."

For the next hour, we rehearsed and rehearsed, so much getting into the parts that I, too, began to believe in Susan's dream. By bedtime I'd become Romeo, and Charlie Hunt's offer was already consigned to the back of my mind.

Up early the next morning, I put on my newly pressed blazer and flannels over one of Bill's starched white shirts. He'd also kindly lent me a pair of his gold cufflinks, saying "Lose those, matey, and I'll have your guts for garters."

Flashing my shirt cuffs, I sauntered into the breakfast room, where I found Sue twirling about in a mid-calf-length cream skirt with a jacket to match. "You look absolutely stunning," I said. "How could Renato not pick you?"

"You look pretty suave yourself," she flattered.

As he'd promised, Bill drove us to the station, paid for our train tickets and gave me a couple of pounds to cover taxi fares. Sue and I sat clutching hands all the way to Waterloo, hardly saying a word. By now, we were Romeo and Juliet, both in body and spirit, star-crossed lovers from the houses of Capulet and Montague, embarked on a fateful journey to Verona. We sat gazing into each other's eyes, murmuring verses from the play, something that did not go unnoticed by our fellow passengers, some of whom smiled in our direction, while others, marginally embarrassed by the spectacle, averted their eyes, shifted in their seats and stared out of the train's rain-streaked windows. We were so oblivious to everything around us, edging ever closer together as we mouthed our lines, we arrived at Waterloo without being aware the passengers in our compartment had already disembarked.

We took the Tube to Piccadilly Circus, where I flagged down a taxi which took us to the address we'd been given in Frith Street. Dropped off outside a faceless office block a good half-hour early, we sheltered from the rain under a large portico at the entrance, shivering both with cold and mounting excitement.

"You scared?" asked Sue, tightening her grip on my arm. "I am."

"Nah," I replied. "I'm bloody terrified. I know we're early, but let's go see what fate has in store."

I pushed open the heavy front door, exposing a steep flight of stairs. I led the way, tramping up three floors, checking all the offices that fanned out from each landing, until I found Renato Castellani's business card tacked under a name plate bearing the title Eros Films Ltd.

"Hang on a sec before you knock, Lancelot," Sue asked, as she ran her hands over her skirt to smooth it down. Delving into her handbag, she pulled out a small mirror and a lipstick. Gazing at her reflection, she quickly applied a touch more colour to her lips before messing about with her hair. Satisfied, she smiled, "Right, Romeo, let's face the music..."

I rapped on the door, more loudly than intended because of nerves. After all, this was show time, and Romeo and Juliet were fired up to give the greatest performance of their lives. Sue and I were on the threshold of fame and fortune; thoughts of rejection consigned to the far reaches of the universe. Not receiving an answer, I knocked once more. This time the door was opened smartly by a smiling woman dressed entirely in white.

"I imagine you must be Mr Robert Monteath Matthews and Miss Susan Kenyon. Sorry to have kept you," she said. "My name is Sophia Amateo. I am Signor Castellani's personal assistant. Do come in and take a seat, please. Renato will see you shortly."

She checked a note on the clip board she was carrying, "Miss Kenyon will be auditioned first." The woman's eyes swept over Sue. I regarded the look of appreciation in them as confirmation that Sue's journey had not been a wild goose chase. Unfortunately, my countenance was not treated with the same approval, leaving me somewhat crestfallen.

"Cheer up, Lancelot," Sue whispered, as we sat down, "you look positively cheesed off."

"No, I'm not. Did you notice the way the woman looked at you? You are definitely going to be chosen. That woman's Castellani's PA, she should know what he's looking for."

"Pish, posh, Romeo." Sue replied, evidently pleased.

We had no time for further discussion. Sophia Amateo emerged from an adjacent room and beckoned to Sue. I just had time to give her a quick kiss, before she got up to follow Sophia. “Good luck, darling,” I said. “Break a leg.” I’d heard the phrase used during my stints in amateur dramatics, although I had no idea what it meant.

Sue blew me a kiss and then was gone, leaving me shaking with apprehension, suddenly fearful that our dream of being selected to act in films was a fantasy. As quickly as I’d convinced myself we were something special, my certainty evaporated.

I sat shivering, twiddling my thumbs, examining my fine fingernails, scuffing my shoes and blinking at the ceiling for what seemed an eternity, but in reality was only about ten minutes, before an ashen-faced Sue faltered towards me, dabbing at her eyes. Behind her Sophia Amateo crooked a finger, inviting me in.

I clutched Sue’s arm in sympathy as I passed. She shook me off. “Go on, Lancelot. Show them what you are made of,” she choked. “They didn’t want me.”

I squared my shoulders and walked into the audition room with more confidence than I felt.

Three straight-faced men wearing dark grey suits confronted me from behind a large table. Terrified, I shuffled about awkwardly until the man in the middle of the group said in an Italian accent, “I am Signor Castellani, Mr Matthews. Will you kindly turn around for me, pliss?” I did as he asked. “Again, pliss,”

I turned about again. There was silence in the room.

Then Castellani spoke once more. “Thank you very much for coming. That will be all. You may go.”

That was it.

My audition had lasted a full minute, a tenth of Susan's. Perhaps I should have left the varnish on my fingernails after all.

Chapter 43

Sue had so convinced herself that Renato Castellani would choose her to play Juliet, she was absolutely broken-hearted not to be selected. I tried to humour her all the way home, but without success. She sat silent, hands folded in her lap, staring blindly out of the window. However hard I tried to make light of what had happened, persuade her to see the funny side, the only response I got, in between little sobbing noises, was "What are we going to do now? What will we do now?"

"It doesn't matter," I tried. "I guess we weren't what Castellani was looking for. I'm sure that's all it was, darling. Maybe that's how auditions are in the film business. Anyway," I said, trying to cheer her, "they gave you a damn sight longer than they gave me."

The corner of Sue's mouth twitched momentarily, which made me think I'd lightened her mood at last. But no, the frown returned, her lips tightened into a thin line and she retreated into herself once more.

Even after we got home, Sue refused to speak to anyone. She immediately ran upstairs to her bedroom and locked the door, leaving me standing at the foot of the stairs together with Bill and Helen, who were equally clearly perplexed. I explained that we'd both failed the audition and that Sue was taking it very badly. As Helen started up the stairs, Bill said, "Leave her for a bit, Mum, she'll be all right soon." Give her time. Give the poor child time." Turning to me, he asked, "Fancy a drink, Bob? I think we all need one."

Beer in hand, I followed Bill and Helen into the drawing room. As I sat warming myself in front of a glowing coal fire, I recounted in detail what had happened that day.

"What are you going to do now?" Bill asked.

"Same as ever," I retorted, "Get my head down, go back to work, forget about being a film star."

Bill took a swig of his beer. "Mind if I ask you a question?"

"No, of course not."

"Well, we got a phone call from Charlie Hunt this morning soon after you'd left. Said to tell you he wouldn't be in the office until Wednesday. He said to remind you he was expecting an answer about the job on Tuesday, but it could now wait 'til he got back." Bill gave me a worried look. "None of my business really, but are you intending to give up your job with Midland? Does Sue know?"

I had planned to talk over my job offer with Sue in private, when the right opportunity arose. Charlie Hunt's phone call had put me on the spot.

"No, I'm not giving up my job, Bill. The reverse, actually. The office is transferring to High Wycombe in March. Charlie's offered me a sales job there. If I accept, Sue and I will move to Buckinghamshire soon after we're married. Charlie asked me to talk it over with Sue and give him an answer by Tuesday. Well, it'll be Wednesday now. Since we didn't pass the audition, I'm going to say yes. If I don't, I'll be out of a job."

“That’s a bit of a pain,” muttered Bill. “I don’t think Sue’ll fancy that, you know. She’s set her heart on moving into a flat with you in London. And, and,” Bill pointed a finger at me, “let’s not forget Sue’s music. She can’t give up her studies. She’s another year to go before she graduates.”

Helen sat perfectly still, not saying a word, listening intently.

What Bill had said was true. Sue’s studies had to come into the equation, but balanced against starting married life without a job; something had to give. I didn’t want to continue living off the Kenyon’s, nor did I wish to look for yet another job. My plan had been to settle down with Sue in High Wycombe. Then, after a while, perhaps find an agent who’d book us for cabarets, weddings and bar mitzvahs on a semi-professional basis, none of which would interfere with my day job.

I’d hoped to find allies in Bill and Helen. However, it was obvious they were not about to support me. I glanced at Bill before replying. In the reflected light of the fire, his expression was stony, unlike the jolly Bill I knew.

“Sue could take a year off from her studies,” I said, tentatively, “or train down to London as she does now. It’s not as if High Wycombe’s *that* far away.”

Helen clapped her hands together. “Bob, you don’t get it. Sue wants to move to London. She loves city life.”

“Always has,” Bill agreed, giving his wife a sugary smile. “And, since we are talking about it, Mum and I were thinking about putting a deposit on a flat in Balham for you as a wedding present. You’d settle the mortgage, of course, but it would be your home.”

Taken completely off balance, I stuttered and stammered, realising I was being out-manoeuvred. However, as I was about to express my thanks and at the same time put my own point of view, Sue appeared at the door, freshly made up and wearing a new frock.

"Sorry, Mum and Dad, for being such a bore," she trilled cheerfully. "Forgive me, Lancelot, don't know what got into me." She gave a forced laugh, "It was only an audition, after all. We should all forget about it, don't you think? I have. Tomorrow's another day."

With that, she went to the drinks cabinet and poured herself a sherry. It was completely out of character to help herself without requesting her father's permission. "Now, then, what was everyone talking about?" she asked, plumping herself down beside me.

"I think Bob should tell you," Bill replied. He sat with his mouth working, his hands fiddling with a pack of cigarettes.

Facing up to the situation, I said, "I had just mentioned to your Mum and Dad I've been offered another job."

"In London?" Sue asked, her face lighting up.

"No, High Wycombe."

"High Wycombe?" In a disbelieving voice, she repeated, "High Wycombe?" Her face now very close up to mine, she narrowed her eyes. "You can't be considering it, can you? You've already got a job with Midland."

Summoning up my courage, I decided to make a stand. No one, it seemed, had any consideration for my opinion or my feelings. It was all about Sue—what Sue wanted, what was best for Sue. I felt left out, incidental to the proceedings, a puppet with the entire Kenyon family pulling the strings.

"Midland is moving to High Wycombe in March," I replied stiffly. "Charlie's promoting me to sales. Four fifty a year and a company car. I haven't said yes yet, Sue, but I am not going to refuse. How can we marry, with me not having a job?"

"I say, Bob, no need to get het up," said Bill getting to his feet, "I'm sure you'll easily find another one. Meantime, we can postpone the wedding for a while, can't we, Mum? It's not as if the wedding invitations have gone out or anything."

"Well," said Sue, downing her drink in one, "if it's to be High Wycombe or nothing, it's nothing." With that she hurried to the door, saying as she went, "And there I was thinking you loved me, Lancelot."

The fire cast tongues of yellow light over the row of photographs standing on the mantelpiece bringing into sharp relief the images of the Kenyon family. Their silver-framed faces seemed to grow and grow in size before I tore my gaze away, but even then I sensed their eyes boring into mine, challenging me to question their judgement.

I realised it was pointless discussing my new job with Bill and Helen any further. I stood a better chance with Sue away from her family. So bidding them goodnight, I said, "I think I'll go to my room now. I'll talk to Sue again tomorrow."

Instead I stopped by Sue's bedroom on the way to mine. I knocked gently before entering. I found her lying on her bed, her face buried in the pillows, quietly sobbing. I went over to her and cradled her head in my arms. She pushed me away roughly. "You don't love me anymore," she cried, "or you'd have talked over the job with me before."

"I was going to tell you after the audition, darling," I explained, feeling miserable. "If we'd passed, I'd have turned it down, don't you see? I haven't had a chance to tell you before now."

Sue lifted her head from the pillows to face me. I was shocked to see how battered and sad she looked, her eyes swimming with tears. "You don't love me anymore, Lancelot," she repeated. Shaking her head, she whimpered,

"Mummy and Daddy were buying us a flat in Balham as a wedding present, so we could live in London."

So Sue already knew, I thought bitterly.

"You wanted to be a singer," she continued, "I was to be your accompanist, remember? I know it would have been tough to start with, but I was happy to put up with that. It was what you wanted and I had faith you'd be famous sometime."

In spite of myself, my resolve wilted. Sue was so distressed, I could no longer bear it. In a moment of weakness, instantly regretted, I heard myself blurt, "Would you like it if I said no to the job?"

Sue sat bolt upright. "You'd do that, Lancelot? For me?" Sue, hugging me tight, cried, "Oh, Bob, I love you! Thank you, thank you darling. I'm so happy."

She was ecstatic; I despaired, knowing I'd made a dreadful mistake. I'd given in to Sue's selfish demands without a fight. If our future depended on my always being subservient to her, what chance of happiness did I have? It prompted the question yet again: was I was ready for marriage?

"Okay, Sue. I'll tell Charlie Hunt on Wednesday, but right now I'm going for a kip. I'm fagged out."

"Oh, my poor darling "said Sue, kissing me. "You go and have a sleep. I'll get up and tell Mummy and Daddy what you've decided. They'll be awfully pleased to hear."

I'd had the stuffing knocked out of me. For a long time I twisted and turned in bed, loathing myself, bitterly regretting what I'd said. I had meant to assert myself, and ended by being spineless. In the quiet of the night, I concluded Charlie Hunt was quite right. Show business was precarious. I was fed up with scraping about for a living. Come what may, I was going to accept Charlie's offer, take the job. But I had misled Sue. She would never forgive me now, and who could blame her? Hurting her was the very last thing I ever intended. The die now cast, there were bound to be consequences. I wondered whether I had the guts to deal with them

Next morning, I joined the family at the breakfast table. There were smiles all around, bonhomie and cheerful banter. For the sake of appearances I forced a smile as well. The day passed in similar fashion, with Helen giving me sweet smiles each time she encountered me. Bill backslapped me at every juncture, and offered me his best whisky. Sue clung to me throughout, kissing me on the cheek, screwing up her nose, and whispering "I love you" until I just wanted to run away and hide, anywhere away from the cloying atmosphere in the household would do.

First thing on Wednesday morning, I faced the music and went straight to Charlie Hunt's office. Charlie was, as ever, welcoming.

"Come in, Bob," he boomed. "How did your audition go?" he asked without preamble.

"No go," I replied.

"So you are going to move with us to High Wycombe, then." It was more a statement than a question.

"Yes, sir."

"Jolly good show. That's settled then."

I left the office at five-thirty with an idea in mind. I called in on Roger Bruce, a chap I knew from the YCs, who rented a semi in Weybridge and only occupied part of it. A travelling salesman for HP Sauce, Roger was a big-boned ruddy-faced Midlander with a great sense of humour and a Vauxhall Velox company car, which attracted the girls.

Luck was with me. Roger was in and, after I explained I was in a bit of a bind and had nowhere to live , said he would put me up in his spare bedroom. "Of course you can stay, old man," he said, looking concerned. "As long as you like. But I say, I'm dashed sorry to hear that Sue and you are having probs. I mean, really sorry."

It was a pig of a night, pitch dark and raining hard by the time I returned home, wet through and dispirited. My heart quailing, I let myself in and crept upstairs unobserved. I knew what I was letting myself in for, so I quickly stuffed my belongings into the tin trunk that had been with me since my school days and scared witless made my way down stairs. I'd hoped to see Sue before running into Bill and Helen, but as luck would have it, I met Bill first, who immediately asked the question I was dreading, "How did it go with Charlie, Bob?"

"Fine," I replied, chewing on my lip. "Where's Sue?" I asked.

"She's with Mum in the kitchen."

The kitchen door was open. Spotting me, Sue ran up and gave me a kiss. "What did Charlie have to say when you turned down the job, darling?" she asked, breathless with excitement.

My left ear began to itch for the first time in months, bringing with it a terrible, desperate compulsion to tear into the ear canal with my fingernails or anything else that would alleviate the itch. It took a great effort of will to restrain myself. "I took the job, Sue," I replied, "I had to. It's for the best."

Out of the corner of my eye I saw Helen throw a dish cloth on the kitchen table, before walking out, giving me a scathing look as she passed me by.

Sue's face had gone white. "You did what?" she asked, her voice icy.

"I accepted the job. I'm sorry I misled you, but I've changed my mind."

"Well, then, Lancelot, so have I. I can't believe how you've let me down."

I watched in disbelief as Sue removed her engagement ring and handed it to me.

"You mean...?"

"Yes, Lancelot. It's over. Goodbye." As a parting shot, for no good reason I could think of other than to humiliate me, she said venomously, "And you can tell that Nick of yours to pay back all the money he's borrowed from Dad."

Sue brushed past me and left the room. It had all been so sudden; I stood fixed to the spot. It was then I tore inside my ear until it bled.

Bill, who had been witness to everything, muttered, "Sorry it's come to this." Putting arm around my shoulder, he said, "You can stay tonight, but I suppose you'd better leave tomorrow, Bob. I'm just so sorry, but you can see how it is."

Roger Bruce drove up the following evening to help me with my trunk. The Kenyon family stayed out of sight in the sitting room as we drove away. Without a backward glance, I followed Roger on my bike, with a bad ear — and still a virgin.

Having settled in with Roger Bruce, I returned to the jeweller from whom I had bought my engagement ring with the aim of selling it back to him. His attitude towards me was quite different from what it was when he sold me the ring. Gone was the oily salesman who'd persuaded me of the bargain I was then getting. Now he was hard as flint, a jeweller's magnifying glass screwed into an eye, making disparaging huffing noises as he turned my ring in his fingers. "Can't give you more than three pounds ten shillings for this," he said at last, as I stood impatient for his decision.

"But I paid you four pounds nineteen shillings and sixpence for it just a couple of months ago. You said I'd got a bargain."

"Ah, the gold band's come in for some harsh treatment since then. Besides, there's a bit of a glut on the market at present, sir. My offer stands, sir, three pounds ten. That's all I can do for you."

The jeweller stood back from his glass counter, a smirk on his face, his hands clasped behind his back, knowing I would accept.

"All right, I'll take it."

My next stop was Milletts, a cheap clothier in the High Street, in whose window I had seen a grey tweed suit I fancied, reduced to three pounds. I haggled the price down by five shillings and emerged from the shop wearing the suit, with my old clothes, bagged up, under my arm. I still had fifteen shillings change in my pocket, which I thought my mother could do with for Christmas. Although I had earlier mentioned the result of the audition—which elicited from her an explosive, "Bloody Eyeties!" as for a moment she forgot her own heritage—I had not as yet informed her about my broken engagement. I thought it was about time I did, so I rode down on my bike to see her.

Instead of fussing about, asking me how to turn on the gas to make a cup of tea, I saw that my mother had now mastered the art. She set about lighting the gas with a long taper without her usual fluster and quickly brewed some tea for us.

"It's easy when you know how," she grinned. "And would you believe, Bobby? I can cook all sorts of things, now that Helen's taught me." Handing me a cup, she said, "And to what do I owe the pleasure of your visit, kind sir?"

"Well, Sue and I have broken up," I said cautiously, before explaining about my new job and the entire Kenyon family's reaction to it.

"Bitch!" was my mother's immediate response. "I don't believe it, she seemed such a nice girl and the Kenyons, such nice people. Oh, I am so sorry for you, darling, you must be awfully upset."

I should have been, of course. Curiously, what I felt was a sense of relief, for throughout my relationship I'd been nervous about getting married.

On one hand, I was saddened by how abruptly my life had changed, with Sue professing undying love for me and breaking off our engagement almost immediately afterwards, but on the other, I was excited about starting a fine new job with prospects. Off with the old and on with the new. Was I really as unfeeling as that? Not really, for being banished by Bill and Helen, after all they had done for me, felt like a lump of lead in my stomach. As for Sue, I missed her dreadfully.

"Sue's still a lovely girl, Mops. But I'll get over it when I move to High Wycombe. Meantime," I said, taking my mother's hand, "stop blubbing, there's always Christmas to look forward to. For the moment, I'm staying with my friend Roger Bruce, but I'll be down on Christmas Day, I promise."

I reached inside my new jacket pocket and retrieved a ten shilling note and five shilling piece, which I gave her. "It's not much Mops, but why not buy yourself a little something to cheer you up?"

She really couldn't help it. "Oh, dahling Bobby," she cried, throwing her arms around my neck, "you are sooh sweet, sooh sweet."

Chapter 44

With Christmas now just a few weeks away, Roger and I spent most of our evenings in various pubs in the area.

"Do you the world of good, Bob. Help you forget," he said. "What's more, you can find any number of dames in pubs, you know."

It was grand to be driven everywhere in a car, sometimes with Roger's new girlfriend, Valerie. The pretty daughter of the owners of Elizabeth Shaw chocolates, a luxury brand beyond my means, she lived in St George's Hill and drove about in a silver-grey Sunbeam Alpine, a sports car into which we sometimes squeezed when we wished to cause a stir. I had a few pounds saved, but, reluctant to drink it all away in case I needed it later on, I nursed no more than a pint and half of brown ale on any given evening. Roger had an enormous capacity for beer and sank several pints, always gathering a mixed audience about him to laugh at his unending stream of extremely funny jokes, with the ladylike Valerie, always perfectly groomed, sipping soft drinks as she listened quietly.

As Roger had said, there were indeed lots of other girls to be seen in pubs, some of whom appeared attracted to me. But for the first time since I could remember I was not interested, even though one or two of them could have unburdened me of my virginal state. Nonetheless, I was having great fun pub-crawling and making the occasional foray to the High Pines Club.

I'd first met Roger there and challenged him to beat me at my party trick of one-armed press-ups. He'd always lost, paying up with good grace and offering to buy me a drink, unlike others who took me on, who cursed when they failed. Since I had a few pennies in my pocket now, I'd given up on challenging the testosterone-fuelled mastiffs frequenting the bar. Even so, some of the rugger buggers still thought they could beat me. This amused Roger, who urged me to take them on and went around with a hat collecting the half-crowns the competitors lost to me, which I intended to use to buy Christmas presents for my mother and my brothers. Under normal circumstances I might have also bought something for Nick, but since he'd upset me by borrowing money from Bill Kenyon, which he'd not paid back, I put the idea from my mind.

Two days prior to Christmas, Roger drove up to Birmingham to spend Christmas with his family, leaving me to fend for myself until he got back on the second of January. This suited me very well, since my firm had a Christmas party arranged for all its employees, before they closed for the holidays. As far as I was aware, only some of the staff were privy to the company's plans to move to High Wycombe in March. For most it would come as a bombshell.

With no Roger to drive me, I was forced to cycle to Chertsey Town Hall where the party was held. I could have taken a bus to Addlestone and then another to Chertsey, but with the weather being so poor, I didn't want to chance being late, most particularly because a little bird had told me I was to be presented with a trophy on the night. In my haste to leave the Kenyons, I had mislaid my invitation. Still, I was convinced the party started at seven-thirty, so I set off in what I thought good time. I was really looking forward to the firm's Christmas party, not having been to one before.

I knew of the Town Hall from old, having once played a small part in a Chertsey Players production *And No Birds Sing*. However, the hall looked quite different from how I remembered it, decked out as it was now with paper streamers and dozens of balloons hanging from the ceiling. The pleasantest surprise of all was to find that the company had splashed out on Harry Geller and his Orchestra to play for us. The fourteen piece band, who I had often heard playing on the radio, was extremely well known. I watched in fascination as the conductor silenced the musicians before striking up Glen Miller's *Take the A train*.

It was obvious I had got the starting time wrong, for about one hundred and fifty people were already assembled. Most of them I recognised, but there were others present, too, who I presumed were Head Office staff. All were partnered, seated at tables around the circumference or on the dance floor. And there was I, alone and palely loitering, wishing Sue was with me.

I saw Charlie Hunt standing by the stage talking to somebody in the wings. He caught my eye and, weaving through jitterbugging couples on the dance floor, came to stand at my side.

"You look lost, Bob", he said amiably. "Found your table yet?"

I shook my head. "I've made an awful balls-up, sir. I thought the party started at seven-thirty, not seven."

"Well, no harm done. Come, let me show you where you are sitting. A waiter will bring you a drink to the table."

Charlie examined the place cards on a long table sitting directly in front of the stage. "Ah, here it is, Bob," he said, pointing to a chair at the very end, "I see you're sitting next to Mrs Chambers from the Buying Office." He gave a loud laugh. "Better watch your step, she's likely to gobble you up."

Of all the people to be sitting next to... Muriel Chambers was built like a battleship and waddled slowly as a river barge. As a gentleman I was expected to dance with her, a prospect I did not relish in the least.

A waiter brought me a beer. I settled into my chair, rapping my feet in time to the music, enjoying every moment of the best live music I'd ever heard. After a short break, Harry Geller, the conductor came to the front of the stage to introduce himself and his orchestra, before putting a clarinet to his lips and playing a racy number I recognised.

After the tune came to an end, his voice came over the loudspeakers. "That was *The Green Cockatoo*, a little something I wrote." Picking up his baton, he said, "And now for some Tommy Dorsey and Glen Miller."

I'd listened to live bands before, at the High Pines and at Friday hops at the Walton Playhouse, but they mostly comprised a drummer, piano and guitar, and sometimes a sax. I was so enchanted by Harry Geller's Orchestra that I only gave Muriel Chambers a smile of recognition, before losing myself in the music. As I listened to Harry Geller's wailing clarinet, tenor saxophones, flutes, guitars, double bass and drums, all I wanted to do was get up onstage and *sing*.

Eventually, the band took another break, returning me to earth and Muriel Chambers. "I could see you loved that, Bob," she said, giving me a smile that made her eyes disappear into the folds of her bunched cheeks. Her chair creaked with her weight as she leant forward to pat my hands . "You haven't eaten a thing. Here..." she stretched out a plump arm and pulled forward a plate with a few egg sandwiches on it, "have some of these. The toads in the 'ole have gone, and the angels on horseback, so you'd better have a scoff of these before they disappear, love."

“Thanks, Muriel, “I said, taking a bite, thinking it was only polite to say a few words. “That was very kind of you. Sorry I was rude. I just got taken up with the band. They are the best I’ve ever heard.”

“Maybe, we can ‘ave a little dance when they come back, then? Well, after the bigwigs have given their speeches.”

“Good idea, Muriel.”

I hoped she had not noticed my lack of enthusiasm. I was still picturing myself hoofing around the floor with Muriel when three men, one of whom was Charlie, climbed up to the stage, where trophies waited on a small table. The hall went quiet as Charlie stepped up to the microphone to acknowledge the band and deliver some opening remarks, ending by introducing the other speakers.

“Mr Robert Flack, our managing director”—Charlie indicated the man on his right, who nodded perfunctorily—"will say a few words, as will Mr Thomas, Midland’s finance director, who’ll tell you of the company’s plans for the future, after which, I shall take great pleasure in making a small presentation to some deserving members of our staff.”

The hall went quiet. Mr Flack, a thin man with a parchment face, wearing a suit a size too big for him, came to the microphone. Clearing his throat, a surprisingly high voice emanated from his bloodless lips, thanking us for our efforts during the year, assuring us that the board of directors appreciated our individual contributions, and wishing us a merry Christmas and a happy New Year. Why hadn’t he mentioned the move to High Wycombe, I wondered?

Mr Thomas stepped forward. Grasping the stand as if he were about to throttle the microphone, he spoke into it from no more than a few inches away. In a gravelly voice, he wished all of us a happy Christmas. Just like Mr Flack, he said nothing about future plans. All he did was grin a lot, before retreating from the microphone to subdued applause.

Perplexed, I looked directly at Charlie Hunt, whose tight lips indicated that he, too, had been expecting more. He forced a smile before speaking into the microphone.

"Come on, come on," his voice boomed, as he attempted to inject a bit of humour into the proceedings. "Pull your crackers and put on your paper hats. Last one to put them on pays a penalty."

He achieved the desired result, for the hall immediately resounded with the noise of crackers. Paper headgear in impossible shapes and sizes emerged to be forced down over heads, tearing, shredding, baulking at piled-high hairdos, all of us in manic haste not to be the last.

"Now, that's better!" shouted Charlie. He lifted a hand and the noise subsided. Laughing, he said, "It gives me great pleasure to dish out these hugely valuable trophies."

Charlie gave a trophy to Midland's spelling bee team and another to a young woman in the office we all admired for collecting money and organising entertainments for disabled children in the area. The captain of the cricket team collected the largest trophy: the lunchtime cricket challenge cup, which Midland had won for the third time in a row.

"Now there's Bob Matthews, our leading wicket-taker this year," continued Charlie. "He bamboozled the opposition with his fluky balls..." Laughter rose to the ceiling. "Now then, ladies and gentlemen, please, our Bob has delicate ears." There was more laughter as he called: "Come on, Bob, collect your cup."

As I took the cup from Charlie, who had moved a pace back from the microphone, he whispered, hardly moving his lips, "Got something to tell you. See you in the gents in ten minutes." Raising his voice again, Charlie said, "Now, how about a clap for Bob?" This was followed instantly by "Ladies and gentlemen, please. I said *a* clap for Bob. And not what those with filthy minds think I said."

Hands loudly bashed tables, women cackled, men roared. It was all great fun at my expense. I didn't mind a bit. Delighted, I returned to my table with my precious cup.

Charlie finally wound up the presentation, exhorting us to drink up, be merry, and enjoy the dancing. I had had my eyes fixed on Charlie ever since he'd whispered to me so mysteriously. He jerked his head slightly in my direction and, taking my cue, I made my way out of the hall and into a corridor where I found him waiting for me outside the loo.

"I'll just check its empty," said Charlie, popping his head round the door. "Okay, Bob. Sorry to be so cloak and dagger, but I thought I owed it you to say that the directors have changed their minds about closing Chertsey. They came to that decision just yesterday. So now you understand why Flack was so tight-lipped."

It was either the smell of urine or Charlie's words. I didn't know which. All I knew was I suddenly felt sick.

"Are you all right, Bob?" asked Charlie, sounding concerned. "Look, son, your job's still safe, I promise you that. What's more, I'll do all I can to ensure you get that sales job sometime this year. Can't say exactly when, but it will be this year. Of that you can be certain. I don't know what else to say to you other than I am terribly sorry for having misled you. It's my fault. I should never have said anything to you, until it was all cut and dried."

Charlie looked so miserable I began to feel sorry for him. "It's okay, sir. At least I've still got a job. You weren't to know and you were only trying to help me decide what I wanted to do: show business or a proper career. I know you were looking after my interests, so there's no more to be said, sir."

"Sure you are okay?"

"Sure, Charlie, sure."

"Well then, I'll be off. Try and enjoy the rest of the evening. I'll see you the day after Boxing Day. We can have a chat and a drink then."

I waited until Charlie disappeared back into the hall, before making my way to my table. While I'd been away, the band had returned and started a slow foxtrot. If ever I was to dance with Muriel, this was it.

"Muriel, may I have the pleasure of a dance?" I asked.

"Ooh, really. You sure?

"Of course. Let's go."

How I managed to trundle around the dance floor with Muriel without tripping over someone's feet, I'll never know. It became even more hazardous when the band switched to a quickstep. Hard as I tried, I was unable to get Muriel into tempo with the music. She swung her upper body about at speed, whilst her hedgehog feet slowly mooched over the floor as if ready to hibernate for the winter.

At least concentrating, as I was forced to do allowed me to forget, temporarily at least, what Charlie had said. That was one benefit. The other was that Muriel's inane chatter about her budgerigars, cats and goldfish kept my mind off my problems.

After three dances, more than duty called for, I returned with Muriel to our table.

"Fancy a drink?" I asked. "From what I see sitting on the bar, your choice is Babycham, Babycham, Babycham or fruit juice. It seems the Advocaat's finished, so it's either that or a beer or a shandy. Which?"

"Would you think me wicked if I asked for a beer?"

"'Course not. I'll go and fetch you one. Pint or a half?"

Muriel covered her mouth with her hands. "Pint, please." Her words so muffled by her fingers, I could hardly make them out. Having had a waiter deliver the beer to us, I sat back to enjoy the band. They played my kind of music. I wondered if I had the courage to ask if I could sing a number, until I suddenly realised the time was approaching a quarter to ten. With only fifteen minutes to go, I racked my brains for a tune I would feel comfortable with, as the band began a waltz. Waltz, waltz, did I know a waltz? The only one to come to mind was a sloppy old piece called *I Wonder Who's Kissing Her Now*. As the last notes of the waltz faded away, to my own amazement, I found myself at the apron of the stage asking Harry Geller if I could sing a number, maybe another waltz.

Harry looked me up and down. "Young man, have you ever sung with a band before?" he asked.

"Yes, I have," I lied.

"Well then, come up onstage and see what you can do. Don't, for goodness sake, mess us up. Okay? A waltz, you said..."

"Can you play *I Wonder Who's Kissing Her Now*?"

"Sure, know it well. Hey, fellas," Harry Geller turned to address the band, "happy with *I Wonder Who's Kissing Her Now*? Yeah? Okay, fine." He then asked me what key I sang it in, which left me poleaxed. I hadn't a clue, but something nagged me to say C.

"C, sir, I replied, and then held my breath.

"Well then, C it is. Let's go."

It was the first time I'd fronted a band. I should have been a nervous wreck, but strangely, I was in complete command of myself. I adjusted the microphone's height to suit me.

Those who had been dancing stood staring, wondering what I was up to. Harry Geller waited patiently until I was ready, before the band struck up with the opening chords of the song. Helpfully, he flicked his baton at the precise moment I was to come in, and I was into the opening bars in perfect time and, God be praised, in the right key.

"I wonder who's kissing her now," I sang. "I wonder who's buying the wine for lips I used to call mine. I wonder if she's ever thinking of me...," and so on to the end, with Harry Geller smiling widely, indicating I should sing a reprise.

I revelled in the applause that came thundering over the footlights. I stood milking every single second of it until it finally died down, with random voices calling for an encore.

"Know anything else, son?" I heard Harry ask.

"The Anniversary Waltz, but I'm not sure of the lyrics," I replied.

"In that case, my advice is call it a day, son. But listen, you've a helluva voice there. I'd like to talk with you after we are done, see what we can do with it, hey?"

I returned to my seat and sat there trembling, while colleagues came up and patted me on my back, all with compliments, any number of variations on "well done" and "didn't know you could sing like that". So enthusiastic was Muriel, she drew my face down and kissed me full on the lips. I felt like gagging.

When the party finally ended, Harry Geller came over to me. "Here's my card, son," he said. "Actually, I think you are as good as Dickie Valentine." He dabbed his damp, swarthy face with a handkerchief pulled from his sleeve, before continuing. "Listen carefully now. If you want a career as a singer you'll need a manager. Have a good think and, if you are really serious about it, I mean really serious, give me a call in the New Year. If I'm to take you on, you'll have to have singing lessons before trying out with my band. How does that sound to you?"

My jaw dropped in astonishment. I was incredulous. "You'd actually be my manager, sir?"

"Harry, Harry, no 'sir' with me, okay?" The tall suave Harry Geller with the sleek black hair took my hand. Smiling, he said, "Let's shake on it, Mr er"...

"Bob Matthews".

Overcome with joy, I pumped his hand so vigorously Harry cried out in mock pain, "Hey, let go, Bob, you're breaking your manager's hand."

After I had shaken the hand of every member of the orchestra and said goodbye to Harry, my bike took wings and raced me home in record time. I simply couldn't believe my luck. Just a few days before, I'd been engaged to be married, and then not. I'd been offered a job which I'd set my heart on, and that had misfired as suddenly. Then Fate in the form of Harry Geller had rescued me from the pit of despair and put me on the path predestined for me. I was to be a singer. I had a manager: the best ever Christmas present in the world. And, what's more, my ear had ceased to itch.

Chapter 45

I was looking forward to spending Christmas Day with my family and also having Boxing Day off before returning to work. I'd decided I'd continue working for Midland until Harry Geller told me I was ready to sing full time with his orchestra. I'd given up on a sales job with the company, the irony of which did not escape me. If the Christmas party had been held a few weeks earlier, I would still have been engaged to be married and living with the Kenyons. It left me wondering whether to cry or not. I missed Sue, but there was no way I would try to contact her again. Things had gone too far for that, now that a new chapter in my life had opened.

I'd managed to buy a second-hand trike as a present for baby Ronald, some colouring pencils and crayons for David, who liked to draw, and a pair of new trousers from Milletts for Richard, which I hoped would fit. In all I had spent around three pounds, which left me a couple of pounds from the amount I'd budgeted to spend on my mother. I knew she loved perfume, make-up, things like that, so I got Roger's girlfriend, Valerie, to help me choose a few small items, which she very kindly wrapped up for me. Unknown to me, she also slipped into the packages some Elizabeth Shaw chocolates for each of my brothers. Her kind gesture was more welcome than she could know, because I was sure my brothers had not tasted chocolate, or sweets of any kind, since they arrived.

There was no way I could wrap or disguise Ronald's tricycle, so again Valerie came to the rescue. She found a cardboard box at her family's factory in Hersham, into which we put all the presents, and then drove me down with it to my mother's little house. I set the box down on the frayed carpet of the tiny sitting room in front of a miniscule Christmas tree. We agreed I should come at ten-thirty on Christmas Day to see the boys open their gifts.

With nothing else to do, I called in to *The Ship*, the public house in whose bar I had whiled away my first miserable Christmas Eve in England. Everything was as I remembered. I wondered for a moment whether the barmaid who had taken pity on me and given me a free drink was still there. She wasn't. But not entirely to my surprise, Nick was at the bar, cigarette holder dangling from his mouth, engaged in conversation with a corpulent man whose frighteningly florid face suggested a close and frequent acquaintance with all the hostelries in town. As I turned to leave, Nick saw me and started with surprise.

"Bob, m'boy, how nice to see you," he called, gesturing for me to join him. "Didn't know *The Ship* was one of your haunts."

"It's not, actually," I replied, taking Nick's hand. "I was at a bit of a loose end, so I came in for a half."

"Half? Not on your life. Landlord," Nick raised his voice, "Two pints please. One bitter, one brown ale". Nick sounded as if he was addressing a private, which I could see made the barman fume.

Nick turned to his florid-faced friend. "Claude, meet my stepson Bob," he said.

"Not really his stepson," I said to Claude, "merely my mother's son." I was furious with Nick, hating him. He had no damned right to call me his stepson. Claude, who could not have cared less who I was, proffered a soft hand and sat back without speaking.

"Well, Bob," said Nick, ignoring the hiatus, "sorry to hear the news about Sue, nevertheless I'm glad I bumped into you. I've been offered the job at the school in Shepperton. Remember? It's the one I told you about. Haven't mentioned it to Alys yet, thought I'd surprise her tomorrow. We'll have to move in a couple of weeks, you know, and Claude here's been very helpful. Found us a cottage on the Thames by Walton Bridge, haven't you, Claude? Belonged to Claude's late mother. Extraordinary, how these things happen. I just popped in for a drink earlier and got talking to Claude and, damn me, if he hasn't got a place we can rent. Isn't that so, Claude?"

"Quite right, Nick," I heard Claude reply, slurring his words, which made me unsure he'd recall anything of the conversation by morning. "The cottage is across the river opposite *The Anglers*. Been empty for ages. Fully furnished, three beds, glad to rent it out to a real gentleman like you."

I was knocked out by the news. I knew my mother would be delighted that Nick had a job at last. Also, that he'd found a suitable home for the family, as well.

"That's great news, Nick, the best present for Mum ever. My turn to buy you a drink next time." Quickly downing my beer, I said goodbye, but I couldn't resist asking Nick if he'd recently met up with Bill Kenyon.

"Haven't set eyes on him for ages" replied Nick, his expression as innocent as a babe's.

Christmas Day dawned picture-postcard perfect. Overnight, snow had fallen, against all the pundits' forecasts.

A light dusting of white covered everything: houses, trees, grass, and the as yet unsullied roads. Smoke rose from a thousand chimneys, the air was crisp and the sun shone brightly. It felt good to be alive.

I was comfortable in Roger's flat, which had a well-equipped kitchen with an up-to-date cooker and tiny fridge. Having managed to scrounge a few eggs from someone at work, I conjured up a three-egg omelette, a big mug of tea and four slices of toast for breakfast, after which I stuffed the meter of the Ascot boiler with coins; the cost of bathing in steaming-hot water halfway up the tub was an extravagance, but for the moment I could afford it. And anyway, wasn't Christmas a time for some indulgence?

As I rubbed myself dry with a bath towel as thick as those of the Kenyons, I was thankful I'd eaten a decent breakfast, certain that my mother's culinary skills were not up to preparing lunch for a family of six.

I suddenly felt mean for not giving Nick a small gift, so I stopped off at *The Ship* on my way to mother's house and bought him a packet of Three Castles cigarettes.

When I eventually arrived, a little later than I'd intended, I was greeted by David and Ronald at the front door, shouting "Happy Christmas, Bob!" As soon as I entered, Richard came forward to wring my hand in a fearsomely tight grip.

"My God, steady on," I said. "Been working out?"

"Just a bit," he smiled, pointing to a set of dumbbells in a corner. "They belong to the hospital. Said if I combined weights with running, it would do me good, make me stronger."

Attracted by the hubbub, my mother came in from the kitchen, followed by Nick holding a dishcloth. My mother reached up on tiptoes to kiss me, giving me one of her special

Hollywood kisses, before going straight to the serious business of the presents.

The tricycle was a huge hit with Ronald, who sat on it shouting "Me! Me! Me!", so happy it brought tears to my eyes. David unwrapped his crayons and chocolates, and tried to scarper, but my mother caught him by the arm.

"You can have these later," she said, extracting the chocolates from his grasp. "Elizabeth Shaw, I see. You've been awfully generous, Bobby."

"No, they're a gift from a friend of a friend of mine," I replied, "Roger's girlfriend, Valerie."

"Must be rich," my mother said. "Do bring her down to see us sometime."

"How did you know I needed trousers, Bob?" asked Richard. "And I've got chocolates, too. Thanks, it's really good of you."

"Now for you Mops," I said, handing over her present, so beautifully wrapped by Valerie.

"Dahling! Makeup, lipstick, scent—I can't believe it," she said, displaying the contents, including a large box of liqueur chocolates. "Must have cost a fortune, you bad boy. Thank you, thank you. I've a little something here for you, too. Here... " She reached behind a chair cushion, where she'd hidden my gift. "I know you need these."

I carefully removed layers of pink tissue paper to expose a pack of six handkerchiefs, which had a Woolworths label and a shilling price tag. I tried not to show my disappointment. After all, this was how my mother was. She'd bought cheap trinkets for friends from Rawalpindi markets, passing them off as precious metal when clearly they were not. Leaving the price tag attached had not been an oversight. She'd meant to show that despite being stony broke she had generously spent an entire shilling on a present for her 'dahling Bobby'.

"Thanks, Mops. How did you guess?" was all I could muster as I tossed Nick's cigarettes over to him.

He mouthed his thanks, giving me a wink, reminding me I was in on his secret.

I figured we would be sitting down to Spam, Spam or Spam, with bread and margarine on the side, and to drink, a bottle of beer. Happily, the vision was inaccurate. My mother returned from the kitchen bearing a decent-sized, steaming hot, roasted chicken. Where she had acquired the bird was to remain a mystery. When I tried to winkle the secret out of her, she put her finger to her lips and smiled, as enigmatic as Mona Lisa. Helen Kenyon had obviously taught my mother well, for the chicken was perfectly cooked and the vegetables equally well done.

As my mother delicately forked the last remnants of the meal into her mouth, the boys asked to be excused and ran off upstairs.

As soon as they had left, Nick stood up and lit a cigarette. "I've an announcement to make," he said, looking at my mother, "even Mummy doesn't know this..."

"Know what, Nick?"

"Just a second, Alys, and I'll tell you. I've a new job. I'm to teach French at a school in Shepperton next term. It's not far from here, although we'll have to move soon. I've found a lovely cottage by the River Thames to rent, so we'll have to leave here in time for the new term in three weeks."

"Why on earth didn't you say something before, Nick?" said my mother, sounding more than a bit aggrieved. "Of course, I'm pleased, but why, oh why, did you keep the news from me? It's too much, really, too much. Why didn't you even have the grace to let me see where we are to live?"

"Sorry, old girl," replied Nick lamely. Thoroughly dejected now, he added, "Just thought it would be a nice surprise for you on Christmas Day."

"Well, you thought wrong," my mother snapped.

I said, "Fancy coming to a pub with me, Richard?"

"Never been inside one."

"First time for everything, little brother."

Chapter 46

In mid-January, Roger told me I had to move out of his flat. His employers, HP Sauce, who owned the property, required my room for a trainee salesman. Then the very next day Charlie Hunt said I and sixty others, all of whom were based in Chertsey, were being made redundant.

Charlie appeared even more dejected than Roger when he gave me the news. I was to leave at the end of the week, Charlie said, with a week's pay in lieu of notice, plus any accrued holiday money due to me. I watched in disbelief as Charlie blew hard into a handkerchief.

"I'm so, so sorry, Bob," he stuttered. "There's nothing I can do about it. Orders from on high, you see. But be sure I'll give you a fine testimonial." With that, he dashed from the room, leaving me shell-shocked.

Actually, I had planned to leave the company as soon as Harry Geller gave me the go-ahead to sing with his band on a permanent basis. I had been thwarted, caught unawares. I was in a real fix. No job and nowhere to live.

The next morning I phoned Harry Geller from a public phone box. I had not heard from him since the Christmas party and needed to know for sure where I stood with him.

"Of course, I meant what I said, Bob," he answered down the line. "But, as I mentioned, before I can let you loose with the band you need some singing lessons. I've been in touch with Madam Davis Reynolds in St John's Wood. She says she's booked up for a few weeks, but she can take you sometime in Feb.

"You're lucky. She's about the best singing teacher in London. And if you are worried about the cost, don't be. I'll take care of it. But I want you to promise me that you'll not miss a single lesson. Is that clear?"

"Of course, Mr Geller."

"Harry. Call me Harry. Ring me again in a week's time. I'll be able to give you a date and time to see her. When she tells me you're ready, maybe in a couple of months, you'll have a go with the band. Maybe even cut a record. Who knows, perhaps audition with the BBC? We'll take it from there. Any problem with that?"

"No, none at all. Thanks, Mr, er, Harry."

I put down the phone. Now as cheerful as any song bird, I cycled over my mother's cottage and asked if I could stay with her for a while.

"Of course, dahling," she replied, "but what a dreadful blow about your job. I think the company was beastly to you. You can have Richard's room. He's been taken on by the army and is off to Catterick for basic training next week."

"Don't worry, Mops, I'll pay for my keep. Is three pounds ten shillings a week, okay?"

"Dahling, how sweet of you," said my mother, promptly thrusting the notes I gave her down of the front of her blouse. "When shall we expect you?"

"Tomorrow evening. I'm sure Roger will drive me over with my stuff after he finishes work."

"Lovely to have you staying with us, dahling," my mother gushed.

Roger, who felt partly responsible for my predicament, readily agreed to take my belongings, suggesting we have a drink afterwards at *The Kings Head* in Shepperton.

"I'm pretty short, Rog," I said. "Well, until I get another job."

"Don't be a chump. My shout, the beer's on me. Least I can do."

The next evening Richard showed me the bedroom I was to share with him, before jogging away down the towpath on one of his five mile runs. Soon after, Roger turned up in his car with my tin trunk. He greeted Nick with a perfunctory handshake before giving my mother, whom I knew he regarded as a character, a big hug. Roger and I then drove off to the pub leaving Nick staring after us, looking most put out.

"I think Nick's pretty cheesed off we didn't ask him to join us," I said to Roger as we drew up in front of *The Kings Head*.

Roger screwed up his face. "I might have done, but he still owes me the ten bob I lent him."

"Christ. Not you, too," I replied, wondering how many others Nick had bummed money from.

The Kings Head, facing a square with a pretty church on one side, was a favourite of Roger's. It was already full with regulars, most of whom Roger seemed to know. I stood at the bar alongside him as he ordered pints of brown and mild for the two of us and chatted in a loud voice to friends perched on bar stools nearby. By the time I had managed a couple of swallows, Roger, a prodigious drinker, had already emptied his jug and was looking at me with a cocked eyebrow, suggesting I have another. I shook my head. I wasn't in Roger's league. He took no notice and ordered another couple of pints. Just as I was thinking a long, hard evening lay ahead, Roger introduced me to a fellow drinker by the name of Henry Branch. During the conversation that followed, he mentioned that he was the pharmaceutical manager of Bayer Products in Molesey. In passing, I said I'd just been made redundant. He pricked up his ears and asked if I'd be interested in a job.

"Nothing grand," Henry intimated. "It's just that I'm looking for a replacement for my lab technician. It just might suit you. Why not come up and see me tomorrow morning and we'll talk about it?"

I couldn't believe my luck. Coincidence and the gift of the gab had come to my rescue once again. I thanked Henry and arranged to meet him at ten. He shrugged off my thanks, saying any friend of Roger's was a friend of his. Roger, looking very pleased, gave me the thumbs up

At around eight o'clock, I suggested to Roger that it might be good idea if I left, making the excuse I didn't have a key to the cottage.

"Fine by me, Bob," Roger said, before turning to Henry. "Now, you just stay there, Henry. It won't take me more than a few minutes to drop Bob off and I'll be back."

I imagine it must have been a heavy night for Henry, for when I arrived for my appointment the next morning he looked distinctly the worse for wear. Rubbing his unshaven jaw, he gave me a lopsided grin. "Boy, that Roger can't half drink," As I followed hard on his heels to his lab, he added, "Must have had ten pints. Mind, I can't talk. Tell you what, Bob, before we go any further let me first show you round the production area, see if you like the setup."

Even if I hated the place, I wasn't about to say so. I needed the job and Henry Branch seemed a nice sort of chap to work for. In the event, the production area was not much to look at, simply a warehouse with a high ceiling. Three sides of its metal-clad walls had huge stainless steel vats attached to them, with what appeared to be electrically driven paddles fixed on top.

"This is where we mostly make cough mixtures," said Henry. "Your job will be to weigh the ingredients according to the daily formula I give you. The vats are filled with a fixed amount of liquid, stirred for as long as the recipe requires and—hey, presto!—the job's done. That's the easy part. The hard bit is cleaning the vats and all the surrounding areas. It's all elbow grease, swabs and chemicals. Pay's three shillings an hour. I make that six quid a week." Henry gave me a searching look, his hands stuffed in the pockets of his white lab coat. "I feel sure you are too good for this, Bob," he said, "but at least it'll keep the wolf from the door for the time being."

I accepted, of course, agreeing to start the following morning at eight.

On the way home, just by the corner of Walton Bridge, I spotted a large poster advertising a grand talent competition at the Odeon cinema on the last Saturday of the month. I dismounted to take a closer look. The first prize was £10, with £5 for the runner up. Late entries were to be submitted in person by the coming weekend. I didn't think twice. I turned around and cycled to the Odeon in the High Street, where I filled in an entry form at the ticket office. I returned to my mother's cottage, thinking £10 would do me very well. It never entered my head that I might not win.

Three days before, I was homeless and out of a job. Already I had somewhere to stay, a new job, a talent competition to win and fame beckoning with Harry Geller and his Orchestra.

Chapter 47

I regarded Bayer's laboratory as my personal rehearsal room and sang my head off all day in preparation for the forthcoming Grand Talent Competition. It was all I could think about as I mixed my medicinal tonics and pushed a mop around the floor. Just as I was about to leave on Friday evening, Henry Branch caught up with me.

"Here, Bob," he said, handing me a phial of colourless liquid. "I've made this up especially for you. I see you smoke a pipe, so I suggest you swallow this stuff before you sing tomorrow evening. It'll clear away any gunge in your lungs or throat. Do Bayer proud and make sure you win."

The Odeon manager had asked all contestants to be at the cinema an hour before the show. When he was satisfied that everything was as it should be, he told us the order in which we were to perform. After a long wait backstage the safety curtain was lowered, signifying that the audience who had been queuing outside in the cold had finally taken their seats.

A mime act was first up. A middle-aged fellow, blacked up for the role, parked himself at the piano and mimed to a recording of Fats Waller's *Honeysuckle Rose*. His gestures and posturing fell short of convincing the audience he was anything like the great man, and he received only desultory applause. One down, seven more to go.

The second act, a little girl who could not have been more than thirteen, sang *Somewhere over the Rainbow*. Dressed up in gauzy pink and looking like something out of Alice in Wonderland, she fluffed her words out of nervousness. Forced to ask the pianist to restart, she broke down and started crying. Finally the manager/her mother/someone led her off the stage, to the accompaniment of sympathetic applause.

The man who came on next, also a singer, fared little better. A cheeky chappie with a thin, black moustache and wearing a dinner suit several sizes too small attempted some sort of operatic aria in a quavering tenor. He, too, got short shrift.

A puppeteer followed, a good-looking young man about my age. He gripped puppets with clownish faces under each arm, and had them tumbling, marching, folding themselves up and spinning like acrobats, leaving the audience in stitches. His well-earned applause made me think I might have to settle for second place after all.

I had been so taken by the skill of puppeteer that I barely took notice of a good-looking girl, who sang very well to a fine reception. Or of a suave fellow who delivered Sinatra's *Singing the Blues* with some panache, only to be let down by reaching for an impossibly high note and going hideously sharp.

After another mime act, it was my turn. I had taken Henry Branch's recommendation and swallowed his magic potion some time before. What he'd claimed for it was true. Miraculously, my sinuses, throat, and larynx were absolutely cleared of gunge, as he called it.

I walked out on stage and adjusted the height of the stand microphone as if I'd done it a million times before. Giving the accompanist a nod, I gazed into darkened auditorium, smiled, spread my hands wide and broke into *Give me your Heart*, a popular number from the film *The Third Man*. On that Saturday night, I sang better than I'd ever done before, my voice soaring, filling the auditorium. I stretched out the last note, sensing I had the audience in my thrall. At the end, I was heady with delirium as loud applause followed me off the stage.

At the conclusion of the programme all the contestants lined up on stage, before stepping forward in turn, to receive their ovations. The puppeteer got the greatest applause and was placed first. I had come second. The cinema manager handed each of us an envelope.

I covered my disappointment with a false smile. "You were terrific," I said to the puppeteer, taking a quick peek inside the envelope to confirm it contained a napkin-sized five pound note. "Sorry, I've forgotten your name."

"Name's Walton. Tony Walton, from Walton," he replied, with a laugh. "Thanks, Bob, but I still think you should have won." He casually thrust his unopened envelope into a trouser pocket, as if he won ten pounds every day. "By the way," he said, "I have a friend here who wants to meet you. You've made quite a hit with Barbara Andrews."

"Barbara Andrews?"

"Yeah, my girlfriend Julie Andrews' mother." Tony looked about. "Ah, there she is, in the wings. Come on over, let me introduce you."

"Hang on a minute. Did you say Julie Andrews is your girlfriend? *The famous Julie Andrews?*"

"The very same," said Tony, as he led over to meet a blowsy woman with flaming red hair and scarlet lips, who welcomed me with the broadest of smiles.

"Bob Matthews," she said, in a rush. "Hello. I'm Barbara Andrews. I must say, you've a very good voice. I just wanted to compliment you. You should make a career of singing, y'know. You've been trained, of course? "

"Well, er, no," I stammered, bowled over by the flattery, awed that I was speaking to Julie Andrews' mother herself. "I am to have some singing lessons soon, though."

"Why not tomorrow?" Barbara laughed. "No, seriously, young Bob," she said. "Come to my house tomorrow afternoon around three. We'll have a sing-song and I'll accompany you. Do you fancy doing that?"

I nodded dumbly.

"Good. Then I'll ask my sister Joan over, as well. Have you heard of the Joan Morris School of Dancing?" Before I could reply, Barbara continued, "If Joan has the time, she can show you how to move around the stage. It's not just the voice that counts, it's the whole performance."

"I don't know what to say," I stammered. "I just don't know how to thank you."

"No need to thank me, Bob," she smiled. "No need at all. Just come on over tomorrow and we'll take it from there. Now, if you'll excuse me, I've got to be off. 'Bye for now." She turned to Tony. "Come, Tony," she said. "Write down my address for Bob and then we'll be off."

Tony grabbed my sheet music from my hands, quickly scribbled, and handed the paper back to me. Taking Tony's arm, Barbara gave me a brilliant smile before waltzing off with him.

I made out from Tony's scrawl that Barbara's address was The Old Meuse, 1 West Grove, Walton. I carefully folded the paper, put it in my jacket pocket, and then cycled home. I thought about telling my mother the extraordinary news, but recalling how she had polished my fingernails prior to my audition in London, I decided on keeping quiet for the time being, in case she insisted on giving me another manicure before my visit to Barbara.

How did the competition go?" she asked, as soon as I got home.

"I came second."

"Who won?"

"A puppeteer."

"A puppeteer!!" my mother shrieked theatrically. "Poor Bob, you must be so disappointed."

"Actually, he was brilliant. Anyway, I won a fiver."

Nick had been half asleep in an armchair, his newspaper spread at his feet. At the mention of a fiver he came instantly awake. "Don't suppose you could spare me ten bob, could you? A loan, mind. Just until Monday when I get paid."

"Okay, Nick. I'll give it you tomorrow. Got to get some sleep now."

I said goodnight and fled to my room. At the first opportunity I'd find somewhere of my own to live.

I slept in until midday and, after swallowing a cup of tea, made off to Walton to find a petrol station that would change my five pound note. I cycled home, handed Nick ten shillings and escaped back to Walton, leaving me a couple of hours to kill. I wandered about in the cold, deserted streets until I came across St Mary's Church. Figuring it had to be warmer than being outside, I entered and found a pew right at the back, where I settled down to read a volume of *Hymns*

Ancient and Modern. I hummed the hymn tunes to myself, remembering most of them from my years in the choir at school. As nostalgia caught hold, I closed my eyes and started to sing rather less quietly than I intended. I felt a light touch on my shoulder. I opened my eyes. An old white-haired priest gave me a gentle smile. "I enjoyed that," he said. "You should come more often, young man."

Gosh, I'm so sorry, sir," I replied, getting to my feet. "I just came in for a bit of warm." I looked at my watch. "I'd better beetle off."

"Stay awhile. You're very welcome, you know."

"No, I can't, sir. I'll be late for an appointment. Thank you, thank you."

"It's for me to thank you," said the priest, shaking my hand as I made to leave.

West Grove, on the border of Hersham and Walton about a mile from the church, had run-down houses on one side, but half way up the other I found a long driveway with fir trees and rhododendrons leading to The Old Meuse. Fizzing with excitement, I cycled to the end of the drive, where I discovered a large, double fronted house, sitting in the middle of an expansive garden with what looked like garages and outbuildings to one side and a small caravan tucked away in a corner.

I knocked at the door. I waited for several minutes before it finally swung open, revealing a stout man with a ginger moustache and thinning ginger hair. Behind him I saw Barbara Andrews beckoning me inside. "So you've found us. Sorry we kept you, Bob. We've just finished lunch," she said. She pushed her way past the man and came forward to greet me. "Meet Ted, my husband," she said, the smell of whisky on her breath.

Ted said "Hi, Bob," exhaling alcoholic fumes. He took my hand, "Good to know ya." Ted's accent sounded American. I learned later that he was a Canadian. "Come on in, come on in."

I followed Ted and Barbara through a hallway and into a long living room with a latticed-glass bay window, hung with floral curtains drawn back to allow the meagre winter light in. The room had been freshly painted white in an effort to mask an earlier, botched attempt at decoration, but dark red stippling still showed through. The bizarre result came as something of a shock. Two sofas and a couple of armchairs tucked away on one side allowed a grand piano pride of place in the greater part of the room.

"This is where we hold our parties," said Barbara, her speech slightly slurred, as she plonked herself down on a chair. "Come sit down. Have a drinkie. Whisky? Beer?"

"Beer, please," I replied, shifting in my chair, uncomfortably aware that my host was slightly drunk.

Barbara gestured to Ted, saying, "Ted, dear, fetch Bob a beer will you, please?" She lolled back in her chair and watched Ted trot off. "Ever hear of Ted and Barbara Andrews?" she asked, cocking her head, her voice casual. "That's how Ted and I were billed when we did music hall and vaudeville. But now that Ted's retired from the business we don't perform much these days. God knows we did it for long enough. Now, I just play the piano for fun and..." Barbara gave raucous laugh, "try and make something of young chaps like you."

Ted returned, gave me a glass of beer, and excused himself. Barbara suggested she'd take me next door to see Joan when I'd finished my drink, so I gulped it down and followed her all the way through the house and into the garden at the back, to a small prefabricated building.

"This is Joan's bung," she said. "I'll just pop in and see her." Pointing to what looked like converted garage immediately adjacent, she said, "You go in there. I'll join you in just a sec."

I did as Barbara asked and found myself in an empty room with a long mirror and a barre. I was still examining my reflection in the mirror when Barbara and her sister entered.

"Vain chump," chortled Barbara, "Come on, meet Joan."

"Hello," said Joan, a slim, fit-looking younger version of her sister, with large bright eyes that scanned me from top to toe. "So, you're Barbara's find," she said, without a trace of irony. "I heard you can sing, but can you dance at all?"

"Only the usual," I replied nervously, wondering what was coming next. "Just ballroom stuff."

"Okay," said Joan, crisply, "go stand in front of that mirror again. Imagine you are about to sing, holding a mike. Then throw one arm out expressively, as if you are giving yourself to the audience. Can you do that?"

Horribly aware of their eyes on me, I pretended to sing on stage, embarrassed by how awkward I appeared in the mirror. At Joan's request, I tried again, this time with a bit more verve.

"No! No!" Joan cried, "Your hands. Your outstretched hand, your fingers, they're like a scarecrow's appendages. Stiff, wooden things. You can do better than that. Come let me show you." She stood directly in front of me, raising her arms fluidly, her wrist and fingers loose, as she demonstrated. "Now you try."

Now feeling even more foolish, I tried to follow Joan's example. After a couple of attempts, she stopped me. "Okay, that's better. Not quite right, but it'll do. Tell you what, Bob,

I'll give you half an hour next Sunday about the same time and we'll go from there."

As I thanked Joan for her kindness, I wondered what had actually been achieved, other than for discovering in her mirrors that I had looked like one of Tony Walton's puppets.

It didn't help that both of them swept out, leaving me standing alone in the middle of the room feeling like some minor player in a French farce, with the cast appearing and disappearing with bewildering speed. I had thought I had been invited there to learn about singing and stagecraft, but as yet Barbara had not asked me to sing a single note. As I stood contemplating whether I should cut my losses and leave, Barbara bustled back into the room and shunted me back to her living room. Giving me a smile, she sat herself at the piano, rippled her fingers across the keys and said, "Sing something for me, Bob. Anything at all. I can't read music, but I can follow you in any key."

Nervous at first, I had a go at singing a couple of popular numbers. Barbara accompanied me beautifully and then, as I gained confidence, I let rip and began to enjoy myself, with Barbara nodding her head enthusiastically as she played. It was a surprise to discover that half an hour had passed, before she called halt.

"That was fun," she said, closing the lid of the piano. "But your timing is hopeless, Bob, half a bar too late after the intro. It's a good job I could follow you, otherwise you'd have made a complete muck of things. You sing in tune and have a nice voice, but you need to improve. Lots and lots and lots of practice is what's required. It's nothing to fuss about. We'll fix it. For starters, I think you should join me at *The Ship* in Shepperton next Saturday evening. I play there most Saturday nights from seven o'clock on. Before coming, practise half a dozen numbers at home. I probably know most of them, and we can then have a go together."

"Are you sure I can do that, Barbara?" I asked, "I've sung in public, but never in a pub."

Barbara interrupted crossly. "So what's the difference? Don't worry your little head, dear, this is Barbara Andrews talking. If I say you can do it, you can do it. And the best part is you won't have to buy a drink all evening."

Barbara got up from her stool. "Let's have a fag and a cuppa and you can tell me all about yourself."

However, instead of my telling Barbara about my life, she filled the time with stories about hers. I learned that Ted Andrews was actually her second husband and that her first, a schoolteacher by the name of Edward Wells, also known as Ted, was Julia's father. I corrected the slip. "You mean, Julie," I said.

"No, no, "She was baptised Julia," replied Barbara. Ted and I had her name officially changed to Julie Andrews when she was about twelve. By then, she was sometimes on the bill with us, and we thought Julie Andrews sounded better than Julia Wells. Also, Ted thought it would make her feel more of a real daughter than a step-daughter."

I said nothing, thinking that if Julie's real father had not been consulted he would have been dreadfully hurt.

Barbara had a pull on her cigarette and then continued. "Strange, I still think of her as Julia, you know." Her eyes wandered in the direction of the bay window. "One day," she mused, "when Julia was very small, Ted asked her to sing a song. We were both stunned when out poured this amazing, adult voice with a phenomenal range. It was so special; Ted immediately started giving Julia, er, Julie, singing lessons to strengthen her voice. When she was ten, she gave her first public performance, singing a duet with Ted." Barbara pulled a handkerchief from her sleeve and dabbed at her eyes. "The poor little thing had to stand on a beer crate just to reach the mike."

"What a lovely story. Gosh, I'd love to meet Julie".

"She's in a show in Portsmouth for two more weeks. But you'll meet her after that, I promise. Now, off you go, young man and remember, next Saturday I'll see you at *The Ship*."

I thanked Barbara and cycled off home. Now that I had Harry Geller and Barbara Andrews to help me, I was surely destined for stardom.

Chapter 48

I had hardly time to step through the door of the house, when my mother accosted me.

"Pam's arriving on Friday," she said. "Yes, darling, she's really coming. Isn't that wonderful?"

"Pam? Sister Pam? How do you know?"

"Her letter says so—"

"What letter?"

"This one," replied my mother, extracting a blue air- mail letter from a pocket in her slacks and waving it under my nose. "Pam sent it six weeks ago. The postman delivered it next door by mistake. Our neighbours have been away in Cornwall and only discovered Pam's letter this afternoon. They were full of apologies when they brought it over."

I took the letter from my mother and began to read.

Dear Mum,

I shall be arriving in Southampton on Friday 26th February on the SS Batory. It's a Polish ship, much cheaper than P&O. No need to come down and collect me. My boyfriend Michael (he sailed to England a few weeks ago on the Strathclyde) is meeting me and will drive me up to you in his father's car. He thinks we should arrive sometime in the afternoon. I hope it doesn't inconvenience you to put me up for a little while until Michael and I get our lives sorted.

Hope you and the boys are all well.

Love, Pam

The brevity, the coldness of Pam's terse letter surprised me at first. But remembering how Nick and my mother had left her behind in Pakistan to fend for herself, I understood. It had been criminal to leave her there. She was only sixteen then. Just a child.

For all the years she had been separated from her family, poor Pam must have scrimped and saved every penny from her typist's job with ICI just to pay her boat fare. I guessed from the tone of her letter how hard it must have been for Pam to ask for help after being so cruelly abandoned. "I wonder who this Michael person is?" said my mother, just as Nick entered the room.

"Yes," he said, stroking his thin moustache, "from the sounds of it, chap must be pretty close to Pam for her to write, quote, 'can I stay with you until Michael and I get our lives sorted,' I'd say pretty close, wouldn't you Bob?"

Instead of answering the question I stared directly at them. I then said, putting heavy emphasis on each word, "I can't wait to see Pam again. Poor Pam. Left alone by herself in Karachi. I had it easy compared to her."

My intention had been to embarrass Nick and my mother, but they gave no sign that they noticed, unless embarrassment caused my mother to change the subject.

"It's such a pity we've so little time to prepare for Pam," she said. "I mean, where is she going to sleep? We've no room."

"Not a problem, darling," Nick replied. "We'll kick David and Ronald into the dining room. The boys can camp on the floor and Pam can have their room. If it means us eating on our laps for a while, so be it."

I clocked in early for work the next morning and got on with mopping up the lab floor. I tried to picture how my sister would look now that she was twenty-one. The last time I'd seen her she was a schoolgirl with pig tails. I remembered sadly how little time I had spent with her during our school holidays, the only girl amongst five brothers. She probably welcomed going back to her boarding school each year, to be with close friends, the only true family she had ever known.

I had about finished disinfecting everything in sight, when the girls who worked in the warehouse next door, followed by Henry Branch, came rushing in to commiserate with me for coming second in the talent show. They all agreed I should have won.

"How did you know the result?" I asked, touched by their comments. "I was going to tell you this morning.

"We were in the audience," smiled Henry, "clapping for you like mad. Didn't tell you we were going in case it put you off."

My doleful mood brightened, I cycled home and discovered all hands were busy, my mother cleaning the house with a fervour I had not previously seen, the boys dusting the furniture and Nick bent over a spade, turning over a flower bed at the front of the house.

My mother greeted me with a kiss and a cheery, "Bob, you can move the dining table and chairs into the shed, then stick Dick's mattress on the floor of the dining room. It's big enough for both the boys. Then, when you've done that I'll come and give you a hand making up Pam's bed."

To see my mother acting like a camp commandant, barking orders and dashing about enthusiastically was a novel experience, and quite the opposite of her manner the previous evening. Had my pointed remarks about Pam being abandoned sparked feelings of remorse? Was the frenetic activity a device to cover her fear of being confronted by my sister?

The following day I received a letter from Harry Geller informing me that Madam Davis Reynolds had agreed to give me a singing lesson on the coming Thursday, the day before Pam arrived. I was to be at Madam's home in St John's Wood at eight on the dot. No ifs, no buts. He had added a postscript, saying that if Madam found my voice up to snuff, I was to have a lesson every Thursday until further notice. There was a second postscript stating in no uncertain terms that I shouldn't let him down. Before signing off with his usual flourish, Harry wrote that my lessons were the precursor to big things: the BBC, and a recording contract

I was thrilled that Harry had kept his word, but apprehensive of meeting the famous Madam Davis Reynolds. Furthermore, although Harry had previously said he'd pay for my lessons, his letter had not made it clear whether I might be required to hand over cash for my lesson and be reimbursed later.

Fortunately, I had the proceeds of the talent show in the money box I kept by my bed. For some reason, I decided to check it and discovered to my horror that all but two pounds of my savings had been stolen. I was sure the boys were not guilty, and whatever I thought about my mother she was not a thief. Nick was the only possible culprit. So I asked him—oh, so very casually—if by chance he'd raided my moneybox as a matter of urgency and forgotten to tell me.

"No, certainly not," he replied straight-faced, looking me directly in the eye. "I'll thank you not to accuse me. You must be mistaken. You've probably spent it and forgotten about it."

"I couldn't have Nick. I won five pounds on Saturday night and today's— what? Tuesday."

Nick looked at me threateningly. I thought for a moment he was going to slap me in the face and bunched my fists ready to deal with him as I'd done before. But instead, he turned on his heel and growled, "Bloody cheek."

All the hate I'd once harboured for the man returned. To make sure there would no re-occurrence, I put my money box in my locker at work. Then I asked Henry Branch to scribble down directions to St John's Wood for me.

"I can do better than that, Bob" he said. "This is a most wonderful map of London, known as the A to Z." He pulled a pocket sized book from a drawer to show me. "And I've also a map of the Underground. Even a duffer like you can't go wrong. Here, let me show you how to use them." By the time Henry had finished explaining, I felt confident enough to find my way around London and to locate the street in which Madam Davis Reynolds lived.

I said nothing to my mother about the theft and made a point of avoiding Nick, to the extent of spending Wednesday night in the pub with my friend Roger until closing time. I'd asked Roger if Nick had ever repaid the money he had lent him. Roger simply shook his head and told me to forget it, since he had. When I told him Pam was coming home, he laughingly said to be sure I introduced him before all others and suggested accompanying Pam and me to *The Ship* on Saturday evening to hear me sing.

"I'd love to meet your sis, Bob," he said. "It'll be fun to see how she reacts to an English pub." He clapped me on the back, "I don't suppose Karachi's anything similar, do you? It'll be wonderful to give her a dose of good old British culture to set her off on the right foot." Roger was a truly good friend, always there for me when I needed him.

I caught the 6.30 train from Walton on Thursday evening, in good time to arrive at Waterloo, get the Tube to St John's Wood and then walk to Madam Davis Reynolds' house. What I had not calculated on was being caught in heavy, freezing rain. By the time I rang the front door bell of my singing teacher's imposing Georgian house, I was soaked to the skin.

The front door, at the top of a flight of stairs, was opened by a short, fussily dressed man wearing a grey waistcoat and jacket over striped trousers. He looked down at me, standing on the step below.

"Mr Matthews? Good gracious. Zo vet you are," he said. "Kom in and get dry, you poor boy. Madam is vaiting for you. Kom, Kom in."

The bedraggled Mr Matthews entered a spacious hallway and was led into a large room. Other than a highly polished grand piano standing in the centre, the room was devoid of furniture.

"Take your coat off," said the man, whom I assumed to be the butler. "I vill bring towel and you can dry yourself. In case you need something else, mein name is Henry."

I removed my jacket and handed it to Henry, who smiled, as he took it from my hands, displaying several gold fillings in a mouth full of uneven teeth. I ran my hands through my wet hair to smooth it down and waited for Henry to return with the promised towel. Meanwhile I remained standing in my wet clothing, feeling ridiculous. Moments later, Henry flounced back into the room bearing a towel and a long, fluffy bathrobe.

"Dry yourself a little and put zis robe on," he said. "It's okay young man, Madam knows how vet you are. Zis robe was her idea."

I took the towel from Henry, rubbed it over the front of my shirt and trousers, finishing with a surreptitious stab at drying my shoes, before quickly slipping on the bathrobe.

In my imagination, I had pictured Madam to be formidable, overbearing, someone who brooked no argument; a bit of a bully in fact. Instead, she turned out to be small; a jolly person with rosy cheeks, penetrating black eyes and wearing a mischievous grin.

"Oh, you poor dear" she said. She put her hand to her mouth, stifling a laugh. "Robert, you're wet through. No matter, as long as the vocal cords are intact. Now, we mustn't waste any time." Wafting a hand in Henry's direction, she said, "Henry lives here and studies *lieder* with me. Going to be as famous as Richard Tauber one day, aren't you, Henry?"

Henry gave a slight bow. "If you say so, Madam. Now I leave you with Robert, yes?"

"Righto, Henry. You buzz off now. Robert will come with me and we'll see what to make of his voice." Madam took me by the elbow and directed me towards the piano, saying, "This once belonged to Dame Nellie Melba."

"Gosh!" I said, hoping I sounded suitably impressed. I had no idea who Tauber was, or for that matter, Nellie Melba.

Madam sat herself down at the piano and played a few chords before turning round to look at me. "Robert, you are such a fright in that robe," she giggled. She tapped middle C on the key board with a finger, "If you can bear it, chuck it off and we'll try a few scales."

Tossing the bathrobe aside, I la-la-la-ed in tune with Madam as she fingered the keys: a semitone lower, then higher, then a full tone up and down the scale before sticking a finger up in the air. "That's it. At least you sing very well in tune, m'dear. Now follow me: do re mi fa sol la ti do."

I did as Madam asked for a full fifteen minutes at full volume, before she stopped again. "Robert," she admonished, "it's beautiful sound we want. Not a bellow. Bel canto is what I teach. Bel canto means beautiful singing. Let's try again. Breathe from the diaphragm, like so." Madam stood up and demonstrated. "See, no movement in the shoulders as I inhale, and exhale. Also, as you sing, allow your breath to float over your vocal cords as they stretch for the higher registers and then thicken as you sing the lower ones. Now, you have a go."

I followed Madam's instructions as best I could for rest of my hour's lesson, with her encouraging me as I sang my scales. "Harry Geller wants you sing with his band," she said, without looking up from the piano. "In my book you'd make a decent opera singer. Now, next week young man, bring some sheet music with you. Meantime practise your breathing won't you? And the last thing I wish to say to you before you leave. If you want a career as a singer, stickability is what's required."

She repeated "stickability, stickability" even as Henry handed me my coat at the door.

My coat had dried out somewhat; I was thankful it felt warm as I put it on. Madam bustled forward and caught my hands in hers. For a moment, I thought she was about to ask me to shell out for the lesson. I was wrong. All she did was to smile, saying, "That was a good first effort Robert, but remember, *stickability*'s the most important thing." I had a momentary sense of unease. Why had Madam found it necessary to repeat the phrase? Nevertheless, I left her house feeling well satisfied by the way my first lesson had gone. On the train home from Waterloo, the words "stickability, stickability" repeated in my head in rhythm with the sound of the wheels running over the tracks.

Chapter 49

My boss gave me time off on Friday afternoon so I could be home to meet my sister, but it was after five when she and her boyfriend finally turned up in an ancient black Austin. My mother and I ran out of the house to greet Pam as she stepped out of the car. Wearing a warm wool coat, she was even prettier than I recalled; petite, with dark curly hair and huge brown eyes, she was a young woman now, no longer a child.

"Sorry we are late, sorry we are late", Pam cried, sounding flustered. Mother grabbed hold of Pam and planted a kiss on her lips, which Pam returned with a faint peck on the cheek. She released herself from our mother's grasp and embraced me. "Hello, big brother," she said, hugging me tight.

David and Ronald were at my side, looking shyly at her. Pam broke away from me and gathered her young brothers in her arms. She kissed both of them in turn. "You've both grown so big, I hardly recognise you," she said, brushing tears from her eyes. Ronald used the back of his hand to scrape his cheek; David shuffled his feet and went bright red.

"Nick would have been here, Pam," my mother interrupted, "but he's still at school I'm afraid."

Ignoring her remark, Pam walked over to the rear of the car, where her boyfriend stood holding a bulky suitcase he'd removed from the boot. "This is my Michael," she said, taking his free hand.

Michael, who was around thirty, a short, barrel-chested man with thinning fair hair, responded half-heartedly, "Pleased to meet you," with just the semblance of a smile. "Sorry I haven't time to meet the family properly. Dad's car broke down in Southampton. Had to call in the AA to fix it. Have to dash back to Hertfordshire as soon as possible."

"Poor boy, poor boy," said my mother, sounding more relieved than sympathetic. "Of course we understand, Michael. Your parents will be awfully worried. But you must come and see us soon. Mustn't he, Pam?"

"Yes, of course," replied Michael, "as soon as I can." He gave Pam a perfunctory hug. "Give me a ring tomorrow, pet. After you've had some rest."

Pam still hung onto Michael's hand. He wrenched it from her grasp before jumping into his car. He blew Pam a kiss and was off before we had time to draw breath. Pam stood frozen, biting her lip. The little I had seen of Michael did not endear him to me. He was too full of himself by half. I wondered what it was Pam saw in him.

I picked up Pam's suitcase and dumped it in the sitting room. Pam sat down on a chair by the window and studied the view across the Thames: *The Anglers* pub on the opposite bank; a tidy row of dinghies moored adjacent to it; a hardy, single sculler pulling against the tide; swans floating serenely on the water and a flotilla of ducks in close escort.

"What a lovely view," Pam said, "but, my, it's cold in England."

"I'll fetch you a blanket, darling," my mother said. She went into a bedroom and returned with a blanket off one of the beds and wrapped it around Pam's knees.

"Thanks, Mum." Pam's stiff expression melted into a nervous smile. "I hope it's all right me staying her for a little. Not putting you out, is it?"

"'Course not darling," replied my mother. She took Pam's hands in hers and looked deep into her eyes. "You can stay just as long as you like. I can't tell you how happy we all are to see you looking so well. So grown up."

"Well, I'll be twenty one next birthday," Pam answered, with an edge to her voice. I feared she was about add something caustic, for instance, how many years she had been left on her own. She obviously thought better of it and changed the direction of the conversation. "Have you heard from Richard?" she asked.

"Oh, yes, he's finished his basic training. He's joined the Royal Engineers, but you may see him very soon. He said he was due some leave."

"I wish he was here, Mum. I really miss him. And how's Geoff? I haven't heard a thing about him for ages."

"Geoff works in London, darling. The last time we saw him was when we first arrived. Haven't heard from him since. Maybe we can get him down to see you. He knows you are here, because the moment I got your letter I wrote and told him you were coming."

Pam looked wistful. "I hope Richard comes soon, before I leave. Michael's applied for a new job in Hertfordshire. If he gets it, we'll marry and I'll move there. Michael's an accountant, you know. We worked in the same office at ICI in Karachi and have been going out for about a year. He asked me to marry him just before he left for the UK. You could say we're engaged," Pam smiled, "although he hasn't bought me a ring as yet. He is going to take me to a jeweller and let me choose one."

"Engaged? You did say engaged? Why, that's wonderful, Pam. Michael does seem such a nice man. When are you planning to get married?"

"Don't know as yet. It depends on Michael. Meantime, I need to get a job, because I've very little money left. Some temporary work to tide me over. The sooner the better."

Having met Michael so briefly, it was perhaps harsh of me to make any kind of judgement about him. However, instinct told me he was no good for Pam and that she was making a big mistake in marrying him. I'd have been happier if she chosen someone else.

"Anyone fancy a cup of tea?" I asked, brightly. "I bet you'd like one, Pam. Sorry no cake, or anything. We've plenty of bread and marge. No doubt you've heard of rationing?"

"Oh, yes, yes, I have. I'm not at all hungry though. Just tea, please, Bob".

The boys stood around looking awkward, not knowing what to say to the sister they barely remembered. As soon I mentioned tea, David said he'd help me make it. David, Ronald and I headed into the kitchen, but we'd hardly time to prepare a tray with cups and saucers, when I heard Nick enter the sitting room. I dashed to the open kitchen door to watch Pam.

"Hello, Pam," said Nick, looming over her. "Had a good trip? Not sea sick or anything? I must say you look awfully well."

"No, I wasn't sea sick. I enjoyed the boat very much, thank you." Pam's reply was cool, her expression neutral.

"Good-oh. Now then, where's your young man, Michael? I'd like to meet him."

"He's not here. He had to hurry back home." Pam replied, her voice now chilly as the tundra. There was no mistaking the subject of Michael was closed to Nick. "Pity," murmured Nick, before asking loudly, "Any chance of a cup of tea, anyone?" He went over to a window seat opposite Pam and sat down. "This place isn't exactly the Ritz, Pam," he said, "but you're welcome to stay as long as you like."

"Thank you, Nick," said Pam, taking a sip from the cup I had placed on a side table beside her. "If nobody minds, maybe Mum can show me where I'm to sleep. I'm awfully tired."

I was sorry Pam was going to bed. I'd been looking forward to catching up with all her news and telling her what I'd been up to. Tired or not, she had made the right decision. I saw her simmering hate for Nick developing into a full blown row if she stayed up.

I decided that when Pam was up and ready on Saturday morning, I'd take her by bus to Walton and point out the Labour Exchange. She could go there after the weekend, sign on for work and get her National Insurance number. If the Labour Exchange had no temporary vacancies, there was always the Alfred Marks Bureau in the High Street who might be a much better bet.

The next morning after we had finished our meagre breakfast, Pam and I walked to the bus stop a quarter of a mile away. By good luck, we had only a few minutes to wait before the bus to Walton drew up. Pam quivered with excitement all the way to the High Street. "England's not at all as I expected," she said over and over again, as she stepped off the bus. "The houses, buildings, everything. So different, so different."

"You'll soon get used to it, Pam. It'll take you no time at all, you'll see."

Pam shivered, “Brrr. Michael said it would cold, but I had no idea how cold. Which reminds me I must phone him. Do you know if there’s somewhere I can phone from?”

“Your wish is my command,” I said, pointing out a phone box at the corner of the High Street, by the Post Office. “For future reference, all the phone boxes are painted red, makes them easy to spot.”

“How sweet,” murmured Pam.

We walked the few yards to the phone box. I inserted tuppence in the box and then showed Pam how to use the phone. I stepped outside as soon as she was connected to Michael. The call lasted barely three minutes, before Pam exited looking tearful.

“Everything all right?” I asked.

“Michael said he was doing something important for his father. He said he was too busy to speak for long,” she replied, clearly upset.

“Ah, well,” I said, “we’ll have another go later on. Meantime, d’you mind waiting here a bit? There’s someone I have to ring.”

I got through to Harry Geller and apologised for not telling him how I’d got on with my singing lesson.

“Madam rang me yesterday,” he said. “She was very pleased with you. I think, after a few more sessions with her, we’ll give you a go with the band at Romano’s, or Quaglino’s in London. Give me a ring in three weeks and we’ll see where we are.”

When I emerged from the phone box, Pam appeared more composed. We then found a tea shop and settled by a window overlooking the High street and talked non-stop for an hour or more as we relived what we’d both gone through. She laughed as I told her of my adventures: The Windmill

Theatre, the film test, my stint as an assistant to a psychiatrist, flatting, Sue Kenyon, just about everything I'd done since I came to England, without mentioning I was on the fringe of the big time in show business, in case she thought I was a big head.

Pam spoke of how she had struggled in her low paid job as a junior typist to make ends meet, her one extravagance to go to the flicks once a month. Other than that, she spent her free time on Karachi's Clifton beach and read every book she could lay her hands on. Even after being promoted, she'd gone without luxuries of any kind until she had saved enough for her boat fare. Only when she met Michael did her life change for the better.

I asked very gently, because of my misgivings over Michael, when they planned to see each other again. She avoided answering other than to say she'd phone him again later and find out. Meanwhile, a job was the most important thing on her mind, so she could pay for her keep. I told her that, although I didn't have much, I would always help her out.

She firmed up that determined chin of hers, clenched my fingers and thanked me. "I've learned to make my own way, Bob," she said. "I'm ready to do anything at all to earn some money."

As I faced my sister across the table, I could not help admiring her determination. Pam was a survivor through and through.

After we had covered just about everything, I suggested she might like to look around the shops. I settled the bill, and together we went up and down both sides of the High Street, with Pam peering into the shop windows we passed.

"There doesn't seem much choice available," she said, pointing to the few items of clothing on display. "So different from the bazaars." She chuckled. "Not a single sari or kameez. But I see from the women's fashions here, my clothes are hopelessly out of date. I suppose I'll have to smarten up when I get a job."

We stopped outside the Labour Exchange, where Pam carefully noted down their opening hours, before heading on to the Alfred Marks employment agency down the road. "I'll try them on Monday," said Pam. "Keep your fingers crossed they've got something suitable for me. Now, if you don't mind, I'd like to go home now. I've got to show willing with Mum and then there's the boys..."

"You need to try phoning Michael again," I said.

"It'll keep. Monday'll do just as well." Pam blinked and reached for a handkerchief.

Although baffled by her response, I thought better than to ask what was troubling her. Instead, I suggested we buy some fish and chips for lunch, which I thought she might like to try. "They are not rationed," I explained, "and there's a shop just around the corner."

"Fish and chips? Oh, yes, please. I'm starving," she cried.

I bought two bobs' worth of cod and chips wrapped in newspaper, enough for the family. On the way home on the bus, I told Pam to be ready at seven that evening, because my friend Roger and I were taking her to the pub.

"A pub? How lovely. I've heard of pubs," she replied, squeezing my hand with excitement.

Nick was out when we arrived back home, so the rest of us made short work of his share of the fish and chips. After lunch, I left Pam with my mother and, not knowing what to do to fill the time until Roger arrived, I retreated to my bedroom and got down to finishing a short story I'd started writing some weeks before.

Roger turned up at seven on the dot and instantly charmed Pam, who had dolled herself up for the occasion. He gave her an extravagant bow from the waist and said, "Glad to see you're so much better-looking than that brother of yours." Smiling, he took Pam by the arm, opened the rear door of his car and ushered her in, while I stood watching. I couldn't help thinking if only, if only...

The lounge bar of *The Ship* was already full of people and fugged up with cigarette smoke. Above the clink of glasses and the general hubbub coming from the press of drinkers, I heard a piano. Roger managed to get us drinks and clear a space for us near Barbara, thumping away at the keys in a corner.

As she caught sight of me, Barbara lifted a hand to acknowledge my presence, then broke into the opening bars of *Give me your Heart*. "Come on, Bob," she rasped loudly, in her tobacco-laden voice, "Sing!"

"Where's the mike?"

"There's no bloody mike, you idiot! Just sing!"

Taken completely off balance, but with Barbara encouraging me, I joined in the chorus with her. Then, as loudly as I could, I sang a reprise that quietened the clamour in the bar. In the hush that followed, Barbara played some well-known Cole Porter standards for me, such as *The Lady is a Tramp.* From somewhere behind me, I heard applause and cries of "More, more, give us another." As I stood uncertainly by the piano, Barbara reached for one of the several glasses lined up on the lid of the piano and took a long swig, before shouting for a bit a quiet for Bob Matthews.

"You must know stuff from *Oklahoma*, Bob," she said, eyeing me. "So, how about *Oh What a Beautiful Morning*?" Without waiting for my reply, she went straight into the opening chorus. Fortunately, I had rehearsed the song with

Sue Kenyon, so I knew it well. I followed up with a couple of numbers from *South Pacific* and *Brigadoon*. Someone in the audience handed me a beer, and Pam came to stand at my side. "I didn't know you could sing like that," she said. "You were good, big brother. You should take it up."

Barbara got up from her stool and clapped me on the back. "Well done, Robert," she said, stretching her back. "But next time we'll practise half a dozen songs before you come on." She laughed, "I'm sorry; it was unfair of me to throw you in at the deep end like that. Anyway, that's what pub singing's all about. You sang well tonight. Johnny Gregson thought so, too. He's the one who bought you the beer. That's him there." I looked where she was pointing and saw a familiar face nod in my direction.

I was astonished. "John Gregson, the famous actor who starred in *Angels One Five*?"

"Yes," replied Barbara. "Johnny lives just across the road, but there's always a film crowd in here on Saturday nights. When shooting's finished at Shepperton studios, this place is always full." She gave a throaty cough, pulled on her cigarette and spluttered, "Now that you're number two on the bill, Bob, you'll never have to buy another drink at *The Ship*." She took another deep drag and blew a perfect smoke circle. "Before I forget, Julie's home. If you like, why not come on over tomorrow about three and you can meet her? But come on, now, I can follow anything. What other songs do you know? We've another half-hour to do."

I replied that I knew a great many of Frank Sinatra's standards and suggested *Singing the Blues.*

"Great, that's what we'll start with," said Barbara, sitting down to play again. She accompanied me for the next thirty minutes, probably twenty minutes too long, for the lounge bar had filled with noise again and it was difficult to sing over it. Besides, I was feeling distinctly woozy after drinking the five pints of beer people had bought me. Roger and Pam had gone to sit by a window at the far end of the bar. She was giggling her head off, presumably at one of his inexhaustible fund of jokes. I was happy that Roger had taken her mind off Michael, at least for a while.

I was relieved when Barbara closed the lid of her piano and said she was off. She slipped on a fur coat, before prodding my chest. “See you tomorrow, Robert,” she said. She gave a regal wave to her fans in the bar and weaved unsteadily out of *The Ship*.

Roger dropped Pam and me home soon after. “See you next Saturday, same time,” he shouted, as he sped off in his car.

Chapter 50

I had told Pam I was meeting Julie Andrews, but the name meant nothing to her. I asked her not to say a word to our mother, to stop her from proclaiming to all and sundry that Julie was her son's best friend.

After Sunday lunch, I got on my bike and set off for Walton, saying to the family I needed the exercise to get rid of my very first hangover. After a couple of miles of hard pedalling in the cold, fresh air, I felt a lot better by the time I arrived outside The Old Meuse a few minutes before three. Thrilled at the prospect of meeting Julie, I parked my bike against a sycamore tree at the entrance to the drive and stood counting the minutes off to three o'clock.

Barbara's Hillman Minx suddenly roared round the blind turning and nearly sent me flying. Screeching to a halt, she wound down her window and shouted, "What the hell?" Recognising me, she called out, "Silly sod, I could have killed you." Shaken, I went over her car to apologise.

"Christ Almighty, Robert, you all right?" she said. "What on earth were you doing standing there? Come on into the house, you naughty boy, and meet Julie." She started up her car and slowly rolled forward to her front door. I followed on close behind, pushing my bike, feeling an absolute fool.

Barbara eased herself out of her car, just as Julie opened the door. Breathing heavily, Barbara grinned at her daughter. “This is Robert, who has just scared the living daylights out of me”.

Julie gave me a big, welcoming smile. “Hello, I’m Julie,” she said, “Mummy’s told me a lot about you. What did you do to frighten her?”

“Er, I was just standing in the wrong place when she drove round the corner. My fault,” I stammered, looking down at my shoes.

“Mummy, tell the truth”, Julie threw up her hands in mock despair. “I’m sure you were driving too fast, as usual.”

Barbara muttered defensively, “Well, maybe a little...” She made a face. “It’s not right; Julie’s always poking fun at her poor mother.”

Julie gave me a grin. “Poor mother indeed.” Standing aside to make way for me, she said, “Come in the warm, Robert. You’ll get cold standing there.”

“My name’s, Bob. Your mum is the only one who calls me Robert.”

“Then Bob it is, Bob,” laughed Julie, before breaking into song, her feet doing a soft shoe shuffle as she sang, “When the rob, rob, robin, comes bob, bob, bobbin’ along.”

I warmed to Julie immediately. How could anyone not? She was friendly, and had a terrific sense of fun. Despite her fame, she was not in the least standoffish or big-headed as I feared she might be.

I followed Barbara and Julie through the hall and into the sitting room. Julie said she was sure I’d like a cup of tea and disappeared into the kitchen to make it.

As soon as Barbara seated herself, she asked, “Robert, how did you enjoy singing at the pub last night?”

"I was scared at first," I replied. "After a while I enjoyed it, but I couldn't have done it without you at the piano, Barbara. Honest, I couldn't."

Barbara looked pleased. "Well, when you've done it as often as I have..." She put her hand to her mouth, as a thought occurred. "Tony will be here soon. Tony Walton, Julie's boyfriend, you met him at the talent show, remember?"

"That's great," I lied, dismayed that I didn't have Julie all to myself.

Julie returned with a tea tray, and when we all had cups, settled herself on an adjacent sofa.

"Mum tells me, your ambition is to sing professionally," said Julie, fixing me with her wide blue eyes, the left one of which had a slight squint.

"Well, yes," I replied, shyly. "I've always loved to sing. It was Harry Geller, my manager, who suggested I take it up professionally. He's even arranged for me to have singing lessons in London. When he thinks I'm ready, I'm going to do some gigs in town."

"I didn't know you had a manager, Robert," interrupted Barbara, sounding aggrieved, "I thought that...well, never mind." She slumped back in her chair, pulled on her cigarette and relapsed into silence.

I squirmed in my seat. "Barbara, I didn't have the opportunity to tell you before."

Sensing an awkward atmosphere developing, Julie broke into the conversation. "Harry Geller?" she said brightly. "Of course, I've heard of Harry Geller and his Orchestra. He's on the radio a lot. And who's your singing teacher, other than mum?"

"Er, she's a Madam Davis Reynolds in St Johns Wood."

"Oh, I'll have to ask my singing teacher, Madame Stiles Allen if she knows of her."

I was astonished. "You still take singing lessons? You?"

"Oh, yes," she said, "singers can never, ever let up. You have to stick at it. Stick it at all the time."

There it was again: *Stick at it, stick at it, stickability, stickability*, the phrase that made me wonder if I had what it took.

I watched as Julie kicked her shoes off and curled her long legs under her. She relaxed against the sofa cushions and lay there smiling. Not conventionally pretty, but with her dark, curling brown hair framing her features Julie was undeniably attractive.

Meanwhile, Bob Matthews, a mere nothing, sat awestruck in the presence of one of the best known singers in the land, a young girl graced with a God-given voice.

Julie at eighteen, had steel behind the girlish façade, I presumed this came from trouping with Ted and Barbara from the age of eleven, always on the move, starring in pantomime for months on end, doing shows all around the country, spending weeks away from home in digs, with personal appearances and singing on the radio in between times. She'd have to be tough to survive such a rigorous way of life.

"Do you play tennis, Bob?" asked Julie casually, eyeing Barbara who had fallen asleep in her chair, I guessed from a surfeit of alcohol at lunch.

"Yes, I do, but I'm hopelessly out of practice. I haven't played since boarding school in the Himalayas."

"Himalayas? Are you an Indian, then?"

"No. I was born and brought up there and only came to England in 1949."

Julie sat up abruptly. "How interesting. You must tell me all about it." So I spent the next half hour or so telling her about my background, with her leaning forward, gripping her knees, listening intently.

"Bob, you should write all this down sometime," she said. "It's another world."

"Actually, I do love to write. I said. "Just short stories, though."

"Me, too. I write in every spare moment I've got."

Having found a common bond, Julie became even more friendly and asked if I'd like to play tennis with her and a couple of girlfriends, Trish and Virginia Waters, the following Sunday. "They've got their own court in the back garden of their house in Walton. We have one, too, but Pops doesn't keep it in good shape."

"Pops?" I enquired.

"Ted, my stepfather. Pops is my name for him," she smiled. "Bob, please say you'll come play doubles with us."

Of course, I jumped at the chance. "Sure Julie, I'd love to," I replied. "But doesn't your boyfriend play?

As soon as Julie had finished explaining that Tony Walton was going off to Canada to complete his National Service in a day or so, and that it would be months before she'd see him again, the front door bell rang.

"That'll be him," said Julie, leaping up to run to the door.

Barbara opened a bleary eye. "Gosh, have I been asleep?" she asked. "Is that Tony at the door?"

Tony stepped into the sitting room, with Julie following behind. Smartly dressed in the grey-blue uniform of a flying officer in the RAF, he leant down to receive a kiss from Barbara.

Straightening up, Tony handed me a mock salute, "Nice to see you again, Bob." He removed his cap from under his arm and placed it on a chair. "Excuse the fancy dress clobber. Julie's never seen me in uniform before". He laughed. "It's her last chance to see me in it before I go to Canada."

"Time I was off then, Tony," I said. "Hope it all goes well with for you and those puppets of yours. I tell you, man, they were bloody marvellous."

"No need to go, Bob," Julie interrupted, "stay awhile, won't you?"

"No thanks, Julie, but I'm still up for tennis next Sunday. That's if you've a spare racquet. What time should I turn up?"

"About three-ish? We can cycle over together. It's only about a mile away."

"Okay, fine, I'll be here." I thanked Barbara for having me and, hesitating a bit, asked, "Shall I come to the pub again next Saturday?"

"Of course, you must, Robert," replied Barbara, patting my hand. "The more you sing, the better your timing will be. I had a devil of a job following you last night. It takes lots of practice you know, so you had better be there."

Perhaps thinking that she'd upset me, Barbara said in a softer tone. "Ask Julie. She has to practise all the time." She blew me a kiss and winked, "See you next week, son".

Chapter 51

Pam immediately struck lucky with the Alfred Marks Bureau, who sent her to be interviewed by a company called OK Bazaars in London. Seeing that she'd previously been employed by ICI and had first class references, the company immediately offered a decently paid job on a three-month trial basis as a secretary to one of the managers.

"I'm so lucky, Bob, I'm starting in a week's time," Pam said, barely able to contain herself. "I can't believe it. They are paying me seven pounds a week, and giving me a week's paid holiday a year. I've done the math, after my train and bus fares, I'll have enough to pay Mummy for my keep and have a couple of pounds left over. Michael will be so pleased."

"When's he coming down to see you?" I asked.

"Soon. Soon," Pam replied, with a slight frown. "He told me on the phone he's lined up some interviews and he'll be down just as soon as he can."

Seeing that she was uncomfortable with the subject, I decided to let it rest, certain that her fiancé was lying for some reason. Poor, poor Pam, I thought. The fellow is a shit.

After Pam came to stay, Nick seemed never to be around. He was either locked away in his bedroom reading newspapers, scribbling notes to God only knew who, or drinking with pals at *The Anglers* across the river. His absence suited me just fine, but I began to feel sorry for my mother, who looked lost and forlorn as she went about doing the chores: cooking and cleaning, tasks which servants had previously done for her. I understood, perhaps for the first time, how hard it must have been for her to adjust to life in England, to move from a privileged life to one of loneliness and drudgery, with no sign of any improvement in her circumstances. Most damaging of all, it was clear that neither Nick nor she had feelings for each other any more.

Occasionally I heard her railing at Nick from behind the closed doors of their bedroom, from which she'd eventually emerge alone, white-faced with rage, to go and stand with her arms crossed, staring at the river. At times like these, I took Pam and the boys for long walks on the tow path and returned home to find Nick had gone to the pub, leaving our mother alone, listlessly turning the pages of ancient *Vogue* magazines, perhaps dreaming of dressing up in fancy clothes again, dancing at glitzy balls at the Rawalpindi Club.

On Thursday, I had my second singing lesson with Madam Davis Reynolds who, after I'd done some breathing exercises and sung scales for the umpteenth time, suggested I bring some music the next time.

"It'll be more fun for you, Bob," she said, "and besides, it'll give me the chance to hear how you deliver a song and to correct any mistakes you make." She got up from her piano stool and wagged a finger in front of my nose. "I'm satisfied you'll make a singer, but no more smoking. I smelt that vile cigarette smoke on your breath the moment you came in to the house. It's no good for the voice. Promise you'll stop?"

I broke my promise to my singing teacher ten minutes after I left her.

On Saturday, Roger accompanied Pam and me over to *The Ship* again, where I desperately tried to keep myself from lagging behind Barbara or coming in half a bar too early. Barbara helped by nodding her head like a metronome, and eventually allowed herself a smile as I finally got the hang of it. Although the applause was as generous as the previous week, as were the pints of beer, I thought more about playing tennis with Julie the following afternoon than on performing.

Unfortunately, the best laid plans, as they say, were ruined; heavy rain fell on Sunday, spoiling any chance of playing tennis. Nevertheless, I cycled over to Julie's house, hoping she didn't mind my keeping her company. She introduced me to her best friends, the sisters Trish and Virginia Waters.

Julie said, "I was sure you'd still come, Bob, so I asked the girls to join us. Maybe we can try and get a game in next week, at the same time. Hope you don't mind?" Mind? I was over the moon. To spend the afternoon flirting with three pretty girls was my idea of fun.

We lounged around for a couple of hours, chatting away about anything and everything, laughing at Julie's anecdotes, often outrageous bits of gossip about well-known comedians and actors with whom she had performed. Later on, Barbara joined the party and sat down at the piano, egging Julie on to sing something for us. We joined in, pleading for her to sing just one song. Julie eventually succumbed and reluctantly went over to join her mother, where they huddled over the piano discussing what she should sing.

Finally, Julie said, "Okay, I'll do the *Polonaise* from *Mignon,*" adding, "Blame Mum. It's her idea. I first sang this in the Starlight Roof revue at the Hippodrome."

Julie stepped forward as Barbara played the introduction, then standing quite relaxed began to sing, her voice soaring, the cadenzas filling the room, concluding the beautiful polonaise with a thrilling, effortless F above top C.

Her magical voice made the hairs on the back of my neck stand on end. I understood at once why she was so famous. Julie's audience of three did not stop clapping until she shyly sat down once more. Gesturing to us to stop the applause, she teased, "Come on, Bob, I've done my bit. Your turn next."

Realising it was futile to refuse, I replied, scared out of my wits, "Okay, I'll have a go."

On cue, Barbara immediately played the opening bars of *Give me Your Heart*. I sang the damn song, which I'd come to hate, and slunk back to my chair, scarlet in the face, ready to bury myself in the biggest hole I could find. But everyone applauded, including Julie, who said without a trace of irony, "Bob, it's true what Mummy told me, you do have a good voice."

To everyone's amusement, Barbara followed up by saying "That was the very first time, Robert, you actually sang in time."

I never got to play tennis the following Sunday, or any other Sunday for four consecutive weeks, because of rain. In the meantime, Julie had accepted to play the lead in *The Boy Friend* on Broadway which was to open in August. I had hoped to see a lot more of her during the summer, but she was immediately cast in another play with music, *Mountain Fire*, which rather scuppered my plans.

After my third singing lesson with Madam Davis Reynolds, she told Harry Geller I was ready for a try-out with his band. When I rang him, something I did every week, he told me to turn up at the Maccabi Club in Golders Green the following

Saturday. "It's a bar mitzvah, lots of dancing and jollies," he said. "We'll give you a shot with one song and see how it goes. The function doesn't start until eight, so if you come along at six, we'll have time for a short rehearsal. Madam said you sang *The Anniversary Waltz* pretty well for her, so I think that's what we'll do. Don't worry, the boys know it already. Oh, yes, before I forget, wear a dinner jacket. You can change into it when you arrive." Harry gave me the address of the venue, stressing that on no account should I be late, and then rang off.

At last a proper engagement, I thought, puzzled by the term bar mitzvah. I hadn't a clue what it meant. Fortunately Henry Branch, my boss, came to my rescue, explaining it was a Jewish custom to celebrate the coming of age of a boy.

Now that Henry had cleared up the mystery for me, I checked out my dinner suit and carefully pressed it, so that the trousers had razor-sharp creases. As I was about to hang up my suit, Pam walked into my bedroom, sat on my bed and began to cry.

"What's up, Pam?" I asked.

"It's Michael," she sobbed, as if her heart would break, "he's dumped me."

"What d'you mean 'dumped' you?"

"He wrote me a letter saying he couldn't marry me, that he didn't love me any more and it was best I forget him. Just that."

"What a bastard! No other explanation?"

"No. None. I really thought Michael loved me. Now what am I to do?"

"I don't know what to say Pam. But I'll tell you now, I never liked Michael from the start. Honest, you're best off without him."

I sat down on the bed alongside her. Not knowing what else I could do, I hugged my poor sister as she rocked back and forth in my arms. Eventually, Pam ceased crying and I saw her firmly set her chin, as she did when she'd made her mind up.

"What's done's done," she said abruptly. "I'll just have to forget Michael and get on with it, won't I? There is nothing else for it."

"Plenty of other fish, Pam..." I ventured.

"As they all say," she replied, brushing the tears from her eyes. She got to her feet. "Don't say anything to Mum. She'll just go on and on about it if she knows. She'll find out soon enough." Smoothing down her frock, she said, "Right, that's me done." As she walked to the door, she laughed bitterly, "Roger's bound to point out some likely replacements for me when we go to the pub on Saturday."

When she had left the room, I thought how wonderful it would have been if Pam and Roger were more than just good friends.

Having forgotten to say to Barbara I wouldn't be singing with her at *The Ship* on Saturday, I cycled to The Old Meuse to explain and also tell her about my first professional engagement.

"Veddings and bar mitzvahs!" she howled. "Robert, is that what your Harry Geller thinks you are only good for? Veddings and bar mitzvahs?" Barbara's hilarity was unexpected; her sharp put-down of Harry Geller a surprise.

Stung, I asked what she meant.

"I couldn't help it, darling," replied Barbara. "It's what Jewish musical-hall comics say to get a laugh. To be available, even for veddings and bar mitzvahs, means times are hard. I didn't intend it as a put-down, honest I didn't. It just struck me as funny."

Harry Branch's A-Z map of London again came in handy when finding my way to Golders Green. It was a great deal further to the north of town than I had anticipated, so I came in for a dressing down from Harry Geller when I turned up at the Maccabi Club fifteen minutes late, with the band set up in a room behind the function hall.

"Never again, Bob Matthews!" he snarled. "Pros are *never* late. Imagine if we hadn't allowed time for rehearsal and we had no singer to front the band. What then?"

I tried to stutter an excuse, but he silenced me under the eyes of the band, saying, "No excuses, no excuses. We've wasted enough time." Seeing I was sufficiently abashed, he cooled down as quickly as he'd flared. "Okay, Bob," he said, as he went around introducing me to the members of the band, who appeared less than interested in me. "I hope you've learnt your lesson. Now climb into your glad rags." He glanced at the valise I'd borrowed from Roger, into which I had carefully folded my dinner suit, and pointed to a corner, saying , "Change there, you've got five minutes."

Agitated, and by now extremely nervous, I climbed awkwardly out of my clothes and donned my dinner suit, aware of laughter from the band as I tried and failed to tie my bow tie properly. After my third attempt, Harry came over, tutting, tied it for me, and stood back to see if it was straight. "I suggest you acquire a clip tie, saves all this malarkey, Bob. Now, if you are ready, let's have a go at *The Anniversary Waltz*. Stand in front. Watch my baton, I'll show you when to come in."

After all the practice I'd had with Barbara, I felt confident enough following Harry. The band struck up and everything went very well, I came in on time, I sang in tune and waited for Harry's reaction after I'd finished.

"Listen, son," he said, "that was good; very good. Do it as well as that when the guests are dancing and you'll be just fine. Well done." Harry swivelled round to face the band, "Take five, guys and have a fag."

From the wings I watched the hall filling up with what appeared to be several entire families: grandparents, parents, children, babies in arms, boys and girls in their teens. In the middle of the room a gaggle of young men and women dressed to the nines surrounded a giggling youth I assumed to be the bar mitzvah boy. Making a terrific din, laughing, clearly having a good time, they cast expectant looks at the music stands on stage, willing the band to materialise.

At ten to eight, the band filed on stage and took their places. Harry had instructed me not to show my face, to stay out of sight until called upon to sing, making me wonder what I'd do to keep myself occupied.

Finally, Harry walked briskly to the stand microphone at the centre of the stage and faced the audience. He drawled confidently, "Good evening ladies and gentlemen, not forgetting young Benjamin Goldfarb, whose bar mitzvah we are celebrating. I hope you have a most enjoyable evening. Now for some music from Harry Geller and his Orchestra."

Harry waved his baton and the band went straight into Glen Miller's *Take the A Train*, the horns and the rhythm section—all top notch musicians—getting everyone's feet tapping.

I sat on a stool, enjoying the music, but after half an hour of twiddling my thumbs, even that began to pall. Another hour passed, by which time I was ready to fall asleep with boredom, but came suddenly alert when Harry announced he had a surprise in store. "I'd like you to give a big hand to Keith Monteath, a well-known singer on All India Radio, whose English debut this is." He made a grand, sweeping gesture in my direction, urging me to make an appearance, "Ladies and gentlemen, I give you Keith Monteath."

It was some time before I realised Harry was referring to me. Filled with confusion, completely taken out of my stride, I went to stand in front of the mike, as the band began to play the introduction to *The Anniversary Waltz.* I glanced at Harry, who gave me a reassuring smile and a wave of his baton. My mind still in ferment, I lost all sense of time and came in late, forcing the band to slow down. I quickened up, catching the band off balance. Dancing couples tripped as I tried to recover the one-two-three beat of the waltz, and I didn't get myself back in time to the music until the second verse. Harry looked furious and the members of the band scowled, as I faltered to the end of the song. Not surprisingly, there was very little in the way of applause, but I did hear a boo or two as I retreated from the stage to my shelter behind the curtain. Humiliated, I was convinced my singing career was over. I put the blame on Harry for not warning me in advance of the revolting new stage name he'd given me. I was furious; Keith Monteath, indeed. It sounded like someone with a speech impediment.

Soon afterwards, the band took a break. Harry strode over to where I sat. I was expecting a volcanic outburst for ruining the reputation of his band, instead of which he addressed me calmly. "Tonight was a serious balls-up, Bob," he said. "I realise I am partly responsible for announcing you as Keith Monteath. I thought I had already mentioned I was giving you a new stage name. Not that there's anything wrong with the name Bob Matthews, but you need a more memorable one, like Keith Monteath." Seeing I was about to dissent, he quickly added, "Or something similar. Anyhow, let's cut to the chase. I know tonight was a one off and I'll tell the band it was my fault. They're pros, they'll understand. Now, we've got a gig at Quaglino's next Saturday. It's a very well-known joint. Top class, the best grub, there's a dance floor; patrons dance if and when they feel like it. Promise I won't refer to you as Keith Monteath again, but how about Robert Monteath? Will that do you?"

I had been listening to Harry, mouth half open with surprise. "That's fine," I said, "but does it mean you'll give me another go?"

"Sure. We all fuck up from time to time, son. Now get the hell out of here and go home. Phone me as usual and I'll fill you in with the details. Here," he pulled a ten shilling note from his pocket, "this'll cover your expenses." I was about to thank him, but he turned his back on me, saying "Bugger off, kid."

Chapter 52

Quaglino's reminded me of the Hotel Quirinale in Rome, where I'd stayed a night on my way over to England, but the restaurant topped the Quirinale and anything I had ever seen before. It obviously catered for a seriously wealthy clientele. Chandeliers, thick carpets, tables set with glittering cutlery and glass—everywhere I looked, opulence on the grand scale. Even the waiters appeared to be a cut above the average, wearing tails and expressionless faces, acknowledging guests with small, deferential bows, silently and expertly going about the business of satisfying the diners' every wish. I wondered if, one day I'd be able to afford to dine in such a place.

There was no stage for the band. A dais at one end of a small dance floor, surrounded by tables, was just about big enough to accommodate Harry's swing quintet for the gig: piano, saxophone, clarinet, drums, double bass.

Earlier, I'd had a successful rehearsal of *The Anniversary Waltz*, which Harry said would be the last number of the night at around eleven o'clock. Having been bored witless waiting in the wings at the Maccabi Club, I had brought a novel with me to pass the long hours. Fortunately, Quaglino's had provided a small anteroom for our band, and a wall clock to keep a close eye on the time.

"I know it's a pain in the arse," Harry said, "hanging about all night, but you'll just have to stick it out, Robert Monteath." He pulled the long cigarette holder from his mouth. "It's called learning on the job. Like, for instance, ignore the noise of cutlery, people laughing, chatting, filling their faces while you sing your song. Remember, here, it's the food they've come for, not to listen to you. When I figure you've learned how to deal with that, I'll call on you to front the band. Until then, chum, hold your horses."

Harry was right; the guests paid no attention to the band. They carried on talking and laughing, and from the band members' faces they did not care either.

I pulled out my paperback and filled two hours reading Hank Janson's execrable prose. At just before eleven I poked my head out of my small room and saw that a few of the guests had taken to the dance floor for the last waltz. I saw Harry glance in my direction; my cue to step out. I heard him introduce me as the well-known singer Robert Monteath, who was going to sing *The Anniversary Waltz* as the finale. There was a smattering of applause when I came to the end of the song. I watched a stout, older woman wearing a tight sequinned dress, detach herself from her dancing partner. She walked over to me and, to my astonishment, handed me a pound note. "That was lovely," she said, "thank you so very much."

Speechless, I looked to see what Harry had to say. Smiling, he nodded, indicating I should accept. I stammered my thanks to the woman. "No, it's for me to thank you," she said. "You made my evening."

Harry put an arm around my shoulder. "Well done, Robert Monteath. I can see the effect you have on old ladies." He laughed. "Let's see if the same thing happens at Romano's next week with younger dames."

"Romano's?"

"Be there Saturday. Bit smaller than this place, so we'll be a quartet for a change. You better be off now or you'll miss your train, chum."

Romano's, also located in the West End of London, turned out not to be in quite the same league as Quaglino's. The younger clientele loved Harry's swing quartet and most of the guests danced until midnight, when the gig ended. Harry let me sing at around ten, so I could go home early.

Earlier, during a break, I mentioned to Harry that I was heartily sick of singing the same two or three songs over and over, and asked him if there was any way I could try out some new ones. I told him, I'd sung lots of other stuff in the pub which had gone down well.

"Yes, it is about time you tried out something different, maybe up-tempo numbers for a change," Harry agreed. "But remember, Robert, singing in strict tempo with a band is streets away from singing in a pub. The prob is you've a day job. So tell me how we find time to rehearse? The only way, as I see it, is for you to practise one new number with the band's pianist every couple of weeks. By the end of the year you'll be singing all night. But, first things first. Phone me if you can take a day off next week, and I'll see if my friend Dick Katz is available. He's about the best session pianist in London. I'll arrange for him to give you a run-through of a few standards at his recording studio in Tin Pan Alley, Denmark Street. How's that sound?"

"Did you say recording studio, Harry?"

"I did. I was thinking that we might even cut a record and punt it over to the BBC."

"BBC?"

"You heard right, son. BBC."

Harry delivered the remark so casually I wondered whether to take him seriously. But, since nothing in his expression suggested he was joking, I took what he said at face value, nearly wetting myself with excitement at the prospect of making a record and having it heard by the BBC.

I couldn't wait to ask my boss if I could have a day off. After examining his schedule, he said Thursday would be fine by him. Kind as ever and keen to have a hand in the making of a star, he allowed me out to ring Harry from a phone box across the road.

"You don't hang around, son, do you?" said Harry dryly down the line. "It so happens Thursday's your lucky day. I had a word with Dick Katz and it's his only free day. So, I'll meet you outside 42 Denmark Street at ten o'clock and we'll go from there. Bring your music with you, just a few of your favourite songs."

When I told my boss, he jumped to his feet, promising to concoct for me some of his magic potion to keep my vocal cords free of mucus, or 'gunge' as he called it. "Remember how well it worked at the talent competition."

True to his word, he gave me a phial of his potion on Wednesday night to use before my session with Dick Katz. "Just as you did the last time, swallow this at least an hour before you sing."

Pam and Mother reacted as if I was already a star when I told them I might be making a record. They threw up their hands and danced around the sitting room, saying they knew I was going to be famous, a star—Mario Lanza, Bing, Sinatra, all rolled into one. Their antics only subsided after I repeated over and over again that it was just a trial run and the record was not for release.

On Thursday, having swallowed my boss's magic potion, I arrived in front of 42 Denmark Street a few minutes early. I stood on the pavement feeling tense, humming to myself, smoking a cigarette to ease my nerves until Harry Geller strolled up ten minutes late.

Looking me up and down, he said, "Not a good idea to smoke, chum. No good for the throat."

Shamefaced, I ground my cigarette under my heel.

"That's the stuff, Robert Monteath," Harry approved. "Now let's go upstairs." He opened the front door and bounded up three flights with me following behind. "Look at you," said Harry, reaching for the door directly facing him, "you're puffed already. I'm twenty years older than you and I'm not. Fags, fags, fags! You'll never be able to hold a note unless you cut them out."

We entered a cavernous room devoid of furniture. A person was bent double over a piece of equipment on a table by an upright piano, so absorbed in adjusting his headphones and twiddling knobs that Harry was forced to shout to get his attention. "Dick!" he bawled. "Get your arse over here and come meet Robert."

Startled, Dick Katz removed his headphones and straightened. A short, sturdy man, he had frizzy ginger hair, a big smile and bad teeth. A half-smoked cigarette hung from his bottom lip. Thumping Harry on the back, he said in a Cockney accent "Good to see you maestro." He stuck a hand out. "Pleased to meet you Robert. Brought some music, have you?" Nodding, I pointed to my valise. "Okay, then, let's get cracking shall we?" he said, walking over to the piano, on the way stubbing out his cigarette on the wooden floor.

"How many numbers have you brought, Robert?" asked Harry. "I've rented the studio for two hours, so I guess we'll only have time for about three."

I pulled out a wad of sheet music. Harry thumbed through them quickly, discarding all the show tunes, leaving to one side the ballads *Answer Me* and *I Believe* and, as an afterthought, Sinatra's *Singing the Blues.*

Harry handed the music to Dick, who was already seated at the piano flexing his fingers, "What d'you think of these?" he asked. "Apart from the Sinatra number, the other tunes are a bit boring," Dick replied, giving me a fierce look. "Robert, haven't you anything with a half-decent beat?"

I shook my head, thoroughly dispirited. Fortunately, Harry came to my rescue. "Dick, the lad's not had much experience," he said, "or any chance to rehearse other stuff with my band. Like I said, this session is to get you to hear Robert and then figure out what his voice is best suited for."

"You're the boss," said Dick. "Okay, Robert, what key?" I replied that C generally suited me best.

"Well, if it's not, I'll transpose. Let's give *Answer Me* a try and we'll see how we get on. Go, take the mike."

As soon as Dick played the opening bars, I steadied myself and came in on time, singing as best and powerfully as I could. When I finished, I could see from Dick's expression he was pleased.

"You sure can belt a song, Robert," he said. "We'll try it again. This time, try and smooth out the breaks between the end of one note and the commencement of another. Legato. Adjust your breathing so the notes meld smoothly and the sound just flows. That's what we're aiming for."

I tried again, and then again, and then again, before Dick finally raised a hand and said, "Now, that was good. See what I mean?"

Harry concurred: "I can't tell you how much better that last effort was, Robert. Now, let's have a shot at *Singing the Blues*.

However many times I sang the number, neither Dick nor Harry were satisfied with my performance. Finally, Harry said, "I think you should stick to big ballads until you get more experience. It's what your voice is best suited for. Now, take a little rest, while Dick and I have a wee chat together."

From where I stood, relaxing, doing breathing exercises, I could hear nothing of their whispered conversation as they huddled over the piano. Finally, Harry stood up and said, "Okay, Robert, now sing *I Believe* and if you make as good a fist of that, we'll record you. How's that?"

Even as I tried to absorb what Harry had said, Dick played the opening chords and I was headlong into the song, my breathing, my timing perfect. But for Harry and Dick once was never good enough, and I had to sing the song three more times before they were happy with the result.

Dick turned to face me. "We've got time for just one more try with both ballads, Robert." He replaced his headphones, went over to his recording machine with its two turntables, and said, "Give me a sec to sort this blessed thing out and we'll go from there." He drew a blank vinyl disc from a carton sitting by the recorder and placed it on one of the turntables. After a minute or two of twiddling knobs, he said, "All right, son. Ready if you are."

After I'd sung both tunes, Dick removed a vinyl 78 record from the turntable, slipped it into a paper sleeve and handed it to me. "It's yours, son. A memento. Good luck, Robert. You're in good hands with Harry."

Harry purred at the compliment. "You did well today, Robert," he said. "However, we think a live audition with the BBC would be better for you. You'd stand a better chance if they see you in person, rather than just listening to your record."

Not knowing how to respond, I carefully placed my record into my valise and clutched it tight against my chest, as if it held the most valuable item in the world. I was dying to hear my recording, but with Harry and Dick in a hurry to leave, I had no choice other than to play it later. The family did not possess a gramophone, so I'd have to wait until I found someone who did.

"Righto, then, Robert," said Harry, "we're all finished for now. But before I forget, on Saturday—that's the day after tomorrow—we've a gig at the American Air Force base in Ruislip. Be there at midday. When you turn up there, speak to the guard at the gate and ask for Sergeant McCluskey. He'll accompany you to the BX where we're setting up."

"BX Ruislip? Where's that?"

"Ruislip. Middlesex. You get there by Tube. Allow an hour from Waterloo. The BX is the Yankee version of our NAAFI." I was still trying to figure out what Harry meant by BX and NAAFI, when I heard him add, "It's not black tie"

"Okay, Harry. What kit do you want me to wear?" I asked.

"Blazer and flannels will do. And, by the way, I've a surprise for you. You'll be meeting a new young singer we're trying out, a girl called Jackie Trent. You'll do *Singing the Blues* for a change and, maybe, the two numbers you did today. Up for that?" Before I could reply, he added, "Okay, well done and see you Saturday. 'Bye for now."

Dick shook my hand. "Good luck, Robert," he said. "Make sure you don't wear out your record, will you?" He backed away, coughing all the way out of the studio and down the stairs under Harry's disapproving eye. I followed, leaving Harry to lock up.

As soon as I was on my train, I pulled out the shiny new 78 and read Dick's scribble on the label. *'I Believe' sung by Robert Monteath, accompanied by Dick Katz on piano'*. On the reverse side, he'd written, *'Answer Me'*. A collector's piece: my very first record.

The first chance I had to listen to my record was on Roger's portable HMV gramophone. After Roger had wound it up and placed the platter on the turntable, all three of us, Pam, Roger and I, sat around it in total silence as if attending a séance. The first sound was that of the steel needle rasping in the vinyl grooves, followed by Dick Katz on the piano, then a high tenor voice unrecognisable as mine, emanating from the speaker. I sat listening in a state of shock. What had Dick Katz done to render my baritone as a castrato?

"Shall we try the other side?" suggested Roger, looking at me out of the corner of his eye. "Could be a duff needle you know."

The reverse was no better. No one spoke. Pam and Roger were acutely embarrassed. No less was I. But I was completely nonplussed and just wanted to run and hide from the world. I tried to speak. I managed a muttered, "That was bloody awful. It didn't even sound like me. Something must have gone wrong in the studio."

"It must have", agreed Pam, putting her arm about me. "Poor Bob."

"Without question," added Roger. "Someone cocked up. It wasn't you. That's for certain."

Roger persuaded me not to break the record into a thousand pieces, suggesting I ask Harry to give me an explanation.

I decided a good time for this would be at the USAAF base in Ruislip on Saturday. I took the Tube all the way to Ruislip station and then walked for a quarter of an hour to the gates of the enormous American base. An armed guard stepped smartly forward from his box and asked me my business. I gave him my name before reading off Sergeant McCluskey's from Harry's note, saying I was with the Harry Geller Orchestra. After looking me up and down, the guard returned to his box and picked up a phone. A few minutes later, Sergeant McCluskey arrived in a Jeep and told me to jump in the back. The sergeant, a tall, bulky, red-faced man in his mid-forties, spoke in a gentle drawl, quite at odds with his intimidating appearance.

"Hey, young fella. You the weddin' singer?"

"Yes, I am, sir."

"You must be rich then, singers fronting bands in the US earn a lotta dough."

"Not me," I replied. "I just get paid my expenses until I get more experience."

Sergeant McCluskey whistled through his teeth. "Shiiit! That all? Sure you are not being taken for a ride? But hey, it's none of my damn business." He brought the Jeep to a halt in front of a colossal Quonset hut, surrounded by others of a similar size. He climbed from his seat and pointed a pudgy finger, "This here is the BX. Inside there's our commissary stocked with just about everything you can think of. A liquor store, dry cleaners and...and, hell, we got it all here. Come on in, I'll show you around."

About to enter Aladdin's cave, I met Harry Geller on his way out, towing a young blonde girl, who looked about fifteen, by the arm. He greeted the sergeant and pushed the young girl forward. "Robert, meet Jackie Trent."

"Pleased to meet you," Jackie said, giving me a shy smile.

Harry clapped his hands. "Okay chaps, intros done. Now, let's take advantage of the quiet and have a little practice.

We've about half an hour before the storm." The sergeant drove off and I followed Harry back into the Quonset hut, past a store with a mind-boggling array of items and into the commissary a good fifty yards beyond. Much bigger than Quaglino's and set with as many tables and chairs, the scale and size of everything took my breath away. Harry pushed on ahead to a makeshift stage, while Jackie and I strove to keep up with his long striding walk .

"This is it, boys and girls," said Harry twirling about. "A big wedding do." Climbing up on stage to where Joe, the band's pianist, sat, Harry called out to Jackie and me. "Come on, chaps, time for business. Robert you go first. Joe, we'll do *Singing the Blues*." I was surprised, for only a few days before he'd said I'd not performed it well.

Joe nodded in my direction; "Okay, Rob, ready when you are," he said. I sang the song through to the end and waited for Harry's reaction. To my surprise, he said "That was good, Robert. Now, one more time."

I sang the same number again. "That'll do fine," said Harry, giving me the thumbs up. "Now you, Jackie." She sang an upbeat number, with all the confidence in the world, in an astonishingly adult voice. I listened in envy as she sang a jazz standard and a ballad, both with perfect phrasing and timing, as if she'd sung with a band all her life. I hurried over to congratulate her, doubting I could ever be in the same league.

"Thanks, Rob," Jackie said softly, her hands clasped in her lap. "I liked your song, too."

I went over to Harry and whispered "Where did you find her, Harry? She's bloody fantastic."

"Jackie's from the Midlands. A pal of mine, her manager, asked me to give her a try out. I think she has a great career ahead of her. Sadly, not with me." Harry paused for a second. "By the way, did you like your record?"

"I was going to ask you about that, Harry. It was bloody awful. What went wrong?"

Harry laughed out loud. "That was Dick's idea of a joke. What he did was to record you on twin turntables, one set normally and one with the frequency turned up really high. That's why the sound register was out of kilter and the quality all to cock on the record he gave you. We made two copies of the master; I've already sent off one to the BBC. The other is yours, I have it here with me."

"Did you say the BBC?" I asked.

"Yup, the very same. Now then, you stay right here and I'll bring you your record." He gave me a pat on the back and strode off, reappearing to hand me the record together with a ten-shilling note to cover my expenses. "I guess you and Jackie must be hungry by now," he said. "Come on let's fetch her. The good sergeant's waiting for us. He's got something for us to eat at the counter next door."

We sat down next to Sergeant McCluskey at a long counter in the adjoining room. I breathed in deeply, savouring the delicious smell coming from behind the serving hatch. "I ordered you guys burgers and fries," said the sergeant. "Hope you like 'em."

"Thank you, but what's a burger, sir?" I asked.

"Never heard of a hamburger, kid?" At first the sergeant looked surprised, before giving me a rueful smile. "Guess I forgot you still have rationing here. We eat hamburgers all the time in the States. Burgers are made of ground steak. The meat is kind of pressed into a pattie and then grilled. Burgers come with fries. You call 'em chips here, I guess."

When the plates appeared, my eyes feasted greedily on the biggest meal of my life: the enormous hamburger, the bun and the mountain of fries. Jackie, eyes wide open, made oohing sounds. Harry, on the other hand, was clearly familiar with hamburgers and wore the superior air of someone who ate them every day of his life.

Sergeant McCluskey leant forward on his stool. "Dig in, guys" he said.

I demolished my hamburger and fries with a pint of Coca-Cola in record time. Even tiny Jackie managed to finish hers. Patting her tummy, she said, "Gosh I'm so full up, Bob, I don't think I'll be able to sing."

At two o'clock, it was time to leave. We thanked Sergeant McCluskey and returned to the stage to find the band busy tuning instruments. Harry told Jackie and me to stay out of sight, saying he'd let us know when he wanted us to come on.

The commissary was filling with tanned young men in uniform, a number of pale English girls, and some older American officers. They raised loud cheers when the bride, in white, and groom, in the dress uniform of a USAAF Major, finally made an entrance. The band immediately struck up *The Wedding March* as the couple made their way through the room and took their places at the head of the centre table.

After everyone had settled down the band commenced playing a series of Glen Miller, Tommy Dorsey and Duke Ellington numbers which, from the enthusiastic response, the American servicemen thoroughly appreciated. Jackie and I sat enjoying the music for a good half hour, before Harry crooked a finger, summoning Jackie to come sing *Chattanooga Choo-Choo,* which brought the house down. My turn came some time after the guests had finished their meal, and my version of *Singing the Blues* got a decent enough reception, which pleased me.

The band took a break, during which Harry told me he didn't require me to sing any more, saying and I could leave now if I wished. I started to protest, but he said my limited repertoire of upbeat songs was the reason. "Can't you see?" he growled. "*I Believe* and *Answer Me* won't go down well with this lot. They're Americans—they like jazz and swing, not crap ballads. Give me a ring next week and I'll let you know the venue of our gigs for the next two months. When you've sung with us for all of those, I'm sure you'll be ready to join the band full time. For the time being, Robert, you've just got to stick at it."

There it was again, the mantra I was sick of hearing; *stick at it, stick, stickability.*

He continued, "Find Sergeant McCluskey, he's around somewhere. He'll see you out. Cheers for now." Harry turned his back on me and returned to chat with members of the band. I said goodbye to Jackie, picked up my precious record and went off in search of the sergeant. I found him back at the counter drinking beer from a frosted glass tumbler; beer with little bubbles in it, like ginger ale.

"Hey, like a beer?" he asked, ordering one up from the barman.

"Yes, please. I've never tried fizzy beer before. Or drunk it cold."

He laughed out loud. "This is how we have it back home. Anyhow, it ain't all that fizzy. Personally, I can't stand flat, warm British beer. I don't know how you guys drink that stuff. "

He handed me a glass. "Takin' a break, kid?"

"I'm done. My boss said for me to find you, just so you can see me out."

"But you only sang once," said the sergeant. "I heard you. You were good, so why not more?"

I took a gulp of my beer, before answering. "Christ only knows. I have to do as Harry says."

"Tough shit. Okay, when you've finished your drink, I'll drop you at the station."

I started to protest, but the kind Sergeant McCluskey shut me up, saying, "No trouble."

He took me in his jeep to the station and, before I could climb out from the vehicle, handed me a note. "It's my address back home," he said, "Bleecker Street, New York. Look me up if you're ever that way. I mean it, now. It was nice knowin' you, kid."

Chapter 53

By the end of May I had sung with Harry Geller's band for eight Saturdays in a row, with the occasional Friday night thrown in, as well. I sang at weddings, bar mitzvahs, at dances and in restaurants all over town, with Harry now calling on me to sing four or five times a night. Even so, he continued to pay me no more than my travelling expenses. I recalled what Sergeant McCluskey had said about singers earning a lot in the US and began to wonder, not for the first time, if Harry was short-changing me.

In the previous month, just before the new school term, Nick had informed the family that not only had he given up teaching, he'd secured a middle-management position at Hackbridge Electrics near Hampton Court. Furthermore, he'd found a larger house for us in Sunbury-on-Thames, also by the river. With a decent position and a decent rate of pay, he was a new man. Rather than spending his spare time in pubs, he stayed at home and helped my mother out around the house. Their relationship became as harmonious as before, which made life for the rest of us much more agreeable.

I didn't care where I lived as long as I could cycle to work. Nick allayed Pam's concern about how long it would take for her to travel from Sunbury to London, by saying was a regular bus service to Hampton Court station which took ten minutes; then only another half an hour by train to Waterloo,

Anxious to see our new home, we all went by bus to view Rose Cottage, a detached thirties house on a corner of the Sunbury Road. In fine fettle, it had four bedrooms, a decent kitchen, a downstairs loo, a separate family bathroom upstairs and a small garden at the back. In terms of space, position and style it was a considerable leg-up from our previous accommodation. There was a school close by for Ronald, and the Hampton Grammar school for David.

For once, life for the family moved on an even plane with no real money worries, enough food on the table and a few new clothes for my mother and the boys. The one exception was me, still doing a menial job and earning barely more than four years before. The business of dashing off to London every Saturday night and occasionally Sundays, too, was taking its toll. I was not enjoying singing with the band any more, or having any kind of fun. There was never time to go to *The Ship* with friends and sing with Barbara Andrews, or even date girls. I was tired, broke and fed up with my life. As I dwelt on how to change things for the better, fate dealt me a bad hand.

Henry Branch and some colleagues had taken to playing cricket on the grass outside Bayer's office building. I was batting at the crease one sunny afternoon in early June, when the bowler delivered a juicy, full toss. I gave it a mighty thump and watched in horror as it flew into the windscreen of the managing director's new Jaguar sitting in the car park. We all ran to inspect the damage. The glass had crazed into a star shape just above the driver's sight line, making the car impossible to drive. Bunched around me, my cricketing pals fell silent, until Henry spoke up. "My God, Bob, there'll be hell to pay. There is nothing for it, you had better own up."

The managing director, Mr Aronstaam, was South African; an Afrikaaner who had always been brusque to the point of rudeness with me. In his country he'd probably have classed me as a Cape Coloured, not quite the lowest of the low, but near enough.

As I headed for the MD's office, those trailing behind in support gradually fell away, their courage wilting as the perpetrator of the dastardly act came ever closer to meeting his doom.

The receptionist showed me into the inner office where Aronstaam stood waiting, already purple in the face.

"Was it you, Matthews, who broke the windscreen of my new Jag?"

I made an attempt to apologise, but he blustered and fumed, in no mood to listen. Overhanging his waistband, his fat stomach wobbled as he menaced me. "If this had been South Africa, I would never have employed you. Go, on, get out! You're sacked. Pick up your cards and leave. I give you ten minutes to leave the premises, or I'll call the police!"

Stunned, I turned about and left the room without a word. As I bade Henry Branch goodbye, I explained what had happened. Unable to look me in the eye—I dare say because he felt he should have stuck up for me—he shook my hand, and repeated over and over again that he was sorry to lose me. Wishing me luck, he blew his nose and retreated back into his lab. Seconds later, he came running out. "Bob," he called, "know Gala Cosmetics do you? They're on the A3 just beyond Hook, on the right. Damn great place."

"Yeah, I know where it is."

"Well, I don't know if you'd be interested, but the chief of the lab there, Freddie Vine, is an old school chum of mine. A couple of nights ago, down at the University Vandals Rugby Club, he mentioned he was looking for a reliable chap to help out in his production department. I could ring him now if you like."

"If you are sure that's all right."

"Sure. I'm sure," Henry said. "Stay there a sec. I'll just be a minute."

He dashed through the open door of his office and picked up the phone. He reappeared moments later with a piece of paper in his hand. "Freddie's phone number," he said. "He told me he can see you now if you like. If not, give him a ring and make an appointment. He's a good bloke. Hope it pans out for you. Meantime, chum, don't worry about your cards and what not. I'll make sure the accounts department sorts everything out, plus cash in lieu of notice and any holiday money due. Pop by after five-thirty and I'll give it to you. That fucking bastard Aronstaam will have left by then. By taxi I imagine."

Things had moved at such a pace, I couldn't quite take in what was happening. I hopped on my bike and headed towards the A3 and Gala Cosmetics, thinking how odd it was that the minute I lost one job, I was immediately found another by some kindly soul. It had never previously occurred that I might have been better off going on the dole for a while and waited for a decent job to come along. I had always taken the first job on offer—menial work that employers couldn't find anyone else to do. And presumably Gala Cosmetics was the same as all the others.

Freddie Vine, who was around thirty years of age and looked very fit, saw me half an hour after I turned up at Gala's premises. "So, you are *the* Bob Matthews, the singer Henry's always going on about," he said, brushing from his forehead a flop of yellow hair. "Come on in and have a chinwag. You obviously know we're looking for someone to help out in the lab. From what Henry's said about you, I think you'll do fine. But there again you might not like us."

Freddie smiled, took me by the elbow and guided me through a double door and into a large production area. A number of white-coated women busily operated filling machines, from which spewed small bottles of red nail varnish ready to be packed into cartons. Waving a hand as we walked, Freddie said, "As you can see, this is where we make nail varnish. Lipsticks, and other odds and sods. Creams and so on are made in another area similar to this. For my sins I'm in charge of production and quality control. Come into my office and I'll whistle up a cup of tea. Bet you are dying for one after your bike ride."

I'd hardly said a word as Freddie burbled on. But as soon as we were seated in his office, he became brisk and businesslike, questioning me at length about the jobs I'd had.

"An interesting CV!" he said at last, as a young woman entered bearing tea. "Bob, you'll do me fine," Freddie continued. "First of all, you'll work on the iridescent nail varnish line. Then, as you get to know the business, you'll progress to lipsticks and creams." He gave me a questioning look. "What d'you think?"

"Fine so far, sir. But what's the pay?" I asked, after gulping down my tea.

"No *sirs* here, Bob. Call me Freddie. You'll get six pounds ten shillings a week, one week paid holiday a year. The hours are...", he paused, "seven a.m. start, four o'clock finish. If you accept, you can start on Monday."

I gulped. "Seven a.m.?"

"Shitty hours, I know, but you and I have got to be here before the girls arrive, so that everything is ready for them to get cracking."

"Okay, Freddie," I said, dreading the thought of waking at six in the winter and cycling to Gala in the pitch black.

"Good show," said Freddie, "We'll get on pretty well I think. Now, before you leave, you might be interested to observe how we make nail varnish." He got to his feet. "This way, Bob."

He led me out of the back to a smaller building, surrounded by barbed wire, about fifty yards away. Freddie fished out a large key from his pocket and opened the padlock on the single front door.

"Take your shoes off, will you, please?" he said, removing his own. I followed his example, without knowing why.

We entered in our stockinged feet. "Gun cotton," said Freddie pointing to half a dozen cylindrical containers. "Nitrocellulose—or dynamite, to you. Hence no shoes. Nails might strike sparks, you see, which is not to be recommended. Otherwise the stuff is safe enough, if you take precautions. Want to take a look?"

He lifted the lid of a container. Reaching inside, he withdrew what appeared to be a wad of thick cotton wool and thrust it under my nose. Freddie laughed as I reared back in alarm. "It's all right, Bob. It's okay to touch it."

As I gingerly poked a finger into the mass, Freddie said, "Actually, nitrocellulose is a liquid mixed with tiny, near-microscopic cotton fibres. In the manufacturing process we grind the fibres even smaller, add plasticizers such as butyl stearate and finally the pigment. If we are making pearl nail varnish, we dissolve fish scales in acetate to achieve that iridescent effect. Mix in the pigment and Bob's your uncle." He replaced the guncotton in the container, and said, "Worry not Bob, we've got specialists who deal with all of this. Your job will be overseeing the production line."

"I was scared for a minute," I replied, exhaling in relief.

"Freddie smiled. "By law, we have lots of safeguards in place. The building has been reinforced, with a roof that'll blow off in the unlikely event of an explosion, leaving the structure intact. Security watches over this place day and night. No one's allowed anywhere near here unless it's with yours truly. Anyway, I'm done for the moment. Any questions?" I shook my head. "Okay," he said, "in that case see you Monday morning."

I didn't bother to cycle all the way home and instead, hung around on the bank of the Thames facing the Mitre Hotel below Hampton Court Bridge, waiting for five-thirty to come along. I sat idly staring into space, until my eye was caught by a girl of about twenty striding across the bridge. With her shoulder-length ash-blonde hair and calf-length filmy white dress she appeared to shimmer in the afternoon sunlight—quite the most beautiful creature I had ever seen in my life. I had a catch in my throat as I watched, spellbound, until she vanished into the crowds milling by the entrance to Hampton Court Palace.

When I finally gave up searching for her in the crowd, I turned about, almost with a sense of loss, and cycled over to Bayer Products to collect my dues. As Henry Branch had predicted, Aronstaam had already left. I went straight to Henry's office, where I found him sitting at his desk fiddling with some papers.

"Freddie phoned me to say he's offered you the job," he said, handing over a large envelope. "I wangled you a bit extra. There's two weeks tax-free wages in there, plus two days extra for luck. I make that fifteen quid or so, old chum." He stuck his hand out. "C'mon, let's go have a drink."

I cried off. Although elated to have so much money, I was not in the mood to celebrate. "Thanks, Henry. Like the Yanks say, can I take a rain check? I feel like going home right now. It's been quite a day."

I cycled home, all the way dreaming of the girl I had seen on Hampton Court Bridge.

Chapter 54

A week or so after I started working for Gala, a highly excited Pam rushed into my bedroom. "You remember that very tall chap you saw me talking to, the last time we were at *The Ship*?" she said, hardly able to contain herself, "Well, he's asked me out. His name's Geoff Bonell. He said he's a photographer with Associated Press. He's taking me to the theatre in London. Isn't that lovely?

I was pleased my sister had found someone else after being so cruelly ditched by Michael. As for me, the grind of getting up so early during the week and then performing every weekend until late had left me little time for girls, other than for playing tennis with Julie's friends, Trish and Virginia Waters. Julie put in the occasional appearance when she had the chance, but as for a steady girlfriend there was none. Eventually I tried my luck with Virginia, or Ginny as we called her. I had found her very attractive and great fun to be with from the start. So the next time I visited her home, I asked her if she fancied taking a cycle ride with me.

"Where to?" she said.

"How about Virginia Water?" I laughed. "Virginia Waters in Virginia Water?"

"My God," she groaned, "Not you, too." But after a second or two, replied, "Okay, why not? I've never been there. It's very far though, isn't it?"

I had no idea, so I tried a shot in the dark. "'Bout fifteen miles, I think, or about an hour or so. We could always stop if you get tired."

Ginny at first appeared dubious and then agreed. "All right, next Sunday afternoon if it's fine. I'll pack some sandwiches for us."

Just then Trish appeared from the direction of the tennis court, to ask if I were up for a game on Sunday, but Ginny chirped "Bob can't. We're going on a cycle ride together."

Trish looked cross. "So I suppose I'll just have to play on my own, then," she sniffed.

Rather than get involved in an argument, I said I'd be off. To my surprise Ginny said goodbye and kissed me. Trish looked on, exuding jealousy from every pore.

We met on Sunday at around three: Ginny in shorts and an open-necked shirt, I in my usual shirt and flannels.

"Won't you be hot in those?' asked Ginny, stuffing packed sandwiches into my pannier. "Don't you possess any shorts? I just wondered, because you always wear long trousers, even when you play tennis."

"No, I don't own a pair. I've always been meaning to buy them and then I forget," I lied, thinking that, now I had the severance cash from Bayer, I'd splash out and buy some shorts the first chance I got. Changing the subject, I said, "Careful how you shove those sandwiches in, I've got a bottle of water in there."

I had worked out a route beforehand: Walton, Weybridge, Chertsey, Staines, Egham, stopping at Runnymede to see the spot by the Thames where King John signed the Magna Carta. It would make a timely place to rest, where I hoped we could neck a bit and...perhaps more. After which, we could cycle on to Virginia Water if Ginny still felt like it. Altogether, I figured we would be back around six-thirty or seven in the evening, unless... I allowed my imagination full rein. It might be about midnight.

Ginny was much fitter than I expected and kept up a good pace. Halfway to Virginia Water, she divulged that Trisha fancied me. Cycling alongside me on her brand-new racing bike, she shouted, “Not that I do,” and then laughed, taking in gulps of air as she pedalled. My five-year-old bike had half as many gears as hers, and she did not seem at all tired when we finally pulled up at Runnymede.

Water meadows swept down to the Thames, where a breeze ruffled the water. Rowing boats and skiffs idled upstream, stately swans sailed by, ducks and ducklings sheltered in the rushes.

We pushed our cycles up as close as we could to the memorial marking the place where King John sealed the Magna Carta in front of his nobles in 1215. I wasn’t exactly a historian, but I had learned about the Magna Carta in school and now stood in awe, and so did Ginny.

After a few minutes, I felt her hand slip into mine. “Come on, let’s eat our sandwiches and have a drink,” she said, pulling me along in the direction of the riverbank, through a gap in the bushes. We laid our bikes down and sprawled out on a patch of springy grass, out of sight of all but the birds flying above.

Ginny had made sandwiches filled with real eggs, not the powdered variety served up at home.

“These are great,” I said, munching away. “I think after this I’ll need a kip.”

“Me, too,” Ginny murmured, lying on her back in the sun with her eyes closed, her baggy shorts hitched up, exposing a length of thigh. She’d also undone a couple of her shirt buttons, showing off her cleavage and the swell of her breasts. It seemed an invitation, but I held back from making a move in case it was all perfectly innocent. It was very hot after all, and I too, had my shirt undone to the waist because of the heat.

I lay down near to Ginny with my arms outstretched and eyes shut. "Good idea, that," she said, also spreading her arms out wide. "I need the rays to get at my white bits." We lay listless for about half an hour with not a word passing between us, until I half rolled on top of her.

"*Pardonez-moi*," she laughed, before shoving me off. In the process, her baggy shorts had ridden up her thighs, giving me a fine view of the curve of her buttocks and a glimpse of her flimsy underwear.

I turned her on her back and kissed her. She flung her arms around my neck and pressed me closer, her tongue in my mouth, driving me wild. I had never for a moment thought the well brought up, Walton-bred Ginny to be as experienced, or as hot, as this.

I began to undo her shirt buttons without any resistance from her, until she suddenly sat upright, pulled the shirt off her back in a single move, saying, "There. That's easier isn't it?"

Finally I, Bob Matthews, was about to lose my virginity and about time too. But I hadn't reckoned on Ginny's bra being so difficult to remove. As hard as my fingers worked to undo the clasp, it simply refused to budge.

By now I was breathing heavily and about ready to wrench the damn thing off, hoping Ginny would reach behind her back and help me out. Instead she irritably thrust me aside, scorning, "You've no *savoir faire* Bob Matthews, and there I was thinking you were sexy."

Ginny clambered to her feet and pulled on her shirt. I watched in dismay as she wandered down to the river and stood staring silently at the water. I was left feeling utterly foolish, not knowing what to do, or what to say. I lit a cigarette to calm myself down and waited for Ginny to return. I was on my second cigarette before she did.

"Sorry, Bob," she said, standing over me. "That was rotten of me. I didn't mean what I said. Honestly, I didn't." There were tears in Ginny's eyes. "I don't suppose you'll want to ever see me again. But I am truly sorry."

"Forget it, Ginny. I have. No need for apologies. Come on, let's pack up and go home."

Heads down over the handlebars, we cycled the entire way back to Walton in silence. I finally deposited Ginny at her front door. She stood there looking hesitant, then gave me a small wave before entering her house.

The Waters sisters never again invited me to play tennis at their home. I now only occasionally met them at the *Gay Adventure*, a shabby social club by the River Mole at Hersham, when Julie happened to come down from London for a break. The club's premises were terribly run down. Even so, I understood why Julie loved the peaceful location; grassy lawns sloping down to the river's edge, a row of weeping willows, and fields of corn beyond as far as the eye could see.

Sometimes, when Julie was home, Barbara asked Roger and me over to the club. We'd sit by the river on warm summer evenings enjoying a quiet drink, chatting about everything and nothing. On one such evening, Julie mentioned she was off to New York in mid-August to rehearse Sandy Wilson's *The Boy Friend*, opening on Broadway in September.

"By the way," she said to me, "Mum's throwing a going away party for me on the fourteenth. You'll come, won't you?"

I was touched Julie had invited me. I quickly worked out the fourteenth of August was a Saturday and Harry was sure to have had a gig lined up for me. I decided he'd just have to do without me for one night. I was not about to miss Julie's party for anything.

Chapter 55

From the very start, I disliked working for Gala Cosmetics. By July's end, I'd had enough. The early morning starts and the boredom of standing by the nail varnish filling station for hours on end checking bottles for defects was doing me in. Freddie Vine detected my loss of interest and kindly had me transferred to the department where creams and unknown unguents were made. There I was more involved in the formulations of the products, but even so the change did little to improve my depression.

I was also fed up to the teeth with travelling all over the place to perform with the band. Once, singing with Harry's band was something to look forward to. Now it was a grind. If Harry had paid me enough to survive on without my day job, I might have felt better. I even began to doubt my chances of ever making it as a recording artist and performing in West End musicals. Just as I'd decided to have it out with Harry one night, he asked to have a word with me.

"Guess what, Bob?" he said, squeezing my arm. "Your record has got you an audition with the BBC on Wednesday, next week. Take the day off and be at Broadcasting House, 22 Portman Place at eleven. Go to Reception and say you've an appointment with Sylvia Cheeseman. She's the one who selects performers for radio programmes. If she likes you, you're made, chum."

Thrilled by the news, I decided it was not the time to talk money with Harry. A successful audition would mean a turnaround in my fortunes. Or so I thought.

On the day prior to the audition I feigned stomach trouble. Freddie Vine ordered me to see my GP and barred me from work until I had the all clear. "This is a sterile environment," he explained, "no bugs allowed."

With cash from Bayer, I had bought myself a navy blue suit from Burton in Kingston for five pounds, and a new tie and white shirt to go with it. I left for my audition with the BBC thinking I looked the bee's knees, only sorry that I hadn't time to ask Henry Branch to make me some of his magic potion.

After my many trips, I had learned to navigate around London, so had no problem finding Portland Place, with the pale stone bulk of Broadcasting House rearing up at one end. Resembling a massive liner with swollen bulwarks, it dominated the skyline. Brushing down my new suit, I entered through the tall double doors. A commissionaire asked me my business before indicating the Reception desk manned by a couple of smartly dressed men. I gave my name, saying I had an appointment with Sylvia Cheeseman.

"Kindly take a seat, sir, Miss Cheeseman is running a trifle late. She apologises for the delay." He glanced up at a wall clock. "She'll see you in fifteen minutes."

Time enough for a smoke to settle my jangling nerves, I thought. I lit a cigarette and settled down. After precisely fifteen minutes, the commissionaire came over to tell me Miss Cheeseman was ready for me in a studio located in the basement. I took the lift and was met at the bottom by a tall woman in her fifties. Her untidy brown hair, dowdy dress and clumpy shoes, didn't impress, but a smile lit up her face as she asked if I was Mr Robert Monteath.

"Yes. It's my stage name. Real name's Matthews," I replied nervously.

"Good. I'm Miss Cheeseman." Her smile widened even more and her eyes twinkled as she looked me over. "Come along, young man," she said. "Follow me into the studio, please, and we'll get cracking."

The studio was bigger than I expected, about thirty feet by thirty, with a proper stage and a stand microphone at the front. A pianist sat at a piano in the well. He nodded as I entered. "Got your music?" he asked. I passed over my sheet music, saying, "It's *Singing the Blues*."

Harry had decided on the tune for me, saying it would go down best with Miss Cheeseman, whose taste he claimed he knew.

"Okey dokey, chum," the pianist said. "Know the number well." His eyes scanned the top sheet. "Good, you've marked the key."

"Robert, I suggest you go on stage and relax a bit, settle your nerves while I go and sit out of the way there," said Miss Cheeseman, pointing to a chair and table some distance from the stage. "Don't mind me. Take your time. Just say when you are ready."

I did as Miss Cheeseman asked and stood by the mike, taking several deep breaths to open my lungs as I'd been taught by Madam Davis Reynolds. My heart rate slowed; my trembling stopped, I was ready to go. "Okay, Miss Cheeseman," I said, taking hold of the mike. I felt completely relaxed as I sang, aware that the audition could make or break me.

"That was very nice, Robert," Miss Cheeseman said, as I came to the end. She clapped, repeating, "Very nice indeed. I am so glad you didn't do a Sinatra impression, though. Young man, we'll call it a day for now. I know how to contact Harry Geller, but if you'd be so kind come down and leave me your address, I shall write you a letter very soon, giving my opinion."

I clambered off the stage, overwhelmed by her old fashioned courtesy, delighted by her encouraging words. I thanked the pianist as I passed him. "You sang okay," he said, handing me back my music. "From Jack that was high praise indeed", smiled Miss Cheeseman"

I wrote down my address. As I expressed my gratitude to Miss Cheeseman, she tut-tutted like a schoolmarm. "It was nice to meet you, Robert." Beyond that, I learned nothing from her.

I met Roger that same evening at the Nordic Club, a new place he'd discovered by the river close to Hampton Court. I'd often cycled passed it on my way to work, but never for a minute thought I could afford to enter. Roger insisted otherwise, saying the beer was at pub prices and that the club maintained a private area for members beside a large public swimming pool.

When I replied membership was surely beyond me, Roger said he'd show me how to get around the problem. So when I turned up on my bike and found the car park full of fancy cars—open topped MGs and such like—I felt sure Roger was having me on. But to my surprise, when I tentatively entered the clubhouse nobody took the slightest notice of me.

The clubhouse itself had not much to commend it: a largish room stuffed with tables and chairs, a small bar at one end and a tiny space for a piano and a drum set. Just a few people sat at the bar; their braying voices reminded me of the Young Conservatives at the High Pines. Others sat on the grass by the pool outside, drinks in hand and sounding jolly.

I spotted Roger lounging by a diving board. I walked around the pool's edge towards him, expecting at any moment to have my collar felt and be told to leave.

"So you found me, then?" said Roger, levering himself upright. "How did the audition go?"

"Okay, I think. I don't suppose I'll hear for a while. The woman who auditioned me said I sang well. I guess that's something."

"Good stuff," said Roger. "Take a seat and I'll get you a beer."

"No, hang on a minute; I'm more interested in how you wangle yourself into a members' club without paying the dues."

"It's so easy," he laughed. "Just come in through the members' entrance as you did. If Bobby Vaughn Jones, the owner, likes the look of you, you're in, no questions asked. If he doesn't, you'll be politely asked to leave."

"I was taking a chance, then?"

"No, not at all. Bobby likes pretty boys," Roger replied, giving me a dig in the ribs. "Seriously, since the pool's Council-owned and for public use, all you do is pay the shilling entrance fee to the attendant. Then use the club's facilities. Simple. No one seems to mind."

"Are you serious?"

"Sure I am. I've swum in the pool and used the club several times these past few weeks. I have never been questioned by anybody. I think we should spend every Sunday here. Lovely pool, no riff-raff, beer at pub prices, a load of nice chicks to look at, what more do you want?"

I stayed for a couple of beers and told Roger I'd see him there again on Sunday, before cycling back home. On the approach to Hampton Court Bridge, at about the same point as I'd seen her before, I saw the most beautiful girl in all the world once more. I almost froze. With her blonde hair flowing free as she walked, she was simply lovely. I dismounted instantly and pretending to examine the chain on my bike, waited for her to come closer. She had enormous brown eyes and endless shapely legs. I very nearly fell over when she smiled at me. I turned to look at her as she passed by, my heart aching as I watched her walk away into the distance.

I dreamt of her that night and every night thereafter. Even as I went through the motions at Gala during the day, she was always in my thoughts.

Bored by overseeing the manufacture of Gala's creams, I became aware I needed to shave my face less and less each day, not for a moment associating the fact with my employment. The hairs on my calves were also vanishing, as were those under my armpits. I didn't think much about it, rather enjoying the sensation of smooth skin, until I casually mentioned the change to an acquaintance at the Nordic Club. He looked at me in alarm, asking if the creams I handled contained hormones. I hadn't any idea, I replied, asking if it was important. He suggested I find out if the formula included oestrogen, a female hormone that could be responsible. He laughingly said I'd turn into a woman, unless I wore gloves at work. The next morning I asked Freddie if any of Gala's creams contained oestrogen.

"No, why do you ask, Bob?" he said, frowning.

"Oh, it's nothing, Freddie. I just wondered that's all."

Unsure that Freddie was being completely truthful, I took to wearing gloves through the day. Soon afterwards my hair loss ceased.

Chapter 56

Sundays at the Nordic Club had become a ritual for Roger and me. Lounging in the members' area, beers in hand, chatting up pretty girls, was a great way to spend the afternoon. Occasionally, we hung around late into the evening, listening to Piano Joe Henderson, a well-known pianist whose girlfriend, film actress and singer Petula Clark, lived up the road in East Molesey. She came to the club occasionally, creating quite a stir, as did Oliver Reed, an up-and-coming actor who spent much of his time at the bar.

One very hot Sunday in early August, a couple of weeks ahead of Julie's party, I saw the most beautiful girl in the world once more. Surrounded by a group of friends, she came to sit a few yards away from me by the swimming pool. My heart raced at the sight of her in a green one-piece swimsuit moulded to her body and I knew in that eureka moment, that this was the girl I would marry.

I continued to stare until Roger touched my arm to get my attention. "What's up, Bob? I've been speaking to you for the last couple of minutes and you haven't heard a word."

I dragged my eyes away. "Sorry Roger," I said, "but I have just seen the girl I am going to marry."

"What girl?" he asked, following my gaze until he had singled her out. "You are a chump, Bob," he said. "You've never seen her before, never spoken to her and already you're going to marry her? You're off your bloody rocker."

"Actually, I've seen her a couple of times on Hampton Court Bridge. Just you wait and see, Rog. She's going to be my wife."

I watched as the girl plunged into the pool and swam a few lengths with a powerful breast stroke, before pulling herself out to perch on the edge of the pool. She caught my eye and smiled in recognition. "Hello," she said, her voice deep and husky, "didn't I see you fixing your bike on the bridge the other day? How's the bike now?"

"It's okay, I've fixed it," I lied, going to jelly.

"Good," she said, "Do you often come here?"

"Roger and I come most Sunday afternoons," I replied.

"See you again, then."

With that, TMBGITW re-joined her friends. Before leaving with her pals at five, she turned around to give me a wave.

I went to the Club on my own the following Sunday. I had just spread my towel on the grass by the pool and lain down on it, when TMBGITW again appeared. She placed her towel alongside mine. "Fancy seeing you here," she said, impishly.

As I got to my feet, she said, "Oh, I thought you were taller." Her fingers went to her mouth. "Sorry, I only saw you lying down before. Nice tan—are you French, by any chance?"

I was annoyed that she'd thought me short when we were about the same height, but I replied, "No, I'm not French." On first meeting me, most people asked where I came from, but she didn't follow up that question. She just said, "My name's Shirley. Shirley Davidson. And yours?"

"Bob Matthews. Nice to meet you." The understatement of the year.

We lay on the grass and talked nonstop. She asked about my life—soon discovering that I had been born in India—about my job, my ambitions. She was nineteen, lived in East Molesey with her parents, worked as a secretary for a surveyor in an office only a hundred yards from Bayer Products, and had no current boyfriend.

When I told her I sang with a band and had made a record, Shirley said she'd love to hear it sometime.

What conceit possessed me I shall never know, but I found myself blurting, "Why not, now? My home's only ten minutes away by bus in Sunbury and we can have some tea as well."

To my amazement, she agreed. "That'll be fun, but I have to get back here by six to meet some friends."

The wonder of it! Shirley, who had the choice of any number of rich chaps who had cars and took her to flashy places, was happy to take the bus to my house for tea.

When we arrived back at Rose Cottage, my mother was charm itself and clearly taken with Shirley. She busied about with cups and teapots, explaining if only she had known, she would have made cucumber sandwiches for us. Nick, who'd lumbered in from the garden, wound the handle of our second-hand portable HMV gramophone—recently bought for the sole purpose of hearing the records of the famous Robert Monteath—and placed my disc on the turntable. When she'd heard both sides, she clapped enthusiastically, saying I sounded a bit like Bing Crosby, a great improvement, as I was tired of being compared to Dickie Valentine.

Shirley and I returned to the Nordic Club soon afterwards to meet her friends. At the entrance to the car park, I took her by surprise and kissed her. Initially, she was pliant in my arms, but she suddenly went rigid. Pushing me away, she cried, "No! Not here, Bob. It's too public."

"I don't care, I'm in love with you. I want to marry you."

Shirley laughed out loud. "Bob, that's mad. I'd like to see you again, but marry you? Don't be so ridiculous." She dissolved into giggles. Then seeing she'd hurt me, she went quiet. "We can meet up again next Sunday," she said.

"You know I'll ask you again, don't you? Okay, see you on Sunday about two. "

"Two? Why so late?

"I could be hung over, that's why. I'm going to Julie Andrews's party on Saturday night. It could be a late one."

"Julie Andrews? You know her?."

"Well, if you promise to marry me, I'll introduce you when she's back from America."

On Friday afternoon after work, my mother handed me a letter. "It's from the BBC," she said, rather redundantly. "See, it's stamped in red over the postmark."

I ripped open the envelope and pulled out a single sheet of note paper. "Come on, darling, tell Mummy what it says," she said, peering over my shoulder as I began to read.

Dear Robert Monteath,

I very much enjoyed meeting you and thought you sang beautifully at your audition. However, after much consideration I am sorry to inform you that we won't be taking this any further.

I have also written to your manager, Harold Geller, suggesting you should apply for another audition with us in a couple of years, by which time you will have gained sufficient experience. Wishing you the very best of luck,

Yours sincerely Sylvia Cheeseman

I stared at the letter, before reading it over once more. Another couple of years before I could try again? Another one hundred and four gigs? No, God, no. I don't think I can stick it for that long.

My mother reached up to give me a kiss. "I'm so sorry, Bobby," she said, loyally. "The BBC's silly not to use you. Really silly. You'll show them one day. I know you will."

There was I thinking Miss Cheeseman had liked my voice. I'd been certain she'd want me to sing on BBC radio; now she wanted me to wait another two years. I'd been a fool to believe I was good enough.

I rang Harry from the nearest phone box. "Harry," I said, "I've just heard from Miss Cheeseman—"

"I know, I know," he interrupted. "I got a letter, too. She's right, you do need a couple of more years' experience."

"But Harry," I tried to explain, "I can barely live on what I earn at Gala. If you'd only put me on the payroll like the other chaps in the band, it would be different. As it is, I'm finding it bloody hard without any extra cash coming in."

After a long pause, he said, "Tell you what, Bob. Let's have a chat when you come up to town tomorrow night."

I'd forgotten to tell him I needed Saturday off. "Er," I stammered, "Can't make tomorrow night, sorry."

"Why not?" he demanded. "You ill or something?"

"No, I'm going to a party. Julie Andrews's party."

"Party!" Harry screamed. "You're going to a fucking party when you are supposed to be working? I don't give a shit if you are going to Julie Andrews's party, or, or, Betty Grable's, or anyone else's. You be there tomorrow night or you can stick it, chum."

I replied stiffly, "I'm sorry Harry. I just want the one night off. I think I've earned it."

"Oh Yeah. Shut your face and listen. I've done a lot for you and this is how you are repaying me? Christ! I wish I'd never bothered." Harry slammed down the phone, leaving me staring at the dead receiver.

His reaction had left me shaking with anger. I had repaid him for my singing lessons and studio recording time several times over. I had worked for him for months on end without pay, and he'd discarded me in seconds. Still simmering, I returned to Rose Cottage to take stock and began to calm down. As I relived what Harry had said, I began to see his point. With such short notice, it was seriously unprofessional to use a party as an excuse for skipping a gig. Although I was relieved not to be at Harry's beck and call any more, I realised my career as a singer was shot.

The following evening, I dressed with particular care. Wearing my new suit and shirt, I set off to the Old Meuse on my bike, planning to arrive at seven thirty, a half hour later than the time on the invitation. The last thing I wanted was to be the first to arrive.

But I had not figured on erratic showbiz timekeeping and found myself the first to turn up after all. Barbara greeted me at the door, appearing flustered.

"You're the first," she said, accusingly, as if punctuality was a crime. Barbara always gave the impression of being in a state. "You better come into the kitchen. You can give us a hand with setting out glasses and things."

"Sure, Barbara. Just tell me what to do and I'll do it," I replied, smiling inwardly; as I followed her into the kitchen, with its untidy pile of nibbles, cheese biscuits, things on dishes, and glasses of all sizes. Crates of beer sat on the floor, with a range of spirits on the counter.

"First, fish out some side plates from the cupboard in the corner and then line up the glasses." she commanded. "After that, be a dear and help Ted out in the sitting room. He's shifting furniture to make space for dancing."

"Yes, boss," I replied, getting on with it.

Barbara threw me a wink. "Good lad. Julie's tarting herself up in her bedroom. She'll be down any minute now," adding fervently, "God, I hope no one else comes just yet."

God granted her wish; there was no sign of guests for another half hour. Julie, in a blue ankle-length gown, came down and helped me out, laying the food on plates, while Ted, her stepfather, already pie-eyed, laid into the whisky in the sitting room.

The first guest to arrive was Joan Regan, the most popular female recording artist of the day, an attractive young Irish woman who I thought, had a rather thin voice. Even so, she apparently raised the blood pressure of many a male—one newspaper reported that, after she had given a concert on an aircraft carrier in Portsmouth, some entrepreneurial naval ratings bottled up Joan's bathwater and sold it for a pound per bottle. So, unsurprisingly, I was anxious to meet her. But she turned out to terribly dull and I certainly wouldn't have offered even tuppence for her bathwater.

The guests, roughly thirty in all, finally arrived and filtered into the kitchen to find their hosts busy greeting people and dishing out drinks. The alcohol-fuelled din in the kitchen rose to such a level that Barbara shooed most of them into the sitting room.

Apart from the Waters sisters, who were, as usual, cool towards me, I knew nobody. Being too shy to mix, I just sat and watched, interested in figuring out who was who on the guest list. Apart from Joan Regan, I failed to recognise a single celebrity. I sat at a pine table in a corner of the kitchen, keeping well out of the way and wishing Shirley was with me.

After half an hour, a short man in a loud suit and a thick American accent plonked himself down on the chair at my side. "Howya doin'?" he said. "Hey, I was just admiring your neck tie." So saying, he waved a pair of scissors under my nose, before slicing my tie right off just under the knot. "Thanks young fella," he said, "I collect ties. This'll go great with my collection."

I watched, speechless, as he walked off, dangling my severed tie. Furious, I asked Julie if she knew the idiot who'd done it.

"I'm so sorry, Bob," Julie replied, as she stared at the ragged piece of material around my neck. "That was Bill Goetz; he's so silly sometimes."

"And who the fuck is Bill Goetz?" I asked, rage getting the better of my manners.

"Oh, the fucker came with Charlie Tucker, my agent," Julie laughed. Her use of the F word would have immediately dispelled the public's notion of her as an innocent English rose, but I knew she was someone who called a spade a bloody spade if she felt like it. "Bill Goetz is Louis B. Meyer's son-in-law and the head of Universal-International in Hollywood; UI's one of the biggest film production companies in the world. I'll ask Charlie Tucker to get Bill to apologise and buy you another tie if you like."

I declined her offer and disposed of the stump of my tie. By about ten o'clock, guests had taken to the floor, dancing sedately to music from a radiogram in the Andrews's garishly decorated sitting room. The party really got going when someone put on Bill Haley and the Comets' *Rock Around the Clock*, the latest craze in music. People began flinging themselves about in time to the music. At last, I joined in and began to enjoy myself.

I had seen Ted and Barbara circulating, but they'd not been visible for a couple of hours, then Ted burst into the sitting room, shouting drunkenly. Red-faced with anger, and carrying a cane, he looked threateningly at the guests, before smashing the chandelier in the hall. He started to throw glasses and other fragile items about. Barbara ran into the room after him, pleading with Ted to calm down, as fearful guests huddled against the sitting room walls.

A horror-stricken Julie cried out at her stepfather, but Ted was not about to settle down. Some people tried to restrain him, but he roared off out of the room; many of the guests headed for the front door, loudly summoning their chauffeurs.

Barbara chased her husband into the kitchen. She stood facing Ted, pleading with him to calm down, but he would have none of it and dashed out of the back door, shouting threats in the direction of Barbara's sister Joan's bungalow.

Ted's shattering moments of madness and mayhem had left Julie distraught and ashen faced. She wept as she ran up the stairs, leaving just one or two of the guests behind to give Barbara support. The coward in me decided it was time to leave. I slipped out of the house and took off on my bike without saying goodbye.

Later, Barbara told me she had been forced to call the police to deal with Ted that night, saying she'd taken out a restraining order and planned to leave him.

Chapter 57

On Sunday afternoon, as planned, Roger picked me up in his car and we drove to the Nordic Club. On the way there, I told him what had happened at the party.

"What a pain," he commented. "You must be so disappointed."

"Yeah, you haven't heard the worst of it yet, Rog. Harry has sacked me."

"What the hell are you going to do now?"

"I've got to face facts, look through the ads, find a job I'd like to do for a change. One that pays well. I've been fiddling about for nearly five years and getting nowhere. If I had carried on singing with Harry I'd have ended up in the poor house. Anyway, there must be more to life than just being a band singer."

"For once you are talking sense," Roger agreed. As we turned into the car park, he added, casually, "Did that girl you fancy come here last Sunday, by any chance?"

"Yes, her name's Shirley, and she's meeting me here today at two. Did I mention I asked her to marry me?"

Roger turned in his seat to face me, “You did what, you silly sod?”

“Asked her to marry me.”

“Bob Matthews, you need locking up.”

We ordered a couple of beers from the bar and took them to our usual spot in the members’ enclosure. I lay down on the grass and closed my eyes. The hands of my watch eventually moved to two o’clock, then twenty past, and Shirley still had not showed.

“She ain’t coming,” Roger said.

At last, Shirley appeared at the side door of the club house. She came straight over.

“I’m sorry to be late,” she said. “I got held up.” Turning to Roger, she said, “Hello, you must be Roger the lodger.”

Once we were in the pool, Shirley asked about the party. “How did it go last night?”

“Bloody awful,” I replied, before explaining how Ted Andrews had ruined the evening. “Fortunately, I had you to look forward to. Have you thought about what I said?”

“What’s that?” Shirley asked.

“Are you going to marry me?”

“Oh, that,” she said, swimming off.

I caught up with her at the far end of the pool. “Yes, that,” I said. Treading water, I ventured, “I know it sounds daft, corny, but it seems I’ve known you all my life.”

“Funny that,” she replied, “I feel the same way, too. I even dreamt of you last night.”

From that moment on, Shirley and I spent all of our free time together and not a day passed without my asking her to marry me. She regarded my professions of undying fealty as my idea of a joke, for she simply ignored them.

Roger was an absolute brick and drove Shirley and me everywhere at weekends: to *The Anchor* in Shepperton where I sang for my supper with Barbara; to *The Gay Adventure* and other places as well. But mostly we spent our time at the Nordic Club, where the price of beer and Shirley's soft drink were just about what I could afford.

Each evening, I scanned the 'Sits Vacant' section of every newspaper I could lay my hands on. It was a full month before I spotted a job I thought would suit me. John Dickinson, the paper manufacturers were looking for a trainee copywriter. Attracted by the salary of £400 per annum, I decided to apply, but there were two problems. First, the job was in Hemel Hempstead, a long way away and second, I had a disastrous work record. With Shirley urging me on, I concocted a masterpiece of a CV that glossed over the truth.

A few days later, to my delight, I received an invitation to go to London for an interview. I made my excuses to my boss at Gala Cosmetics and headed for Holborn where Mr John Horwood, the company's advertising copy chief, took charge of the interview.

Fortunately, Mr Horwood appeared more interested in why I wished to be an advertising copywriter and in my ability to write clear English, rather than what I had been up to before.

"Now, Mr Matthews," he said, suddenly producing a lady's high heeled shoe, "use your imagination and tell me how you'd extol the virtues of this shoe in an ad."

I let out a deep breath. "Well, sir," I replied, as heaven-sent inspiration struck, "I wouldn't."

“No?” queried Mr. Horwood, pushing his glasses down his nose to look at me “So what would you do?”

“As it’s a woman’s shoe, I might concentrate on beautiful feet and write about how much prettier they’d look in those shoes, rather than just describe the shoes —I presume there’d be pictures that would do that.”

“Bravo, Mr Matthews, that was really imaginative, considering I threw you a googly.” Mr Horwood looked me straight in the eye and asked, “How do I know you can write decent English?”

I had brought a couple of my short stories with me, so I produced one from my pocket. Mr Horwood ran his eyes over the first two paragraphs.

“All right, I’m satisfied you can write pretty well, so we won’t waste time. You’ve got the job if you are still interested,” he said.

“Sir, I’m really interested,” I replied. “The only problem is I don’t have anywhere to live in Hemel, so it might take me a while before I can join you.”

“Worry not, friend, that’s all sorted. We’ve already checked with a Salvation Army couple who keep digs for our trainees. It’s only a five minute bus ride from the office. Three guineas a week, all in. If you accept, we’ll send you a formal letter and you can start in a couple of weeks.”

Chapter 58

Following my interview with Mr Horwood, an official letter arrived from John Dickinson and Co. I was to report to the head office in Apsley, Hertfordshire, on Monday 15th October at 9a.m. Mr Horwood sent a note telling me he'd arranged digs at 2 Orchard Close, Kings Langley and that the Jacksons, were expecting me some time on Saturday the 13th. Roger was present when I opened the letter and insisted on driving Shirley and me to Kings Langley to help me settle in.

I gave in my notice to Gala immediately and, on the 13th, the three of us pulled up outside 2 Orchard Close at four o'clock. Almost before the car's wheels had stopped turning, we were greeted at the door of their small bungalow by Major Tom Jackson of the Salvation Army and his wife Amy. A jolly couple, they immediately ushered us inside and plied us with tea and cake. We were then invited to look over my bedroom in the loft. Tom led the way up the ladder into a surprisingly large loft. Furnished with a bed, a small wardrobe, dressing table and wash stand, my room contained everything I could have wished for. Tom tactfully returned downstairs to allow us some privacy but Roger was itching to be off. "I'll give you two lovebirds another five minutes alone," he said, descending the ladder.

Shirley and I fell on the bed. "Nice, soft bed, this," she said, nuzzling up to me. "We could be really cosy up here."

"God, I want so much to make love to you."

"Me, too," Shirley replied, wrapping her arms tight around me, pulling me even closer to give me a lingering kiss that set my nerve ends on fire.

"But when darling?" I gasped. "And where? A hotel's no good. They'd want proof we're married."

"Roger's flat?"

"No. He's funny about that sort of thing."

"Then what can we do? I want my first time to be somewhere nice."

"It'll be my first time, too."

"I'd never have believed it before, but now I know it's true," she said, serious now. Cupping my face in her hands, she said, quietly, "I love my Bob, but I'd better be off now in case the Jacksons think we're already at it."

"I'll write you every day."

"I will, too."

We found the Jacksons waiting for us by the open front door. Roger was already sitting at the wheel of his car. Shirley said a hasty goodbye to the Jacksons, and blew me a kiss before joining Roger in the front. He pipped the horn, gave me a wave and was away with a roar.

"Now, young man," said Amy, steering me into the kitchen, "come and have some supper. I've made you a lovely rice pudding."

"Hope you like rice pudding," said Tom, giving me wink.

"Oh, yes I do," I replied, "Haven't had one for years."

After telling me the rules of the house (no smoking, no lady visitors in my room and certainly no alcohol) Amy informed me breakfast was at a quarter to eight every day of the week, including Sundays. By now, desperate for a smoke, I asked to be excused. Claiming I needed some fresh air, but not for a moment fooling the Jacksons, I went outside and lit up. Afterwards, I said goodnight to them and received a fervent, 'God bless you', in return.

Next morning, after a generous breakfast, Tom said he'd show me around the area on the back of his 250c.c Triumph motorcycle. Belying his sixty years, white hair and portly frame, he roared around the roads, with me on the back, clinging to his waist for dear life. On the way, he pointed out John Dickinson's, Apsley Mills, an immense Victorian paper mill that also housed the company's head office, overlooking the Grand Union canal.

"That was fun wasn't it?" asked Tom, when we returned after our frantic ride. He scraped at his wind-blown hair, and then marched into the house. "Fancy a cuppa, son? Amy and I are off to the Citadel soon." He explained, "It's what we call our church hall."

On Monday morning, at a quarter to nine, I arrived at John Dickinson's head office. The friendly young man at reception asked me to wait, saying, "Mr Horwood will be down shortly, sir."

Not long after, Mr Horwood bounded down the broad set of stairs at one end of the hallway. "'Morning, Mr Matthews", he said, cheerfully. "So you found us all right? Come, meet the rest of the team." I followed him up the stairs, through a large office, where a couple of dozen people were settling at their desks. He opened a glazed door into a much smaller office beyond with windows offering views of the canal.

A young man, just a few years older than me and wearing a tight fitting three piece suit, sat at a desk alongside a bespectacled female in her early thirties. “Team,” said Mr Horwood, addressing them cheerfully, “this is the Mr Matthews I told you was joining us. It’s Robert, isn’t it?” he said, turning to me.

“I’m generally known as Bob,” I replied, sheepishly.

“I’m Betty Royle, nice to meet you,” said the woman giving me a shy smile; her colleague merely grunted, “Sam Jenkins.”

Introductions over, Mr Horwood walked me over to his desk by the window, saying I should call him John. Seating me opposite him, he told me Sam and Betty wrote advertising copy for Basildon Bond, the UK’s best known writing paper, and also for Churston Deckle, which was much more expensive.

“As for you, m’lad,” he continued, “you will first learn everything about the dies, embossed seals and labels JD makes. Then, when you’re ready I’ll let you loose on ads in the trade press. Writing about labels is as boring as hell, but we all have to serve our apprenticeship.”

“In that corner bookcase, you’ll find books, magazines, catalogues, advertisements etc, on the subject of seals and labels. Get stuck into them. That’s your desk there,” he said, pointing to one in the corner, “Just shout if you need help.”

As John predicted, I found seals and labels exceedingly boring. At the same time, I was staggered by how many varieties there were and the uses to which they could be put.

A tea lady came round at eleven. I saw that everybody had downed tools, including John, Sam and Betty. After finishing their cups of tea, they walked about the office puffing on cigarettes. I asked Sam where the loo was.

“Ah, you can’t have been given your own key,” he said, fetching one out from his trouser pocket. “Obviously,

Personnel haven't filled you in yet. The company has lots of rules and regs, such as separate canteens for workers and executives. We're executives, just so you know," he said, puffing himself up. "Executives have keys to the toilets on this floor. Workers use the loos downstairs. Which is as it should be," he said.

Betty gave Sam a look of disgust. "Bob, don't take any notice of him," she said, "we all know he's a self-important prig." Ignoring her, Sam stubbed out his cigarette and sat down at his desk and began to hum loudly. John Horwood, who obviously missed nothing, pursed his lips. "Now, now, team, cut it out, please, and Sam, stop that bloody noise. You don't want to give Bob the wrong impression on his first day."

Around four, John asked me how I was getting on. I told him I had read up on everything to do with the company's cameo embossed seals and labels. "Well then," he said, "let's give you a little test, shall we?" After posing all sorts of questions about seals, the metal dies and insets, packaging and a myriad other things, he whistled softly. "Fast learner, aren't you? Good stuff. Tell you what, if you can bear it, spend another day mugging up and then jig up an article day after tomorrow, 1,000 -1200 words, for *Packaging News*. You'll find old copies of the mag in the files. Think you're up to it?"

"I'm ready to have a go, John. But I've only ever written short stories, not articles."

"That's where a copy chief comes in, son. Don't worry, I'll hold your hand."

Dead on five-thirty, the factory gates opened and hundreds of workers burst through like a herd of bison. Some rode off on bikes, others filed onto a line of waiting buses, but the majority filled the pavements on both sides of the road and walked away in the direction of Hemel Hempstead. I had never seen so many people together at one time.

I got home at six and was handed a cup of tea and a biscuit by Amy, who asked how my first day had gone. Tom said, "Don't mean to pry, Bob, we're just interested. The last young man we had here hated his job from day one. Funny that. He was only with us a couple of weeks."

I saw that Tom's right hand clasped a trumpet. He gave a slightly embarrassed smile, "Got some practice in before you got back. My trumpet makes such a din, I thought it best to get it over and done with in case it bothered you."

"Good Lord, no!" I protested, "I love music, please, please, play something. Anything."

Tom began playing *Abide with Me*, which I knew well from my choir days. The sound of his music filled the house and I sang along until the last brassy notes died away.

"Tom, that was wonderful!" I exclaimed. "Where did you learn to play like that?"

"Oh, I've played in Salvation Army bands since I was about sixteen," Tom said mildly, laying down his trumpet on the kitchen table. "You should come and have a listen to the band sometime."

"Please Tom, don't mind me. Play your trumpet whenever you feel like it. I just love to hear it."

After supper, again more than I could eat, I went upstairs to write a long letter to Shirley. I told her how well my first day had gone and filled a couple of pages saying how much I loved her, how much I was already missing her, how much I wanted to make love to her, and had she figured out where? Signing off with a dozen kisses I scribbled a final P.S. 'When will you marry me?'

Chapter 59

My second day was as boring as the first. I spent hours reading turgid articles on the subject of packaging and the use of seals to enhance the end product, making notes as I went along for my first draft.

Betty invited me to join her in the staff canteen for lunch, but I wasn't hungry after my big breakfast. Instead, I went down to sit by the canal. I smoked a couple of cigarettes and sat viewing barges being loaded with paper from the mill. A soft mist was rising off the water, blurring the landscape on the far bank. As I began to drift off, I realised that it was only a year ago that Sue Kenyon had broken off our engagement. But for my narrow escape I'd never have met Shirley, for whom I yearned every second of the day. She'd already told me she was too young to marry, but I was prepared to wait, knowing we were meant to be together for the rest of our lives.

When I returned to the office, I started typing up, one finger at a time, my article for *Packaging News*. My typewriter was an old Imperial with a worn ribbon and a couple of eccentric keys that hardly made an impression on the paper. John Horwood noticed I was having difficulty with it, so he passed his new Remington over for me to use. "Let me set it up for you," he said, "the margin indents like so, and of course, double spacing dear boy. I see you've been single spacing. When submitting something to a publisher, remember, always use double space. You'll soon get the hang of it."

I got down about five hundred words by five-thirty and left for home feeling very pleased with myself. There were two letters waiting for me; one from my mother and the other from Shirley. I opened my mother's first, which, apart from saying she missed me, mentioned not much else.

Shirley's letter on the other hand, contained some surprising news. Her father had recently retired from the police force and her parents were soon off Scotland. They had mentioned they'd like to see me again before they left. On the two previous occasions I had met them, I'd found them delightful. He, a tall, broad shouldered Scot with a craggy face, was as gentle as his appearance was forbidding. She was small, spry, and always smiling; the perfect mother earth who'd taught Shirley to cook, sew and make her own clothes while she was still at school.

Shirley surprised me still further by saying; she and Pam planned to share a flat in Surbiton after her parents had left. "I get on so well with Pam," she wrote, "and I'm so happy she's found a lovely boyfriend in Geoffrey Bonell. She wants to leave home because she's not getting on with your mother and Nick, so it's better off all round we move in together. Best news of all, my darling, Mum and Dad have bought me a dear little Vespa scooter as an advance twentieth birthday present. By the time you come down in couple of weeks I'll have learned how to ride it. Then I can teach you!"

I fell asleep holding Shirley's letter dreaming she was in my eyrie with me.

I finished off my article the following day and nervously handed it over to John. He read it through without a word.

Finally, as was his habit, he gave his spectacles a rub before speaking. “It’s fine, Bob, reads well, but for your obsession with commas. Far too many, spread like peas in a greengrocer’s shop. But that’s easily sorted. Come, let me show you.” He undid the cap of his fountain pen and struck through more than twenty superfluous commas in my article of 1200 words and then explained exactly the reasons why he’d deleted each and every one of them. It was a salutary lesson for me. Finally, he sat back in his chair and smiled. “Now, off you go, Bob, type it up again. Then we’ll submit it to *Packaging News* and see how we go. Good job.”

Glowing with pleasure, I returned to my desk, fancying myself a Joseph Conrad and Ernest Hemingway combined. I was a writer now: far better that than a mere band singer.

Two weeks after my article had been submitted to *Packaging News*, John summoned me to his desk. “You’re a fully blown copywriter now,” he said, waving a letter from the editor of the trade magazine. “Your article has been accepted. And they want more of the same.” I was thrilled—my very first time in print. I went over to Betty and told her of my success. I heard Sam saying, sourly, “*Packaging News* is so short of fillers, they’ll take anything.” His remark so incensed Betty, she rounded on him in a rage. “You’re just a jealous bastard, Sam Jenkins. Of the first, bloody water!” she shouted, bringing John Horwood to his feet.

“That was uncalled-for, Sam,” John said, sounding furious. “And, in any case, Bob,” he added, turning to me, “it’s quite untrue.” Fixing Sam with a stare, he continued, “I think Bob deserves an apology, don’t you?” He waited until Sam finally muttered a grudging, “Sorry.”

“Right, then,” said John, not quite done yet, “There’ll be hell to pay if I hear such stuff from you again. Got that? This is my department, not a kindergarten playground.

Understood?" Sam stood awkwardly by his desk, eyes looking everywhere but at his boss.

From that day, I avoided Sam. What puzzled me was why he disliked me so much. I decided to ask Betty.

"All I can think is that, when John advertised your job, he and Sam had just had a massive blow-up," she replied. "John had told Sam to buck up and called him a lazy sod, which he is. Maybe Sam thought he was going to get the push and you were to be his replacement. So when you turned up, he was just plain jealous. When I joined a couple of years ago, he was nasty to me, too, for a while. Just ignore him."

On pay day, someone from Accounts came round handing out our pay packets, but Sam Jenkins was nowhere to be seen. Nor was he the next day, or the one after. I asked John if Sam was sick.

"No, Sam's been sacked," he said. "The powers-that-be want the details kept quiet for some reason. Sam was reported by a female member of staff for inappropriate behaviour of a sexual nature. I've spent the last few days going through all his stuff and seen where he's got to with his ads and layouts. You're taking over from him, so you'll be handling the Basildon Bond account in future."

Although I was pleased not to be dealing with Sam any more, I was astonished my boss had enough confidence in me to take over Basildon Bond; it was a tremendous responsibility.

"Sure I can do it, John?" I asked.

"Piece of cake my boy, piece of cake," he replied, removing his glasses to give them a rub.

I had been flat broke the entire month of October after shelling out three guineas rent to the Jacksons every week. But now I was flush enough to visit Shirley for the weekend and still have some cash to put by for Christmas presents. I wrote to her saying I'd be on the train arriving at Hampton Court at seven-thirty on the coming Friday.

Shirley, who was waiting on the platform, rushed forward to put her arms around my neck. Her eyes gleaming with excitement, she said, "Bob, come and take a look at my lovely Vespa. It's parked just outside."

She pointed to a green Vespa in the car park. Every inch of it shone. "What do you think? Isn't she sweet?" she enthused, before levering away the foot rest and kick-starting the engine. The engine burst into life with a satisfying pop, pop, pop, as she called, "Hop on the back, we'll drive over to your Mum's."

"Hang on!" I shouted, "You've only a learner's licence."

"Look, no L plates," she replied, "I passed my test yesterday. I applied for it the day I got the Vespa and it came through in three weeks."

I needn't have been concerned; the little scooter easily dealt with our combined weight. Shirley revved the engine as if she had ridden a scooter all her life, and we were off and away over Hampton Court Bridge at around thirty miles an hour and then on to Sunbury at nearly fifty, before stopping outside Rose Cottage.

My mother welcomed me in with wide open arms and kissed me in her usual dramatic style, a bemused Ronald at her side. Glancing at Shirley, my mother said, "No one else is in, I'm afraid. Pam's out with her boyfriend and David's doing a special project at school."

"And Nick?"

"Oh, Nick," my mother said, "he'll be in soon for his supper. He usually stops off for a drink on the way home."

Feeling sorry that my mother had been left with only Ronald for company, I gave her a hug. “Mum,” I said, gritting my teeth, “Shirley and I are supposed to be seeing Roger at the Nordic about now, so we’d better be off. I won’t be late back, I promise.”

“Don’t worry about me,” she said, “It’s fine. I expected you to be with Shirley tonight. You’d better take a key just in case.” Handing it to me, she said, “Off you go then. Enjoy yourselves, have some fun and be careful on that scooter, Shirley.”

“I feel bad, leaving your Mum,” said Shirley, starting the scooter’s engine.

“Me, too,” I echoed insincerely, as we rode off.

“Did I tell you Roger’s got a new girlfriend?” Shirley shouted over her shoulder. “You’ll meet her tonight at the Nordic.”

We arrived at the club ten minutes later. Shirley and I dismounted and she waltzed in, proudly showing off her escort, the famous advertising executive, Bob Matthews.

Roger spotted us immediately. Striding over, he called out, “Hello Shirls. And Matthews, you old reprobate. Glad you made it. Come, meet Anne.”

Pretty, with near black hair and blue eyes, Anne was as quietly spoken as Roger was loud. It was clear from the way her soft eyes followed his every move she was extremely fond of him.

As much as I enjoyed meeting Anne and seeing my friend again, I so much wanted to be alone with Shirley. I turned to look at her and just melted. I decided we had to leave Roger and Anne and find somewhere by the Thames where we wouldn’t be interrupted.

"We'd better be off," I said, "It's nearly eleven." Hoping Roger understood what I was getting at, I added, somewhat unconvincingly, "It's late for Shirley to drop me off on her scooter and then ride back home alone." Roger leapt to his feet, saying, "Nonsense, Anne and I'll drive you to Sunbury. We'll drop off Shirley back here, pick up her scooter and follow her home in the car."

There was no point in arguing. Shirley gazed at me ruefully as we walked out to Roger's car. We sat silent all the way to Rose Cottage, staring out of the windows, burning with frustration.

As I thanked Roger and Anne for giving me a lift home, he said, "See you tomorrow night, lover boy. We'll pick up Shirley first and then come over to you at eight. Barbara's looking forward to seeing you at The Ship."

Chapter 60

Shirley and I had agreed that I should spend all day Saturday with my family. I wandered down to the kitchen, expecting to find my mother there and the table set for breakfast. But the house was silent. Then at ten o'clock , Pam, Nick, my mother, David and Ronald came down all together to greet me. "You're up early, darling," said my mother, "I forgot to tell you, we all sleep in late at weekends."

After breakfast, Pam disappeared to get herself ready to meet Geoff Bonell at midday. Nick limped off to the sitting room to light the fire, the single source of heat in the house. David cycled off on my bike without permission, saying his school was competing in a rugby match and he couldn't miss it. Ronald vanished into the back garden, leaving me to help my mother wash the dishes and clear up. After her fulsome greeting of the night before, she was unusually quiet, leaving me with the impression she was worried about something.

"What's bothering you, Mum?" I asked. "You're very quiet."

"Oh, it's nothing, really," she replied, "I was just thinking, with Pam going away to live with Shirley, and you gone, too, the house is going to feel really empty."

"What else, Mum?" I persisted, aware she was holding something back.

"It's Nick," she said, "our GP's told him he has a problem with his back that could be very serious. It's to do with nerve damage in the spine, he says. He might even have to go to hospital, which means he could be given the push from his job. Then where would we be?"

I managed a smile, hugged her tightly and said, trying to lift her mood, "Nick's a tough bloke, mum. He'll be fine, you'll see."

She gave me a sad smile and continued with the chores.

Pam hurried downstairs to greet Geoff Bonell the instant the front door bell rang. She, five foot nothing, he six foot five, she looked like a tiny child as she put out her cheek for him and was given a chaste kiss in return. "Bob, I don't think you ever met Geoff at *The Ship*, did you?" she said. I shook my head.

"Well, I heard you sing there often enough though, Bob," said Geoff amiably, looking down at me from his great height.

I could see Pam was anxious to be away. "Geoff's taking me shopping to buy a few bits and pieces for my flat," she said, leaving the house arm in arm with her beau.

It was a totally wasted day. Nick slept most of it, my mother retreated to her bedroom and Ronald occasionally put in a noisy appearance. Other than that, I was left on my own, feeling angry and thoroughly dispirited, waiting impatiently for eight o'clock so I could see my darling Shirley.

Roger arrived on the dot of eight, with Shirley and Anne aboard. I scrambled into his car, gasping with relief, "Rog, thank God you're here. I've had such a bloody awful day." Both girls made sympathetic noises as I settled myself beside Shirley in the back.

Being a Saturday night, The Ship was packed with regulars and film people from Shepperton Studios. As we fought our way in, I heard Barbara start playing the opening bars of *Where is Your Heart* which, for some obscure reason, she regarded as my signature tune. I was expected to break into song the moment I heard it, but on this occasion the noise in the bar was too great to attempt it. So, instead, I pressed through to where Barbara sat at her piano and kissed her on the cheek.

"Where have you been, you naughty bugger?" she chuckled, affectionately, "haven't seen you for ages. "Have you brought that lovely girl of yours?" she asked, looking around for her.

"Yes, I'm here," replied Shirley, "and Roger and Anne, too. The whole gang's here."

"What are you going to sing tonight, Bob?" asked Barbara, her fingers on the piano keys.

"It's too noisy right now, Barbara. Maybe later."

Barbara looked around the bar. "OK then— tell you what, let's all go on to *The Treglos* when the pub closes. Do you know it? There's dancing there on Saturday nights."

Just before last orders at ten thirty, Barbara banged down the lid of the piano and got to her feet, saying, "Bob, we'll have a sing at *The Treglos* later."

Noticing how Barbara listed when we walked out of the pub together, Roger insisted he drive her to *The Treglos* but Barbara flatly refused. We stood helpless, as she fumbled in her handbag for her keys before getting into her car. To our surprise and relief, she turned the car expertly out of the car park and drove down the road in the direction of Walton Bridge as if perfectly sober. We knew she'd had too much to drink, but she had driven the route so many times I guessed she drove on auto-pilot.

We pulled up outside *The Treglos* a couple of minutes after Barbara, who stood waiting in the hall for us. A run-down, small hotel on the Surrey bank of the Thames, it was where people went to drink on weekdays after the pubs closed. The hotel also had a tiny sprung floor where dances were held every Saturday until midnight. By my watch, we had about an hour and half to go.

Barbara, unsurprisingly, was well known to the doorman, who refused her shilling entrance fee, and then kindly waved us all in without charge, saying it was so late it wouldn't be proper.

"Righto, then, chaps," said Barbara, "you all go off to the bar. Meanwhile, I'll chat up my friend Charlie Hastings who's playing piano tonight, so that Bob can have a sing with the band."

"Do I really have to?" I asked, reluctantly. "I'd rather be dancing with Shirley, Barbara."

"Just one song," she replied, "for me."

"You really don't have to sing," said Shirley, her eyes on Barbara staggering down a stairway to the dance floor below.

"I know," I replied, "but I can't refuse her. She's been so kind to me."

Downstairs, there was a small bar at one end of the sprung dance floor, and a trio of musicians, piano, guitar and drums, sitting on a dais at the other. Barbara stood bent over the pianist, talking animatedly. A waiter brought the drinks, beer for Roger and me, soft drinks for the girls. Fringing the floor, there were about twenty tables like ours, where staid, middle aged couples engaged in muted conversation sat waiting for the band to start playing.

Meantime, I sat stiffly in my seat, willing the pianist to refuse Barbara's request for me to sing.

It was not to be. Barbara took over the piano and again began playing my 'signature tune'. She beckoned me to the microphone, and I had no option than accept it with good grace and sing the damn song. The guests got up from their seats to dance the slow foxtrot. The audience seemed to enjoy my performance and requested an encore. Bowing myself off, I returned to our table. No sooner had the band struck up with a quickstep than I took Shirley in my arms. We were lost in a world of our own as we spun about the floor.

The band stopped for a short break between tunes. The house lights dimmed: Barbara was at the piano again. She gave me a broad grin and started to play *The Anniversary Waltz*, I knew just for Shirley and me. I got up and swept the loveliest girl in the world on to the dance floor. Holding her close, I whispered, "Darling, please marry me. I can't live without you. I love you more than anything else in the world." Even more softly, I heard her reply, "I will."

I was so used to rejection, it took a couple of circuits of the dance floor before I realised I'd not misheard her. I braked sharply and asked her to repeat what she'd said. "Yes, I will," she replied, her eyes filling with tears of happiness.

I was torn between laughing and crying as I led her off the floor to tell Roger and Anne that Shirley had agreed to be my wife. Roger immediately called for a toast, patting me on the back, pumping my hand, saying, "That's fabulous! Come on, let's tell Barbara, shall we?"

Barbara was just as delighted. Taking both of my hands, she said, "Lucky, lucky, boy, Congratulations, both of you." She planted a great big kiss on Shirley's cheek, saying, "I've a lovely idea. Come home with me. I've got an engagement present for you both."

"What's that?" I asked.

"Never you mind, young man, it's a surprise," she replied, screwing up her face at me. "No, Roger and Anne, not for you. My present's just for these two."

Shirley and I were mystified. Shrugging, we looked at each other, not knowing whether we should chance our luck and let ourselves to be driven to The Old Meuse by a drunk. In the end we accepted, anxious to discover what surprise Barbara had in store for us. We need not have been concerned about the journey. Driving as impeccably as before, Barbara chattered nonsense like a mynah bird all the way home.

Drawing up in front of her darkened house, Barbara got out of her car. "Stay where you are!" she shouted, as she let herself in; "I'll be back in a sec."

"What d'you think this is all about?" asked Shirley nervously.

"Can't imagine at this time of night. I hope she's not wasting our time."

Barbara re-emerged from her house, carrying a sort of bundle in her arms. We watched, bewildered as she vanished into the darkness beyond the house.

A few minutes later, she returned to the car holding a torch. "Come on, you two, come with me."

We followed her over pebbles to where Julie's white touring caravan was parked by the garage. "Come, come, come," she said; a hen clucking her chicks into their coop. "Here's my present." Opening the door of the caravan with a flourish, she ushered us up the steps. "I've made up the bed," she said. "Off you go now. See you in the morning. Sleep well my darlings."

Postscript

I was twenty five and Shirley twenty one when we married just over a year later. I had resigned from John Dickinson and was now working as a copywriter with Kodak, earning a decent £500 per annum, which enabled us, with our combined salaries, to save enough over the next couple of years to buy our first house, a newly built semi-detached house in Hersham, Surrey. By the age of thirty one, I was a director of a vending machine company and living in a five bedroom house in East Molesey, Surrey which we'd had built for us.

At forty, I was appointed managing director of a Hamburg based international coffee manufacturer, responsible for both the U.S and U.K markets. Although we had taken a circuitous route, the Himalayan Hillbilly had finally dun good!

Five years after we married, our daughter Kerri was born. Viki arrived two years later, followed by Abigail after another couple of years.

This book is dedicated to my three lovely daughters and six grand-children, Samantha, Lottie, Tiggy, Daisy, Henry and Archie.

Not forgetting my nephew Matt Carter (Jaguarskills.com) who designed the cover of my book.